Baked Apples with
Dates, page 227

Dill-Lemon Chicken, page 11

"The *Fix-It and Forget-It* series is the country's bestselling crockpot cookbook series.

"The six books in the series compile edited versions of recipes contributed by everyday cooks and have sold more than nine million copies."
— *Publishers Weekly*

"The author who came in second to Rachael Ray in total foodie sales was Phyllis Pellman Good, who does not have a TV show."
— *Summary of Bestsellers*
Publishers Weekly

"One reason why the books are so popular is that they aren't intended for folks who dabble in cooking as a hobby or a whim.

"'The audience that I have in mind is those who have to cook every day of the week,' says Good."
— *Los Angeles Times*

"Good's books have sold more in the United States than the *combined* works of popular Food Network hosts Ina Garten, Giada De Laurentiis, and Jamie Oliver."
— *The New York Times*
Front-page feature

"One of the losses in our lives is that it's so hard to sit down at the dinner table, night after night, and have parents and children eating together," says Phyllis Pellman Good.

"With the slow cooker, you can prepare food early and bring everyone together at the table," she says. "It helps immensely."
— *The Associated Press*

Fix-It and FORGET-It®

Cooking Light
for Slow Cookers

REVISED & UPDATED

600
Healthy, Low-Fat Recipes for Your Slow Cooker

Phyllis Good

Good Books

New York, New York

Cover illustration and illustrations throughout the book by Cheryl Benner

FIX-IT AND FORGET-IT® COOKING LIGHT FOR SLOW COOKERS: REVISED AND UPDATED

Table of Contents

Welcome to Fix-It and Forget-It Cooking Light, Revised and Updated

Yes, now you can have it all: Food from your slow cooker that is scrumptious, quick, easy to prepare—and low-fat!

We work at portion control here...

You'll notice that our serving sizes are quite modest. So if you'd like to manage your weight, *Fix-It and Forget-It Cooking Light, Revised and Updated* will help with portions and healthy ingredients.

Ideal slow-cooker sizes...

The ideal slow-cooker size given with each recipe is just a suggestion. I went big in most cases so that you aren't faced with a pot that's running over. (On the other hand, be aware of the fact that your food may get too dry if your pot is less than half full.)

Some raw vegetables stand up and take a lot of room. As they cook, they quiet down and sink together. So some recipes with an abundance of uncooked vegetables suggest a larger cooker than other recipes which yield the same number of servings.

Slow cookers are great for carry-in meals and pot-lucks. But who wants an overflowing pot in the back of a vehicle? So, again, I tilted toward the larger size.

Phyllis Good

Cooking times do vary...

New slow cookers are generally faster than old ones. If your cooker is relatively new, go with the lesser amount of cooking time when a range of times is given.

Mark up this cookbook!

When you've found the perfect cooking time for a recipe—write it in your cookbook. When you've discovered the right size slow cooker for a recipe, write that next to the recipe. And when you've made a tasty and compatible go-along for a dish, note it next to the recipe.

Personalize this cookbook—and it will be your companion in the kitchen and in your effort to eat healthfully.

Calculating the nutritional analyses...

The recipe analyses are based on the lesser amount of an ingredient when a range of amounts is given. Optional ingredients are not included in the analyses. Only those items on a recipe's list of ingredients are part of that recipe's analysis. (If a recipe's procedure or Notes suggest serving it with pasta or potatoes, for example, those foods are not calculated in the analysis.)

Feast healthfully. Your family and friends—your waistline and your heart—will thank you!

Tips for Using Your Slow Cooker: A Friendly Year-Round Appliance

1. What to buy

- A good standard size for a household of four is a 4-quart slow cooker. If you often cook for more, or you like to prepare sizable roasts, turkey breasts, or chicken legs and thighs, you'll want a 6-quart cooker.
For parties or buffets, a 1½- to 2-quart size works well for dips and snacks.

- Cookers which allow you to program "On," the length of the cooking time, and "Off," are convenient. If your model doesn't include that feature, you might want to get a digital appliance timer, which gives you that option. Make sure the timer is adequate for the electrical flow that your cooker demands.

- A baking insert, a cooking rack, a temperature probe, and an insulated carrying tote are all useful additions offered with some models. Or you can buy some of them separately by going to the manufacturers' websites.

2. Learn to know your slow cooker

- Some newer slow cookers cook at a very high temperature. You can check the temperature of your slow cooker this way:
  1. Place 2 quarts of water in your slow cooker.
  2. Cover. Heat on Low 8 hours.
  3. Lift the lid. Immediately check the water temp with an accurate thermometer.
  4. The temperature of the water should be 185°F. If the temperature is higher, foods may overcook and you should reduce the overall cooking time. If the temperature is lower, your foods will probably not reach a safe temperature quickly enough, and the cooker should be discarded.

3. Maximizing what a slow cooker does best

• Slow cookers tend to work best when they're ⅔ full. You many need to increase the cooking time if you've exceeded that amount, or reduce it if you've put in less than that.

• Cut the hard veggies going into your cooker into chunks of about equal size. In other words, make your potato and carrot pieces about the same size. Then they'll be done cooking at nearly the same time. Softer veggies, like bell peppers and zucchini, cook faster, so they don't need to be cut as small. But again, keep them similar in size to each other so they finish together.

• Because raw vegetables are notoriously tough customers in a slow cooker, layer them over the bottom and around the sides of the cooker, as much as possible. That puts them in more direct contact with the heat.

• There are consequences to lifting the lid on your slow cooker while it's cooking. To compensate for the lost heat, you should plan to add 15-20 minutes of cooking time for each time the lid was lifted off.
On the other hand, moisture gathers in a slow cooker as it works. To allow that to cook off, or to thicken the cooking juices, take the lid off during the last half hour of cooking time.

• Use only the amount of liquid called for in a recipe. In contrast to an oven or a stovetop, a slow cooker tends to draw juices out of food and then harbor it.
Of course, if you sense that the food in your cooker is drying out, or browning excessively before it finishes cooking, you may want to add ½ cup of *warm* liquid to the cooker.

• Important variables to remember that don't show up in recipes:
  · The fuller your slow cooker, the longer it will take its contents to cook.
  · The more densely packed the cooker's contents are, the longer they will take to cook.
  · The larger the chunks of meat or vegetables, the more time they will need to cook.

4. Debunking the myths

• Slow cookers are *a handy year-round appliance*. They don't heat up a kitchen in warm weather. They allow you to escape to the pool or lake or lawn or gardens—so why not let them work for you when it's hot outdoors. A slow cooker fixes your dinner while you're at your child's soccer game, too.

So don't limit its usefulness. Remember the dozens of recipes-beyond-beef-stew in this collection!

One more thing—a slow cooker provides a wonderful alternative if your oven is full—no matter the season.

• You can overdo food in a slow cooker. If you're tempted to stretch a recipe's 6-hour stated cooking time to 8 or 10 hours, you may be disappointed in your dinner. Yes, these cookers work their magic using slow, moist heat. Yes, many dishes cook a long time. But these outfits have their limits.

For example, chicken can overcook in a slow cooker. Especially boneless, skinless breasts. But legs and thighs aren't immune either. Once they go past the falling-off-the-bone stage, they are prone to move on to deeply dry.

Cooked pasta and sour cream do best if added late in the cooking process, ideally 10 minutes before the end of the cooking time if the cooker is on high; 30 minutes before the end of the cooking time if it's on low.

5. Safety

• A working slow cooker gets hot on the outside—and I mean the outer electrical unit as well as the inner vessel. Make sure that curious and unsuspecting children or adults don't grab hold of either part. Use oven mitts when lifting any part of a hot cooker.

• To prevent a slow cooker from bubbling over, either when it's sitting still on a counter, or when it's traveling to a carry-in dinner, fill the cooker only ⅔ full.

If you're going to exceed that limit, pull out your second slow cooker (what—you have only one?!) and divide the contents between them.

6. Adapting stove-top or oven recipes for a slow cooker

• Many stove-top and oven recipes can be adapted for a slow cooker. If you want to experiment, use these conversion factors:
- · Low (in a slow cooker) = 200°F approximately (in an oven).
- · High (in a slow cooker) = 300°F approximately (in an oven).
- · In a slow cooker, 2 hours on Low = 1 hour, approximately, on High.

7. More than one slow cooker?!

• If you run the food services for an active household, or if you often have guests, consider having more than one slow cooker. If you own two different sizes, you can do sides or appetizers or desserts in the smaller one. Or you may want two of similar, or the same, size so you can double the portions of your favorite dishes.

Chicken and Turkey Main Dishes

One-Pot Easy Chicken

Jean Robinson
Cinnaminson, NJ

Makes 6 servings

Prep. Time: 25 minutes
Cooking Time: 6-8 hours
Ideal slow-cooker size: 6-qt.

6-8 medium-sized potatoes, quartered
1-2 large onions, sliced
3-5 carrots, cubed
1 tsp. garlic salt
¼ tsp. black pepper
5 lbs. chicken, skin removed (quarters *or* legs and thighs work well)
1 small onion, chopped
¾ tsp. black pepper
2 tsp. whole cloves
2 tsp. garlic salt
1 Tbsp. chopped fresh oregano
1 tsp. dried rosemary
½ cup lemon juice

1. Mix together potatoes, sliced onions, carrots, 1 tsp. garlic salt, and ¼ tsp. black pepper in bottom of slow cooker.

2. Rinse and pat chicken dry. In bowl mix together chopped onions, ¾ tsp. black pepper, cloves, and 2 tsp. garlic salt. Dredge chicken in seasonings. Place in slow cooker over vegetables.

3. In small bowl mix together oregano, rosemary, and lemon juice. Pour over chicken.

4. Cover. Cook on low 6-8 hours, or until vegetables are soft and chicken juices run clear.

—— PER SERVING ——
- 470 calories
  (200 calories from fat)
- 22g total fat
  (6g saturated, 0g trans)
- 215mg cholesterol
- 1120mg sodium
- 50g total carbohydrate
  (7g fiber, 7g sugar)
- 82g protein
- 100%DV vitamin A
- 40%DV vitamin C
- 10%DV calcium
- 30%DV iron

Note:

This is a lifesaver when the grandchildren come for a weekend. I get to play with them, and dinner is timed and ready when we are.

Use your slow cooker to cook a hen, turkey, or roast beef for use in salads or casseroles. The meat can even be frozen when you put it in the slow cooker. Set the cooker on Low, and let the meat cook all night while you sleep.

Julia B. Boyd, Memphis, TN

Chicken and Sun-Dried Tomatoes

Joyce Shackelford
Green Bay, WI

Makes 8 servings

Prep. Time: 15 minutes
Cooking Time: 4-6 hours
Ideal slow-cooker size: 6-qt.

1 Tbsp. olive oil
3 lbs. boneless, skinless chicken breasts, cut in 8 serving pieces
2 garlic cloves, minced
½ cup white wine
1½ cups fat-free, low-sodium chicken stock
1 tsp. dried basil
½ cup chopped, sun-dried tomatoes, cut into slivers

1. Heat oil in skillet. Add several pieces of chicken at a time, but make sure not to crowd the skillet so the chicken can brown evenly.
2. Transfer chicken to slow cooker as it finishes browning.
3. Add garlic, wine, chicken stock, and basil to skillet. Bring to a boil. Scrape up any bits from the bottom of the pan.
4. Pour over chicken. Scatter tomatoes over the top.
5. Cover. Cook on low 4-6 hours.

—— PER SERVING ——
• 320 calories
  (70 calories from fat)
• 8g total fat
  (2g saturated, 0g trans)
• 145mg cholesterol
• 230mg sodium
• 2g total carbohydrate
  (0.5g fiber, 1g sugar)
• 54g protein
• 0%DV vitamin A
• 0%DV vitamin C
• 4%DV calcium
• 15%DV iron

Greek Chicken

Judy Govotsus
Monrovia, MD

Makes 8 servings

Prep. Time: 20 minutes
Cooking Time: 5-10 hours
Ideal slow-cooker size: 6-qt.

6 medium-sized potatoes, quartered
3 lbs. chicken pieces, skin removed
2 large onions, quartered
1 whole bulb garlic, minced
½ cup water
3 tsp. dried oregano
1 tsp. salt
½ tsp. black pepper
1 Tbsp. olive oil

1. Place potatoes in bottom of slow cooker. Add chicken, onions, and garlic.
2. In small bowl mix water with oregano, salt, and pepper.
3. Pour over chicken and potatoes. Top with oil.
4. Cover. Cook on high 5-6 hours or on low 9-10 hours.

—— PER SERVING ——
• 430 calories
  (70 calories from fat)
• 8g total fat
  (2g saturated, 0g trans)
• 145mg cholesterol
• 430mg sodium
• 31g total carbohydrate
  (4g fiber, 3g sugar)
• 56g protein
• 0%DV vitamin A
• 30%DV vitamin C
• 6%DV calcium
• 20%DV iron

Twenty-Clove Chicken

Nancy Savage
Factoryville, PA

Makes 6 servings

Prep. Time: 20 minutes
Cooking Time: 5-6 hours
Ideal slow-cooker size: 4-qt.

¼ cup dry white wine
2 Tbsp. chopped dried parsley
2 tsp. dried basil leaves
1 tsp. dried oregano
pinch of crushed red pepper flakes
20 cloves of garlic (about 2 bulbs)
4 celery ribs, chopped
6 boneless, skinless chicken breast halves
1 lemon, juice and zest
fresh herbs, *optional*

1. Combine wine, dried parsley, dried basil, dried oregano, and dried red pepper flakes in large bowl.
2. Add garlic cloves and celery. Mix well.
3. Transfer garlic and celery to slow cooker with slotted spoon.
4. Add chicken to herb mixture one piece at a time. Coat well. Place chicken on top of vegetables in slow cooker.
5. Sprinkle lemon juice and zest over chicken. Add any remaining herb mixture.
6. Cover. Cook on low 5-6 hours or until chicken is no longer pink in center.

7. Garnish with fresh herbs if desired.

—— PER SERVING ——
- 170 calories (30 calories from fat)
- 3.5g total fat (1g saturated, 0g trans)
- 75mg cholesterol
- 90mg sodium
- 7g total carbohydrate (2g fiber, 1g sugar)
- 28g protein
- 4%DV vitamin A
- 10%DV vitamin C
- 6%DV calcium
- 10%DV iron

Tip:

For browned chicken, sauté uncooked breasts in large skillet in 1 Tbsp. olive oil over medium heat. Cook for 5 minutes on each side, or until golden brown. Then proceed with steps above.

Lemon Chicken

Judi Manos
West Islip, NY
Joette Droz
Kalona, IA
Cindy Krestynick
Glen Lyon, PA

Makes 6 servings

Prep. Time: 15 minutes
Cooking Time: 3½-4½ hours
Ideal slow-cooker size: 5-qt.

6 boneless, skinless chicken breast halves
1 tsp. dried oregano
½ tsp. seasoned salt
¼ tsp. black pepper
¼ cup water
3 Tbsp. lemon juice
2 garlic cloves, minced
2 tsp. chicken bouillon granules

2 tsp. fresh parsley, minced

1. Pat chicken dry with paper towels.
2. Combine oregano, seasoned salt, and pepper. Rub over chicken.
3. Brown chicken in a nonstick skillet over medium heat.
4. Place chicken in slow cooker.
5. Combine water, lemon juice, garlic, and bouillon in skillet. Bring to a boil, stirring to loosen browned bits. Pour over chicken.
6. Cover. Cook on low 3-4 hours.
7. Baste chicken. Add parsley.
8. Remove lid and cook 15-30 minutes longer, allowing juices to thicken slightly.
9. Serve chicken and juices over rice.

—— PER SERVING ——
- 150 calories (30 calories from fat)
- 3g total fat (1g saturated, 0g trans)
- 75mg cholesterol
- 320mg sodium
- 1g total carbohydrate (0g fiber, 0g sugar)
- 27g protein
- 2%DV vitamin A
- 4%DV vitamin C
- 2%DV calcium
- 6%DV iron

Tip:
If you want to make sure the chicken absorbs the flavors of the sauce as fully as possible, cut it into 1-inch cubes just before placing in slow cooker.

Dill-Lemon Chicken

Vera Schmucker
Goshen, IN

Makes 4 servings

Prep. Time: 15 minutes
Cooking Time: 3-4 hours
Ideal slow-cooker size: 4-qt.

1 cup fat-free sour cream
1 Tbsp. fresh dill, minced
1 tsp. lemon pepper seasoning
1 tsp. lemon zest
4 boneless, skinless chicken breast halves

1. Combine sour cream, dill, lemon pepper, and lemon zest in a small bowl. Spoon one-fourth of the sour cream-lemon-dill mixture into bottom of slow cooker.
2. Arrange chicken breasts on top in a single layer.
3. Pour remaining sauce over chicken. Spread evenly.
4. Cover. Cook on low 3-4 hours or until juices run clear.

—— PER SERVING ——
- 200 calories (35 calories from fat)
- 4g total fat (1.5g saturated, 0g trans)
- 80mg cholesterol
- 230mg sodium
- 10g total carbohydrate (0g fiber, 5g sugar)
- 30g protein
- 8%DV vitamin A
- 0%DV vitamin C
- 10%DV calcium
- 6%DV iron

When using fresh herbs you may want to experiment with the amounts to use, because the strength is enhanced in the slow cooker, rather than becoming weaker.

Annabelle Unternahrer, Shipshewana, IN

"Baked" Chicken

Eileen Eash
Carlsbad, NM

Makes 8 servings

Prep. Time: 20 minutes
Cooking Time: 6-8 hours
Ideal slow-cooker size: 5- or 6-qt.

3 lbs. chicken pieces
1 cup flour
1 tsp. salt
½ tsp. coarse black pepper
¼ tsp. garlic powder
1 tsp. Montreal chicken
  seasoning
1 Tbsp. parsley flakes
2 Tbsp. canola oil
1 cup water

1. Remove skin from chicken. Rinse. Pat dry.
2. Combine remaining ingredients, except oil and water, in good-sized bowl.
3. Toss chicken pieces with seasoned flour mixture.
4. Brown chicken lightly in skillet in oil.
5. Place in slow cooker. Pour water around the outside wall of the cooker.
6. Cover. Cook on low 6-8 hours.

—— PER SERVING ——
• 350 calories
  (60 calories from fat)
• 7g total fat
  (2g saturated, 0g trans)
• 145mg cholesterol
• 450mg sodium
• 12g total carbohydrate
  (0g fiber, 0g sugar)
• 54g protein
• 2%DV vitamin A
• 2%DV vitamin C
• 4%DV calcium
• 15%DV iron

Slow-Cooker Barbecued Chicken

Charlotte Shaffer
East Earl, PA

Makes 6 servings

Prep. Time: 20 minutes
Cooking Time: 6-8 hours
Ideal slow-cooker size: 3- or 4-qt.

1 lb. frying chicken, cut up and skin removed (organic *or* free-range, if possible)
10¾-oz. can condensed tomato soup
¾ cup onion, chopped
¼ cup vinegar
3 Tbsp. brown sugar
1 Tbsp. Worcestershire sauce
½ tsp. salt
¼ tsp. dried basil

1. Place chicken in slow cooker.
2. Combine all remaining ingredients and pour over chicken, making sure that the sauce glazes all the pieces.
3. Cover. Cook on low 6-8 hours.

—— PER SERVING ——
• 170 calories
  (40 calories from fat)
• 4.5 total fat
  (1g saturated, 0g trans)
• 45mg cholesterol
• 550mg sodium
• 16g total carbohy-drate
  (0.5g fiber, 11g sugar)
• 17g protein
• 6%DV vitamin A
• 20%DV vitamin C
• 2%DV calcium
• 10%DV iron

Barbecued Chicken Breasts

Jeanne Allen
Rye, CO

Makes 8 servings

Prep. Time: 10 minutes
Cooking Time: 3-8 hours
Ideal slow-cooker size: 4-qt.

8 boneless, skinless
  chicken breast halves
8-oz. can low-sodium
  tomato sauce
8-oz. can water (use the
  tomato sauce can you've
  just emptied)
2 Tbsp. brown sugar
2 Tbsp. prepared mustard
2 Tbsp. Worcestershire sauce
¼ cup cider vinegar
½ tsp. salt
¼ tsp. black pepper
dash of garlic powder
dash of dried oregano
3 Tbsp. onion, chopped

1. Place chicken in slow cooker sprayed with nonfat cooking spray. Overlap chicken as little as possible.
2. Combine remaining ingredients. Pour over chicken.
3. Cover. Cook on low 6-8 hours or on high 3-4 hours.
4. To thicken the sauce a bit, remove the lid during the last hour of cooking.

—— PER SERVING ——
• 170 calories
  (30 calories from fat)
• 3g total fat
  (1g saturated, 0g trans)
• 75mg cholesterol
• 470mg sodium
• 7g total carbohydrate
  (0.5g fiber, 5g sugar)
• 27g protein
• 2%DV vitamin A
• 4%DV vitamin C
• 2%DV calcium
• 8%DV iron

Chicken Breasts with Rosemary

Marla Folkerts
Holland, OH

Makes 4 servings

Prep. Time: 10 minutes
Cooking Time: 3-6 hours
Ideal slow-cooker size: 3- or 4-qt.

4 boneless, skinless
 chicken breast halves
 (4 ozs. each)
1½ tsp. balsamic vinegar
1 tsp. minced garlic
1 Tbsp. grated lemon rind
¼ tsp. salt
⅛ tsp. black pepper
½ cup dry white wine, *or*
 reduced-sodium chicken
 broth
1 tsp. finely chopped fresh,
 or ½ tsp. dried, crumbled
 rosemary leaves
½ cup fresh tomato, diced

1. Place chicken breasts in slow cooker.
2. Mix together vinegar, garlic, lemon rind, salt, pepper, and wine. Pour over chicken.
3. Cover. Cook on low 6 hours or on high 3 hours.
4. One-half hour before the end of the cooking time, stir in rosemary and fresh tomato.

—— PER SERVING ——
• 170 calories   • 3g total carbohydrate
 (30 calories from fat)   (0.5g fiber, 1g sugar)
• 3 total fat   • 27g protein
 (1g saturated, 0g trans) • 4%DV vitamin A
• 75mg cholesterol   • 8%DV vitamin C
• 210mg sodium   • 2%DV calcium
                                        • 6%DV iron

Southwestern Chicken

Joyce Shackelford
Green Bay, WI

Makes 6 servings

Prep. Time: 10 minutes
Cooking Time: 3-8 hours
Ideal slow-cooker size: 6-qt.

2 15¼-oz. cans corn,
 drained
15-oz. can black beans,
 rinsed and drained
16-oz. jar chunky salsa,
 divided
6 boneless, skinless
 chicken breast halves
1 cup low-fat shredded
 cheddar cheese

1. Combine corn, black beans, and ½ cup salsa in slow cooker.
2. Top with chicken. Pour remaining salsa over chicken.
3. Cover. Cook on high 3-4 hours or low 7-8 hours.
4. Sprinkle with cheese. Cover and cook 5 minutes more for cheese to melt.

—— PER SERVING ——
• 370 calories   • 43g total carbohydrate
 (50 calories from fat)   (7g fiber, 7g sugar)
• 6g total fat   • 39g protein
 (2g saturated, 0g trans) • 6%DV vitamin A
• 75mg cholesterol   • 10%DV vitamin C
• 1210mg sodium   • 15%DV calcium
                                        • 20%DV iron

Tip:
This dish goes well with rice.

Slow-Cooker Tex-Mex Chicken

Kim Stoltzfus
Parkesburg, PA

Makes 6 servings

Prep. Time: 15-20 minutes
Cooking Time: 2-6 hours
Ideal slow-cooker size: 3½-qt.

1 lb. boneless skinless
 chicken breasts, cut into
 ¾"-wide strips
2 Tbsp. dry taco seasoning
 mix
2 Tbsp. flour
1 green pepper, cut into
 strips
1 red pepper, cut into strips
1 cup frozen corn
1½ cups chunky salsa
1 cup nonfat Mexican-style
 cheese, shredded

1. Toss chicken with seasoning and flour in slow cooker.
2. Gently stir in vegetables and salsa.
3. Cook on low 4-6 hours, or on high 2-3 hours, until chicken and vegetables are cooked through but are not dry or mushy.
4. Stir before serving.
5. Serve topped with cheese.

—— PER SERVING ——
• 170 calories   • 15g total carbohydrate
 (20 calories from fat)   (3g fiber, 5g sugar)
• 2g total fat   • 22g protein
 (0.5g saturated,   • 25%DV vitamin A
 0g trans)   • 70%DV vitamin C
• 45mg cholesterol   • 30%DV calcium
• 860mg sodium   • 6%DV iron

Artichoke-Tomato Chicken

Barbara Jean Fabel
Wausau, WI

Makes 4 servings

Prep. Time: 10 minutes
Cooking Time 4-6 hours
Ideal slow-cooker size: 3-qt.

1 yellow onion, thinly
   sliced
14-oz. jar marinated
   artichoke hearts,
   drained
14-oz. can low-sodium
   peeled tomatoes
6 Tbsp. red wine vinegar
1 tsp. minced garlic
½ tsp. salt
½ tsp. black pepper
4 boneless, skinless
   chicken breast halves

1. Combine all ingredients
except chicken in slow
cooker.
2. Place chicken in cooker,
pushing down into vegetables
and sauce until it's as covered
as possible.
3. Cover. Cook on low 4-6
hours.
4. Serve over rice.

—— PER SERVING ——
• 270 calories   • 18g total carbohydrate
  (80 calories from fat)   (4g fiber, 4g sugar)
• 8g total fat   • 31g protein
  (1g saturated, 0g trans) • 4%DV vitamin A
• 75mg cholesterol   • 30%DV vitamin C
• 900mg sodium   • 6%DV calcium
                • 6%DV iron

Chicken and Apples

Jean Butzer
Batavia, NY

Makes 6 servings

Prep. Time: 20 minutes
Cooking Time: 7-8 hours
Ideal slow-cooker size: 5- or 6-qt.

6-oz. can frozen orange
   concentrate, thawed
½ tsp dried marjoram leaves
dash ground nutmeg
dash garlic powder
1 onion, chopped
6 skinless, boneless
   chicken breast halves
3 Granny Smith apples,
   cored and sliced
¼ cup water
2 Tbsp. cornstarch

1. In a small bowl, combine
orange juice concentrate,
marjoram, nutmeg, and garlic
powder.
2. Place onions in bottom
of slow cooker.
3. Dip each chicken breast
into the orange mixture to
coat. Then place in slow
cooker over onions.
4. Pour any remaining
orange juice concentrate
mixture over the chicken.
5. Cover. Cook on low 6-7
hours.
6. Add apples and cook on
low 1 hour longer.
7. Remove chicken, apples,
and onions to a serving platter.
8. Pour the sauce that
remains into a medium
saucepan.

9. Mix together water
and cornstarch. Stir into the
juices.
10. Cook over medium
heat, stirring constantly until
the sauce is thick and bubbly.
11. Serve the sauce over the
chicken.

—— PER SERVING ——
• 240 calories   • 24g total carbohydrate
  (30 calories from fat)   (2g fiber, 19g sugar)
• 3g total fat   • 28g protein
  (1g saturated, 0g trans) • 2%DV vitamin A
• 75mg cholesterol   • 20%DV vitamin C
• 65mg sodium   • 4%DV calcium
                • 6%DV iron

Tip:
You can also thicken the
sauce by adding cornstarch
and water mixture to the
sauce in the slow cooker.
Cook on high 10-15 minutes
until thickened.

Cran-Apple Chicken

Joyce Shackellord
Green Bay, WI

Makes 6 servings

Prep. Time: 10 minutes
Cooking Time: 6-8 hours
Ideal slow-cooker size: 5- or 6-qt.

6 boneless, skinless
   chicken breast halves
1 cup fresh *or* frozen
   cranberries
1 green apple, peeled,
   cored, and sliced
1 Tbsp. brown sugar
1 cup unsweetened apple
   juice *or* cider

1. Place chicken in slow cooker.

2. Sprinkle with cranberries and apples.

3. Mix brown sugar and apple juice. Pour over chicken and fruit.

4. Cover. Cook on low 6-8 hours.

—— PER SERVING ——
- 190 calories
  (30 calories from fat)
- 3g total fat
  (1g saturated, 0g trans)
- 75mg cholesterol
- 65mg sodium
- 13g total carbohydrate
  (2g fiber, 11g sugar)
- 27g protein
- 0%DV vitamin A
- 20%DV vitamin C
- 2%DV calcium
- 6%DV iron

Sweet 'n' Sour Chicken Over Rice

Carol Eberly
Harrisonburg, VA

Makes 6 servings

Prep. Time: 10-15 minutes
Cooking Time: 6½-7½ hours
Ideal slow-cooker size: 5 qt.

1 lb. baby carrots
1 medium onion, cut into wedges
6 boneless, skinless chicken breast halves
20-oz. can unsweetened pineapple chunks
⅓ cup brown sugar
1 Tbsp. low-sodium soy sauce
2 tsp. chicken bouillon granules
½ tsp. salt
½ tsp. ground ginger
¼ tsp. garlic powder

3 Tbsp. cornstarch
¼ cup water
3 cups cooked long-grain enriched rice

1. Layer carrots and onion in slow cooker. Top with chicken.

2. Drain pineapple, reserving juice. Place pineapple chunks over chicken.

3. Mix together pineapple juice, brown sugar, soy sauce, chicken bouillon, salt, ginger, and garlic. Pour over top.

4. Cook on low 6-7 hours.

5. Combine cornstarch and water. Gradually stir into slow cooker.

6. Cook 30 minutes longer or until sauce is thickened.

7. Serve over rice.

—— PER SERVING ——
- 330 calories
  (20 calories from fat)
- 2.5g total fat
  (0.5g saturated, 0g trans)
- 35mg cholesterol
- 760mg sodium
- 59g total carbohydrate
  (3g fiber, 29g sugar)
- 17g protein
- 200%DV vitamin A
- 20%DV vitamin C
- 4%DV calcium
- 15%DV iron

Hawaiian Chicken

Leona M. Slabaugh
Apple Creek, OH

Makes 6-8 servings

Prep. Time: 30 minutes
Cooking Time: 3-8 hours
Ideal slow-cooker size: 3- to 5-qt.

3 lbs. boneless, skinless chicken breast halves
16-oz. can pineapple slices, drained
15-oz. can mandarin oranges, drained
2 Tbsp. cornstarch
3 Tbsp. brown sugar, packed
2 Tbsp. lemon juice
¼ tsp. salt
¼ tsp. ground ginger

1. Arrange chicken in slow cooker.

2. Mix remaining ingredients together in a medium bowl.

3. Spoon over chicken evenly.

4. Cover. Cook on low 6-8 hours or on high 3 hours, or until meat is tender but not dry.

—— PER SERVING ——
- 240 calories
  (35 calories from fat)
- 4g total fat
  (1g saturated, 0g trans)
- 95mg cholesterol
- 160mg sodium
- 14g total carbohydrate
  (1g fiber, 11g sugar)
- 35g protein
- 10%DV vitamin A
- 25%DV vitamin C
- 2%DV calcium
- 8%DV iron

Sweet 'n' Sour Chicken Over Potatoes

Dorothy VanDeest
Memphis, TN

Makes 8 servings

Prep. Time: 20-30 minutes
Cooking Time: 4-6 hours
Ideal slow-cooker size: 5-qt.

3 medium-sized potatoes, peeled and sliced thin
4 whole chicken breasts, skinned and halved
1 cup orange juice
2 Tbsp. brown sugar
1 tsp. dried basil
¼ tsp. nutmeg
2 Tbsp. cider vinegar
dried parsley flakes
17-oz. can pineapple chunks in water, drained
chopped fresh parsley

1. Place sliced potatoes in slow cooker. Arrange chicken breasts over potatoes.
2. Combine orange juice, brown sugar, basil, nutmeg, and vinegar. Pour over chicken.
3. Sprinkle dried parsley flakes over chicken.
4. Cover and cook on low 4-6 hours.
5. Remove chicken breasts and potatoes from sauce and arrange on a warm platter.
6. Add pineapple chunks to sauce remaining in slow cooker. Cook on high until they are at serving temperature.
7. Pour sauce over chicken and potatoes. Garnish with chopped parsley.

— PER SERVING —
• 180 calories
  (15 calories from fat)
• 1.5 total fat
  (0g saturated, 0g trans)
• 35mg cholesterol
• 40mg sodium
• 25g total carbohydrate
  (3g fiber, 10g sugar)
• 15g protein
• 8%DV vitamin A
• 30%DV vitamin C
• 2%DV calcium
• 8%DV iron

Orange Chicken Leg Quarters

Kimberly Jensen
Bailey, CO

Makes 8 servings

Prep. Time: 25-30 minutes
Cooking Time: 5¼-6¼
Ideal slow-cooker size: 5- to 6-qt.

4 chicken drumsticks, skin removed
4 chicken thighs, skin removed
1 cup strips of green and red bell peppers
½ cup fat-free, low-sodium chicken broth
½ cup prepared orange juice
½ cup ketchup
2 Tbsp. soy sauce
1 Tbsp. light molasses
1 Tbsp. prepared mustard
½ tsp. garlic salt
11-oz. can mandarin oranges
2 tsp. cornstarch
1 cup frozen peas
2 green onions, sliced

1. Place chicken in slow cooker. Top with pepper strips.
2. Combine broth, juice, ketchup, soy sauce, molasses, mustard, and garlic salt. Pour over chicken.
3. Cover. Cook on low 5-6 hours.
4. Remove chicken and vegetables from slow cooker. Keep warm.
5. Measure out 1 cup of cooking sauce. Put in saucepan and bring to boil.
6. Drain oranges, reserving 1 Tbsp. juice. Stir cornstarch into reserved juice. Add to boiling sauce in pan.
7. Add peas to sauce and cook, stirring continually 2-3 minutes, until sauce thickens and peas are warm. Stir in oranges.
8. Arrange chicken pieces on platter of cooked white rice, fried cellophane noodles, or lo mein noodles. Pour orange sauce over chicken and rice or noodles. Top with sliced green onions.

— PER SERVING —
• 170 calories
  (40 calories from fat)
• 4g total fat
  (1g saturated, 0g trans)
• 45mg cholesterol
• 520mg sodium
• 18g total carbohydrate
  (2g fiber, 11g sugar)
• 16g protein
• 10%DV vitamin A
• 30%DV vitamin C
• 4%DV calcium
• 10%DV iron

Company Chicken

Jeanne Allen
Rye, CO

Makes 6 servings

Prep. Time: 15-20 minutes
Cooking Time: 3-8 hours
Ideal slow-cooker size: 6-qt.

1 envelope liquid Butter
  Bud mix
6 boneless, skinless
  chicken breast halves
6 fat-free mozzarella
  cheese slices
10¾-oz. can cream of
  mushroom soup
¼ cup water
6-oz. package stuffing mix

1. Prepare liquid Butter
Bud mix according to package
directions.
2. Place chicken breasts
in slow cooker sprayed with
nonfat cooking spray.
3. Top each breast with a
slice of cheese.
4. Combine soup and
water. Pour over chicken.
5. Toss the stuffing mix, its
seasoning packet, and prepared Butter Buds together.
Sprinkle over chicken breasts.
6. Cover. Cook on low 6-8
hours or on high 3-4 hours.

—— PER SERVING ——
• 350 calories   • 30g total carbohydrate
  (60 calories from fat) (1g fiber, 3g sugar)
• 7g total fat   • 39g protein
  (2g saturated, 0g trans) • 0%DV vitamin A
• 80mg cholesterol   • 0%DV vitamin C
• 1310mg sodium   • 45%DV calcium
                        • 10%DV iron

Tip:
  For additional seasoning,
add 1 tsp. dried sage to Step 5.

Spicy Italian
Chicken

Ilene Bontrager
Arlington, KS

Makes 6 servings

Prep. Time: 20 minutes
Cooking Time: 4¼-5¼ hours
Ideal slow-cooker size: 5-qt.

1 medium-sized onion,
  chopped
½ cup fat-free Italian
  dressing
½ cup water
¼ tsp. salt
½ tsp. garlic powder
1 tsp. chili powder
½ tsp. paprika
¼ tsp. black pepper
6 boneless, skinless
  chicken breast halves
2 Tbsp. cornstarch
2 Tbsp. cold water

1. Spray the inside of the
slow cooker with nonfat
cooking spray. Combine all
ingredients except chicken,
cornstarch, and 2 Tbsp. cold
water in slow cooker.
2. Add chicken. Turn to
coat.
3. Cover. Cook on low 4-5
hours.
4. Remove chicken and
keep warm.
5. In a saucepan, combine
cornstarch and cold water.
6. Add cooking juices
gradually. Stir and bring to a
boil until thickened.
7. Place chicken over
noodles or rice. Top with
sauce.

—— PER SERVING ——
• 180 calories   • 7g total carbohydrate
  (30 calories from fat) (0.5g fiber, 3g sugar)
• 3.5g total fat   • 27g protein
  (1g saturated, 0g trans) • 2%DV vitamin A
• 75mg cholesterol   • 0%DV vitamin C
• 550mg sodium   • 2%DV calcium
                        • 6%DV iron

Tip:
  The flavor of the chicken
improves if you marinate it in
the Italian dressing for a few
hours before cooking.

Super Easy Chicken

Mary Seielstad
Sparks, NV

Makes 4 servings

Prep. Time: 5 minutes
Cooking Time: 5-6 hours
Ideal slow-cooker size: 4-qt.

4 boneless, skinless
  chicken breast halves
1 pkg. dry Italian dressing
  mix
1 cup warm water *or*
  chicken stock

1. Place chicken in slow
cooker. Sprinkle with dressing mix. Pour water around
chicken.
2. Cover. Cook on low 5-6
hours, or until juices run
clear.

—— PER SERVING ——
• 160 calories   • 6g total carbohydrate
  (30 calories from fat) (0g fiber, 4g sugar)
• 3g total fat   • 27g protein
  (1g saturated, 0g trans) • 0%DV vitamin A
• 75mg cholesterol   • 0%DV vitamin C
• 650mg sodium   • 2%DV calcium
                        • 6%DV iron

Chicken and Veggie Bake

Sara Puskar
Abingdon, MD

Makes 8 servings

Prep. Time: 15 minutes
Cooking Time: 4-8 hours
Ideal slow-cooker size: 4-qt.

8 boneless, skinless
  chicken breast halves
black pepper to taste
1 tsp. garlic powder
16-oz. bottle fat-free Italian
  salad dressing, *divided*
2 15-oz. cans whole
  potatoes, drained
1 lb. frozen Italian veggies,
  or green beans
8-oz. can water chestnuts,
  optional

1. Sprinkle chicken with pepper and garlic powder.
2. Put chicken in bottom of slow cooker. Pour half of salad dressing over meat, making sure that all pieces are glazed.
3. Add potatoes, vegetables, and water chestnuts. Pour remaining salad dressing over, again making sure that the vegetables are all lightly coated.
4. Cover. Cook on high 4 hours or on low 7-8 hours.

—— PER SERVING ——
• 200 calories
  (35 calories from fat)
• 3.5g total fat
  (1g saturated, 0g trans)
• 75mg cholesterol
• 480mg sodium
• 12g total carbohydrate
  (3g fiber, 2g sugar)
• 29g protein
• 50%DV vitamin A
• 4%DV vitamin C
• 4%DV calcium
• 10%DV iron

Chicken Italiano

Mary C. Casey
Scranton, PA

Makes 6 servings

Prep. Time: 15-20 minutes
Cooking Time: 3½-6 hours
Ideal slow-cooker size: 4-qt.

2 large whole boneless,
  skinless chicken breasts,
  each cut in 3 pieces
¾ tsp. salt
¼ tsp. black pepper
½ tsp. dried oregano
½ tsp. dried basil
2 bay leaves
26-oz. jar low-sodium
  meatless spaghetti sauce

1. Place chicken in bottom of slow cooker.
2. Sprinkle seasonings over chicken.
3. Pour sauce over seasoned meat, stirring to be sure chicken is completely covered.
4. Cover. Cook on low 6 hours or on high 3½-4 hours.
5. Serve over pasta.

—— PER SERVING ——
• 120 calories
  (30 calories from fat)
• 3.5g total fat
  (0g saturated, 0g trans)
• 25mg cholesterol
• 820mg sodium
• 10g total carbohydrate
  (2g fiber, 5g sugar)
• 11g protein
• 10%DV vitamin A
• 6%DV vitamin C
• 4%DV calcium
• 6%DV iron

Variation:
  You may substitute 2 1-lb. cans of diced tomatoes, undrained, for the spaghetti sauce. Or use 2 cups diced fresh tomatoes and 1-lb. can crushed tomatoes for the spaghetti sauce.

Slow-Cooked Italian Chicken

Dorothy VanDeest
Memphis, TN

Makes 8 servings

Prep. Time: 15 minutes
Cooking Time: 6½-8½ hours
Ideal slow-cooker size: 5 qt.

3 lbs. boneless, skinless
  chicken breast pieces
1 pkg. dry Italian dressing
  mix
10¾-oz. can 98% fat-free
  cream of mushroom soup
4-oz. can mushrooms,
  drained
8 ozs. fat-free sour cream
  or fat-free plain yogurt

1. Place chicken in slow cooker.
2. Mix together Italian dressing mix, soup, and mushrooms. Stir into chicken.
3. Cook on low 6-8 hours.
4. With a slotted spoon, lift chicken out of cooker. Place in a covered dish and keep warm. Combine cooking juices with sour cream or yogurt in slow cooker. Cover and heat until warmed through, about 15 minutes.
5. When ready to serve, place chicken on bed of rice or noodles and pour sauce over top.

—— PER SERVING ——
• 340 calories
  (70 calories from fat)
• 7 total fat
  (2.5g saturated,
  0g trans)
• 150mg cholesterol
• 750mg sodium
• 11g total carbohydrate
  (0g fiber, 4g sugar)
• 55g protein
• 4%DV vitamin A
• 0%DV vitamin C
• 8%DV calcium
• 10%DV iron

Zesty Chicken Breasts

Barb Yoder
Angola, IN

Makes 6 servings

Prep. Time: 20 minutes
Cooking Time: 3-8 hours
Ideal slow-cooker size: 4-qt.

6 chicken breast halves
2 14½-oz. cans diced
   tomatoes, undrained
1 small can jalapeños, sliced
   and drained, *optional*
¼ cup reduced-fat, creamy
   peanut butter
2 Tbsp. fresh cilantro,
   chopped, *optional*

1. Remove skin from chicken, but leave bone in.
2. Mix all ingredients, except chicken in medium-sized bowl.
3. Pour one-third of sauce in bottom of slow cooker sprayed with nonfat cooking spray. Place chicken on top.
4. Pour remaining sauce over chicken.
5. Cover. Cook on high 3-4 hours or on low 6-8 hours.
6. Remove from slow cooker gently. Chicken will be very tender and will fall off the bones.

—— PER SERVING ——
• 230 calories   • 11g total carbohydrate
  (60 calories from fat)   (4g fiber, 5g sugar)
• 7g total fat   • 31g protein
  (1.5g saturated,   • 8%DV vitamin A
  0g trans)   • 10%DV vitamin C
• 75mg cholesterol   • 10%DV calcium
• 650mg sodium   • 8%DV iron

Parmesan Chicken

Karen Waggoner
Joplin, MO

Makes 8 servings

Prep. Time: 15 minutes
Cooking Time: 4-4½ hours
Ideal slow-cooker size: 4- or 5-qt.

8 boneless, skinless
   chicken breast halves
   (about 2 lbs.)
½ cup water
1 cup fat-free mayonnaise
½ cup grated fat-free
   Parmesan cheese
2 tsp. dried oregano
¼ tsp. black pepper
¼ tsp. paprika

1. Place chicken and water in slow cooker.
2. Cover. Cook on high 2 hours.
3. Mix remaining ingredients. Spread over chicken.
4. Cover. Cook on high 2-2½ hours.

—— PER SERVING ——
• 180 calories   • 4g total carbohydrate
  (35 calories from fat)   (0.5g fiber, 2g sugar)
• 4g total fat   • 28g protein
  (1g saturated, 0g trans)   • 2%DV vitamin A
• 75mg cholesterol   • 0%DV vitamin C
• 400mg sodium   • 8%DV calcium
   • 6%DV iron

Baked Chicken Breasts

Nadine L. Martinitz
Salina, KS

Makes 6 servings

Prep. Time: 20 minutes
Cooking Time: 4-10 hours
Ideal slow-cooker size: 4- or 5-qt.

3 whole chicken breasts,
   skin removed and
   halved
10¾-oz. can low-sodium
   condensed cream of
   chicken soup
½ cup cooking sherry
4-oz. can sliced
   mushrooms, drained
1 tsp. Worcestershire sauce
1 tsp. dried tarragon leaves
   or dried rosemary
¼ tsp. garlic powder

1. Rinse chicken breasts and pat dry. Place in slow cooker.
2. Combine remaining ingredients and pour over chicken breasts, making sure that all pieces are glazed with the sauce.
3. Cover and cook on low 8-10 hours or on high 4-5 hours.
4. Serve over mashed potatoes or noodles.

—— PER SERVING ——
• 340 calories   • 11g total carbohydrate
  (70 calories from fat)   (0g fiber, 4g sugar)
• 7 total fat   • 55g protein
  (2.5g saturated,   • 4%DV vitamin A
  0g trans)   • 0%DV vitamin C
• 150mg cholesterol   • 8%DV calcium
• 750mg sodium   • 10%DV iron

Chicken "Delite"

Rose Hankins
Stevensville, MD

Makes 8 servings

Prep. Time: 20 minutes
Cooking Time: 6-8 hours
Ideal slow-cooker size: 5- or 6-qt.

8 boneless, skinless
  chicken breast halves
1 cup onion, chopped
½ cup celery, chopped
2 chicken bouillon cubes
2 cups water
2 cups steamed rice
¼ cup fresh parsley

1. Combine all ingredients
except rice and fresh parsley
in slow cooker.
2. Cover. Cook on low 6-8
hours.
3. Add steamed rice and
parsley, stir, and cook for 10
more minutes.

—— PER SERVING ——
- 30 calories
  (15 calories from fat)
- 2g total fat
  (0g saturated, 0g trans)
- 35mg cholesterol
- 340mg sodium
- 14g total carbohydrate
  (0.5g fiber, 2g sugar)
- 15g protein
- 2%DV vitamin A
- 2%DV vitamin C
- 2%DV calcium
- 6%DV iron

Variation:
You can substitute brown
rice or pasta in place of the
steamed rice.

Chicken Delicious

Janice Crist
Quinter, KS

Makes 12 servings

Prep. Time: 20 minutes
Cooking Time: 8-10 hours
Ideal slow-cooker size: 6-qt.

12 boneless, skinless
  chicken breast halves
¼ cup lemon juice
1 tsp. salt
½ tsp. black pepper
¼ tsp. celery salt
¼ tsp. paprika
10¾-oz. can fat-free,
  low-sodium cream of
  mushroom soup
10¾-oz. can fat-free, low-
  sodium cream of celery
  soup
⅓ cup dry sherry, *or* white
  wine
grated fat-free, low-sodium
  Parmesan cheese

1. Mix together lemon
juice, salt, black pepper,
celery salt, and paprika in
medium-sized bowl. Stir in
mushroom and celery soups
and sherry or wine.
2. Dip each chicken
breast half in seasoned soup
mixture, then place chicken
pieces in slow cooker.
3. When all chicken is
in cooker, pour remaining
soup mixture over chicken.
Sprinkle with cheese.
4. Cover. Cook on low 8-10
hours.
5. Serve with rice.

—— PER SERVING ——
- 160 calories
  (35 calories from fat)
- 3.5g total fat
  (1g saturated, 0g trans)
- 75mg cholesterol
- 470mg sodium
- 2g total carbohydrate
  (0g fiber, 0g sugar)
- 27g protein
- 0%DV vitamin A
- 0%DV vitamin C
- 2%DV calcium
- 6%DV iron

Creamy Slow-Cooker Chicken

Sara Harter Fredette
Williamsburg, MA

Makes 6 servings

Prep. Time: 10 minutes
Cooking Time: 6¼-8¼ hours
Ideal slow-cooker size: 4-qt.

6 boneless, skinless
  chicken breast halves
10¾-oz. can fat-free,
  low-sodium cream of
  mushroom soup
1 pkg. low-sodium dry
  mushroom soup mix
¼-½ cup fat-free sour
  cream
4-oz. can mushrooms,
  drained

1. Stir together mushroom
soup and dry soup mix. Dip
each chicken breast half in
mixture and then place in
slow cooker.
2. Pour remaining soup
mix over chicken pieces.
3. Cover. Cook on low 6-8
hours.
4. Just before serving,
stir in sour cream and
mushrooms. Cover. Turn

cooker to high and heat for 10 minutes.

5. Serve over noodles.

—— PER SERVING ——

- 200 calories (45 calories from fat)
- 5g total fat (1.5g saturated, 0g trans)
- 75mg cholesterol
- 620mg sodium
- 8g total carbohydrate (0g fiber, 1g sugar)
- 28g protein
- 0%DV vitamin A
- 0%DV vitamin C
- 4%DV calcium
- 6%DV iron

Tip:

Leftover sauce makes a flavorful topping for grilled hamburgers.

Mandarin Orange Chicken

Ann VanDoren
West Lady Lake, FL

Makes 4 servings

Prep. Time: 10 minutes
Cooking Time: 4¼-5¼ hours
Ideal slow-cooker size: 3- or 4-qt.

4 boneless, skinless chicken breast halves
1 medium-sized onion, thinly sliced
¼ cup orange juice concentrate
1 tsp. poultry seasoning
½ tsp. salt
11-oz. can mandarin oranges, drained, with 3 Tbsp. juice reserved
2 Tbsp. flour

1. Place chicken in slow cooker.
2. Combine onion, orange juice concentrate, poultry seasoning, and salt. Pour over chicken.
3. Cover. Cook on low 4-5 hours.
4. Remove chicken and keep warm. Reserve cooking juices.
5. In a saucepan, combine 3 Tbsp. reserved mandarin orange juice and flour. Stir until smooth.
6. Stir in cooking juices. Bring to a boil. Stir and cook for 2 minutes to thicken.
7. Stir in mandarin oranges. Pour over chicken.
8. Serve with rice or pasta.

—— PER SERVING ——

- 240 calories (30 calories from fat)
- 3.5g total fat (1g saturated, 0g trans)
- 75mg cholesterol
- 360mg sodium
- 25g total carbohydrate (1g fiber, 20g sugar)
- 28g protein
- 10%DV vitamin A
- 30%DV vitamin C
- 4%DV calcium
- 10%DV iron

Creamy Comforting Chicken and Rice

Elaine Patton
West Middletown, PA

Makes 12 servings

Prep. Time: 15 minutes
Cooking Time: 4-6 hours
Ideal slow-cooker size: 4-qt.

10¾-oz. can low-sodium, low-fat cream of chicken soup
10¾-oz. can low-sodium, low-fat cream of celery soup
10¾-oz. can low-sodium, low-fat cream of mushroom
3 soup cans fat-free milk (use the soup cans you've just emptied of soup)
1½ cups long-grain uncooked rice
3 lbs. boneless, skinless chicken breasts, trimmed of fat, uncooked, and cut into cubes
1 envelope dry onion-soup mix

1. Whisk soups and milk together in slow cooker until smooth.
2. Mix uncooked rice into liquid.
3. Arrange chicken pieces over rice, pushing chicken down into liquid.
4. Sprinkle with dry onion soup mix.
5. Cover. Cook 4 hours on low. Check to see if rice and chicken are cooked. If not, cover and continue cooking another hour. Then check again. Cover and cook up to another hour if needed.

—— PER SERVING ——

- 290 calories (40 calories from fat)
- 4.5g total fat (1.5g saturated, 0g trans)
- 65mg cholesterol
- 570mg sodium
- 31g total carbohydrate (1g fiber, 5g sugar)
- 28g protein
- 6%DV vitamin A
- 0%DV vitamin C
- 15%DV calcium
- 10%DV iron

To make your own cream of mushroom or celery soup, please turn to pages 264-265.

Apricot Mustard Chicken

Lee Ann Hazlett
Delavan, WI

Makes 6 servings

Prep. Time: 20 minutes
Cooking Time: 2½-6 hours
Ideal slow-cooker size: 5- or 6-qt.

11½-oz. can apricot nectar
2 Tbsp. Dijon mustard
1 clove garlic, minced
¼ tsp. fresh ginger, grated
¼ tsp. cayenne pepper
¼ tsp. ground allspice
¼ tsp. turmeric
¼ tsp. ground cardamom
6 boneless, skinless
    chicken breast halves
4 cups prepared couscous
    or wild rice (blended is
    good, too)

1. Combine all ingredients except chicken and couscous in slow cooker.

2. Add chicken, turning pieces to make sure all sides are covered in sauce.

3. Cover. Cook on low 5-6 hours or on high 2½-3 hours.

4. Remove chicken and arrange over warm couscous or rice. Pour the sauce over the chicken and serve.

—— PER SERVING ——
• 300 calories   • 33g total carbohydrate
  (35 calories from fat)   (2g fiber, 8g sugar)
• 4g total fat   • 31g protein
  (1g saturated, 0g trans)   • 15%DV vitamin A
• 75mg cholesterol   • 2%DV vitamin C
• 200mg sodium   • 4%DV calcium
   • 10%DV iron

Golden Chicken and Noodles

Betty B. Dennison
Grove City, PA

Makes 8-10 servings

Prep. Time: 25 minutes
Cooking Time: 6-7 hours
Ideal slow-cooker size: 5-qt.

2 10¾-oz. cans 98% fat-free
    cream of chicken soup
½ cup water
¼ cup lemon juice
1 Tbsp. Dijon mustard
1½ tsp. garlic powder
¼-½ tsp. black pepper,
    according to your taste
    preference
6 large carrots, sliced
8 boneless chicken breast
    halves
8 cups hot, cooked egg
    noodles
parsley, if desired

1. Combine cream of chicken soup, water, lemon juice, mustard, garlic powder, pepper, and carrots in slow cooker.

2. Cut the chicken breast halves into quarters or smaller chunks. Stir into mixture in cooker.

3. Cover. Cook on low 6-7 hours.

4. Serve over egg noodles.

—— PER SERVING ——
• 450 calories   • 51g total carbohydrate
  (90 calories from fat)   (3g fiber, 5g sugar)
• 10g total fat (2.5g   • 37g protein
  saturated, 0g trans)   • 200%DV vitamin A
• 130mg cholesterol   • 10%DV vitamin C
• 740mg sodium   • 6%DV calcium
   • 25%DV iron

Tip:
If you prefer a thicker sauce, and if you are willing to add a few more calories and carbs to your meal, remove the cooked chicken from the slow cooker after Step 3. Keep warm. Remove ½ cup cooking juices from cooker and allow to cool for a few minutes. Stir 2-3 Tbsp. flour or cornstarch into juices until smooth. Then stir back into juices in cooker. Cover and cook another 15 minutes, until juices are thickened. Stir in chicken and serve.

Honey Chicken

Donna Lantgen
Rapid City, SD

Makes 6 servings

Prep. Time: 10 minutes
Cooking Time: 4-6 hours
Ideal slow-cooker size: 5- or 6-qt.

**6 boneless, skinless
   chicken breast halves**
½ cup light soy sauce
½ cup honey
2 Tbsp. sesame seeds,
   optional

1. Mix together soy sauce, honey, and sesame seeds, if desired.
2. Place chicken in slow cooker, spooning 2 Tbsp. of soy-honey-seeds mixture over each breast. Pour any remaining sauce over top after all chicken is in the cooker.
3. Cook on low 4-6 hours, or until meat juices run clear.

—— PER SERVING ——
- 170 calories
  (15 calories from fat)
- 1.5g total fat
  (0g saturated, 0g trans)
- 35mg cholesterol
- 740mg sodium
- 25g total carbohydrate
  (0g fiber, 22g sugar)
- 15g protein
- 0%DV vitamin A
- 0%DV vitamin C
- 2%DV calcium
- 6%DV iron

Low-Fat Glazed Chicken

Martha Hershey
Ronks, PA
Jean Butzer
Batavia, NY

Makes 6 servings

Prep. Time: 15-20 minutes
Cooking Time: 3¼-6¼ hours
Ideal slow-cooker size: 4 qt.

**6-oz. can frozen
   concentrated orange
   juice, thawed**
½ tsp. dried marjoram
¼ tsp. nutmeg
¼ tsp. garlic powder
**6 skinless chicken breast
   halves**
¼ cup water
2 Tbsp. cornstarch

1. Mix orange juice concentrate with marjoram, nutmeg, and garlic powder.
2. Dip chicken breasts in sauce. Place in slow cooker.
3. Pour remaining orange juice mixture over chicken.
4. Cover and cook on low 6 hours or on high 3-4 hours.
5. Remove chicken from slow cooker and keep warm on a platter.
6. Pour remaining liquid in a saucepan.
7. Mix the cornstarch in water and pour into saucepan. Cook until thickened, stirring continually.
8. Pour sauce over the chicken and serve with rice or noodles.

—— PER SERVING ——
- 130 calories
  (15 calories from fat)
- 1.5g total fat
  (0g saturated, 0g trans)
- 35mg cholesterol
- 35mg sodium
- 13g total carbohydrate
  (0g fiber, 11g sugar)
- 14g protein
- 2%DV vitamin A
- 30%DV vitamin C
- 2%DV calcium
- 4%DV iron

Variations:

1. To add texture and flavor, add 3 Granny Smith apples, cored and sliced, immediately following Step 4. Continue cooking 1 more hour on low. Then remove chicken and apples and keep warm while proceeding to Step 6.
2. If you are not concerned about sodium intake, you may increase the garlic powder to ½ tsp., or add ½ tsp. salt to Step 1.

Coq au Vin

Nancy Savage
Factoryville, PA

Makes 6 servings

Prep. Time: 30 minutes
Cooking Time: 5¼-6¼ hours
Ideal slow-cooker size: 4- or 5-qt.

4 slices turkey bacon
1½ cups frozen pearl onions
1 cup fresh, sliced, button
　mushrooms
1 clove garlic, minced
1 tsp. dried thyme leaves
¼ tsp. coarse ground black
　pepper
6 boneless, skinless
　chicken breast halves
½ cup dry red wine
¾ cup fat-free, low-sodium
　chicken broth
¼ cup tomato paste
3 Tbsp. flour

1. Cook bacon in medium skillet over medium heat. Drain and cut up.

2. Layer ingredients in slow cooker in the following order: onions, crumbled bacon, mushrooms, garlic, thyme, pepper, chicken, wine, and broth.

3. Cover. Cook on low 5-6 hours.

4. Remove chicken and vegetables. Cover. Keep warm.

5. Ladle ½ cup cooking liquid into small bowl. Allow to cool slightly.

6. Turn slow cooker to high. Cover.

7. Mix removed liquid, tomato paste, and flour until smooth.

8. Return tomato mixture to slow cooker.

9. Cover. Cook 15 minutes or until thickened.

10. Serve chicken and sauce over egg noodles, if desired.

—— PER SERVING ——
• 230 calories
　(45 calories from fat)
• 5g total fat
　(1.5g saturated,
　0g trans)
• 80mg cholesterol
• 230mg sodium
• 11g total carbohydrate
　(2g fiber, 4g sugar)
• 31g protein
• 6%DV vitamin A
• 6%DV vitamin C
• 4%DV calcium
• 15%DV iron

Delicious Chicken & Vegetables

Tina Goss
Duenweg, MO

Makes 6 servings

Prep. Time: 20-25 minutes
Cooking Time: 3½-5 hours
Ideal slow-cooker size: 4- or 5-qt.

1 cup fresh mushrooms,
　sliced
2 carrots, sliced
2 onions, sliced
2 celery ribs with leaves,
　cut in 1" sections
6 boneless, skinless
　chicken breast halves
1 tsp. salt
½ tsp. black pepper
dash of red pepper flakes
1 cup water
½ cup white wine
½ tsp. dried basil
2 tsp. dried parsley

1. Combine mushrooms, carrots, onions, and celery in slow cooker.

2. Lay chicken breasts on top.

3. Mix together salt, black pepper, red pepper flakes, water, and wine. Pour over chicken and vegetables. Sprinkle with basil and parsley.

4. Cover. Cook on high 3½-5 hours.

5. To serve, place chicken in center of platter. Using slotted spoon, place vegetables around the chicken. Serve remaining broth in a gravy bowl.

—— PER SERVING ——
• 190 calories
　(30 calories from fat)
• 3.5g total fat
　(1g saturated, 0g trans)
• 75mg cholesterol
• 470mg sodium
• 7g total carbohydrate
　(2g fiber, 4g sugar)
• 28g protein
• 100%DV vitamin A
• 2%DV vitamin C
• 4%DV calcium
• 8%DV iron

Variations:

If you'd like more vegetables, add another ½ cup mushrooms, 1 more carrot, 1 more onion, and an additional celery rib. You may need to add another hour to the cooking time so that the vegetables are done to your liking.

Autumn Chicken and Veggies

Nanci Keatley
Salem, OR

Makes 6 servings

Prep. Time: 20 minutes
Cooking Time: 4-6 hours
Ideal slow-cooker size: 6-qt.

2 yellow onions, chopped
2 parsnips, cut into
 ½"-thick slices
3 carrots, cut into ½"-thick
 slices
1 lb. celery root, cut into
 chunks
½ tsp. salt
¼-½ tsp. pepper
6 5-oz. boneless, skinless
 chicken breast halves
salt to taste, *optional*
pepper to taste, *optional*
1 tsp. tarragon
1 cup low-sodium, nonfat
 chicken broth
½ cup white wine

1. Place vegetables in
slow cooker. Stir in salt and
pepper. Mix well.
2. Lay chicken pieces over
vegetables.
3. Season with salt and
pepper if you wish. Sprinkle
with tarragon.
4. Pour broth and wine
around the chicken pieces, so
as not to disturb the seasonings.
5. Cover. Cook on low 4-6
hours, or until vegetables and
chicken are tender and done
to your liking.

—— PER SERVING ——
• 270 calories
 (35 calories from fat)
• 4g total fat
 (1g saturated, 0g trans)
• 80mg cholesterol
• 380mg sodium
• 23g total carbohydrate
 (5g fiber, 7g sugar)
• 32g protein
• 0%DV vitamin A
• 30%DV vitamin C
• 8%DV calcium
• 10%DV iron

Tip:
 We like this with mashed
potatoes or some good French
bread.

Smothered Chicken

Marilyn Mowry
Irving, TX

Makes 4 servings

Prep. Time: 25-30 minutes
Cooking Time: 6-8 hours
Ideal slow-cooker size: 4- or 5-qt.

4 boneless, skinless chicken
 breast halves, each ¼ lb.
 in weight
flour as needed (about 3
 Tbsp.)
1 Tbsp. vegetable oil
½ tsp. salt
¼ tsp. black pepper
2 cups carrots, cut in ½"
 diagonal slices
1 cup onion, cut in ¼" slices
1 garlic clove, minced
2 4-oz. cans mushrooms,
 drained
¼ cup flour
14½-oz. can fat-free, low-
 sodium chicken broth
1 Tbsp. fresh thyme,
 chopped, *or* 1 tsp. dried
 thyme
chopped fresh chives,
 optional

1. Dredge chicken in flour
to coat. Sauté in hot oil in
skillet, just until browned.
Season with salt and pepper.
2. Arrange chicken in slow
cooker.
3. Combine remaining
ingredients, except thyme and
chives, in slow cooker.
4. Cook on low 6-8 hours
or until vegetables are tender.
Stir in fresh herbs and serve.

—— PER SERVING ——
• 310 calories
 (70 calories from fat)
• 7 total fat (1.5g
 saturated, 0g trans)
• 75mg cholesterol
• 930mg sodium
• 26g total carbohydrate
 (6g fiber, 7g sugar)
• 34g protein
• 250%DV vitamin A
• 10%DV vitamin C
• 6%DV calcium
• 20%DV iron

Variation:
 You may skip Step One for
a healthier meal.

Slow-Cooked Chicken & Mushroom Stew

Joette Proz
Kalona, IA

Makes 4 servings

Prep. Time: 15-20 minutes
Cooking Time: 6-8 hours
Ideal slow-cooker size: 4- or 5-qt.

10¾-oz. can 98% fat-free cream of mushroom soup
half a soup can water
4 boneless, skinless chicken breast halves
½ tsp. salt
¼ tsp. black pepper
½ lb. fresh, medium-sized, white mushrooms, *or a variety of mushrooms, including portabella, cut-up*
1 cup baby carrots
2 ribs celery, cut into small pieces
½ tsp. garlic powder

1. Combine soup and water in slow cooker.
2. Cut chicken into 2" chunks. Sprinkle with salt and pepper. Place in slow cooker.
3. Add mushrooms, carrots, celery, and garlic powder. Stir gently to mix.
4. Cover. Cook on low 6-8 hours, or until chicken is done and internal temperature reaches 170°.
5. Serve with rice.

—— PER SERVING ——
• 230 calories (50 calories from fat)
• 5g total fat (1.5g saturated, 0.5g trans)
• 75mg cholesterol
• 900mg sodium
• 14g total carbohydrate (2g fiber, 4g sugar)
• 30g protein
• 150%DV vitamin A
• 8%DV vitamin C
• 6%DV calcium
• 10%DV iron

Variations:

If you're a mushroom lover, double the amount of mushrooms! You may want to increase the salt, pepper, and garlic powder if you add mushrooms.

To make your own cream of mushroom or celery soup, please turn to pages 264-265.

Roasted Chicken

Kristen Allen
Houston, TX

Makes 4 servings

Prep. Time: 25 minutes
Cooking Time: 6-8 hours
Ideal slow-cooker size: 4- or 5-qt.

1 medium-sized onion, cut in 8 pieces
1 lb. boneless, skinless chicken breasts
3-4 carrots, peeled and each cut into 4 pieces
2 potatoes, cleaned and cut into chunks
4 ribs celery, each cut into 4 pieces
1 pkg. herb-with-garlic dry soup mix
10¾-oz. can 98% fat-free cream of mushroom soup

1. Place onions on bottom of slow cooker. Place chicken on top.
2. Add carrots, potatoes, and celery. Sprinkle dry soup mix over all.
3. Spread mushroom soup over top.
4. Cover. Cook on low 6-8 hours.

—— PER SERVING ——
• 460 calories (70 calories from fat)
• 8g total fat (2.5g saturated, 0.5g trans)
• 100mg cholesterol
• 1070mg sodium
• 53g total carbohydrate (5g fiber, 7g sugar)
• 42g protein
• 200%DV vitamin A
• 20%DV vitamin C
• 8%DV calcium
• 15%DV iron

Chicken Dinner

Doris Perkins
Mashpee, MA

Makes 4 servings

Prep. Time: 25 minutes
Cooking Time: 4-8 hours
Ideal slow-cooker size: 5- or 6-qt.

4 medium-sized potatoes,
 cut into chunks
4 carrots, sliced
1 large onion, chopped
4 cabbage wedges
1 can cream of mushroom
 soup
½ cup water
4 boneless, skinless
 chicken breast halves

1. Layer vegetables in bottom of slow cooker.
2. In small bowl, mix together soup and water. Spoon half of mixture over vegetables.
3. Place chicken over soup and vegetables.
4. Add remaining diluted soup.
5. Cook on high 4 hours or on low 7-8 hours, or until vegetables are done.

—— PER SERVING ——
- 530 calories
 (80 calories from fat)
- 9g total fat (2.5g
 saturated, 0g trans)
- 80mg cholesterol
- 780mg sodium
- 76g total carbohydrate
 (18g fiber, 20g sugar)
- 41g protein
- 300%DV vitamin A
- 200%DV vitamin C
- 30%DV calcium
- 35%DV iron

Variation:
 If your diet allows, you may want to add 1 tsp. salt and ½ tsp. black pepper to soup and water mixture in Step 2.

Chicken and Vegetable Casserole

Cindy Krestynick
Glen Lyon, PA

Makes 8 servings

Prep. Time: 25 minutes
Cooking Time: 3-4 hours
Ideal slow-cooker size: 5-qt.

8 boneless, skinless
 chicken breast halves
2 cups potatoes, peeled
 and quartered
3-4 carrots, peeled and cut
 in chunks
1 onion, chopped
1 rib celery, chopped
1 cup frozen lima beans
1⅓ cups water
½ tsp. salt
¼ tsp. black pepper
10¾-oz. can cream of
 chicken soup

1. Rinse chicken. Pat dry. Place in slow cooker.
2. Scatter potatoes, carrots, onion, celery, lima beans, water, salt, and pepper over top.
3. Pour cream of chicken soup over all.
4. Cover. Cook on low 6-8 hours.

—— PER SERVING ——
- 190 calories
 (35 calories from fat)
- 4g total fat
 (1g saturated, 0g trans)
- 40mg cholesterol
- 500mg sodium
- 20g total carbohydrate
 (4g fiber, 4g sugar)
- 17g protein
- 100%DV vitamin A
- 10%DV vitamin C
- 4%DV calcium
- 10%DV iron

Variations:
 Add more vegetables if you like.

If you are not concerned about your sodium intake, you may want to increase the salt to ¾ tsp. and/or add ½ tsp. seasoning salt or Mrs. Dash's seasoning in Step 2.

Chicken Soft Tacos

Kristen Allen
Houston, TX

Makes 6 servings

Prep. Time: 10 minutes
Cooking Time: 5-6 hours
Ideal slow-cooker size: 5- or 6-qt.

1-1½ lbs. frozen, boneless,
 skinless chicken breasts
14½-oz. can low-sodium
 diced tomatoes with
 green chilies
1 envelope low-sodium
 taco seasoning

1. Place chicken breasts in slow cooker.
2. Mix tomatoes and taco seasoning. Pour over chicken.
3. Cover. Cook on low 5-6 hours.
4. Serve in soft tortillas. Top with salsa, low-fat shredded cheddar cheese, guacamole if your diet allows, and fresh tomatoes.

—— PER SERVING ——
- 100 calories
 (20 calories from fat)
- 2.5g total fat
 (0.5g saturated,
 0g trans)
- 50mg cholesterol
- 300mg sodium
- 2g total carbohydrate
 (0.5g fiber, 1g sugar)
- 18g protein
- 0%DV vitamin A
- 0%DV vitamin C
- 2%DV calcium
- 4%DV iron

Marinated Chicken Tenders

Elsie Schlabach
Millersburg, OH

Makes 8 servings

Marinating Time: 3 hours
Prep. Time: 30 minutes
Cooking Time: 2-3 hours
Ideal slow-cooker size: 6-qt.

3 lbs. chicken tenders
15-oz. bottle fat-free Italian salad dressing
1 Tbsp. vegetable oil
2½ cups flour
½ tsp. salt
½ tsp. Lawry's Seasoned Salt

1. Rinse chicken. Pat dry.
2. Cut chicken tenders into 1" square pieces and place in a 9 x 13 pan.
3. Pour Italian dressing over meat and marinate for at least 3 hours.
4. Place flour and seasonings in a sturdy plastic bag. Add one-third of the cubed chicken. Toss until all pieces are well coated.
5. Remove chicken (reserve flour mixture in plastic bag). Brown in vegetable oil in skillet. Remove chicken with slotted spoon. Place in slow cooker.
6. Repeat steps 4 and 5 with remaining chicken.
7. Cover. Cook on low 2-3 hours.

—— PER SERVING ——
- 410 calories
  (80 calories from fat)
- 9g total fat
  (2.5g saturated,
  0g trans)
- 145mg cholesterol
- 990mg sodium
- 24g total carbohydrate
  (1g fiber, 4g sugar)
- 56g protein
- 0%DV vitamin A
- 0%DV vitamin C
- 6%DV calcium
- 15%DV iron

Fruited Chicken Curry

Jan Mast
Lancaster, PA

Makes 6 servings

Prep. Time: 15 minutes
Cooking Time: 4½-6½ hours
Ideal slow-cooker size: 6-qt.

3 lbs. uncooked, boneless, skinless chicken breasts, cut in chunks
¼ tsp. salt
¼ tsp. pepper
29-oz. can peach halves in natural, no-sugar-added syrup
1 Tbsp. curry powder
1 garlic clove, minced
1 Tbsp. dried onion
½ cup low-sodium, nonfat chicken broth
½ cup prunes, pitted
3 Tbsp. cornstarch
3 Tbsp. cold water

1. Place chicken pieces in slow cooker. Season with salt and pepper.
2. Drain peaches. Reserve syrup.
3. In a small bowl combine curry, garlic, dried onion, and broth. Stir in ½ cup reserved peach syrup.
4. Pour curry sauce over chicken.
5. Cover. Cook on low 3-4 hours, or until chicken is tender but not dry or mushy.
6. Remove chicken from cooker and keep warm on a platter.
7. Turn cooker to high and stir in prunes.
8. In a small bowl, dissolve cornstarch in cold water and stir until smooth. Stir into hot broth in cooker.
9. Cover. Cook on high 10-15 minutes, or until broth is slightly thickened.
10. Stir in peach halves. Cover. Heat an additional 10-15 minutes.
11. Serve chicken with warm fruited curry sauce.

—— PER SERVING ——
- 360 calories
  (50 calories from fat)
- 5g total fat
  (1.5g saturated,
  0g trans)
- 125mg cholesterol
- 220mg sodium
- 30g total carbohydrate
  (3g fiber, 19g sugar)
- 47g protein
- 15%DV vitamin A
- 10%DV vitamin C
- 4%DV calcium
- 15%DV iron

Curried Chicken

Sharon Miller
Holmesville, OH

Makes 7 servings

Prep. Time: 10 minutes
Cooking Time: 4½-6½ hours
Ideal slow-cooker size: 4-qt.

1½ lbs. uncooked boneless
   skinless chicken breasts,
   cubed
2½ cups apples, finely
   chopped
10¾-oz. can 98% fat-free
   cream of mushroom
   soup, undiluted
4-oz. can mushroom pieces
1 medium-sized onion,
   chopped
½ cup skim milk
2-3 tsp. curry powder,
   according to your taste
   preference
¼ tsp. paprika
1 cup peas, thawed

1. Combine all ingredients
except peas in greased slow
cooker.
2. Cook on low 4-6 hours.
3. Add peas.
4. Cook an additional 30
minutes.
5. Serve over noodles or
rice if desired.

——— PER SERVING ———
• 200 calories   • 20g total carbohydrate
  (35 calories from fat)   (4g fiber, 11g sugar)
• 4g total fat   • 22g protein
  (1g saturated, 0g trans) • 6%DV vitamin A
• 55mg cholesterol   • 4%DV vitamin C
• 490mg sodium   • 6%DV calcium
                        • 8%DV iron

Chicken Curry

Michelle Steffen
Harrisonburg, VA

Makes 6 servings

Prep. Time: 20-30 minutes
Cooking Time: 2 hours
Ideal slow-cooker size: 4-qt.

1 large tart cooking apple,
   unpeeled, cored, and
   diced
1 large onion, finely
   chopped
3 ribs celery, thinly
   sliced
1-2 Tbsp. curry powder,
   according to your taste
   preference
1-2 Tbsp. canola oil
½ tsp. salt
¼ tsp. black pepper
2 cups chicken breast,
   cooked and diced
1-2 cups low-fat, low-
   sodium chicken broth

1. Sauté apple, onion,
celery, and curry powder
in skillet in canola oil until
tender and glazed.
2. Season with salt and
pepper. Combine in slow
cooker with chicken and
chicken broth.
3. Cover. Cook on high
30 minutes, and then on low
90 minutes.
4. Serve over cooked brown
rice or sweet potatoes. Top
with your choice of raisins,
pineapple tidbits, toasted
almond slivers, plain yogurt,
and toasted coconut.

——— PER SERVING ———
• 220 calories   • 28g total carbohydrate
  (40 calories from fat)   (2g fiber, 4g sugar)
• 4g total fat   • 17g protein
  (1g saturated, 0g trans) • 0%DV vitamin A
• 35mg cholesterol   • 0%DV vitamin C
• 170mg sodium   • 4%DV calcium
                        • 10%DV iron

Chicken Jambalaya

Martha Ann Auker
Landisburg, PA

Makes 6 servings

Prep. Time: 25 minute
Cooking Time: 4-6 hours
Ideal slow-cooker size: 5-qt.

1 lb. uncooked boneless, skinless chicken breasts, cubed
3 cups fat-free chicken broth
¾ cup water
1½ cups uncooked brown rice
4 ozs. reduced-fat, smoked turkey sausage, diced
½ cup celery with leaves, thinly sliced
½ cup onion, chopped
½ cup green bell pepper, chopped
2 tsp. Cajun seasoning
2 garlic cloves, minced
⅛ tsp. hot pepper sauce, *optional*
1 bay leaf
14½-oz. can no-salt diced tomatoes, undrained

1. In a large nonstick skillet, sauté chicken 2-3 minutes.
2. Stir together remaining ingredients in slow cooker.
3. Add sautéed chicken.
4. Cover. Cook on low 4-6 hours.

—— PER SERVING ——
• 370 calories
 (60 calories from fat)
• 7g total fat
 (1.5g saturated,
 0g trans)
• 75mg cholesterol
• 620mg sodium
• 42g total carbohydrate
 (4g fiber, 4g sugar)
• 34g protein
• 4%DV vitamin A
• 10%DV vitamin C
• 10%DV calcium
• 15%DV iron

Variation:
You can substitute 1 cup low-sodium tomato juice for ¾ cup water.

Low-Fat Chicken Cacciatore

Dawn Day
Westminster, CA

Makes 10 servings

Prep. Time: 20 minutes
Cooking Time: 5-6 hours
Ideal slow-cooker size: 3-qt.

2 lbs. uncooked boneless, skinless chicken breasts, cubed
½ lb. fresh mushrooms
1 bell pepper, chopped
1 medium-sized onion, chopped
12-oz. can low-sodium chopped tomatoes
6-oz. can low-sodium tomato paste
12-oz. can low-sodium tomato sauce
½ tsp. dried oregano
½ tsp. dried basil
½ tsp. garlic powder
½ tsp. salt
½ tsp. black pepper

1. Combine all ingredients in slow cooker.
2. Cover. Cook on low 5-6 hours.
3. Serve over rice or whole wheat, or semolina, pasta.

—— PER SERVING ——
• 200 calories
 (30 calories from fat)
• 3.5g total fat (1g
 saturated, 0g trans)
• 75mg cholesterol
• 500mg sodium
• 10g total carbohydrate
 (2g fiber, 4g sugar)
• 30g protein
• 10%DV vitamin A
• 20%DV vitamin C
• 6%DV calcium
• 10%DV iron

Variations:
You can substitute 2 cups fresh diced tomatoes for 12-oz. can tomatoes.
If you are not concerned about increasing your sodium intake, you may want to use 1 tsp. salt instead of ½ tsp.

Cape Breton Chicken

Joanne Kennedy
Plattsburgh, NY

Makes 5 servings

Prep. Time: 25 minutes
Cooking Time: 5-6 hours
Ideal slow-cooker size: 4-qt.

4 uncooked boneless,
   skinless chicken breast
   halves, cubed
1 medium-sized onion,
   chopped
1 small-medium-sized
   green bell pepper,
   chopped
1 cup celery, chopped
1 qt. low-sodium stewed,
   or crushed, tomatoes
1 cup water
½ cup tomato paste
2 Tbsp. Worcestershire
   sauce
2 Tbsp. brown sugar
1 tsp. black pepper

1. Combine all ingredients
in slow cooker.
2. Cover. Cook on low 5-6
hours.
3. Serve over rice.

—— PER SERVING ——
• 240 calories
   (25 calories from fat)
• 2.5g total fat
   (0.5g saturated,
   0g trans)
• 60mg cholesterol
• 190mg sodium
• 27g total carbohydrate
   (6g fiber, 16g sugar)
• 25g protein
• 30%DV vitamin A
• 40%DV vitamin C
• 10%DV calcium
• 25%DV iron

Chicken and Bean Torta

Vicki Dinkel
Sharon Springs, KS

Makes 6 servings

Prep. Time: 25 minutes
Cooking Time: 4-5 hours
Ideal slow-cooker size: 4- or 5-qt.

1 lb. uncooked boneless,
   skinless chicken breasts
1 medium-sized onion
½ tsp. garlic salt
¼ tsp. black pepper
15-oz. can ranch-style
   black beans, drained
   and rinsed
15-oz. can low-sodium
   diced tomatoes with
   green chilies
4 tortillas
1½ cups grated low-fat
   cheddar cheese
salsa
fat-free sour cream
lettuce
tomatoes

1. Cut chicken in small
pieces. Brown with onion in
nonstick skillet. Drain well.
2. Season with garlic salt
and pepper. Stir in beans and
tomatoes.
3. Place strips of foil on
bottom and up sides of slow
cooker forming an X. Spray
foil and cooker lightly with
nonfat cooking spray.
4. Place 1 tortilla on
bottom of cooker. Spoon on
one-third of chicken mixture
and one-quarter of cheese.

5. Repeat layers, ending
with a tortilla sprinkled with
cheese on top.
6. Cover. Cook on low 4-5
hours.
7. Remove to platter using
foil strips as handles. Gently
pull out foil and discard.
8. Serve with salsa, sour
cream, lettuce, and tomatoes.

—— PER SERVING ——
• 510 calories
   (90 calories from fat)
• 10g total fat (3.5g
   saturated, 0.5g trans)
• 75mg cholesterol
• 1250mg sodium
• 60g total carbohydrate
   (9g fiber, 11g sugar)
• 45g protein
• 20%DV vitamin A
• 30%DV vitamin C
• 45%DV calcium
• 25%DV iron

Variation:
   If your diet allows, use
mild Rotel tomatoes in place
of the tomatoes with green
chilies.

Italian Chicken Stew

Mary Longenecker
Bethel, PA

Makes 4 servings

Prep. Time: 25-30 minutes
Cooking Time 3-6 hours
Ideal slow-cooker size: 5- or 6-qt.

2 uncooked boneless, skinless chicken breast halves, cut in 1½" pieces
19-oz. can cannellini beans, drained and rinsed
15½-oz. can kidney beans, drained and rinsed
14½-oz. can low-sodium diced tomatoes, undrained
1 cup celery, chopped
1 cup carrots, sliced
2 small garlic cloves, coarsely chopped
1 cup water
½ cup dry red wine, *or* low-fat chicken broth
3 Tbsp. tomato paste
1 Tbsp. sugar
1½ tsp. dried Italian seasoning

1. Combine chicken, cannellini beans, kidney beans, tomatoes, celery, carrots, and garlic in slow cooker. Mix well.
2. In medium bowl, combine all remaining ingredients. Mix well. Pour over chicken and vegetables. Mix well.
3. Cover. Cook on low 5-6 hours or on high 3 hours.

—— PER SERVING ——
- 340 calories
  (25 calories from fat)
- 2.5g total fat
  (0.5g saturated,
  0g trans)
- 35mg cholesterol
- 1460mg sodium
- 53g total carbohydrate
  (14g fiber, 12g sugar)
- 29g protein
- 100%DV vitamin A
- 20%DV vitamin C
- 20%DV calcium
- 25%DV iron

Chicken Tortilla Casserole

Jeanne Allen
Rye, CO

Makes 8-10 servings

Prep. Time: 30 minutes
Cooking Time: 3-6 hours
Ideal slow-cooker size: 5- or 6-qt.

4 whole boneless, skinless chicken breasts, cooked and cut in 1" pieces (reserve ¼ cup broth chicken was cooked in)
10 6" flour tortillas, cut in strips about ½" wide x 2" long, *divided*
2 medium-sized onions, chopped
1 tsp. canola oil
10¾-oz. can fat-free chicken broth
10¾-oz. can 98% fat-free cream of mushroom soup
2 4-oz. cans mild green chilies, chopped
1 egg
1 cup low-fat cheddar cheese, grated

1. Pour reserved chicken broth in slow cooker sprayed with nonfat cooking spray.
2. Scatter half the tortilla strips in bottom of slow cooker.
3. Mix remaining ingredients together, except the second half of the tortilla strips and the cheese.
4. Layer half the chicken mixture into the cooker, followed by the other half of the tortillas, followed by the rest of the chicken mix.
5. Cover. Cook on low 4-6 hours or on high 3-5 hours.
6. Add cheese to top of dish during last 20-30 minutes of cooking.
7. Uncover and allow casserole to rest 15 minutes before serving.

—— PER SERVING ——
- 280 calories
  (70 calories from fat)
- 7g total fat
  (2.5g saturated,
  1g trans)
- 65mg cholesterol
- 570mg sodium
- 28g total carbohydrate
  (2g fiber, 3g sugar)
- 23g protein
- 2%DV vitamin A
- 2%DV vitamin C
- 20%DV calcium
- 15%DV iron

To make your own cream of mushroom or celery soup, please turn to pages 264-265.

Chickenetti

Miriam Nolt
New Holland, PA

Ruth Hershey
Paradise, PA

Makes 10 servings

Prep. Time: 15-20 minutes
Cooking Time: 2-3 hours
Ideal slow-cooker size: 6- 7-qt.

1 cup fat-free, low-sodium chicken broth
16-oz. pkg. spaghetti, cooked
4-6 cups cubed and cooked chicken, *or* turkey, breast
10¾-oz. can fat-free, low-sodium cream of mushroom soup *or* cream of celery soup
1 cup water
¼ cup green bell peppers, chopped
½ cup diced celery
½ tsp. black pepper
1 medium-sized onion, grated
½ lb. fat-free white *or* yellow American cheese, cubed

1. Put chicken broth into very large slow cooker. Add spaghetti and chicken.
2. In large bowl, combine soup and water until smooth. Stir in remaining ingredients; then pour into slow cooker.
3. Cover. Cook on low 2-3 hours.

—— PER SERVING ——
• 210 calories
 (25 calories from fat)
• 3g total fat
 (1g saturated, 0g trans)
• 50mg cholesterol
• 630mg sodium
• 20g total carbohydrate
 (1g fiber, 4g sugar)
• 24g protein
• 0%DV vitamin A
• 0%DV vitamin C
• 20%DV calcium
• 6%DV iron

Variation:
If your diet allows, you may want to add ½ tsp. salt to Step 2, when stirring together the diluted soup and chopped vegetables.

Chicken and Dumplings

Annabelle Unternahrer
Shipshewana, IN

Makes 5-6 servings

Prep. Time: 25 minutes
Cooking Time: 2½-3½ hours
Ideal slow-cooker size: 3- or 4-qt.

1 lb. uncooked boneless, skinless chicken breasts, cut in 1" cubes
1 lb. frozen vegetables of your choice
1 medium-sized onion, diced
2 12-oz. jars fat-free low-sodium chicken broth, *divided*
1½ cups low-fat buttermilk biscuit mix

1. Combine chicken, vegetables, onion, and chicken broth (reserve ½ cup, plus 1 Tbsp., broth) in slow cooker.

2. Cover. Cook on high 2-3 hours.
3. Mix biscuit mix with reserved broth until moistened. Drop by tablespoonfuls over hot chicken and vegetables.
4. Cover. Cook on high 10 minutes.
5. Uncover. Cook on high 20 minutes more.

—— PER SERVING ——
• 330 calories
 (70 calories from fat)
• 8g total fat
 (2g saturated, 0g trans)
• 65mg cholesterol
• 600mg sodium
• 31g total carbohydrate
 (5g fiber, 7g sugar)
• 33g protein
• 6%DV vitamin A
• 10%DV vitamin C
• 10%DV calcium
• 20%DV iron

Variation:
For a less brothy stew, add another ½ pound vegetables.

Chicken Ginger

Dianna R. Milhizer
Brighton, MI

Makes 6 servings

Prep. Time: 30 minutes
Cooking Time: 4-6 hours
Ideal slow-cooker size: 6-qt.

6 uncooked chicken breast
   halves, cut-up
1 cup carrots, diced
½ cup minced onion
½ cup low-sodium soy sauce
¼ cup rice vinegar
¼ cup sesame seeds
1 Tbsp. ground ginger, *or*
   ¼ cup grated gingerroot
¾ tsp. salt
1 tsp. sesame oil
2 cups broccoli florets
1 cup cauliflower florets

1. Combine all ingredients
except broccoli and cauliflower in slow cooker.
2. Cover. Cook on low
3-5 hours. Stir in broccoli
and cauliflower and cook an
additional hour.
3. Serve over brown rice.

—— PER SERVING ——
- 230 calories
  (60 calories from fat)
- 7g total fat (1.5g
  saturated, 0g trans)
- 75mg cholesterol
- 1090mg sodium
- 12g total carbohydrate
  (4g fiber, 4g sugar)
- 31g protein
- 100%DV vitamin A
- 30%DV vitamin C
- 10%DV calcium
- 15%DV iron

Variations:
  You can use a variety of
vegetables that are in season for
this recipe—zucchini, celery,
Chinese peas, and turnips.
Chop or slice them and add
during the last hour of cooking.

Easy Chicken
a la King

Jenny R. Unternahrer
Wayland, IA

Makes 6 servings

Prep. Time: 20 minutes
Cooking Time 3-6 hours
Ideal slow-cooker size: 4-qt.

1½ lbs. uncooked boneless,
  skinless chicken breast
10¾-oz. can fat-free, low-
  sodium cream of chicken
  soup
3 Tbsp. flour
¼ tsp. black pepper
9-oz. pkg. frozen peas and
  onions, thawed and
  drained
2 Tbsp. chopped pimentos
½ tsp. paprika

1. Cut chicken into bite-
sized pieces and place in slow
cooker.
2. Combine soup, flour, and
pepper. Pour over chicken.
Do not stir.
3. Cover. Cook on high 2½
hours or low 5-5½ hours.
4. Stir in peas and onions,
pimentos, and paprika.
5. Cover. Cook on high
20-30 minutes.

—— PER SERVING ——
- 280 calories
  (70 calories from fat)
- 7g total fat
  (2g saturated, 0g trans)
- 100mg cholesterol
- 510mg sodium
- 13g total carbohydrate
  (2g fiber, 0g sugar)
- 39g protein
- 10%DV vitamin A
- 10%DV vitamin C
- 4%DV calcium
- 15%DV iron

Variations:
  1. Add ¼-½ cup chopped
green peppers to Step 2.
     Sharon Brubaker
     Myerstown, PA

  2. If your diet allows, you
may want to add ½ tsp. salt to
the mixture in Step 2.

Chicken and Rice
Casserole

Wanda Roth
Napoleon, OH

Makes 8 servings

Prep. Time: 20 minutes
Cooking Time: 3-7 hours
Ideal slow-cooker size: 6-qt.

1 cup long-grain rice,
  uncooked
3 cups water
2 tsp. low-sodium chicken
  bouillon granules
10¾-oz. can fat-free, low-
  sodium cream of chicken
  soup
2 cups chopped, cooked
  chicken breast
¼ tsp. garlic powder

*Lightly grease your slow cooker before adding casserole
ingredients.*
     Sara Wilson, Blairstown, MO

1 tsp. onion salt
1 cup grated, fat-free
   cheddar cheese
16-oz. bag frozen broccoli,
   thawed

1. Combine all ingredients
except broccoli in slow
cooker.
2. One hour before end of
cooking time, stir in broccoli.
3. Cook on high a total of
2-3 hours or on low a total of
4-6 hours.

—— PER SERVING ——
• 200 calories
   (20 calories from fat)
• 2.5g total fat (0.5g
   saturated, 0g trans)
• 30mg cholesterol
• 960mg sodium
• 25g total carbohydrate
   (2g fiber, 1g sugar)
• 18g protein
• 15%DV vitamin A
• 20%DV vitamin C
• 20%DV calcium
• 10%DV iron

Tip:
   If casserole is too runny as
the end of the cooking time
nears, remove lid from slow
cooker for 15 minutes while
continuing to cook on high.

Marinated Asian Chicken Salad

Lee Ann Hazlett
Delavan, WI

Makes 8 servings

Prep. Time: 40 minutes
Cooking Time: 3-8 hours
Ideal slow-cooker size: 5- or 6-qt.

Marinade:
   3 cloves minced garlic
   1 Tbsp. fresh ginger,
      grated
   1 tsp. dried red pepper
      flakes
   2 Tbsp. honey
   3 Tbsp. low-sodium soy
      sauce

6 boneless, skinless
   chicken breast halves,
   uncooked

Dressing:
   ½ cup rice wine vinegar
   1 clove garlic, minced
   1 tsp. fresh ginger, grated
   1 Tbsp. honey

Salad:
   1 large head lettuce,
      shredded
   2 carrots, julienned
   ½ cup roasted
      peanuts, chopped
   ¼ cup cilantro,
      chopped
   ½ package maifun
      rice noodles, fried
      in hot oil

1. Mix Marinade ingredi-
ents in a small bowl.
2. Place chicken in slow
cooker and pour marinade
over chicken, coating each
piece well.
3. Cover. Cook on low 6 to
8 hours or high 3 to 4 hours.
4. Remove chicken from
slow cooker and cool. Reserve
juices. Shred chicken into
bite-sized pieces.
5. In a small bowl, combine
Dressing ingredients with ½
cup of the juice from the slow
cooker.
6. In a large serving bowl
toss together the shredded
chicken, lettuce, carrots, peanuts, cilantro, and noodles.
7. Just before serving,
drizzle with the salad dressing. Toss well and serve.

—— PER SERVING ——
• 130 calories
   (20 calories from fat)
• 2.5g total fat (0.5g
   saturated, 0g trans)
• 55mg cholesterol
• 250mg sodium
• 6g total carbohydrate
   (0g fiber, 4g sugar)
• 21g protein
• 8%DV vitamin A
• 2%DV vitamin C
• 2%DV calcium
• 6%DV iron

Variation:
   You may substitute chow
mein noodles for the maifun
noodles.

Sloppy Janes

Nadine Martinitz
Salina, KS

Makes 6 servings

Prep. Time: 10-15 minutes
Cooking Time: 2-4 hours
Ideal slow-cooker size: 4- or 5-qt.

1 lb. ground turkey
1 small onion, chopped
1 small green bell pepper,
   chopped
14½-oz. can low-sodium
   diced tomatoes
3 Tbsp. brown sugar
2 tsp. Worcestershire sauce
1½ tsp. ground cumin
1 tsp. chili powder
½ tsp. salt

1. Brown turkey in nonstick skillet, stirring to break into small pieces.

2. Add onion and pepper to meat in skillet, cooking a few more minutes. Drain off drippings.

3. Transfer meat mixture to slow cooker.

4. Stir in tomatoes, brown sugar, Worcestershire sauce, and seasonings.

5. Cover and cook until flavors are well blended, 2 hours on high or 4 hours on low.

6. To serve, fill 6 whole wheat sandwich rolls each with ½ cup turkey mixture.

—— PER SERVING ——
• 160 calories
  (35 calories from fat)
• 4g total fat
  (1g saturated, 0g trans)
• 50mg cholesterol
• 370mg sodium
• 13g total carbohydrate
  (2g fiber, 7g sugar)
• 18g protein
• 15%DV vitamin A
• 35%DV vitamin C
• 6%DV calcium
• 15%DV iron

Barbecued Chicken Sandwiches

Brittany Miller
Millersburg, OH

Makes 15 servings

Prep. Time: 25-30 minutes
Cooking Time: 4-5 hours
Ideal slow cooker size: 5-qt.

3 lbs. uncooked boneless,
   skinless chicken breast
   chunks
1 cup ketchup
1 small onion, chopped
¼ cup water
¼ cup cider vinegar
2 Tbsp. Worcestershire sauce
1 Tbsp. brown sugar
1 garlic clove, minced
1 bay leaf
2 tsp. paprika
1 tsp. dried oregano
1 tsp. chili powder
½ tsp. salt
½ tsp. pepper

1. Place chicken in slow cooker.

2. In a medium-sized mixing bowl, combine ketchup, onion, water, vinegar, Worcestershire sauce, brown sugar, garlic, bay leaf, and seasonings. Pour over chicken.

3. Cover. Cook on low 3-4 hours, or until meat is tender.

4. Discard bay leaf.

5. Remove chicken to large bowl. Shred meat with 2 forks. Return chicken to slow cooker.

6. Stir shredded chicken and sauce together thoroughly.

7. Cover. Cook on low 30 minutes. Remove lid. Continue cooking 30 more minutes, allowing sauce to cook off and thicken.

—— PER SERVING ——
• 120 calories
  (20 calories from fat)
• 2g total fat (0.5g
  saturated, 0g trans)
• 50mg cholesterol
• 320mg sodium
• 6g total carbohydrate
  (0g fiber, 5g sugar)
• 19g protein
• 8%DV vitamin A
• 6%DV vitamin C
• 2%DV calcium
• 6%DV iron

Note:

This is enough chicken and sauce to fill 15 whole wheat sandwich rolls.

Turkey Barbecue

Mary B. Sensenig
New Holland, PA

Makes 10 servings

Prep. Time: 10-20 minutes
Cooking Time: 4-5 hours
Ideal slow cooker size: 3- or 4-qt.

4 cups turkey breast, cut in
　1" cubes, uncooked
½ cup chopped onion
½ cup chopped celery
1 cup ketchup
½ cup water
1 tsp. dried mustard
2 Tbsp. brown sugar
½ tsp. salt
2 Tbsp. vinegar
2 Tbsp. Worcestershire
　sauce

1. Mix all ingredients
together in slow cooker.
2. Cover. Cook on high
1 hour.
3. Turn cooker to low and
cook 3-4 more hours.

—— PER SERVING ——
• 160 calories
　(10 calories from fat)
• 1g total fat
　(0g saturated, 0g trans)
• 75mg cholesterol
• 470mg sodium
• 9g total carbohydrate
　(0g fiber, 8g sugar)
• 28g protein
• 6%DV vitamin A
• 8%DV vitamin C
• 2%DV calcium
• 10%DV iron

Note:
　This Barbecue will fill 10
whole wheat sandwich rolls.

Turkey Cacciatore

Dorothy VanDeest
Memphis, TN

Makes 6 servings

Prep. Time: 20 minutes
Cooking Time: 4 hours
Ideal slow cooker size: 4-qt.

2½ cups cut-up cooked
　turkey
1 tsp. salt
dash pepper
1 Tbsp. dried onion flakes
1 green bell pepper, seeded
　and finely chopped
1 clove garlic, finely
　chopped
15-oz. can low-sodium
　whole tomatoes, mashed
4-oz. can sliced
　mushrooms, drained
2 tsp. tomato paste
1 bay leaf
¼ tsp. dried thyme
2 Tbsp. finely chopped
　pimento

1. Combine all ingredients
well in slow cooker.
2. Cover. Cook on low 4
hours.

—— PER SERVING ——
• 130 calories
　(15 calories from fat)
• 1.5g total fat (0.5g
　saturated, 0g trans)
• 55mg cholesterol
• 590mg sodium
• 9g total carbohydrate
　(2g fiber, 3g sugar)
• 19g protein
• 15%DV vitamin A
• 50%DV vitamin C
• 4%DV calcium
• 15%DV iron

Tip:
　This is good served over
rice or pasta.

Cranberry-Orange Turkey Breast

Lee Ann Hazlett
Delavan, WI

Makes 9 servings

Prep. Time: 20 minutes
Cooking Time: 3½-8 hours
Ideal slow-cooker size: 6-qt.

½ cup orange marmalade
16-oz. can whole
　cranberries in sauce
2 tsp. orange zest, grated
3-lb. uncooked turkey
　breast

1. Combine marmalade,
cranberries, and zest in a
bowl.
2. Place turkey breast in
slow cooker and pour half
the orange-cranberry mixture
over turkey.
3. Cover. Cook on low 7-8
hours or on high 3½-4 hours,
until turkey juices run clear.
4. Add remaining half of
orange-cranberry mixture for
last half hour of cooking.
5. Remove turkey to warm
platter and allow to rest for 15
minutes before slicing.
6. Serve with orange-
cranberry sauce.

—— PER SERVING ——
• 270 calories
　(10 calories from fat)
• 1g total fat
　(0g saturated, 0g trans)
• 125mg cholesterol
• 90mg sodium
• 18g total carbohydrate
　(2g fiber, 16 sugar)
• 46g protein
• 0%DV vitamin A
• 4%DV vitamin C
• 2%DV calcium
• 15%DV iron

Fruited Turkey and Yams

Jean M. Butzer
Batavia, NY

Makes 8 servings

Prep. Time: 30-40 minutes
Cooking Time: 3-8 hours
Ideal slow cooker size: 5- or 6-qt.

2 lbs. (about 3) uncooked skinless turkey thighs, cut in half lengthwise
2 large (3 cups) yams, *or* sweet potatoes, cut crosswise into ½"-thick slices
1 cup mixed chopped dried fruit
1 tsp. chopped garlic
½ tsp. salt
¼ tsp. pepper
¾ cup orange juice
¼ cup chopped fresh parsley

1. Brown turkey thighs in nonstick skillet over medium-high heat, turning once.
2. Meanwhile, place yams in slow cooker. Top with turkey thighs.
3. Sprinkle with dried fruit, garlic, salt, and pepper.
4. Gently pour orange juice over top, being careful not to disturb fruit and seasonings.
5. Cover. Cook on low 6-8 hours or on high 3-4 hours, just until turkey is tender.
6. Slice; then sprinkle with parsley before serving.

— PER SERVING —
- 270 calories
  (50 calories from fat)
- 6g total fat
  (2g saturated, 0g trans)
- 70mg cholesterol
- 260mg sodium
- 26g total carbohydrate
  (3g fiber, 16g sugar)
- 25g protein
- 180%DV vitamin A
- 35%DV vitamin C
- 6%DV calcium
- 15%DV iron

Turkey Thighs, Acorn Squash, and Apples

Mary E. Wheatley
Mashpee, MA

Makes 9 servings

Prep. Time: 35 minutes
Cooking Time: 6-8 hours
Ideal slow cooker size: 6-qt.

2 lbs. acorn squash, peeled, seeded, and cut into 1"- thick rings
6 medium-sized Granny Smith, *or* other tart, apples cored and cut into ½"-thick rings
4 uncooked turkey thighs, skin and fat removed
salt and pepper to taste
1 shallot, *or* small onion, chopped
½ cup apple juice, *or* cider
1 Tbsp. apple brandy
3 Tbsp. brown sugar
1 tsp. ground cinnamon
½ tsp. ground allspice

1. Spray inside of slow cooker with nonstick spray. Layer in squash, followed by apple rings.
2. Place turkey thighs on top. Sprinkle with salt, pepper, and shallot or onion.
3. In a small bowl, combine apple juice, brandy, brown sugar, cinnamon, and allspice. Pour over turkey.
4. Cover. Cook on low 6-8 hours, or just until turkey and squash are tender.

— PER SERVING —
- 430 calories
  (110 calories from fat)
- 12g total fat
  (3.5g saturated, 0g trans)
- 140mg cholesterol
- 135mg sodium
- 33g total carbohydrate
  (6g fiber, 18g sugar)
- 48g protein
- 8%DV vitamin A
- 20%DV vitamin C
- 10%DV calcium
- 25%DV iron

Terrific Turkey Breast

Dawn Day
Westminster, CA

Makes 10 servings

Prep. Time: 30 minutes
Cooking Time: 6¼-8¼ hours
Ideal slow-cooker size: 5-qt.

2½-lb. uncooked turkey breast
2 Tbsp. canola oil
2 cups onions, chopped
2 garlic cloves, chopped
1 tsp. black pepper
1 tsp. salt
1 tsp. dried rosemary
½ tsp. dried sage
2 cups fat-free, low-sodium chicken broth
½ cup white wine, *optional*
¼ cup flour, *optional*

1. Brown turkey breast in oil in skillet. Remove from skillet and place in slow cooker.
2. Sauté onions and garlic in reserved drippings. Stir in seasonings, broth, and wine and mix well.
3. Pour seasoned broth over turkey in slow cooker.
4. Cover. Cook on low 6-8 hours or just until turkey is tender.
5. Remove turkey from cooker and allow to rest for 10 minutes on warm platter.
6. Remove 1 cup broth from cooker and place in bowl. Mix ¼ cup flour into broth in bowl until smooth. Stir back into broth in cooker until smooth. Cover and cook on high for 10 minutes, or until broth is thickened.
7. Meanwhile, slice turkey. Serve with gravy or au jus.

— PER SERVING —
- 160 calories
  (50 calories from fat)
- 5g total fat
  (1.5g saturated,
  0g trans)
- 55mg cholesterol
- 310mg sodium
- 3g total carbohydrate
  (0.5g fiber, 2g sugar)
- 22g protein
- 0%DV vitamin A
- 4%DV vitamin C
- 2%DV calcium
- 8%DV iron

Turkey with Mushroom Sauce

Judi Manos
West Islip, NY

Makes 12 servings

Prep. Time: 25 minutes
Cooking Time: 7-8 hours
Ideal slow-cooker size: 6-qt.

1 large uncooked boneless, skinless turkey breast, halved
2 Tbsp. butter, melted
2 Tbsp. dried parsley
½ tsp. dried oregano
½ tsp. salt
¼ tsp. black pepper
½ cup white wine
1 cup fresh mushrooms, sliced
2 Tbsp. cornstarch
¼ cup cold water

1. Place turkey in slow cooker. Brush with butter.
2. Mix together parsley, oregano, salt, pepper, and wine. Pour over turkey.
3. Top with mushrooms.
4. Cover. Cook on low 7-8 hours or just until turkey is tender.
5. Remove turkey and keep warm.
6. Skim any fat from cooking juices.
7. In a saucepan, combine cornstarch and water until smooth. Gradually add cooking juices. Bring to a boil. Cook and stir 2 minutes until thickened.
8. Slice turkey and serve with sauce.

— PER SERVING —
- 100 calories
  (20 calories from fat)
- 2.5g total fat
  (1.5g saturated,
  0g trans)
- 45mg cholesterol
- 140mg sodium
- 2g total carbohydrate
  (0g fiber, 0g sugar)
- 16g protein
- 2%DV vitamin A
- 0%DV vitamin C
- 0%DV calcium
- 6%DV iron

Chopping dried fruit can be difficult. Make it easier by spraying your kitchen scissors with nonstick cooking spray before chopping. Fruits won't stick to the blade.

Cyndie Marrara, Port Matilda, PA

Lemony Turkey Breast

Joyce Shackelford
Green Bay, WI
Mrs. Carolyn Baer
Conrath, WI

Makes 12 servings

Prep. Time: 15 minutes
Cooking Time: 7-8 hours
Ideal slow-cooker size: 6-qt.

5-lb. uncooked bone-in turkey breast, cut in half and skin removed
1 medium-sized lemon, halved
1 tsp. lemon-pepper seasoning
1 tsp. garlic salt
4 tsp. cornstarch
½ cup fat-free, reduced-sodium chicken broth

1. Place turkey, meaty side up, in slow cooker sprayed with nonfat cooking spray.
2. Squeeze half of lemon over turkey. Sprinkle with lemon pepper and garlic salt.
3. Place lemon halves under turkey.
4. Cover. Cook on low 7-8 hours or just until turkey is tender.
5. Remove turkey. Discard lemons.
6. Allow turkey to rest 15 minutes before slicing.

—— PER SERVING ——
- 190 calories
  (10 calories from fat)
- 1g total fat
  (0g saturated, 0g trans)
- 110mg cholesterol
- 260mg sodium
- 1g total carbohydrate
  (0g fiber, 0g sugar)
- 40g protein
- 0%DV vitamin A
- 0%DV vitamin C
- 2%DV calcium
- 10%DV iron

Tip:
To make gravy, pour cooking liquid into a small bowl. Skim the fat. In saucepan, combine cornstarch and broth until smooth. Gradually stir in cooking liquid. Bring to a boil. Cook and stir for 2 minutes. Serve over turkey slices.

Easy and Delicious Turkey Breast

Gail Bush
Landenberg, PA

Makes 6 servings

Prep. Time: 10 minutes
Cooking Time: 6-8 hours
Ideal slow-cooker size: 5- or 6-qt.

1 uncooked turkey breast, skin removed
15-oz. can whole-berry cranberry sauce
1 envelope low-sodium dry onion soup mix
½ cup orange juice
½ tsp. salt
¼ tsp. black pepper

1. Place turkey breast in slow cooker.
2. Combine remaining ingredients. Pour over turkey.
3. Cover. Cook on low 6-8 hours.

—— PER SERVING ——
- 250 calories
  (5 calories from fat)
- 1g total fat
  (0g saturated, 0g trans)
- 85mg cholesterol
- 360mg sodium
- 29g total carbohydrate
  (1g fiber, 19g sugar)
- 31g protein
- 0%DV vitamin A
- 0%DV vitamin C
- 2%DV calcium
- 10%DV iron

Some newer slow cookers cook at a very high temperature. You can check the temperature of your slow cooker this way:

1. Place 2 quarts of water in your slow cooker.
2. Cover. Heat on Low 8 hours.
3. Lift the lid. Immediately check the water temp with an accurate thermometer.
4. The temperature of the water should be 185°F. If the temperature is higher, foods may overcook and you should reduce the overall cooking time. If the temperature is lower, your foods will probably not reach a safe temperature quickly enough, and the cooker should be discarded.

Italian Turkey Sandwiches

Joette Droz
Kalona, IA
Barbara Walker
Sturgis, SD

Makes 10 servings

Prep. Time: 20 minutes
Cooking Time: 7-8 hours
Ideal slow-cooker size: 6-qt.

5½-lb. uncooked bone-in turkey breast, skin removed
½ cup green bell pepper, chopped
1 medium-sized onion, chopped
¼ cup chili sauce
3 Tbsp. white vinegar
2 Tbsp. dried oregano *or* Italian seasoning
4 tsp. beef bouillon granules

1. Place turkey breast, green pepper, and onion in slow cooker.
2. Combine chili sauce, vinegar, oregano, and bouillon. Pour over turkey and vegetables.
3. Cover. Cook on low 7-8 hours, or until meat juices run clear and vegetables are tender.
4. Remove turkey, reserving cooking liquid. Shred the turkey with 2 forks.
5. Return to cooking juices and mix well.
6. For each serving, spoon approximately ½ cup onto a kaiser or hard sandwich roll.

—— PER SERVING ——

- 270 calories
  (30 calories from fat)
- 3g total fat
  (0.5g saturated, 0g trans)
- 50mg cholesterol
- 760mg sodium
- 35g total carbohydrate
  (2g fiber, 5g sugar)
- 24g protein
- 4%DV vitamin A
- 10%DV vitamin C
- 8%DV calcium
- 20%DV iron

Turkey Enchiladas

Joyce Shackelford
Green Bay, WI

Makes 8 servings

Prep. Time: 20 minutes
Cooking Time: 4-5 hours
Ideal slow-cooker size: 3-qt.

10-oz. turkey breast, roasted
10-oz. can low-sodium tomato sauce
4-oz. can chopped green chilies
1 cup onions, chopped
2 Tbsp. Worcestershire sauce
1-2 Tbsp. chili powder
¼ tsp. garlic powder
8 7" flour tortillas

1. Remove skin from turkey. Place in slow cooker.
2. Combine tomato sauce, chilies, onions, Worcestershire sauce, chili powder, and garlic powder. Pour over turkey.
3. Cover. Cook on low 4-5 hours.
4. Remove turkey. Shred with fork and return to cooker.
5. Spoon about ½ cup turkey mixture down center of each tortilla. Fold bottom of tortilla over filling and roll up. Add Toppings of your choice.

—— PER SERVING ——

- 180 calories
  (40 calories from fat)
- 4.5g total fat
  (1g saturated, 0g trans)
- 20mg cholesterol
- 490mg sodium
- 24g total carbohydrate
  (3g fiber, 3g sugar)
- 12g protein
- 10%DV vitamin A
- 10%DV vitamin C
- 8%DV calcium
- 10%DV iron

Optional Toppings:
green onions, chopped
ripe olives, sliced
tomatoes, chopped
shredded low-fat cheddar cheese
fat-free sour cream
lettuce, shredded

Broccoli Turkey Supreme

Karen Waggoner
Joplin, MO

Makes 8 servings

Prep. Time: 20 minutes
Cooking Time: 2-2½ hours
Ideal slow-cooker size: 5- or 6-qt.

4 cups cooked turkey
  breast, cubed
10¾-oz. can condensed
  cream of chicken soup
10-oz. pkg. frozen broccoli
  florets, thawed and
  drained
6.9-oz. pkg. low-sodium
  plain rice mix
1½ cups fat-free milk
1 cup fat-free chicken
  broth
1 cup celery, chopped
8-oz. can sliced water
  chestnuts, drained
¾ cup low-fat mayonnaise
½ cup onions, chopped

1. Combine all ingredients
in slow cooker.
2. Cook on high 2-2½
hours, or until rice is tender.

—— PER SERVING ——
- 380 calories
  (100 calories from fat)
- 11g total fat
  (2.5g saturated,
  0g trans)
- 70mg cholesterol
- 630mg sodium
- 37g total carbohydrate
  (3g fiber, 9g sugar)
- 32g protein
- 10%DV vitamin A
- 20%DV vitamin C
- 10%DV calcium
- 10%DV iron

Turkey Fajitas

Carol Ambrose
McMinnville, OR

Makes 10 servings

Prep. Time: 10-15 minutes
Cooking Time: 2-4 hours
Ideal slow cooker size: 2½-qt.

2½ lbs. uncooked turkey
  tenderloins
1¼-oz. envelope taco
  seasoning mix
1 celery rib, chopped
1 onion, chopped
14½-oz. can low-sodium
  mild diced tomatoes and
  green chilies, undrained
1 cup (4 oz.) shredded
  nonfat cheddar cheese
10 7½" flour tortillas
Toppings: lettuce, nonfat
  sour cream, chopped
  tomatoes

1. Cut turkey into 2½"-long
strips. Place in zip-lock plastic
bag.
2. Add taco seasoning to
bag. Seal and shake to coat
meat.
3. Empty seasoned turkey
into slow cooker. Add celery,
onion, and tomatoes. Stir
together gently.
4. Cover. Cook on high 2-4
hours, or just until turkey is
cooked through and tender.
5. Stir in cheese.
6. Warm tortillas according
to package directions. Spoon
turkey mixture evenly in
center of each tortilla, and
roll up.
7. Serve with Toppings.

—— PER SERVING ——
- 300 calories
  (45 calories from fat)
- 5g total fat
  (1g saturated, 0g trans)
- 45mg cholesterol
- 900 mg sodium
- 29 g total carbohydrate
  (2g fiber, 2g sugar)
- 36g protein
- 6%DV vitamin A
- 4%DV vitamin C
- 10%DV calcium
- 15%DV iron

Turkey Meat Loaf

Martha Ann Auker
Landisburg, PA

Makes 8 servings

Prep. Time: 30 minutes
Cooking Time: 4-5 hours
Ideal slow-cooker size: 4-qt.

1½ lbs. lean ground turkey
2 egg whites
⅓ cup ketchup
1 Tbsp. Worcestershire sauce
1 tsp. dried basil
½ tsp. salt
½ tsp. black pepper
2 small onions, chopped
2 potatoes, finely shredded
2 small red bell peppers,
  finely chopped

1. Combine all ingredients
in a large bowl.
2. Shape into a loaf to fit
in your slow cooker. Place in
slow cooker.
3. Cover. Cook on low 4-5
hours.

—— PER SERVING ——
- 200 calories
  (60 calories from fat)
- 7g total fat
  (2g saturated, 0g trans)
- 65mg cholesterol
- 380mg sodium
- 16g total carbohydrate
  (2g fiber, 4g sugar)
- 17g protein
- 20%DV vitamin A
- 40%DV vitamin C
- 4%DV calcium
- 10%DV iron

Turkey Lasagna

Rhoda Atzeff
Lancaster, PA

Makes 10 servings

Prep. Time: 20-30 minutes
Cooking Time: 5 hours
Ideal slow cooker size: 5-qt.

1 lb. 95% lean ground turkey
1 onion, chopped
⅛ tsp. garlic powder
2 15-oz. cans low-sodium tomato sauce
6-oz. can tomato paste
½ tsp. salt
1 tsp. dried oregano, *or* ½ tsp. dried oregano and 1 tsp. dried basil
12 oz. fat-free cottage cheese
½ cup grated low-fat Parmesan cheese
12 oz. shredded nonfat mozzarella cheese
12 oz. lasagna noodles, uncooked

1. Brown ground turkey and onions in nonstick skillet.
2. Stir garlic powder, tomato sauce, tomato paste, salt, and herbs into browned turkey in skillet.
3. In a good-sized mixing bowl, blend together cottage cheese, Parmesan cheese, and mozzarella cheese.
4. Spoon ⅓ of meat sauce into slow cooker.
5. Add ⅓ of uncooked lasagna noodles, breaking to fit.
6. Top with ⅓ of cheese mixture. You may have to use a knife to spread it.
7. Repeat layers two more times.
8. Cover. Cook on low 5 hours.
9. Allow to stand 10 minutes before serving.

—— PER SERVING ——
- 340 calories
  (40 calories from fat)
- 4g total fat
  (1g saturated, 0g trans)
- 45mg cholesterol
- 730mg sodium
- 44g total carbohydrate
  (3g fiber, 10g sugar)
- 31g protein
- 20%DV vitamin A
- 25%DV vitamin C
- 35%DV calcium
- 15%DV iron

Note:

I tried this on my brothers. It is a delicious dish, but I thought their raves were maybe a bit overdone. But it was a good feeling to know it pleased them. I overheard my one brother calling another brother in Virginia and telling him about it!

Southern Barbecue Spaghetti Sauce

Mrs. Carolyn Baer
Conrath, WI
Lavina Hochstedler
Grand Blanc, MI

Makes 12 servings

Prep. Time: 30 minutes
Cooking Time: 3-4 hours
Ideal slow-cooker size: 4- or 5-qt.

1 lb. lean ground turkey
2 medium-sized onions, chopped
1½ cups sliced fresh mushrooms
1 medium-sized green bell pepper, chopped
2 garlic cloves, minced
14½-oz. can diced tomatoes, undrained
12-oz. can tomato paste
8-oz. can tomato sauce
1 cup ketchup
½ cup fat-free beef broth
2 Tbsp. Worcestershire sauce
2 Tbsp. brown sugar
1 Tbsp. ground cumin
2 tsp. chili powder
12 cups hot cooked spaghetti

1. In a large nonstick skillet, cook the turkey, onions, mushrooms, green pepper, and garlic over medium heat until meat is no longer pink. Drain.
2. Transfer to slow cooker. Stir in tomatoes, tomato paste, tomato sauce, ketchup, broth, Worcestershire sauce, brown sugar, cumin, and chili powder. Mix well.
3. Cook on low 3-4 hours. Serve over spaghetti.

—— PER SERVING ——
- 330 calories
  (20 calories from fat)
- 2g total fat
  (0g saturated, 0g trans)
- 15mg cholesterol
- 530mg sodium
- 60g total carbohydrate
  (6g fiber, 10g sugar)
- 20g protein
- 30%DV vitamin A
- 20%DV vitamin C
- 6%DV calcium
- 20%DV iron

Swedish Meatballs

Connie Slagle
Roann, IN

Makes 4 servings

Prep. Time: 40 minutes
Cooking Time: 4½-6½ hours
Ideal slow-cooker size: 4-qt.

3 slices bread, cubed
1 cup evaporated skim
   milk, *divided*
1 Tbsp. butter
¼ cup shallots, minced
½ lb. lean ground turkey
1 egg, slightly beaten
½ tsp. salt
¼-½ tsp. black pepper,
   according to your taste
   preference
¼ cup, plus 2 Tbsp., flour,
   divided
1 cup fat-free, low-sodium
   chicken broth
1 Tbsp. low-sodium
   Worcestershire sauce

1. In a mixing bowl, toss
bread cubes and ½ cup milk.
Let stand 5 minutes.

2. In a skillet, melt butter.
Add shallots and cook 2
minutes over medium heat.

3. Add shallots, meat, egg,
salt, and pepper to bread and
milk mixture.

4. Mix well; then shape
into equal-sized balls.

5. Place ¼ cup flour on
waxed paper. Roll meatballs
in flour, coating evenly.

6. Place meatballs in slow
cooker. Add chicken broth
and Worcestershire sauce.

7. Cover. Cook on low 4-6
hours.

8. Mix remaining 2 Tbsp.
flour with remaining ½ cup
milk (and a small amount of
water if desired) until smooth.
Remove meatballs to warm
platter. Stir thickened milk
into cooking juices until
smooth. Cover and cook on
high 10 minutes, or until
juices are thickened.

9. Stir meatballs back into
sauce and heat through. Serve
over noodles or rice.

—— PER SERVING ——
• 220 calories
  (70 calories from fat)
• 8g total fat
  (2g saturated, 0g trans)
• 85mg cholesterol
• 610mg sodium
• 20g total carbohydrate
  (2g fiber, 8g sugar)
• 19g protein
• 10%DV vitamin A
• 0%DV vitamin C
• 20%DV calcium
• 10%DV iron

Saucy Meatballs

Michelle Steffen
Harrisonburg, VA

Makes 6 servings

Prep. Time: 40 minutes
Cooking Time: 3-4 hours
Ideal slow-cooker size: 3-qt.

½ lb. lean ground turkey
1 cup oat bran
1 clove garlic, crushed
2 Tbsp. water
1 Tbsp. low-sodium soy
   sauce
3 egg whites
½ cup onions, diced
½ cup low-sodium chili
   sauce
½ cup grape jelly
¼ cup Dijon mustard

1. Combine turkey, oat bran,
garlic, water, soy sauce, egg
whites, and onions. Shape into
24 balls (1 Tbsp. per ball).

2. Place meatballs on baking sheet and bake at 350° for
15-20 minutes until browned.
(They can be made ahead and
frozen.)

3. Mix together chili sauce,
grape jelly, and Dijon mustard.

4. Combine thawed meat-
balls and sauce in slow cooker.

5. Cover. Cook on low 3-4
hours.

—— PER SERVING ——
• 210 calories
  (45 calories from fat)
• 5g total fat
  (1g saturated, 0g trans)
• 30mg cholesterol
• 650mg sodium
• 36g total carbohydrate
  (3g fiber, 22g sugar)
• 12g protein
• 0%DV vitamin A
• 0%DV vitamin C
• 4%DV calcium
• 10%DV iron

BBQ Balls

Judy Moore
Pendleton, IN

Makes 5 servings

Prep. Time: 40 minutes
Cooking Time: 2 hours
Ideal slow-cooker size: 4-qt.

1 lb. 99% fat-free ground turkey
2 eggs
1 cup uncooked minute rice
1 medium-sized onion, chopped
1-lb. can cranberry sauce
14-oz. bottle ketchup
2 Tbsp. Worcestershire sauce
½ tsp. garlic powder

1. Blend ground turkey, eggs, rice, and onion. Form into ¾" balls.
2. Bake at 400° for 20 minutes or until brown. Drain.
3. Combine cranberry sauce, ketchup, Worcestershire sauce, and garlic powder in a small bowl.
4. Place meatballs in slow cooker. Pour sauce over top. Stir to coat.
5. Cover. Cook on low 2 hours.

—— PER SERVING ——
- 270 calories
  (30 calories from fat)
- 3.5g total fat (0.5g saturated, 0g trans)
- 110mg cholesterol
- 1090mg sodium
- 37g total carbohydrate
  (2g fiber, 15g sugar)
- 27g protein
- 10%DV vitamin A
- 10%DV vitamin C
- 4%DV calcium
- 15%DV iron

Tip:
You can add a little of the sauce to the meatball mixture for extra flavor.

Sloppy Joes Italia

Nanci Keatley
Salem, OR

Makes 12 servings

Prep. Time: 25 minutes
Cooking Time: 3-4 hours
Ideal slow-cooker size: 4- or 5-qt.

1½ lbs. ground turkey, browned in nonstick skillet
1 cup onions, chopped
2 cups low-sodium tomato sauce
1 cup fresh mushrooms, sliced
2 Tbsp. Splenda
1-2 Tbsp. Italian seasoning, according to your taste preference
12 reduced-calorie hamburger buns
12 slices low-fat mozzarella cheese, *optional*

1. Place ground turkey, onions, tomato sauce, and mushrooms in slow cooker.
2. Stir in Splenda and Italian seasoning.
3. Cover. Cook on low 3-4 hours.
4. Serve ¼ cup Sloppy Joe mixture on each bun, topped with cheese, if desired.

—— PER SERVING ——
- 200 calories
  (50 calories from fat)
- 6g total fat
  (1.5g saturated, 0g trans)
- 45mg cholesterol
- 680mg sodium
- 25g total carbohydrate
  (4g fiber, 6g sugar)
- 15g protein
- 8%DV vitamin A
- 4%DV vitamin C
- 4%DV calcium
- 15%DV iron

Ground Turkey Potato Dinner

Marjorie Yoder Guengerich
Harrisonburg, VA

Makes 6 servings

Prep. Time: 25 minutes
Cooking Time: 4-8 hours
Ideal slow-cooker size: 4- or 5-qt.

1 lb. ground turkey
5 cups raw potatoes, sliced
1 onion, sliced
½ tsp. salt
dash of black pepper
14½-oz. can cut green beans, undrained
4-oz. can mushroom pieces, undrained, *optional*
10¾-oz. can cream of chicken soup

1. Crumble uncooked ground turkey into slow cooker.
2. Add potatoes, onions, salt, and pepper.
3. Add beans and mushrooms. Pour soup over top.
4. Cover. Cook on high 4 hours or on low 6-8 hours.

—— PER SERVING ——
- 250 calories
  (40 calories from fat)
- 4g total fat
  (1g saturated, 0g trans)
- 35mg cholesterol
- 900mg sodium
- 31g total carbohydrate
  (5g fiber, 3g sugar)
- 24g protein
- 2%DV vitamin A
- 20%DV vitamin C
- 6%DV calcium
- 15%DV iron

Cabbage Joe

Sue Hamilton
Minooka, IL

Makes 6 servings

Prep. Time: 30 minutes
Cooking Time: 4-5 hours
Ideal slow-cooker size: 5-qt.

1 lb. lean ground turkey
3 cups cabbage, shredded
2 cups barbecue sauce

1. Brown turkey in a nonstick skillet over medium heat.
2. Combine cabbage, turkey, and sauce in slow cooker.
3. Cover. Cook on low 4-5 hours.

── PER SERVING ──
- 230 calories
  (60 calories from fat)
- 7g total fat (1.5g saturated, 0g trans)
- 60mg cholesterol
- 1210mg sodium
- 26g total carbohydrate
  (2g fiber, 21g sugar)
- 14g protein
- 8%DV vitamin A
- 10%DV vitamin C
- 4%DV calcium
- 10%DV iron

Tip:
Use as sandwich filling, if you wish, in rolls.

Kielbasa and Cabbage

Mary Ann Lefever
Lancaster, PA

Makes 4 servings

Prep. Time: 10-15 minutes
Cooking Time: 8 hours
Ideal slow cooker size: 4- or 5-qt.

1 lb. turkey kielbasa cut into 2"-thick chunks
4 large white potatoes, cut into chunks
1-lb. head green cabbage, shredded
1 qt. whole tomatoes (strained if you don't like seeds)
onion, thinly sliced, *optional*

1. Layer kielbasa, then potatoes, and then cabbage into slow cooker.
2. Pour tomatoes over top.
3. Top with sliced onions if you wish.
4. Cover. Cook on high 8 hours, or until meat is cooked through and vegetables are as tender as you like them.

── PER SERVING ──
- 480 calories
  (35 calories from fat)
- 4g total fat
  (1g saturated, 0g trans)
- 40mg cholesterol
- 1020mg sodium
- 88g total carbohydrate
  (15g fiber, 22g sugar)
- 24g protein
- 50%DV vitamin A
- 260%DV vitamin C
- 15%DV calcium
- 25%DV iron

Turkey Hash

Joy Sutter
Iowa City, IA

Makes 6 servings

Prep. Time: 30 minutes
Cooking Time: 3 hours
Ideal slow-cooker size: 5-qt.

¾ lb. lean ground turkey
1 cup onions, sliced
1 cup carrots, cut julienne-style
2 cups canned tomatoes with juice
2 cups low-sodium tomato juice
6 ozs. uncooked long-grain white rice
2 tsp. chili powder
¼ tsp. black pepper, freshly ground

1. Brown ground turkey in nonstick skillet breaking up chunks with a wooden spoon.
2. Combine all ingredients in slow cooker.
3. Cook on high 3 hours.

── PER SERVING ──
- 250 calories
  (50 calories from fat)
- 5g total fat
  (1.5g saturated, 0g trans)
- 45mg cholesterol
- 130mg sodium
- 36g total carbohydrate
  (4g fiber, 8g sugar)
- 14g protein
- 200%DV vitamin A
- 20%DV vitamin C
- 6%DV calcium
- 20%DV iron

Cheesy Stuffed Green Peppers

Jean Moore
Pendleton, IN

Makes 8 servings

Prep. Time: 40 minutes
Cooking Time: 3-9 hours
Ideal slow-cooker size: 4- or 6-qt.,
(large enough so that all peppers
sit on the bottom of the cooker)

8 small green bell peppers,
   tops removed and seeded
10-oz. pkg. frozen corn
¾ lb. 99% fat-free ground
   turkey
¾ lb. extra-lean ground
   beef
8-oz. can low-sodium
   tomato sauce
½ tsp. garlic powder
¼ tsp. black pepper
1 cup shredded low-fat
   American cheese
½ tsp. Worcestershire
   sauce
¼ cup onions, chopped
3 Tbsp. water
2 Tbsp. ketchup

1. Wash peppers and drain well. Combine all ingredients except water and ketchup in mixing bowl. Stir well.
2. Stuff peppers ⅔ full with ground meat mixture.
3. Pour water in slow cooker. Arrange peppers on top.
4. Pour ketchup over peppers.
5. Cover. Cook on high 3-4 hours or on low 7-9 hours.

—— PER SERVING ——
• 200 calories   • 21g total carbohydrate
  (35 calories from fat)   (4g fiber, 7g sugar)
• 4g total fat (1.5g   • 23g protein
  saturated, 0g trans)   • 20%DV vitamin A
• 30mg cholesterol   • 100%DV vitamin C
• 530mg sodium   • 20%DV calcium
                   • 10%DV iron

Variations:
   For a zestier flavor, use 99% fat-free Italian turkey sausage instead of ground turkey, and use 1 cup salsa instead of tomato sauce.

Zucchini-Vegetable Pot

Edwina Stoltzfus
Narvon, PA

Makes 6 servings

Prep. Time: 40 minutes
Cooking Time: 3-4 hours
Ideal slow-cooker size: 3½- or 4-qt.

½ lb. ground turkey
2 cups zucchini, diced
2 ribs celery, chopped
¼ cup green bell peppers,
   chopped
1 large onion, chopped
2 large tomatoes, chopped
¼ cup long-grain rice,
   uncooked
¾ tsp. salt
¼ tsp. garlic salt
⅛ tsp. nutmeg
¼ tsp. black pepper
1 tsp. Worcestershire sauce

1. Brown turkey in non-stick skillet.
2. Meanwhile, place vegetables in slow cooker. Top with rice and ground turkey.
3. Sprinkle seasonings over top.
4. Cover. Cook on high 3-4 hours.

—— PER SERVING ——
• 80 calories   • 9g total carbohydrate
  (5 calories from fat)   (2g fiber, 3g sugar)
• 1g total fat   • 11g protein
  (0g saturated, 0g trans) • 0%DV vitamin A
• 15mg cholesterol   • 10%DV vitamin C
• 380mg sodium   • 2%DV calcium
                   • 6%DV iron

Turkey Slow-Cooker Pizza

Evelyn L. Ward
Greeley, CO

Ann Van Doren
Lady Lake, FL

Makes 8 servings

Prep. Time: 25 minutes
Cooking Time: 3 hours
Ideal slow-cooker size: 6-qt.

1 Tbsp. olive oil
1½ lbs. 99% fat-free ground turkey
¼ cup onions, chopped
28-oz. jar fat-free, low-sodium spaghetti sauce
4½-oz. can sliced mushrooms, drained
1-1½ tsp. Italian seasoning, according to your taste preference
12-oz. pkg. wide egg noodles, slightly under-cooked
2 cups fat-free, shredded mozzarella cheese
2 cups low-fat, low-sodium, shredded cheddar cheese

1. In a large skillet, cook turkey and onions in olive oil until no longer pink. Drain.
2. Stir in spaghetti sauce, mushrooms, and Italian seasoning.
3. Spray slow cooker with nonfat cooking spray. Spread ¼ of meat sauce in pot.
4. Cover with ⅓ of noodles. Top with ⅓ of cheeses.
5. Repeat layers twice.
6. Cover. Cook on low 3 hours. Do not overcook.

—— PER SERVING ——
- 360 calories
  (70 calories from fat)
- 8g total fat
  (2g saturated, 0g trans)
- 60mg cholesterol
- 1290mg sodium
- 23g total carbohydrate
  (3g fiber, 8g sugar)
- 48g protein
- 15%DV vitamin A
- 8%DV vitamin C
- 100%DV calcium
- 15%DV iron

Tip:

You may create your own Italian seasoning by combining equal parts dried basil, oregano, rosemary, marjoram, thyme, and sage. Mix well. Stir in a tightly covered jar in a dry and dark place.

Turkey Macaroni

Jean Moore
Pendleton, IN

Jeanne Allen
Rye, CO

Makes 6 servings

Prep. Time: 25 minutes
Cooking Time: 3-6 hours
Ideal slow-cooker size: 5-qt.

1 tsp. vegetable oil
1½ lbs. 99% fat-free ground turkey
2 10¾-oz. cans condensed low-sodium tomato soup, undiluted
16-oz. can corn, drained
½ cup onions, chopped
4-oz. can sliced mushrooms, drained
2 Tbsp. ketchup
1 Tbsp. prepared mustard
¼ tsp. black pepper
¼ tsp. garlic powder
2 cups dry macaroni, cooked and drained

1. Heat oil in medium skillet. Brown turkey. Drain.
2. Combine all ingredients except macaroni in slow cooker. Stir to blend. Cover.
3. Cook on high 3-4 hours or on low 4-6 hours. Stir in cooked and drained macaroni 15 minutes before serving.

—— PER SERVING ——
- 300 calories
  (40 calories from fat)
- 4.5g total fat
  (0g saturated, 0g trans)
- 45mg cholesterol
- 420mg sodium
- 38g total carbohydrate
  (3g fiber, 4g sugar)
- 34g protein
- 8%DV vitamin A
- 30%DV vitamin C
- 2%DV calcium
- 20%DV iron

If a recipe calls for cooked noodles, macaroni, etc., cook them before adding to the cooker. Don't overcook; instead, cook just till slightly tender.

If cooked rice is called for, stir in raw rice with the other ingredients. Add 1 cup extra liquid per cup of raw rice. Use long grain converted rice for best results in all-day cooking.

Mrs. Don Martins, Fairbank, IA

Sausage Pasta

Rose Hankins
Stevensville, MD

Makes 6 servings

Prep. Time: 30 minutes
Cooking Time: 6-8 hours
Ideal slow-cooker size: 5-qt.

1 lb. turkey sausage, cut in
  1" chunks
1 cup green *and/or* red bell
  peppers, chopped
1 cup celery, chopped
1 cup red onions, chopped
1 cup green zucchini,
  chopped
8-oz. can tomato paste
2 cups water
14-oz. can tomatoes,
  chopped
¼ cup cooking wine
1 Tbsp. Italian seasoning
1 lb. cooked pasta

1. Combine all ingredients
except pasta in slow cooker.
2. Cover. Cook on low 6-8
hours.
3. Add pasta 10 minutes
before serving.

—— PER SERVING ——
• 220 calories   • 27g total carbohydrate
  (60 calories from fat)   (4g fiber, 5g sugar)
• 7g total fat   • 14g protein
  (2g saturated, 0g trans) • 15%DV vitamin A
• 55mg cholesterol   • 20%DV vitamin C
• 730mg sodium   • 6%DV calcium
   • 15%DV iron

Tip:
If diets allow, enjoy this
served with a thick slice of
Italian bread for each person.
Sprinkle with olive oil and
garlic. Broil 1-2 minutes.

Now That's Lasagna

Shirley Unternahrer
Wayland, IA

Makes 12 servings

Prep. Time: 30 minutes
Cooking Time: 3¾ hours
Ideal slow cooker size: 6-qt.

1 lb. turkey sausage
1 small onion, chopped
1 small bell pepper,
  chopped
1 qt. low-sodium tomato
  juice, *divided*
15 lasagna noodles,
  uncooked, *divided*
12 oz. fat-free cottage
  cheese, *divided*
3 cups grated fat-free
  mozzarella cheese
28-oz. jar low-sodium, low-
  fat spaghetti sauce of
  your choice, *divided*

1. Brown sausage in skillet.
Drain off half the drippings.
2. Add chopped onions
and peppers to skillet. Sauté
3 minutes in drippings with
meat.
3. Pour 1 cup tomato juice
into slow cooker as first layer.
4. Add a layer of 5
uncooked lasagna noodles.
Break to fit inside curved
edges of slow cooker.
5. Spread with half of
cottage cheese as next layer.
6. Spoon half of meat/veg-
gie mix over cottage cheese.
7. Sprinkle with 1 cup
mozzarella cheese
8. Spoon half of spaghetti

sauce over grated cheese.
9. Add another layer of 5
lasagna noodles.
10. Add remaining cottage
cheese, followed by a layer of
remaining meat and onions.
11. Add remaining 5
noodles.
12. Top with remaining
spaghetti sauce and half of
remaining mozzarella cheese.
13. Pour rest of tomato
juice slowly around edge of
cooker and its ingredients.
14. Cover. Cook on high 3½
hours.
15. Remove lid and top
with remaining mozzarella
cheese. Cook another 15
minutes.
16. Allow Lasagna to rest
15-20 minutes before serving.

—— PER SERVING ——
• 360 calories   • 43g total carbohydrate
  (50 calories from fat)   (4g fiber, 13g sugar)
• 5g total fat   • 33g protein
  (1.5g saturated,   • 25%DV vitamin A
  0g trans)   • 50%DV vitamin C
• 40mg cholesterol   • 35%DV calcium
• 880mg sodium   • 10%DV iron

Red Rice

Nadine L. Martinitz
Salina, KS

Makes 6-8 servings

Prep. Time: 20 minutes
Cooking Time 2-6 hours
Ideal slow-cooker size: 4-qt.

5 slices turkey bacon
1 large onion, chopped
2 16-oz. cans sodium-free diced tomatoes
1 cup uncooked long-grain rice
1 cup low-fat turkey ham, finely chopped
¼ tsp. salt
¼ tsp. black pepper
1½ tsp. garlic powder, *optional*
2 tsp. dried parsley flakes
1 tsp. dried oregano
1 Tbsp. hot sauce, *optional*

1. Sauté turkey bacon in skillet. Remove and cut up.
2. Cook onion in drippings until transparent.
3. Combine bacon, onions, tomatoes, rice, turkey ham, and seasonings in slow cooker.
4. Cover and cook on low 4-6 hours or on high 2-3 hours.

—— PER SERVING ——
- 170 calories
  (35 calories from fat)
- 4 total fat
  (12.5g saturated, 0g trans)
- 25mg cholesterol
- 600mg sodium
- 26g total carbohydrate
  (2g fiber, 5g sugar)
- 9g protein
- 10%DV vitamin A
- 10%DV vitamin C
- 4%DV calcium
- 10%DV iron

Noodleless Lasagna

Nanci Keatley
Salem, OR

Makes 4 servings

Prep. Time: 30 minutes
Cooking Time: 4-4½ hours
Ideal slow-cooker size: 4- or 5-qt.

1½ lbs. fat-free ground turkey
1½ cups meat-free, low-sodium spaghetti sauce
8 ozs. sliced mushrooms
1½ cups fat-free ricotta cheese
1 egg, beaten
1 cup grated mozzarella cheese (part skim), *divided*
1½ tsp. Italian seasoning
10 slices turkey pepperoni

1. Brown ground turkey in a nonstick skillet.
2. Add spaghetti sauce and mushrooms and mix with meat.
3. Pour half of turkey mixture into slow cooker sprayed with nonfat cooking spray.
4. In a small bowl, mix together the ricotta cheese, egg, ¼ cup of mozzarella, and the Italian seasoning. Beat well with a fork.
5. Lay half of pepperoni slices on top of turkey mixture.
6. Spread half of cheese mixture over pepperoni.
7. Repeat layers, finishing by sprinkling the remaining mozzarella on top.
8. Cover. Cook on low 4-4½ hours.

—— PER SERVING ——
- 480 calories
  (130 calories from fat)
- 15g total fat
  (5g saturated, 0g trans)
- 190mg cholesterol
- 2070mg sodium
- 19g total carbohydrate
  (2g fiber, 8g sugar)
- 67g protein
- 10%DV vitamin A
- 6%DV vitamin C
- 30%DV calcium
- 25%DV iron

Variation:

If you are not concerned about increasing your sodium intake, you could add ½ tsp. salt and an additional cup of spaghetti sauce to Step 2.

Frequently Asked Questions about Slow-Cooker Cooking

Q. Is browning the meat necessary, even if the recipe calls for it?

A. No, it's not essential. You can skip this step if you're short on time.

But if you have time, doing so has some benefits:

1.) You get greater depth of flavor;

2.) If you're browning ground beef or sausage, you can drain off the drippings before adding the meat to your slow cooker. That means you don't have that extra fat content in your finished dish.

Beef Main Dishes

Swiss Steak with Carrots and Tomatoes

Becky Harder
Monument, CO

Makes 6 servings

Prep. Time: 25 minutes
Cooking Time: 5-7 hours
Ideal slow-cooker size: 4- or 5-qt.

2-lb. lean beef round steak, cut 1" thick
¼ cup flour
1 tsp. salt
1 rib celery, chopped
2 carrots, pared and chopped
¼ cup onions, chopped
½ tsp. Worcestershire sauce
2 cups whole tomatoes
½-1 cup low-sodium tomato juice
½ cup grated, low-fat, low-sodium American cheese, *optional*

1. Cut steak into six serving pieces. Dredge in flour mixed with salt. Place in slow cooker.
2. Add chopped vegetables and Worcestershire sauce.
3. Pour tomatoes over meat and vegetables.
4. Cover. Cook on low 5-7 hours.
5. Just before serving sprinkle with grated cheese, if desired.

—— PER SERVING ——
• 270 calories
  (70 calories from fat)
• 8g total fat
  (3g saturated, 0g trans)
• 95mg cholesterol
• 690mg sodium
• 11g total carbohydrate
  (2g fiber, 5g sugar)
• 37g protein
• 100%DV vitamin A
• 6%DV vitamin C
• 15%DV calcium
• 30%DV iron

A slow cooker is perfect for less tender meats such as a round steak. Because the meat is cooked in liquid for hours, it turns out tender and juicy.

Carolyn Baer, Conrath, WI
Barbara Sparks, Glen Burnie, MD

Swiss Steak with Onion, Peppers, and Tomatoes

Nadine Martinitz
Salina, KS
Hazel L. Propst
Oxford, PA

Makes 10 servings

Prep. Time: 30 minutes
Cooking Time: 6-8 hours
Ideal slow-cooker size: 5- or 6-qt.

3-lb. lean round steak
⅓ cup flour
2 tsp. salt
½ tsp. black pepper
2 Tbsp. vegetable oil
1 large onion, *or more,* sliced
1 large bell pepper, *or more,* sliced
14½-oz. can low-sodium stewed tomatoes, *or 3-4 fresh tomatoes, chopped*
water

1. Cut meat into 10 pieces. Pound both sides. Mix together flour, salt, and pepper. Dredge each piece of meat on both sides in flavored flour.
2. Sauté meat in oil over medium heat on top of stove, until browned. Transfer to slow cooker.
3. Brown onion and pepper in pan drippings. Add tomatoes and bring to boil. Stir pan drippings loose. Pour over steak. Add water to completely cover steak.
4. Cover. Cook on low 6-8 hours.

—— PER SERVING ——
• 190 calories
  (60 calories from fat)
• 7g total fat
  (2g saturated, 0g trans)
• 70mg cholesterol
• 510mg sodium
• 7g total carbohydrate
  (1g fiber, 3g sugar)
• 23g protein
• 0%DV vitamin A
• 0%DV vitamin C
• 2%DV calcium
• 20%DV iron

Variations:
To add some flavor, stir your favorite dried herbs into Step 3. Or add fresh herbs just before serving.

Three-Pepper Steak

Renee Hankins
Narvon, PA

Makes 14 servings

Prep. Time: 30 minutes
Cooking Time: 5-8 hours
Ideal slow cooker size: 4- or 5-qt.

4 bell peppers—one red, one orange, one yellow, and one green (*or any combination of colors*), each cut into ¼"-thick slices
2 garlic cloves, sliced
2 large onions, sliced
1 tsp. ground cumin
½ tsp. dried oregano
1 bay leaf
3-lb. beef flank steak, cut in ¼-½"-thick slices across the grain
salt to taste
2 14½-oz. cans low-sodium diced tomatoes in juice
jalapeño chilies, sliced, *optional*

1. Place sliced bell peppers, garlic, onions, cumin, oregano, and bay leaf in slow cooker. Stir gently to mix.
2. Put steak slices on top of vegetable mixture. Season with salt.
3. Spoon tomatoes with juice over top. Sprinkle with jalapeño pepper slices if you wish. Do not stir.
4. Cover. Cook on low 5-8 hours, depending on your slow cooker. Check after 5 hours to see if meat is tender. If not, continue cooking until tender but not dry.

—— PER SERVING ——
• 180 calories
  (50 calories from fat)
• 6g total fat
  (2.5g saturated, 0g trans)
• 40mg cholesterol
• 125mg sodium
• 10g total carbohydrate
  (2g fiber, 4g sugar)
• 21g protein
• 25%DV vitamin A
• 140%DV vitamin C
• 4%DV calcium
• 15%DV iron

Fruited Flank Steak

Jean Butzer
Batavia, NY

Makes 5 servings

Prep. Time: 15 minutes
Cooking Time: 4-6 hours
Ideal slow-cooker size: 4- or 5-qt.

1 lb. flank steak
¼ tsp. salt
dash of black pepper
30-oz. can fruit cocktail in light syrup
1 Tbsp. vegetable oil
1 Tbsp. lemon juice

¼ **cup low-sodium teriyaki sauce**
1 tsp. red wine vinegar
1 clove garlic, minced

1. Place flank steak in slow cooker. Sprinkle with salt and pepper.
2. Drain fruit cocktail, saving ¼ cup syrup.
3. Combine ¼ cup syrup with remaining ingredients, except fruit.
4. Pour syrup mixtures over steak.
5. Cover. Cook on low 4-6 hours.
6. Add drained fruit during last 10 minutes of cooking time.
7. Cut meat into thin slices across the grain to serve.

—— PER SERVING ——
- 250 calories
  (70 calories from fat)
- 7g total fat
  (2g saturated, 0g trans)
- 55mg cholesterol
- 710mg sodium
- 28g total carbohydrate
  (2g fiber, 25g sugar)
- 19g protein
- 8%DV vitamin A
- 2%DV vitamin C
- 2%DV calcium
- 15%DV iron

Chianti-Braised Short Ribs

Veronica Sabo
Shelton, CT

Makes 8 servings

Prep. Time: 30-40 minutes
Cooking Time: 6 hours
Ideal slow-cooker size: 5- or 6-qt.

8 meaty beef short ribs on bone (4-5 lbs.)
salt to taste
pepper to taste
1 Tbsp. vegetable oil
1 onion, finely chopped
2 cups Chianti wine
2 tomatoes, seeded and chopped
1 tsp. tomato paste
salt to taste
pepper to taste

1. Season ribs with salt and pepper.
2. Add vegetable oil to large skillet. Brown half the ribs 7-10 minutes, turning to brown all sides. Drain and remove to slow cooker.
3. Repeat browning with second half of ribs. Drain and transfer to slow cooker.
4. Pour off all but one tablespoon drippings from skillet.
5. Sauté onion in skillet, scraping up any browned bits, until slightly softened, about 4 minutes.
6. Add wine and tomatoes to skillet. Bring to a boil.
7. Carefully pour hot mixture into slow cooker.
8. Cover. Cook on low 6 hours, or until ribs are tender.
9. Transfer ribs to serving plate and cover to keep warm.
10. Strain cooking liquid from slow cooker into a measuring cup.
11. Skim off as much fat as possible.
12. Pour remaining juice into skillet used to brown ribs. Boil sauce until reduced to one cup.
13. Stir in tomato paste until smooth.
14. Season to taste with salt and pepper.
15. Serve sauce over ribs or on the side.

—— PER SERVING ——
- 250 calories
  (110 calories from fat)
- 13g total fat
  (4.5g saturated,
  0.5g trans)
- 55mg cholesterol
- 45mg sodium
- 5g total carbohydrate
  (1g fiber, 2g sugar)
- 18g protein
- 0%DV vitamin A
- 10%DV vitamin C
- 2%DV calcium
- 15%DV iron

Slow-Cooked Coffee Beef Roast

Mrs. Carolyn Baer
Conrath, WI

Makes 12 servings

Prep. Time: 30 minutes
Cooking Time: 5-6 hours
Ideal slow-cooker size: 4- or 5-qt.

1½ lbs. boneless beef sirloin
  tip roast, cut in half
2 tsp. canola oil
1½ cups sliced fresh
  mushrooms
½ cup sliced green onions
2 garlic cloves, minced
1½ cups brewed coffee
1 tsp. liquid smoke, *optional*
½ tsp. salt
½ tsp. chili powder
¼ tsp. black pepper
¼ cup cornstarch
½ cup cold water

1. In a large nonstick skillet, brown roast over medium-high heat on all sides in oil. Transfer roast to slow cooker.

2. In the same skillet, sauté mushrooms, onions, and garlic until tender.

3. Stir coffee, liquid smoke if desired, salt, chili powder, and pepper into vegetables. Pour over roast.

4. Cook on low 5-6 hours or until meat is tender.

5. Remove roast and keep warm.

6. Pour cooking juices into a 2-cup measuring cup; skim fat.

7. Combine cornstarch and water in skillet until smooth. Gradually stir in 2 cups cooking juices.

8. Bring to a boil; cook and stir for 2 minutes or until thickened. Serve with sliced beef.

—— PER SERVING ——
• 100 calories
  (30 calories from fat)
• 3.5g total fat
  (1g saturated, 0g trans)
• 35mg cholesterol
• 120mg sodium
• 4g total carbohydrate
  (0.5g fiber, 1g sugar)
• 12g protein
• 0%DV vitamin A
• 2%DV vitamin C
• 0%DV calcium
• 8%DV iron

Machaca Beef

Jeanne Allen
Rye, CO

Makes 12 servings

Prep. Time: 20 minutes
Cooking Time: 5-6 hours
Ideal slow-cooker size: 4-qt.

1½-lb. lean beef roast
1 large onion, sliced
4-oz. can chopped green
  chilies
2 low-sodium beef bouillon
  cubes
1½ tsp. dry mustard
½ tsp. garlic powder
¾ tsp. seasoning salt
½ tsp. black pepper
1 cup low-sodium salsa

1. Combine all ingredients except salsa in slow cooker. Add just enough water to cover.

2. Cover cooker and cook on low 5-6 hours, or until beef is tender. Drain and reserve liquid.

3. Shred beef using two forks to pull it apart.

4. Combine beef, salsa, and enough of the reserved liquid to make your desired consistency.

5. Use your filling for burritos, chalupas, quesadillas, or tacos.

—— PER SERVING ——
• 80 calories
  (20 calories from fat)
• 2.5g total fat
  (1g saturated, 0g trans)
• 30mg cholesterol
• 400mg sodium
• 3g total carbohydrate
  (0g fiber, 1g sugar)
• 10g protein
• 0%DV vitamin A
• 0%DV vitamin C
• 2%DV calcium
• 8%DV iron

Note:

After living in New Mexico for the past 30 years, I get homesick for New Mexican cuisine now that I live in Colorado. I keep memories of New Mexico alive by cooking foods that remind me of home.

Browning meat in another pan means an extra step, but it adds a lot to a recipe's appearance and flavor.
Mary Puskar, Forest Hill, MD

Spicy Beef Roast

Karen Ceneviva
Seymouor, CT

Makes 10 servings

Prep. Time: 15-20 minutes
Cooking Time: 3-8 hours
Ideal slow cooker size: 4- or 5-qt.

3-lb. eye of round roast, trimmed of fat
1-2 Tbsp. cracked black peppercorns
2 cloves garlic, minced
3 Tbsp. balsamic vinegar
¼ cup reduced-sodium soy sauce
2 Tbsp. Worcestershire sauce
2 tsp. dry mustard

1. Rub cracked pepper and garlic onto roast. Put roast in slow cooker.
2. Make several shallow slits in top of meat.
3. In a small bowl, combine remaining ingredients. Spoon over meat.
4. Cover. Cook on low 6-8 hours, or on high 3-4 hours, just until meat is tender but not dry.

—— PER SERVING ——
- 150 calories
  (30 calories from fat)
- 3g total fat
  (1g saturated, 0g trans)
- 40mg cholesterol
- 320mg sodium
- 2g total carbohydrate
  (0g fiber, 1g sugar)
- 26g protein
- 0%DV vitamin A
- 2%DV vitamin C
- 4%DV calcium
- 15%DV iron

Note:
Once when I had made this roast for friends, my son said—in front of all the guests—"Mom, you always cook so well and you have a smile while you're doing it." That's the kind of comment you don't forget. And this roast is that good!

Old World Sauerbraten

C. J. Slagle
Roann, IN

Angeline Lang
Greeley, CO

Makes 12 servings

Prep. Time: 10 minutes
Marinating Time: 24-36 hours
Cooking Time: 6¼-8¼ hours
Ideal slow-cooker size: 5-qt.

4-lb. lean beef rump roast
1 cup water
1 cup vinegar
1 lemon, sliced but unpeeled
10 whole cloves
1 large onion, sliced
4 bay leaves
5 whole peppercorns
2 Tbsp. salt
2 Tbsp. sugar
12 low-fat gingersnaps, crumbled

1. Place meat in deep ceramic or glass bowl.
2. Combine water, vinegar, lemon, cloves, onion, bay leaves, peppercorns, salt, and sugar. Pour over meat. Cover and refrigerate 24-36 hours. Turn meat several times while marinating.
3. Place beef in slow cooker. Pour 1 cup marinade over meat.
4. Cover. Cook on low 6-8 hours. Remove meat.
5. Strain meat juices and return to pot. Turn to high. Stir in gingersnaps. Cover and cook on high 10-14 minutes.
6. Allow meat to rest for 15 minutes. Slice. Then pour finished sauce over meat to serve.

—— PER SERVING ——
- 200 calories
  (60 calories from fat)
- 6g total fat
  (2g saturated, 0g trans)
- 70mg cholesterol
- 1250mg sodium
- 13g total carbohydrate
  (1g fiber, 6g sugar)
- 23g protein
- 0%DV vitamin A
- 0%DV vitamin C
- 2%DV calcium
- 20%DV iron

Plum Roast

Shirley Unternahrer
Wayland, IA

Makes 9 servings

Prep. Time: 10-15 minutes
Cooking Time: 6-8 hours
Ideal slow cooker size: 6-qt.

3-lb. eye of round beef
  roast, trimmed of fat
12-oz. can cola
½ tsp. salt
1 large onion, sliced
1 rib celery, sliced
1 whole clove garlic
2 cups fresh plums, cut up

1. Layer first six ingredients into slow cooker in order.
2. Cover. Cook on high 6-8 hours, or just until roast is tender but not dry.
3. Add plums for last hour of cooking. Cover.

—— PER SERVING ——
- 220 calories
  (45 calories from fat)
- 4.5g total fat
  (1.5g saturated,
  0g trans)
- 60mg cholesterol
- 180mg sodium
- 11g total carbohydrate
  (1g fiber, 9g sugar)
- 34g protein
- 4%DV vitamin A
- 8%DV vitamin C
- 2%DV calcium
- 15%DV iron

Pepsi Pot Roast

Mrs. Don Martins
Fairbank, IA

Makes 12 servings

Prep. Time: 10 minutes
Cooking Time: 6-8 hours
Ideal slow-cooker size: 5- or 6-qt.

3-lb. pot roast
2 10¾-oz. cans fat-free,
  low-sodium cream of
  mushroom soup
1 envelope dry onion soup
  mix
2 16-oz. bottles diet cola

1. Place meat in slow cooker.
2. In large bowl mix together mushroom soup, dry onion soup mix, and cola. Pour over roast in cooker.
3. Cover. Cook on low 6-8 hours.

—— PER SERVING ——
- 170 calories
  (60 calories from fat)
- 7g total fat
  (2g saturated,
  0.5g trans)
- 70mg cholesterol
- 430mg sodium
- 4g total carbohydrate
  (0g fiber, 0g sugar)
- 23g protein
- 0%DV vitamin A
- 0%DV vitamin C
- 2%DV calcium
- 15%DV iron

Root Vegetables and Pot Roast

Rosemarie Fitzgerald
Gibsonia, PA

Makes 8-10 servings

Prep. Time: 30 minutes
Cooking Time: 6¼-8¼ hours
Ideal slow-cooker size: 5-qt.

2 beef bouillon cubes
¼ cup boiling water
14½-oz. can low-sodium
  diced *or* stewed tomatoes
1 cup dry red wine *or*
  burgundy
1.8-oz. box dry leek soup
  mix
1 Tbsp. Worcestershire
  sauce
4 cloves garlic, crushed *or*
  sliced
1 tsp. dried rosemary
1 tsp. dried thyme
1 tsp. dried marjoram
3-lb. lean boneless beef
  pot roast, rolled and tied
2½ cups sliced carrots
½ cup parsnips, peeled,
  halved crosswise
4 Tbsp. flour
⅓ cup cold water

1. Dissolve bouillon cubes in boiling water. Pour into slow cooker.
2. Stir in tomatoes, wine, dry soup mix, Worcestershire sauce, garlic, and herbs.
3. Add meat. Roll in liquid to coat.
4. Put vegetables around meat.
5. Cover. Cook on low 6-8 hours or just until meat and

For more flavorful gravy, first brown the meat in a skillet. Scrape all browned bits from the bottom of the skillet and add to the slow cooker along with the meat.

Carolyn Baer, Conrath, WI

vegetables are tender, but not dry or mushy.

6. Remove meat to plate. Cover to keep warm. Turn slow cooker to high.

7. Whisk flour into ⅓ cup cold water. Stir into liquid in cooker and cook, covered, for 10 minutes.

8. Serve meat sliced with vegetables on the side and gravy.

—— PER SERVING ——
- 260 calories
  (70 calories from fat)
- 7g total fat (2.5g saturated, 0g trans)
- 80mg cholesterol
- 740mg sodium
- 16g total carbohydrate
  (3g fiber, 5g sugar)
- 29g protein
- 100%DV vitamin A
- 10%DV vitamin C
- 6%DV calcium
- 25%DV iron

Variation:

You could add 5 red or white potatoes, quartered, to Step 4.

Italian Pot Roast

Betty Chalker
Dalhart, TX

Makes 8 servings

Prep. Time: 15 minutes
Cooking Time: 2-3½ hours
Ideal slow-cooker size: 6-qt.

1-lb. boneless round roast
1 medium-sized onion, sliced
¼ tsp. salt
¼ tsp. black pepper
2 8-oz. cans no-salt-added tomato sauce
.7 oz. pkg. dry Italian salad dressing mix

---

1. Slice roast in quarters for even cooking and to distribute the flavors better. Place in slow cooker.

2. Cover with sliced onions.

3. In small bowl, stir together remaining ingredients and pour over meat and onions.

4. Cook on high 2 hours, or on high 30 minutes and then low 3 hours, or until meat is tender.

5. Shred meat and serve in sauce over rice or mashed potatoes.

—— PER SERVING ——
- 100 calories
  (25 calories from fat)
- 3g total fat
  (1g saturated, 0g trans)
- 35mg cholesterol
- 720mg sodium
- 8g total carbohydrate
  (1g fiber, 5g sugar)
- 12g protein
- 10%DV vitamin A
- 10%DV vitamin C
- 2%DV calcium
- 10%DV iron

Dilled Pot Roast

Kathryn Yoder
Minot, ND

Makes 8 servings

Prep. Time: 15 minutes
Cooking Time: 5¼-6¼ hours
Ideal slow-cooker size: 4- or 5-qt.

2¾-lb. beef pot roast
1 tsp. salt
¼ tsp. black pepper
2 tsp. dried dill weed, *divided*
¼ cup water
2 Tbsp. wine vinegar
4 Tbsp. flour
½ cup water
2 cups fat-free sour cream

---

1. Sprinkle both sides of beef with salt, pepper, and 1 tsp. dill weed. Place in slow cooker.

2. Add ¼ cup water and vinegar.

3. Cover. Cook on low 5-6 hours.

4. Remove meat from pot. Turn cooker to high.

5. Stir flour into ½ cup water. Stir into meat drippings.

6. Stir in additional 1 tsp. dill weed if you wish.

7. Cover. Cook on high 5 minutes.

8. Stir in sour cream.

9. Cover. Cook on high another 5 minutes.

10. Slice beef and serve with sour cream sauce.

—— PER SERVING ——
- 270 calories
  (80 calories from fat)
- 8g total fat
  (3g saturated, 0g trans)
- 100mg cholesterol
- 390mg sodium
- 13g total carbohydrate
  (0g fiber, 5g sugar)
- 34g protein
- 0%DV vitamin A
- 0%DV vitamin C
- 6%DV calcium
- 20%DV iron

Autumn Brisket

Karen Ceneviva
Seymour, CT

Makes 9 servings

Prep. Time: 20-30 minutes
Cooking Time: 3-8 hours
Ideal slow-cooker size: 6-qt.

3-lb. boneless beef brisket
pepper to taste
1½-lb. head cabbage, cut
   into wedges
1½ lbs. sweet potatoes, cut
   into 1" pieces
1 large onion, cut in
   wedges
pepper to taste
2 medium Granny Smith
   apples, cored and each
   cut into 8 wedges
2 10¾-oz. cans low-sodium,
   low-fat cream of celery
   soup
1 cup water
2 tsp. caraway seeds,
   optional

1. Place brisket in slow
cooker.
2. Shake pepper over meat
to taste.
3. Top with cabbage, sweet
potatoes, and onion.
4. Season to taste with
pepper.
5. Place apple wedges over
vegetables.
6. In a medium bowl
combine soup, water, and
caraway seeds if you wish.
7. Spoon mixture over
brisket and vegetables.
8. Cover. Cook on high 3-4
hours, or on low 6-8 hours, or
until brisket and vegetables
are fork-tender, but not dry or
mushy.

—— PER SERVING ——
• 330 calories
   (70 calories from fat)
• 8 total fat
   (2.5g saturated,
   0g trans)
• 65mg cholesterol
• 350mg sodium
• 31g total carbohydrate
   (6g fiber, 13g sugar)
• 34g protein
• 240%DV vitamin A
• 70%DV vitamin C
• 15%DV calcium
• 20%DV iron

Spiced Pot Roast

Janie Steele
Moore, OK

Makes 16 servings

Prep. Time: 30 minutes
Cooking Time: 3-4 hours
Ideal slow-cooker size: 6-qt.

1 Tbsp. olive oil
2-lb. boneless beef top
   round roast
2 cups apple juice
16-oz. can tomato sauce
2 small onions, chopped
3 Tbsp. white vinegar
1 Tbsp. salt
¾ tsp. ground ginger, *or*
   1 Tbsp. fresh gingerroot,
   minced
2-3 tsp. ground cinnamon
¼ cup cornstarch
1 cup water

1. Brown roast in olive oil
on all sides in a skillet. Then
place in slow cooker.
2. Combine juice, tomato
sauce, onions, vinegar, salt,
ginger, and cinnamon. Pour
over roast.
3. Cook on high 2-3 hours.
4. Mix cornstarch and water
until smooth. Remove roast
from cooker and keep warm
on a platter. Stir cornstarch
water into juices in cooker.
5. Return roast to cooker
and continue cooking 1 hour
on high, or until meat is done
and gravy thickens.

—— PER SERVING ——
• 150 calories
   (45 calories from fat)
• 5g total fat
   (1.5g saturated,
   0g trans)
• 50mg cholesterol
• 640mg sodium
• 9g total carbohydrate
   (less than 1g fiber,
   5g sugar)
• 17g Protein
• 6%DV vitamin A
• 4%DV vitamin C
• 2%DV calcium
• 15%DV iron

Variation:
   This recipe also works well
with a pork roast.

Smoked
Beef Brisket

Joy Martin
Myerstown, PA

Makes 8 servings

Prep. Time: 30 minutes
Cooking Time: 4-5 hours
Ideal slow cooker size: 3- to 4-qt.

2½ lbs. beef brisket
1 Tbsp. liquid smoke
½ tsp. salt
½ tsp. pepper
2 cups chopped onion
1½ lbs. red potatoes, cut in
   quarters
½ cup ketchup
2 tsp. prepared Dijon
   mustard
½ tsp. celery seed

1. Cut brisket in half. Rub both pieces with liquid smoke, salt, and pepper.

2. Place brisket halves in slow cooker. Top with onion and potatoes.

3. In a small bowl, combine ketchup, mustard, and celery seed. Spread over meat.

4. Cover. Cook on low 4-5 hours, or until meat is tender but not dry.

5. Remove brisket and keep warm.

6. Transfer cooking juices to a blender. Cover and process until smooth. (Cover lid of blender with thick towel and hold it on tightly while using.) Serve juices with brisket.

—— PER SERVING ——
- 270 calories
  (60 calories from fat)
- 6g total fat
  (2.5g saturated,
  0g trans)
- 60mg cholesterol
- 400mg sodium
- 20g total carbohydrate
  (2g fiber, 5g sugar)
- 31g protein
- 2%DV vitamin A
- 20%DV vitamin C
- 4%DV calcium
- 20%DV iron

Wine Tender Roast

Rose Hankins
Stevensville, MD

Makes 10 servings

Prep. Time: 15 minutes
Cooking Time: 6-8 hours
Ideal slow cooker size: 4- or 5-qt.

3-lb. eye of round beef roast
3 cups thinly sliced onions
1½ cups chopped apples, peeled *or* unpeeled

3 cloves garlic, chopped
1 cup red wine
salt and pepper

1. Put roast in slow cooker. Layer onions, apples, and garlic on top of roast.

2. Carefully pour wine over roast without disturbing its toppings.

3. Sprinkle with salt and pepper.

4. Cover. Cook on low 6-8 hours, or until meat is tender but not dry.

—— PER SERVING ——
- 210 calories
  (40 calories from fat)
- 4g total fat
  (1.5g saturated,
  0g trans)
- 55mg cholesterol
- 40mg sodium
- 7g total carbohydrate
  (1g fiber, 4g sugar)
- 30g protein
- 0%DV vitamin A
- 6%DV vitamin C
- 2%DV calcium
- 15%DV iron

Low-Fat Slow-Cooker Roast

Charlotte Shaffer
East Earl, PA

Makes 10 servings

Prep. Time: 15 minutes
Cooking Time: 3-8 hours
Ideal slow-cooker size: 6-qt.

3-lb. boneless beef roast
4 carrots, cut into 2" pieces
4 potatoes, cut into quarters
2 onions, quartered
1 cup fat-free, low-sodium beef broth
1 tsp. garlic powder
½ tsp. Mrs. Dash seasoning

½ tsp. salt
½ tsp. black pepper

1. Place roast in slow cooker.

2. Add carrots around edges, pushing them down so they reach the bottom of the cooker.

3. Add potatoes and onions.

4. Mix together broth and seasonings and pour over roast.

5. Cover. Cook on low 6-8 hours or on high 3-4 hours.

—— PER SERVING ——
- 260 calories
  (60 calories from fat)
- 7 total fat
  (2g saturated, 0g trans)
- 80mg cholesterol
- 180mg sodium
- 20g total carbohydrate
  (3g fiber, 4g sugar)
- 30g protein
- 80%DV vitamin A
- 20%DV vitamin C
- 2%DV calcium
- 20%DV iron

Tips:

1. You may brown the roast in a nonstick skillet on all sides before placing in cooker for added flavor.

2. If you want gravy, and if your diet allows, add a second cup of fat-free beef broth to Step 4. Remove roast from cooker at end of cooking time and keep warm on a platter. Turn cooker to high until cooking juices come to a boil. Meanwhile, mix ¼ cup flour into ½ cup cold water until smooth. When cooking juices boil, stir in flour water, stirring constantly until smooth and thickened. Serve with sliced beef.

All-Day Roast

Moreen Weaver
Bath, NY

Makes 9 servings

Prep. Time: 15-20 minutes
Cooking Time: 4-6 hours
Ideal slow-cooker size: 6-qt.

4 carrots, cut in 1" chunks
5 medium potatoes, cut in
   1" chunks
1 lb. frozen, *or* fresh, green
   beans
1 large onion, cut in wedges
1½ cups water
3-lb. eye of round beef roast
2 cloves garlic, minced
salt to taste
pepper to taste
10¾-oz. can low-fat,
   low-sodium cream of
   mushroom soup
2 Tbsp. Worcestershire
   sauce
1 pkg. low-sodium dry
   onion soup mix, beef *or*
   mushroom flavor

1. Place vegetables and
water into slow cooker.
2. Place beef roast on top of
vegetables.
3. Sprinkle garlic over
meat, followed by salt and
pepper to taste.
4. Spoon cream of mushroom
soup over seasoned meat.
5. Gently pour Worcester-
shire sauce over soup.
6. Sprinkle with dry onion
soup mix.
7. Cover. Cook on high 2-3
hours.
8. Reset temperature to
low. Continue cooking 2-3

more hours, or until vegetables and meat are fork-tender
but not dry or mushy.

—— PER SERVING ——
• 310 calories
  (50 calories from fat)
• 5g total fat
  (2g saturated, 0g trans)
• 65mg cholesterol
• 370mg sodium
• 27g total carbohydrate
  (4g fiber, 5g sugar)
• 37g protein
• 100%DV vitamin A
• 35%DV vitamin C
• 8%DV calcium
• 20%DV iron

Succulent Steak

Betty B. Dennison
Grove City, PA

Makes 6 servings

Prep. Time: 25 minutes
Cooking Time: 4¼-5¼ hours
Ideal slow-cooker size: 4-qt.

1½ lbs. round steak, cut
   ½"-¾" thick
¼ cup flour
½ tsp. salt
¼ tsp. black pepper
¼ tsp. paprika
2 onions, sliced
4-oz. can sliced
   mushrooms, drained
½ cup fat-free, low-sodium
   beef broth
2 tsp. Worcestershire sauce
2 Tbsp. flour
3 Tbsp. water

1. Mix together ¼ cup
flour, salt, pepper, and
paprika.
2. Cut steak into 6 pieces.
Dredge meat in seasoned
flour until lightly coated.
3. Layer half of onions,
half of steak, and half of
mushrooms into slow cooker.
Repeat.
4. Combine beef broth and
Worcestershire sauce. Pour
over mixture in slow cooker.
5. Cover. Cook on low 4-5
hours.
6. Remove steak to serving
platter and keep warm. Mix
together 2 Tbsp. flour and
water. Stir into juices in
cooker and cook on high until
thickened, about 10 minutes.
Pour over steak and serve.

—— PER SERVING ——
• 190 calories
  (50 calories from fat)
• 6g total fat
  (2g saturated, 0g trans)
• 70mg cholesterol
• 340mg sodium
• 10g total carbohydrate
  (1g fiber, 2g sugar)
• 24g protein
• 0%DV vitamin A
• 0%DV vitamin C
• 0%DV calcium
• 20%DV iron

*Roasting bags work well in the slow cooker. Simply
fill with meat and vegetables and cook as directed in slow
cooker recipes. Follow manufacturer's directions for filling
and sealing bags.*
                                    Charlotte Shaffer, East Earl, PA

Hungarian Goulash

Elaine Patton
West Middletown, PA

Makes 8 servings

Prep. Time: 15 minutes
Cooking Time: 4-6 hours
Ideal slow-cooker size: 6-qt.

2 lbs. round steak, cut into ¾" cubes
1 cup onions, chopped
1 clove garlic, pressed
2 Tbsp. flour
½ tsp. salt
½ tsp. pepper
1 tsp. paprika
¼ tsp. dried thyme, crushed
1 bay leaf
14½-oz. can low-sodium stewed *or* diced tomatoes
1 cup fat-free sour cream

1. Place steak cubes, onions and garlic in slow cooker.
2. Stir in flour and mix to coat steak cubes and vegetables.
3. Add salt, pepper, paprika, thyme, bay leaf, and tomatoes. Stir well.
4. Cover. Cook on low 4-6 hours, or until meat is tender but not dry.
5. Add sour cream 30 minutes before end of cooking time. Stir in thoroughly.
6. Serve slow cooker contents over cooked noodles or brown rice.

—— PER SERVING ——
- 210 calories
  (40 calories from fat)
- 4.5g total fat
  (1.5 saturated, 0g trans)
- 70mg cholesterol
- 300mg sodium
- 14g total carbohydrate
  (2g fiber, 3g sugar)
- 28g protein
- 10%DV vitamin A
- 15%DV vitamin C
- 8%DV calcium
- 20%DV iron

Beef Burgundy

Joyce Kaut
Rochester, NY

Makes 8 servings

Prep. Time: 25 minutes
Cooking Time: 4¼-6¼ hours
Ideal slow-cooker size: 4-qt.

2 slices lean turkey bacon, cut in squares
2 lbs. lean sirloin tip, *or* round, steak, cubed
¼ cup flour
1 tsp. salt
½ tsp. seasoning salt
¼ tsp. dried marjoram
½ tsp. dried thyme
¼ tsp. black pepper
1 garlic clove, minced
1 low-sodium beef bouillon cube, crushed
1 cup burgundy wine
¼ lb. fresh mushrooms, sliced
2 Tbsp. cornstarch
2 Tbsp. cold water

1. Cook bacon in nonstick skillet until browned. Remove bacon, reserving drippings.
2. Coat beef with flour and brown on all sides in bacon drippings.
3. Combine steak, bacon drippings, bacon, seasonings, garlic, bouillon, and wine in slow cooker.
4. Cover. Cook on low 4-6 hours.
5. Add mushrooms.
6. Dissolve cornstarch in water. Add to slow cooker.
7. Cover. Cook on high 15 minutes.
8. Serve over noodles.

—— PER SERVING ——
- 180 calories
  (45 calories from fat)
- 5g total fat (1.5 saturated, 0g trans)
- 55mg cholesterol
- 630mg sodium
- 7g total carbohydrate
  (0g fiber, 1g sugar)
- 18g protein
- 0%DV vitamin A
- 0%DV vitamin C
- 2%DV calcium
- 15%DV iron

Variation:
If your diet allows, you may want to increase the salt to 1½ tsp. or the seasoning salt to 1 tsp.

Corned Beef

Elaine Vigoda
Rochester, NY

Makes 12 servings

Prep. Time: 20 minutes
Cooking Time: 4-8 hours
Ideal slow-cooker size: 5- or 6-qt.

3 large carrots, cut into
    chunks
1 cup chopped celery
1 tsp. salt*
½ tsp. black pepper*
1 cup water
4-lb. corned beef
1 large onion, cut into pieces
4 potatoes, peeled and
    chunked
half a small head of
    cabbage, cut in wedges

1. Place carrots, celery,
seasonings, and water in slow
cooker.
2. Add beef. Cover with
onions.
3. Cover. Cook on low 4-6
hours or on high 2-3 hours.
(If your schedule allows, this
dish has especially good taste
and texture if you begin it on
high for 1 hour, and then turn
it to low for 4-5 hours, before
going on to Step 4.)
4. Lift corned beef out
of cooker and add potatoes,
pushing them to bottom of
slow cooker. Return beef to
cooker.
5. Cover. Cook on low 1 hour.

6. Lift corned beef out
of cooker and add cabbage,
pushing the wedges down
into the broth. Return beef to
cooker.
7. Cover. Cook on low
1 more hour.
8. Remove corned beef.
Cool and slice on the diagonal. Serve surrounded by
vegetables.

—— PER SERVING ——
• 340 calories
  (130 calories from fat)
• 15g total fat
  (5g saturated, 0.5g
  trans)
• 75mg cholesterol
• 1110mg sodium
• 35g total carbohydrate
  (7g fiber, 6g sugar)
• 19g protein
• 80%DV vitamin A
• 40%DV vitamin C
• 8%DV calcium
• 20%DV iron

* If the corned beef that
you buy includes a spice
packet, use either it or the
salt and pepper called for in
this recipe. **Do not use both.**
(The nutritional analysis for
this recipe was based on the
1 tsp. salt and ½ tsp. black
pepper specified here, and not
on a spice packet.)

Tip:
    Horseradish is a tasty
condiment to serve alongside
this dish.

CC Roast
(Company's Coming)

Anne Townsend
Albuquerque, NM

Makes 8 servings

Prep. Time: 20 minutes
Cooking Time: 6-8 hours
Ideal slow-cooker size: 4- or 5-qt.

3-lb. boneless pot roast
2 Tbsp. flour
1 Tbsp. prepared mustard
1 Tbsp. chili sauce
1 Tbsp. Worcestershire
    sauce
1 tsp. red cider vinegar
1 tsp. sugar
4 potatoes, sliced
2 onions, sliced

1. Place pot roast in slow
cooker.
2. Make a paste with the
flour, mustard, chili sauce,
Worcestershire sauce, vinegar,
and sugar. Spread over roast.
3. Top with potatoes and
then the onions.
4. Cover. Cook on low 6-8
hours.

—— PER SERVING ——
• 320 calories
  (70 calories from fat)
• 8g total fat
  (3g saturated, 0g trans)
• 100mg cholesterol
• 160mg sodium
• 24g total carbohydrate
  (3g fiber, 3g sugar)
• 36g protein
• 0%DV vitamin A
• 20%DV vitamin C
• 2%DV calcium
• 25%DV iron

Make sure you cut potatoes small enough so they cook thoroughly.
Trudy Kutter, Corfu, NY

Beef Roast with Mushroom Barley

Sue Hamilton
Minooka, IL

Makes 6 servings

Prep. Time: 15 minutes
Cooking Time: 4-5 hours
Ideal slow-cooker size: 6-qt.

1 cup dry pearl barley (not quick-cook)
½ cup onion, diced
6½-oz. can mushrooms, undrained
1 tsp. garlic, minced
1 tsp. Italian seasoning
¼ tsp. black pepper
2-lb. eye of round beef roast
1¾ cups low-sodium, fat-free beef broth

1. Put barley, onion, mushrooms with liquid, and garlic in slow cooker.
2. Sprinkle seasoning and pepper over top.
3. Add roast. Pour broth over all.
4. Cover. Cook 4-5 hours on low, or until meat is fork-tender and barley is also tender.

—— PER SERVING ——
• 320 calories
  (50 calories from fat)
• 5g total fat
  (2g saturated, 0g trans)
• 60mg cholesterol
• 180mg sodium
• 28g total carbohydrate
  (6g fiber, 1g sugar)
• 38g protein
• 0%DV vitamin A
• 0%DV vitamin C
• 2%DV calcium
• 20%DV iron

Tip:
Serve with mashed potatoes. They'll benefit from the delicious broth in this dish.

Easy Company Beef

Joyce B. Suiter
Garysburg, NC

Makes 12 servings

Prep. Time: 10 minutes
Cooking Time: 5-6 hours
Ideal slow-cooker size: 4-qt.

3 lbs. lean stewing beef, cubed
10¾-oz. can fat-free, low-sodium cream of mushroom soup
7-oz. jar mushrooms, undrained
½ cup red wine
1 envelope dry onion soup mix

1. Combine all ingredients in slow cooker.
2. Cover. Cook on low 5-6 hours.
3. Serve over noodles, rice, or pasta.

—— PER SERVING ——
• 130 calories
  (40 calories from fat)
• 4.5g total fat
  (1.5g saturated, 0g trans)
• 45mg cholesterol
• 370mg sodium
• 4g total carbohydrate
  (0g fiber, 0g sugar)
• 16g protein
• 0%DV vitamin A
• 0%DV vitamin C
• 2%DV calcium
• 10%DV iron

Beef Stroganoff

Gloria Julien
Gladstone, MI

Makes 6 servings

Prep. Time: 15 minutes
Cooking Time: 3¼-4¼ hours
Ideal slow-cooker size: 4-qt.

1½ lbs. lean beef stewing meat, trimmed of fat
1 onion, chopped
1 clove garlic, minced
1 tsp. salt
¼ tsp. black pepper
1 lb. fresh mushrooms
10¾-oz. can 98% fat-free cream of mushroom soup
1 cup water
1 cup fat-free sour cream

1. Combine all ingredients except sour cream in slow cooker.
2. Cook on low 3-4 hours.
3. Stir in sour cream.
4. Cook on high for a few minutes to heat sour cream.

—— PER SERVING ——
• 240 calories
  (70 calories from fat)
• 7g total fat (2.5g saturated, 0.5g trans)
• 75mg cholesterol
• 800mg sodium
• 15g total carbohydrate
  (1g fiber, 6g sugar)
• 27g protein
• 6%DV vitamin A
• 2%DV vitamin C
• 8%DV calcium
• 20%DV iron

Tip:
This saucy dish works well served over no-yolk noodles.

To make your own cream of mushroom or celery soup, please turn to pages 264-265.

63

Slow-Cooker Stroganoff

Evelyn Page
Rapid City, SD

Makes 10 servings

Prep. Time: 20 minutes
Cooking Time: 3-4 hours
Ideal slow-cooker size: 5- or 6-qt.

1½-lb. round steak,
 trimmed of fat
¼ cup flour
½ tsp. black pepper
½ tsp. salt
1 tsp. garlic, minced
1 small onion, chopped
1 Tbsp. low-sodium soy
 sauce
1 beef bouillon cube
10¾-oz. can 98% fat-free
 cream of mushroom soup
1 cup water
8-oz. pkg. fat-free cream
 cheese, cubed

1. Cut steak into strips 1"
long and ½" wide.
2. Mix with flour, pepper,
salt, and garlic.
3. Combine with onion,
soy sauce, bouillon, soup, and
water in slow cooker.
4. Cook on low 3-4 hours,
stirring occasionally.

5. Add cream cheese cubes
during last 30 minutes of
cooking.
6. Serve over cooked wide
noodles.

—— PER SERVING ——
• 140 calories
 (40 calories from fat)
• 4.5g total fat
 (1.5g saturated,
 0g trans)
• 45mg cholesterol
• 760mg sodium
• 8g total carbohydrate
 (0g fiber, 1g sugar)
• 18g protein
• 4%DV vitamin A
• 2%DV vitamin C
• 6%DV calcium
• 10%DV iron

Milk products such as cream, milk, and sour cream can curdle and separate when cooked for a long period. Add them during the last 10 minutes if cooking on High, or during the last 20-30 minutes if cooking on Low.

Mrs. J. E. Barthold, Bethlehem, PA
Marilyn Yoder, Archbold, OH

Tuscan Beef Stew

Karen Ceneviva
Seymour, CT

Makes 8 servings

Prep. Time: 15 minutes
Cooking Time: 3-5 hours
Ideal slow-cooker size: 4-qt.

10½-oz. can low-sodium
 tomato soup
10½-oz. can low-sodium,
 fat-free beef broth
½ cup water
1 tsp. dry Italian seasoning
½ tsp. garlic powder
14½-oz. can low-sodium
 Italian diced tomatoes
3 large carrots (¾ lb.), cut
 into 1" pieces
2 lbs. stewing beef, cut into
 1" cubes
2 15½-oz. cans white
 kidney (cannellini)
 beans, rinsed and
 drained

1. Mix all ingredients,
except beans, in slow cooker.
2. Cover. Cook on high 3
hours, or on low 4-5 hours, or
until vegetables and beef are
tender.
3. Stir in beans. Cover.
Cook on high for final 10
minutes of cooking time.

—— PER SERVING ——
• 330 calories
 (70 calories from fat)
• 7g total fat
 (2.5g saturated,
 0g trans)
• 65mg cholesterol
• 350mg sodium
• 31g total carbohydrate
 (7g fiber, 6g sugar)
• 35g protein
• 100%DV vitamin A
• 20%DV vitamin C
• 10%DV calcium
• 35%DV iron

Veal Hawaiian

Dorothy VanDeest
Memphis, TN

Makes 4 servings

Prep. Time: 15 minutes
Cooking Time: 3-4 hours
Ideal slow-cooker size: 4-qt.

1½ lbs. boneless veal shoulder, trimmed of all fat and cut into 1" cubes
1 cup water
¼ cup sherry
2 Tbsp. low-sodium soy sauce
1 tsp. ground ginger
1 tsp. artificial sweetener

1. Lightly brown veal in a nonstick skillet.
2. Combine remaining ingredients in slow cooker. Stir in veal.
3. Cover. Cook on low 3-4 hours.

—— PER SERVING ——
- 220 calories
  (60 calories from fat)
- 7g total fat
  (3g saturated, 0g trans)
- 130mg cholesterol
- 470mg sodium
- 1g total carbohydrate
  (0g fiber, 0g sugar)
- 32g protein
- 0%DV vitamin A
- 0%DV vitamin C
- 4%DV calcium
- 10%DV iron

Variation:
You may substitute pork shoulder for the veal.
This is tasty served over rice.

Sturdy Sauerkraut Dinner

Gloria Julien
Gladstone, MI

Makes 10 servings

Prep. Time: 15 minutes
Cooking Time: 4-5 hours
Ideal slow-cooker size: 6-qt.

1 lb. beef stewing meat, trimmed of fat
1 lb. pork roast, cubed and trimmed of fat
2 10¾-oz. cans 98% fat-free cream of mushroom soup
1 envelope dry onion soup mix
27-oz. can sauerkraut
2 cups skim milk
12-oz. pkg. kluski (or extra-sturdy) noodles

1. Combine all ingredients except noodles in slow cooker.
2. Cook on low 4-5 hours.
3. Add uncooked noodles 2 hours before serving, or cook noodles fully, drain, and stir into Dinner 15 minutes before serving.

—— PER SERVING ——
- 300 calories
  (60 calories from fat)
- 7g total fat
  (2.5g saturated, 0.5g trans)
- 95mg cholesterol
- 780mg sodium
- 33g total carbohydrate
  (2g fiber, 4g sugar)
- 25g protein
- 2%DV vitamin A
- 2%DV vitamin C
- 8%DV calcium
- 15%DV iron

Hamburger Cabbage

Donna Lantgen
Rapid City, SD

Makes 6 servings

Prep. Time: 20 minutes
Cooking Time: 4-5 hours
Ideal slow-cooker size: 4- or 5-qt.

1 lb. extra-lean ground beef
1 medium-sized head cabbage, cut in bite-sized pieces, *or* shredded, whichever you prefer
1 small onion, diced
1 tsp. salt
¼ tsp. black pepper
1 cup ketchup

1. Brown beef in nonstick skillet.
2. Place half the cut cabbage in the cooker. Top with half the onions.
3. Place beef over vegetables and sprinkle with half the seasonings.
4. Top with remaining cabbage, onions, and seasonings.
5. Spread ketchup over all.
6. Cook on low 4-5 hours, or until vegetables are done to your liking.

—— PER SERVING ——
- 210 calories
  (70 calories from fat)
- 7g total fat
  (3g saturated, 0g trans)
- 30mg cholesterol
- 560mg sodium
- 20g total carbohydrate
  (4g fiber, 9g sugar)
- 18g protein
- 10%DV vitamin A
- 40%DV vitamin C
- 8%DV calcium
- 15%DV iron

65

Slow-Cooked Cabbage Rolls

Rebecca Meyerkorth
Wamego, KS

Makes 8 servings

Prep. Time: 30-45 minutes
Cooking Time: 4-6 hours
Ideal slow-cooker size: 3- or 4-qt.

large head of cabbage
¼ cup Egg Beaters
8-oz. can tomato sauce
¾ cup minute rice,
    uncooked
½ cup green bell pepper,
    chopped
½ cup (approx. 15) crushed
    low sodium, low-fat
    crackers
1 envelope low-sodium dry
    onion soup mix
1½ lbs. 95% fat-free ground
    beef
46-oz. can low-sodium
    vegetable juice
½ cup reduced fat grated
    Parmesan cheese,
    optional

1. Cook whole head of cabbage in boiling water just until outer leaves begin to loosen. Pull off 16 large leaves. Drain well. (Use remaining leaves for another meal.)

2. Cut out thick veins from bottoms of reserved leaves.

3. Combine Egg Beaters, tomato sauce, rice, green pepper, cracker crumbs, and dry soup mix in a bowl.

4. Crumble beef over mixture and mix well.

5. Place approximately ¼ cup of mixture on each cabbage leaf.

6. Fold in sides, beginning from cut end.

7. Roll up completely to enclose meat.

8. Secure each roll with a toothpick.

9. Place cabbage rolls in 3- or 4-quart slow cooker.

10. Pour vegetable juice over rolls.

11. Cover and cook on low 4-6 hours, or until rice is fully cooked, or filling reaches 160°.

12. Just before serving, sprinkle each roll with cheese if you wish.

—— PER SERVING ——
- 280 calories
  (50 calories from fat)
- 6 total fat
  (2.5 saturated, 0 trans)
- 55 cholesterol
- 630mg sodium
- 33g total carbohydrate
  (6g fiber, 13g sugar)
- 23g protein
- 60%DV vitamin A
- 190%DV vitamin C
- 15%DV calcium
- 25%DV iron

Stuffed Cabbage

Miriam Nolt
New Holland, PA

Makes 8 servings

Prep. Time: 25 minutes
Cooking Time: 4-6 hours
Ideal slow-cooker size: 5-qt.

4 cups water
12 large cabbage leaves,
    cut from head at base
    and washed
1 lb. lean ground beef *or*
    lamb
½ cup rice, cooked
½ tsp. salt
¼ tsp. black pepper
¼ tsp. dried thyme
¼ tsp. nutmeg
¼ tsp. cinnamon
6-oz. can tomato paste
¾ cup water

1. Boil 4 cups water in saucepan. Turn off heat. Soak cabbage leaves in water for 5 minutes. Remove. Drain. Cool.

2. Combine ground beef, rice, salt, pepper, thyme, nutmeg, and cinnamon.

3. Place 2 Tbsp. of mixture on each cabbage leaf. Roll firmly. Stack in slow cooker.

4. Combine tomato paste and ¾ cup water. Pour over stuffed cabbage.

5. Cover. Cook on low 4-6 hours.

—— PER SERVING ——
- 140 calories
  (50 calories from fat)
- 5g total fat
  (2g saturated, 0g trans)
- 20mg cholesterol
- 220mg sodium
- 10g total carbohydrate
  (2g fiber, 2g sugar)
- 13g protein
- 10%DV vitamin A
- 20%DV vitamin C
- 4%DV calcium
- 10%DV iron

Casserole for Skinnies

Betty Moore
Plano, IL

Makes 6 servings

Prep. Time: 20 minutes
Cooking Time: 4-6 hours
Ideal slow-cooker size: 5- or 6-qt.

1 small head cabbage, chopped
2 large onions, diced
6-8 ribs celery, chopped
1½-2 lbs. extra-lean ground beef
2 15-oz. cans low-sodium stewed tomatoes
2 14½-oz. cans green beans, drained
1 tsp. dried basil
1 tsp. dried oregano
½ tsp. dried thyme
3-4 cups water

1. Combine all ingredients in slow cooker.
2. Cook on low 4-6 hours, or until meat is fully cooked.

—— PER SERVING ——
• 370 calories
 (130 calories from fat)
• 14g total fat (6g saturated, 0.5g trans)
• 55mg cholesterol
• 530mg sodium
• 26g total carbohydrate
 (9g fiber, 14g sugar)
• 36g protein
• 20%DV vitamin A
• 60%DV vitamin C
• 15%DV calcium
• 40%DV iron

Variations:
1. You may substitute 1½-2 lbs. lean stewing meat instead of ground chuck.
2. You may also substitute 1½-2 lbs. ground turkey instead of ground beef.

Hamburger, Cabbage & Potato Dinner

Becky Frey
Lebanon, PA

Makes 6-8 servings

Prep. Time: 20 minutes
Cooking Time: 6-8 hours
Ideal slow-cooker size: 5- or 6-qt.

1 lb. extra-lean ground beef
6 medium potatoes, quartered
1 medium-sized head of cabbage, cut in chunks
¾ tsp. salt
½ tsp. black pepper
2 cups water

1. Brown ground beef in nonstick skillet.
2. Layer in slow cooker potatoes, cabbage, and hamburger. Sprinkle seasonings over each layer.
3. Pour water over top.
4. Cover. Cook on low 6-8 hours or until vegetables are tender.

—— PER SERVING ——
• 250 calories
 (50 calories from fat)
• 6g total fat
 (2g saturated, 0g trans)
• 20mg cholesterol
• 75mg sodium
• 34g total carbohydrate
 (6g fiber, 4g sugar)
• 16g protein
• 4%DV vitamin A
• 80%DV vitamin C
• 8%DV calcium
• 15%DV iron

Beef-Vegetable Casserole

Edwina Stoltzfus
Narvon, PA

Makes 8 servings

Prep. Time: 20 minutes
Cooking Time: 2-3 hours
Ideal slow-cooker size: 5-qt.

1 lb. extra-lean ground beef, *or* turkey
1 medium-sized onion, chopped
½ cup celery, chopped
4 cups cabbage, chopped
2½ cups canned stewed tomatoes, slightly mashed
1 Tbsp. flour
1 tsp. salt
1 Tbsp. sugar
¼-½ tsp. black pepper, according to your taste preference

1. Sauté meat, onion, and celery in nonstick skillet until meat is browned.
2. Pour into slow cooker.
3. Top with layers of cabbage, tomatoes, flour, salt, sugar, and pepper.
4. Cover. Cook on high 2-3 hours.

—— PER SERVING ——
• 140 calories
 (50 calories from fat)
• 5g total fat
 (2g saturated, 0g trans)
• 20mg cholesterol
• 710mg sodium
• 10g total carbohydrate
 (2g fiber, 6g sugar)
• 13g protein
• 8%DV vitamin A
• 20%DV vitamin C
• 8%DV calcium
• 10%DV iron

Mexicali Round Steak

Marcia S. Myer
Manheim, PA

Makes 6 servings

Prep. Time: 20 minutes
Cooking Time: 5-6 hours
Ideal slow-cooker size: 5-qt.

1½ lbs. round steak,
  trimmed of fat
1 cup frozen corn, thawed
½-1 cup fresh cilantro,
  chopped, according to
  your taste preference
½ cup low-sodium, fat-free
  beef broth
3 ribs celery, sliced
1 large onion, sliced
20-oz. jar salsa
15-oz. can black beans, *or*
  pinto beans, rinsed and
  drained
1 cup fat-free cheddar
  cheese

1. Cut beef into 6 pieces.
Place in slow cooker.
2. Combine remaining
ingredients, except cheese,
and pour over beef.
3. Cover. Cook on low 5-6
hours.
4. Sprinkle with cheese
before serving.

—— PER SERVING ——
• 290 calories
  (60 calories from fat)
• 6g total fat
  (2g saturated, 0g trans)
• 70mg cholesterol
• 900mg sodium
• 26g total carbohydrate
  (7g fiber, 2g sugar)
• 35g protein
• 20%DV vitamin A
• 20%DV vitamin C
• 25%DV calcium
• 25%DV iron

Cowtown Favorite

Jean H. Robinson
Cinnaminson, NJ

Makes 10 servings

Prep. Time: 25 minutes
Cooking Time: 3-5 hours
Ideal slow-cooker size: 4-qt.

2½ lbs. boneless beef, cut
  in 1"-square pieces and
  trimmed of fat
1 tsp. black pepper
½ tsp. salt
1 Tbsp. flour
1 medium-sized onion,
  sliced thin
3 large potatoes, peeled
  and chopped
3 cups carrots, cut in ½"
  slices
1 rib celery, chopped
2 cups green beans, cut in
  1" pieces
2 14-oz. cans low-sodium
  stewed tomatoes,
  undrained
10¾-oz. can low-sodium
  tomato soup
2 Tbsp. minute tapioca

1. Combine black pepper,
salt, and flour in a plastic
bag. Add half the beef cubes.
Shake to coat. Place beef
in slow cooker. Shake the
remaining cubes, and then
add them to the cooker.
2. Layer onions, potatoes,
carrots, celery, and green
beans on top of meat.
3. Mix tomatoes, soup, and
tapioca together. Pour over
meat and vegetables.
4. Cover. Cook on high 3
hours or on low 4-5 hours.

—— PER SERVING ——
• 260 calories
  (50 calories from fat)
• 6g total fat
  (2g saturated, 0g trans)
• 70mg cholesterol
• 190mg sodium
• 26g total carbohydrate
  (5g fiber, 7g sugar)
• 25g protein
• 200%DV vitamin A
• 30%DV vitamin C
• 6%DV calcium
• 25%DV iron

Beef and Beans

Barbara L. McGinnis
Hobe Sound, FL

Makes 10 servings

Prep. Time: 20 minutes
Cooking Time: 5-6 hours
Ideal slow-cooker size: 4-qt.

2½ lbs. beef, trimmed of
  fat and cut into ¾" pieces
15½-oz. can kidney beans,
  drained and rinsed
15½-oz. can great northern
  beans, drained and rinsed
2 14½-oz. cans diced
  tomatoes with garlic and
  onions, undrained
1 tsp. salt
½ tsp. black pepper

1. Combine all ingredients
in slow cooker.
2. Cover. Cook on low 5-6
hours, or until beef is tender.
3. Serve over cooked rice.

—— PER SERVING ——
• 250 calories
  (50 calories from fat)
• 6g total fat
  (2g saturated, 0g trans)
• 70mg cholesterol
• 650mg sodium
• 19g total carbohydrate
  (5g fiber, 4g sugar)
• 29g protein
• 6%DV vitamin A
• 6%DV vitamin C
• 10%DV calcium
• 20%DV iron

10-Layer Slow-Cooker Dish

Norma Saltzman
Shickley, NE

Makes 8 servings

Prep. Time: 25 minutes
Cooking Time: 3-6 hours
Ideal slow-cooker size: 5-qt.

1½ lbs. lean ground chuck
6 medium-sized potatoes,
   thinly sliced
1 medium onion,
   thinly sliced
½ tsp. salt
½ tsp. black pepper
15-oz. can corn, undrained
15-oz. can peas, undrained
¼ cup water
10¾-oz. can fat-free,
   low-sodium cream
   of mushroom soup

1. Brown ground chuck in nonstick skillet. Then create the following layers in the slow cooker.
2. Layer 1: one-fourth of potatoes, mixed with one-half the onions, salt, and pepper.
3. Layer 2: half-can of corn.
4. Layer 3: one-fourth of potatoes.
5. Layer 4: half-can of peas.
6. Layer 5: one-fourth of potatoes, mixed with one-half the onions, salt, and pepper.
7. Layer 6: remaining corn.
8. Layer 7: remaining potatoes.
9. Layer 8: remaining peas and water.
10. Layer 9: ground chuck.
11. Layer 10: soup.
12. Cover. Cook on high 3-4 hours or on low 6 hours.

— PER SERVING —
• 370 calories
  (90 calories from fat)
• 9g total fat
  (3.5g saturated,
  0.5g trans)
• 30mg cholesterol
• 720mg sodium
• 49g total carbohydrate
  (7g fiber, 6g sugar)
• 25g protein
• 0%DV vitamin A
• 30%DV vitamin C
• 4%DV calcium
• 25%DV iron

When cooking meats and vegetables together, especially when cooking on Low, place the vegetables on the bottom where they will be kept moist.

Roseann Wilson, Albuquerque, NM

Goulash with Vegetables

Mrs. Audrey L. Kneer
Williamsfield, IL

Makes 7 servings

Prep. Time: 15 minutes
Cooking Time: 4-5 hours
Ideal slow-cooker size: 4-qt.

1 lb. extra-lean ground beef
1 medium-sized onion,
   chopped
1 clove garlic, chopped
14½-oz. can low-sodium
   diced tomatoes
16-oz. can kidney beans,
   drained
½ cup green bell pepper,
   chopped
1 cup celery, chopped
1 tsp. salt
1 Tbsp. Worcestershire sauce
½ tsp. paprika
1 Tbsp. sugar
1 bay leaf
¼ tsp. black pepper

1. Brown lean ground beef, onion, and garlic in a nonstick skillet over medium heat.
2. Combine all ingredients in slow cooker.
3. Cover. Cook on low 4-5 hours.
4. Serve over or with mashed potatoes.

— PER SERVING —
• 190 calories
  (60 calories from fat)
• 6g total fat
  (2.5g saturated,
  0g trans)
• 25mg cholesterol
• 800mg sodium
• 17g total carbohydrate
  (4g fiber, 5g sugar)
• 18g protein
• 2%DV vitamin A
• 10%DV vitamin C
• 8%DV calcium
• 15%DV iron

Wild Rice Casserole

Carolyn Baer
Coranth, WI

Makes 8 servings

Soaking Time: 8 hours or overnight
Prep. Time: 35-40 minutes
Cooking Time: 3-4 hours
Ideal slow-cooker size: 3- or 4-qt.

1 cup uncooked wild rice
½ lb. loose turkey sausage
1 lb. 95% lean ground beef
1 medium onion, chopped
1 cup celery, chopped
1 green bell pepper, chopped
2-3 medium carrots, grated
2 tsp. light soy sauce
1 tsp. Worcestershire sauce
10¾-oz. can low-sodium, low-fat cream of mushroom soup
10¾-oz. can low-sodium, low-fat cream of chicken soup
1 cup sliced mushrooms, *optional* (undrained if using canned mushrooms)
½ cup water, *or* more

1. Wash and soak rice overnight.
2. Brown sausage and beef together in large skillet.

3. Drain off drippings. Place meat in slow cooker.
4. Drain rice.
5. Add rice, chopped onion, celery, green pepper, and carrots to slow cooker.
6. Stir in soy sauce, Worcestershire sauce, soups, and mushrooms if you wish.
7. Mix in water.
8. Cover. Cook on high 1 hour. Stir. If dish seems somewhat dry, add another ½ cup water.
9. Cover. Cook on low 2 hours.
10. Or cook on low a total of 4 hours.

—— PER SERVING ——

• 260 calories (60 calories from fat)
• 7g total fat (2.5g saturated, 0g trans)
• 55mg cholesterol
• 560mg sodium
• 28g total carbohydrate (3g fiber, 4g sugar)
• 21g protein
• 60%DV vitamin A
• 25%DV vitamin C
• 6%DV calcium
• 10%DV iron

To make your own cream of mushroom or celery soup, please turn to pages 264-265.

Ground Beef Casserole

Lois J. Cassidy
Willow Street, PA

Makes 8 servings

Prep. Time: 20 minutes
Cooking Time: 5-8 hours
Ideal slow-cooker size: 6-qt.

1½ lbs. lean ground chuck
6-8 potatoes, sliced
water and ½ tsp. cream of tartar
1 medium-sized onion, sliced
1 clove garlic, minced
½ tsp. salt
½ tsp. dried basil
½ tsp. dried thyme
¼ tsp. black pepper
14½-oz. can cut green beans with juice
10¾-oz. can fat-free, low-sodium cream of mushroom soup

1. Crumble uncooked ground chuck in bottom of slow cooker.
2. Slice potatoes into mixing bowl filled with water mixed with cream of tartar to keep potatoes from turning dark. Stir together; then drain potatoes and discard water.
3. Add potatoes, onion, garlic, salt, basil, thyme, and black pepper to cooker.
4. Pour beans over all. Spread can of mushroom soup over beans.
5. Cover. Cook on low 5-8 hours.

- 340 calories
  (80 calories from fat)
- 9g total fat (3.5g
  saturated, 0.5g trans)
- 30mg cholesterol
- 610mg sodium
- 43g total carbohydrate
  (6g fiber, 3g sugar)
- 23g protein
- 0%DV vitamin A
- 20%DV vitamin C
- 6%DV calcium
- 20%DV iron

Tips:

1. If you have time, brown the chuck in a nonstick skillet before putting it in the slow cooker.

2. For a creamier dish, mix half a soup can of water with the mushroom soup before placing over beans.

Beef Stew

Barbara L. McGinnis
Hobe Sound, FL

Makes 8 servings

Prep. Time: 30 minutes
Cooking Time: 6½ hours
Ideal slow-cooker size: 5-qt.

1½ lbs. boneless, beef chuck
  roast, trimmed of fat
1 envelope dry low-sodium
  onion soup mix
½ tsp. black pepper
6 cups water
2 cups potatoes, peeled
  and cubed
8 medium-sized carrots,
  cut into chunks
1 medium-sized onion,
  chopped
1 cup frozen peas, thawed
1 cup frozen corn, thawed
5 Tbsp. cornstarch
6 Tbsp. cold water

1. Place beef in slow cooker. Sprinkle with soup mix and pepper.

2. Pour water around meat.

3. Cover. Cook on low 4 hours.

4. Remove roast and let stand 5 minutes.

5. Add vegetables to slow cooker. Cube beef and return to slow cooker.

6. Cover. Cook on low 1½ hours, or until veggies are tender.

7. Combine cornstarch and cold water until smooth. Stir into stew.

8. Cover. Cook on high 1 more hour.

——— PER SERVING ———
- 240 calories
  (40 calories from fat)
- 4.5g total fat
  (1.5g saturated,
  0g trans)
- 50mg cholesterol
- 170mg sodium
- 31g total carbohydrate
  (5g fiber, 7g sugar)
- 21g protein
- 300%DV vitamin A
- 20%DV vitamin C
- 4%DV calcium
- 20%DV iron

Welcome-Home
Slow-Cooker Stew

Rhonda L. Burgoon
Collingswood, NJ

Makes 6 servings

Prep. Time: 15 minutes
Cooking Time: 3 hours
Ideal slow-cooker size: 4- or 5-qt.

1 lb. lean beef, cubed
2 cups low-sodium diced
  canned tomatoes,
  undrained
1 cup nonfat, low-sodium
  beef broth
¼ cup red wine
1 Tbsp. Worcestershire sauce
1 bay leaf
1 tsp. dried thyme
1 tsp. dried rosemary
1 tsp. dried marjoram
1 Tbsp. garlic, crushed
½ tsp. black pepper
1 onion, diced
2-3 medium-sized potatoes,
  diced
1 cup carrots, chopped

1. Combine all ingredients in slow cooker.

2. Cover. Cook on high 3 hours.

——— PER SERVING ———
- 170 calories
  (35 calories from fat)
- 4g total fat (1.5g
  saturated, 0g trans)
- 45mg cholesterol
- 300mg sodium
- 15g total carbohydrate
  (3g fiber, 5g sugar)
- 18g protein
- 100%DV vitamin A
- 20%DV vitamin C
- 8%DV calcium
- 15%DV iron

Variation:

If your sodium count allows, you may want to add ¼-½ tsp. salt to Step 1.

Beef Barley Stew

Bonita Ensinberger
Albuquerque, NM

Makes 6 servings

Prep. Time: 20 minutes
Cooking Time: 4-5 hours
Ideal slow-cooker size: 5-qt.

½ lb. lean round steak, cut in ½" cubes
4 carrots, peeled and cut in ¼" slices
1 cup yellow onions, chopped
½ cup green bell peppers, coarsely chopped
1 clove garlic, minced
½ lb. fresh button mushrooms, quartered
¾ cup dry pearl barley
½ tsp. salt
¼ tsp. ground black pepper
½ tsp. dried thyme
½ tsp. dried sweet basil
1 bay leaf
5 cups fat-free, low-sodium beef broth

1. Combine all ingredients in slow cooker.
2. Cover. Cook on low 4-5 hours.

— PER SERVING —
• 220 calories
  (45 calories from fat)
• 5g total fat
  (1g saturated, 0g trans)
• 25mg cholesterol
• 520mg sodium
• 29g total carbohydrate
  (6g fiber, 5g sugar)
• 16g protein
• 200%DV vitamin A
• 20%DV vitamin C
• 4%DV calcium
• 15%DV iron

Beef and Beans over Rice

Robin Schrock
Millersburg, OH

Makes 8 servings

Prep. Time: 20 minutes
Cooking Time: 3½-4½ hours
Ideal slow-cooker size: 4-qt.

1½ lbs. boneless, round steak
1 Tbsp. prepared mustard
1 Tbsp. chili powder
½ tsp. salt, *optional*
¼ tsp. black pepper
1 garlic clove, minced
2 14½-oz. cans low-sodium diced tomatoes
1 medium-sized onion, chopped
1 beef bouillon cube, crushed
16-oz. can kidney beans, rinsed and drained

1. Cut steak into thin strips.
2. Combine mustard, chili powder, salt if you wish, pepper, and garlic in a bowl.
3. Add steak. Toss to coat.
4. Transfer to slow cooker. Add tomatoes, onion, and bouillon.
5. Cover. Cook on low 3-4 hours.
6. Stir in beans. Cook 30 minutes longer.
7. Serve over rice.

— PER SERVING —
• 190 calories
  (40 calories from fat)
• 4.5g total fat
  (1.5g saturated, 0g trans)
• 50mg cholesterol
• 870mg sodium
• 15g total carbohydrate
  (4g fiber, 4g sugar)
• 21g protein
• 10%DV vitamin A
• 8%DV vitamin C
• 0%DV calcium
• 15%DV iron

Brevard Stew

David R. Britchfield
Melbourne, FL

Makes 10 servings

Prep. Time: 20-25 minutes
Cooking Time: 4-5 hours
Ideal slow-cooker size: 5-qt.

1½ lbs. lean stewing beef, cut in 1" cubes
1 cup onions, chopped
1 Tbsp. olive oil
3 medium-sized potatoes, cut in 1" cubes
28-oz. can low-sodium crushed tomatoes, undrained
16-oz. can cream-style corn, drained and rinsed
16-oz. can low-sodium lima beans, drained and rinsed
16-oz. can low-sodium cut carrots, drained and rinsed
1 Tbsp. Worcestershire sauce
¾ tsp. salt
½ tsp. dried marjoram leaves
4 slices bacon, cooked and crumbled
¼ tsp. red pepper sauce

1. In a large skillet, brown beef and onions in olive oil over medium heat until beef is brown on all sides. Drain.

2. Combine all ingredients except bacon and red pepper sauce in slow cooker sprayed with nonfat cooking spray. Mix well.

3. Cover. Cook on low 4-5 hours.

4. Stir bacon and red pepper sauce into stew just before serving.

—— PER SERVING ——

- 270 calories
  (60 calories from fat)
- 7g total fat
  (2g saturated, 0g trans)
- 45mg cholesterol
- 530mg sodium
- 35g total carbohydrate
  (6g fiber, 5g sugar)
- 20g protein
- 100%DV vitamin A
- 20%DV vitamin C
- 6%DV calcium
- 25%DV iron

Veggie Beef Stew

Irene Hull
Anderson, IN

Makes 5 servings

Prep. Time: 25 minutes
Cooking Time: 2½-3½ hours
Ideal slow-cooker size: 3- or 4-qt.

¾ lb. lean stewing meat, trimmed of fat and cut into ½" cubes
2 tsp. canola oil
14½-oz. can low-sodium, low-fat beef broth
14½-oz. can low-sodium stewed tomatoes
1½ cups butternut squash, peeled and cubed
1 cup frozen corn
½ cup carrots, chopped

dash of salt
dash of black pepper
dash of dried oregano
2 Tbsp. cornstarch
¼ cup water

1. In a skillet, brown stewing meat in canola oil over medium heat. Transfer to slow cooker.

2. Add beef broth, vegetables, salt, pepper, and oregano.

3. Cover. Cook on high 2-3 hours.

4. Combine cornstarch and water until smooth. Stir into stew.

5. Cover. Cook on high 30 minutes.

—— PER SERVING ——

- 200 calories
  (50 calories from fat)
- 5g total fat
  (1.5g saturated, 0g trans)
- 40mg cholesterol
- 180mg sodium
- 22g total carbohydrate
  (4g fiber, 6g sugar)
- 17g protein
- 150%DV vitamin A
- 20%DV vitamin C
- 6%DV calcium
- 15%DV iron

Best Everyday Stew

Elizabeth L. Richards
Rapid City SD

Makes 8 servings

Prep. Time: 25 minutes
Cooking Time: 5-6 hours
Ideal slow-cooker size: 6-qt.

2¼ lbs. flank steak, 1½" thick
8 red potatoes, small to medium in size
10 baby carrots

1 large clove garlic, diced
1 medium-sized to large onion, chopped
1 cup baby peas
3 ribs celery, cut in 1" pieces
3 cups cabbage, in chunks
2 8-oz. cans low-sodium tomato sauce
1 Tbsp. Worcestershire sauce
2 bay leaves
¼-½ tsp. dried thyme, according to your taste preference
¼-½ tsp. dried basil, according to your taste preference
¼-½ tsp. dried marjoram, according to your taste preference
1 Tbsp. parsley
2 cups water *or* more, if desired
4 cubes beef *or* vegetable bouillon

1. Trim flank steak of fat. Cut in 1½" cubes. Brown slowly in nonstick skillet.

2. Quarter potatoes.

3. Combine all ingredients in large slow cooker.

4. Cover. Cook on high 1 hour. Turn to low and cook 4-5 additional hours.

—— PER SERVING ——

- 260 calories
  (60 calories from fat)
- 7g total fat
  (2g saturated, 0g trans)
- 75mg cholesterol
- 1330mg sodium
- 22g total carbohydrate
  (4g fiber, 6g sugar)
- 29g protein
- 40%DV vitamin A
- 20%DV vitamin C
- 6%DV calcium
- 25%DV iron

Tip:

Let all soups and stews sit overnight in refrigerator and skim off any fat in the morning.

Gone-All-Day Dinner

Susan Scheel
West Fargo, ND

Makes 8 servings

Prep. Time: 15-20 minutes
Cooking Time: 4-6 hours
Ideal slow-cooker size: 5-qt.

1 cup uncooked wild rice, rinsed and drained
1 cup celery, chopped
1 cup carrots, chopped
2 4-oz. cans mushrooms, drained
1 large onion, chopped
½ cup slivered almonds
3 beef bouillon cubes
2½ tsp. seasoned salt
2 lbs. boneless round steak, cut in bite-sized pieces
3 cups water

1. Layer ingredients in slow cooker in order listed. Do not stir.
2. Cover. Cook on low 4-6 hours.
3. Stir before serving.

—— PER SERVING ——
• 300 calories
  (90 calories from fat)
• 10g total fat
  (2g saturated, 0g trans)
• 70mg cholesterol
• 1110mg sodium
• 24g total arbohydrate
  (4g fiber, 3g sugar)
• 28g protein
• 80%DV vitamin A
• 2%DV vitamin C
• 4%DV calcium
• 20%DV iron

Hearty Beef Stew

Laurie Sylvester
Ridgely, MD

Makes 8 servings

Prep. Time: 20 minutes
Cooking Time: 4-6 hours
Ideal slow-cooker size: 5- or 6-qt.

2 lbs. lean stewing beef, cubed
2 Tbsp. quick-cooking tapioca
2 ribs celery
4 onions, quartered
1 Tbsp. sugar
4 carrots, cut up
4 potatoes, cubed
16-oz. can string beans, undrained
10¾-oz. can low-sodium tomato soup
½ cup water
1 tsp. salt
½ tsp. black pepper
1 Tbsp. fresh parsley

1. Combine all ingredients except parsley in slow cooker.
2. Cover. Cook on low 4-6 hours. Stir in parsley just before serving.

—— PER SERVING ——
• 300 calories
  (60 calories from fat)
• 6g total fat
  (2g saturated, 0g trans)
• 70mg cholesterol
• 440mg sodium
• 35g total carbohydrate
  (5g fiber, 10g sugar)
• 26g protein
• 100%DV vitamin A
• 30%DV vitamin C
• 6%DV calcium
• 25%DV iron

Lotsa Tomatoes Beef Stew

Bernice A. Esau
North Newton, KS

Makes 6 servings

Prep. Time: 20-25 minutes
Cooking Time: 4-6 hours
Ideal slow-cooker size: 6- or 7-qt.

2 lbs. extra-lean stewing beef cubes, trimmed of fat
5-6 carrots, cut in 1" pieces
1 large onion, cut in chunks
3 ribs celery, sliced
6 medium-sized tomatoes, cut up and gently mashed
½ cup quick-cooking tapioca
1 whole clove, *or* ¼-½ tsp. ground cloves
1 tsp. dried basil
½ tsp. dried oregano
2 bay leaves
2 tsp. salt
½ tsp. black pepper
3-4 potatoes, cubed

1. Place all ingredients in slow cooker. Mix together well.
2. Cover. Cook on low 4-6 hours.

—— PER SERVING ——
• 400 calories
  (70 calories from fat)
• 8g total fat
  (2.5g saturated, 0g trans)
• 90mg cholesterol
• 110mg sodium
• 48g total carbohydrate
  (7g fiber, 10g sugar)
• 34g protein
• 200%DV vitamin A
• 50%DV vitamin C
• 60%DV calcium
• 30%DV iron

A word of caution — it is a common mistake to add too much liquid.   *Mrs. J. E. Barthold, Bethlehem, PA*

Tip:

Tip:

Add 2-3 Tbsp. instant mashed potatoes during the last 30 minutes of cooking if the cooking juices are too thin.

Fruity Vegetable Beef Stew

Esther S. Martin
Ephrata, PA

Mrs. Carolyn Baer
Conrath, WI

Makes 4 servings

Prep. Time: 25 minutes
Cooking Time: 3½-4½ hours
Ideal slow-cooker size: 4-qt.

¾ lb. lean beef stewing meat, cut into ½" cubes
2 tsp. canola oil
14½-oz. can fat-free beef broth
14½-oz. can stewed tomatoes, cut up
1½ cups butternut squash, peeled and cubed
1 cup frozen corn, thawed

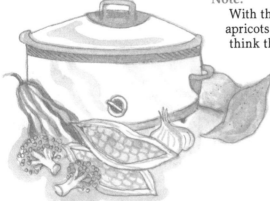

6 dried apricot, *or* peach, halves, quartered
½ cup carrots, chopped
1 tsp. dried oregano
¼ tsp. salt
¼ tsp. black pepper
2 Tbsp. cornstarch
¼ cup water
2 Tbsp. fresh parsley, minced

1. Brown meat in oil in a nonstick skillet over medium heat.
2. Combine meat, broth, tomatoes, squash, corn, apricots, carrots, oregano, salt, and pepper in slow cooker.
3. Cook on low 3-4 hours, or until vegetables and meat are tender.
4. Combine cornstarch and water until smooth. Stir into stew.
5. Cook on high 30 minutes, or until stew is thickened.
6. Add parsley just before serving.

—— PER SERVING ——
• 280 calories   • 35g total carbohydrate
  (60 calories from fat)   (5g fiber, 13g sugar)
• 7g total fat (1.5g   • 23g protein
  saturated, 0g trans)   • 150%DV vitamin A
• 50mg cholesterol   • 20%DV vitamin C
• 510mg sodium   • 8%DV calcium
   • 20%DV iron

Note:

With the sweet flavor from apricots and squash we think this dish has a South American or Cuban flair. The addition of corn makes it even more hearty.

Makes-A-Meal Slow-Cooker Stew

Sharon Wantland
Menomonee Falls, WI

Makes 6 servings

Prep. Time: 25 minutes
Cooking Time: 4-5 hours
Ideal slow-cooker size: 4- or 5-qt.

1½ lbs. beef stewing meat
1 medium-sized onion, chopped
4 carrots, peeled and cut in slices
2 ribs celery, cut in pieces
4 medium-sized potatoes, peeled and cut in cubes
28-oz. can sodium-free whole tomatoes, undrained
10½-oz. can fat-free beef broth
1 Tbsp. Worcestershire sauce
2 Tbsp. dried parsley flakes
1 bay leaf
1 tsp. salt
¼ tsp. black pepper
2 Tbsp. quick-cooking tapioca

1. Brown beef cubes over medium heat in nonstick skillet. Transfer to slow cooker.
2. Add remaining ingredients. Stir to blend.
3. Cook on low 4-5 hours.

—— PER SERVING ——
• 240 calories   • 30g total carbohydrate
  (40 calories from fat)   (5g fiber, 6g sugar)
• 4.5g total fat   • 21g protein
  (1.5g saturated,   • 150%DV vitamin A
  0g trans)   • 30%DV vitamin C
• 50mg cholesterol   • 6%DV calcium
• 520mg sodium   • 20%DV iron

German Dinner

Sharon Miller
Holmesville, OH

Makes 6 servings

Prep. Time: 15 minutes
Cooking Time: 4-5 hours
Ideal slow-cooker size: 4- or 5-qt.

32-oz. bag sauerkraut,
  drained
1 lb. extra-lean ground
  beef
1 small green bell pepper,
  grated
2 11½-oz. cans V8 juice
½ cup chopped celery,
  optional

1. Combine all ingredients in slow cooker.
2. Cook for 1 hour on high, and then on low 3-4 hours.

— PER SERVING —
• 170 calories
  (60 calories from fat)
• 7g total fat
  (3g saturated, 0g trans)
• 30mg cholesterol
• 1160mg sodium
• 10g total carbohydrate
  (4g fiber, 3g sugar)
• 17g protein
• 10%DV vitamin A
• 40%DV vitamin C
• 6%DV calcium
• 25%DV iron

Tangy Barbecue Sandwiches

Lavina Hochstedler
Grand Blanc, MI
Lois M. Martin
Lititz, PA

Makes 18 sandwiches

Prep. Time: 25 minutes
Cooking Time: 5-6 hours
Ideal slow-cooker size: 6-qt.

3 cups chopped celery
1 cup chopped onions
1 cup low-sodium ketchup
1 cup low-sodium barbecue
  sauce
1 cup water
2 Tbsp. vinegar
2 Tbsp. Worcestershire sauce
2 Tbsp. brown sugar
1 tsp. chili powder
1 tsp. salt
½ tsp. black pepper
½ tsp. garlic powder
4-lb. lean boneless chuck
  roast

1. Combine all ingredients except roast in slow cooker. When well mixed, add roast.
2. Cover. Cook on low 5-6 hours.
3. Remove roast. Cool and shred meat. Return to sauce. Heat well.
4. Serve on buns.

— PER SERVING —
• 300 calories
  (60 calories from fat)
• 7g total fat
  (2g saturated, 0g trans)
• 60mg cholesterol
• 840mg sodium
• 36g total carbohydrate
  (4g fiber, 10g sugar)
• 24g protein
• 0%DV vitamin A
• 0%DV vitamin C
• 8%DV calcium
• 20%DV iron

Pork and Beef Barbecue

Susan Scheel
West Fargo, ND

Makes 14 servings

Prep. Time: 25 minutes
Cooking Time: 3-4 hours
Ideal slow-cooker size: 5- or 6-qt.

8-oz. can tomato sauce
½ cup brown sugar, packed
¼ cup chili powder, *or less*
¼ cup cider vinegar
2 tsp. Worcestershire sauce
1 tsp. salt
1 lb. lean beef stewing
  meat, cut into ¾" cubes
1 lb. lean pork tenderloin,
  cut into ¾" cubes
3 green bell peppers,
  chopped
3 large onions, chopped

1. Combine tomato sauce, brown sugar, chili powder, cider vinegar, Worcestershire sauce, and salt in slow cooker.
2. Stir in meats, green peppers, and onions.
3. Cover. Cook on high 3-4 hours.
4. Shred meat with two forks. Stir all ingredients together well.
5. Serve on buns.

— PER SERVING —
• 270 calories
  (50 calories from fat)
• 6g total fat
  (1.5g saturated,
  0.5g trans)
• 40mg cholesterol
• 480mg sodium
• 38g total carbohydrate
  (3g fiber, 14g sugar)
• 18g protein
• 20%DV vitamin A
• 20%DV vitamin C
• 8%DV calcium
• 20%DV iron

Beef Sandwiches

Robin Schrock
Millersburg, OH

Makes 12 servings

Prep. Time: 30 minutes
Cooking Time: 5-7 hours
Ideal slow-cooker size: 4- or 5-qt.

2-lb. boneless beef roast
3 medium-sized onions, chopped
2 cups red wine vinegar
3 bay leaves
½ tsp. salt, *optional*
¼ tsp. ground cloves
½ tsp. garlic powder

1. Cut roast in half. Place in slow cooker.
2. Combine onions, vinegar, bay leaves, salt, cloves, and garlic powder. Pour over roast.
3. Cover. Cook on low 5-7 hours.
4. Discard bay leaves.
5. Remove meat. Shred with a fork.
6. Serve on hamburger buns.

— PER SERVING —
- 230 calories
  (50 calories from fat)
- 6g total fat (1.5g saturated, 0g trans)
- 45mg cholesterol
- 330mg sodium
- 27g total carbohydrate (4g fiber, 4g sugar)
- 19g protein
- 0%DV vitamin A
- 0%DV vitamin C
- 0%DV calcium
- 15%DV iron

Variations:
If you prefer a somewhat sweeter flavoring, and your diet allows, you may want to add ¼ cup brown sugar, ½ cup raisins, or several tablespoons of Splenda to Step 2.

Beef Pitas

Dede Peterson
Rapid City, SD

Makes 2 servings

Prep. Time: 15 minutes
Cooking Time: 2-3 hours
Ideal slow-cooker size: 2-qt.

½ lb. beef *or* pork, cut into small cubes
½ tsp. dried oregano
dash of black pepper
1 cup fresh tomatoes, chopped
2 Tbsp. fresh green bell peppers, diced
¼ cup nonfat sour cream
1 tsp. red wine vinegar
1 tsp. vegetable oil
2 large pita breads, heated and cut in half

1. Place meat in slow cooker. Sprinkle with oregano and black pepper.
2. Cook on low 2-3 hours.
3. In a separate bowl, combine tomatoes, green peppers, sour cream, vinegar, and oil.
4. Fill pitas with meat. Top with vegetable- and sour-cream mixture.

— PER SERVING —
- 380 calories
  (80 calories from fat)
- 9g total fat
  (2.5g saturated, 0g trans)
- 75mg cholesterol
- 410mg sodium
- 44g total carbohydrate (3g fiber, 6g sugar)
- 30g protein
- 20%DV vitamin A
- 20%DV vitamin C
- 10%DV calcium
- 25%DV iron

French Dip

Loretta Weisz
Auburn, WA

Makes 12 servings

Prep. Time: 10 minutes
Cooking Time: 5-6 hours
Ideal slow-cooker size: 4- or 5-qt.

2-lb. beef top round roast, trimmed
3 cups water
1 cup light soy sauce
1 tsp. dried rosemary
1 tsp. dried thyme
1 tsp. garlic powder
1 bay leaf
3 whole peppercorns

1. Place roast in slow cooker. Add water, soy sauce, and seasonings.
2. Cover. Cook on low 5-6 hours.
3. Remove meat from broth. Thinly slice or shred. Keep warm.
4. Strain broth and skim off fat. Pour broth into small cups for dipping.
5. Serve beef on rolls.

— PER SERVING —
- 260 calories
  (60 calories from fat)
- 7g total fat
  (2g saturated, 0g trans)
- 70mg cholesterol
- 630mg sodium
- 20g total carbohydrate (1g fiber, 1g sugar)
- 26g protein
- 0%DV vitamin A
- 0%DV vitamin C
- 4%DV calcium
- 20%DV iron

Slow-Cooker Fajita Stew

Sara Puskar
Abingdon, MD

Nancy Wagner Graves
Manhattan, KS

Makes 8 servings

Prep. Time: 20 minutes
Cooking Time: 4¼-5¼ hours
Ideal slow-cooker size: 3- or 4-qt.

2½ lbs. boneless beef top
   round steak
1 onion, chopped
1-oz. envelope dry fajita
   seasoning mix (about 2
   Tbsp.)
14-oz. can diced tomatoes,
   undrained
1 red bell pepper, cut into
   1" pieces
¼ cup flour
¼ cup water

1. Trim excess fat from beef and cut into 2" pieces. Combine with onion in slow cooker.

2. Mix together fajita seasoning and undrained tomatoes. Pour over beef.

3. Place cut-up peppers on top.

4. Cover. Cook on low 4-5 hours, or until beef is tender.

5. Combine flour and water in a small bowl. Stir well to mix.

6. Gradually add to slow cooker.

7. Cover. Cook on high 15-20 minutes until thickened, stirring occasionally.

—— PER SERVING ——
• 320 calories
  (60 calories from fat)
• 7g total fat (2.5g
  saturated, 0g trans)
• 85mg cholesterol
• 330mg sodium
• 31g total carbohydrate
  (2g fiber, 3g sugar)
• 31g protein
• 20%DV vitamin A
• 20%DV vitamin C
• 4%DV calcium
• 25%DV iron

Tip:
   This is delicious served over hot rice.

Slow-Cooked Steak Fajitas

Virginia Graybill
Hershey, PA

Makes 12 servings

Prep. Time: 25-30 minutes
Cooking Time: 4½-6½ hours
Ideal slow-cooker size: 4-qt.

1½ lbs. beef flank steak
15-oz. can low-sodium diced
   tomatoes with garlic and
   onion, undrained
1 jalapeño pepper, seeded
   and chopped *
2 garlic cloves, minced
1 tsp. ground coriander
1 tsp. ground cumin
1 tsp. chili powder
½ tsp. salt
2 medium-sized onions,
   sliced
2 medium-sized green bell
   peppers, julienned
2 medium-sized sweet red
   bell peppers, julienned
1 Tbsp. fresh parsley,
   minced
2 tsp. cornstarch
1 Tbsp. water
12 6" flour tortillas,
   warmed
¾ cup fat-free sour cream
¾ cup low-sodium salsa

1. Slice steak thinly into strips across grain. Place in slow cooker.

2. Add tomatoes, jalapeño, garlic, coriander, cumin, chili powder, and salt.

3. Cover. Cook on low 3-4 hours.

4. Add onions, peppers, and parsley.

5. Cover. Cook on low 1-2 hours longer, or until meat is tender.

6. Combine cornstarch and water until smooth. Gradually stir into slow cooker.

7. Cover. Cook on high 30 minutes, or until slightly thickened.

8. Using a slotted spoon, spoon about ½ cup of meat mixture down the center of each tortilla.

9. Add 1 Tbsp. sour cream and 1 Tbsp. salsa to each.

10. Fold bottom of tortilla over filling and roll up.

—— PER SERVING ——
• 250 calories
  (60 calories from fat)
• 7g total fat
  (2g saturated, 0g trans)
• 35mg cholesterol
• 570mg sodium
• 31g total carbohydrate
  (2g fiber, 4g sugar)
• 16g protein
• 30%DV vitamin A
• 60%DV vitamin C
• 10%DV calcium
• 20%DV iron

*When cutting jalapeño peppers, use rubber or plastic gloves to protect your hands. Avoid touching your face.

Slow-Cooker Enchiladas

Robin Schrock
Millersburg, OH

Makes 6 servings

Prep. Time: 30-45 minutes
Cooking Time: 2-3 hours
Ideal slow-cooker size: 4-qt.

1 lb. lean ground beef
1 cup onions, chopped
½ cup green bell pepper, chopped
16-oz. can pinto, *or* kidney, beans, rinsed and drained
10-oz. can diced tomatoes and green chilies
1 cup water
1 tsp. chili powder
16-oz. can black beans, rinsed and drained
½ tsp. ground cumin
½ tsp. salt
¼ tsp. black pepper
dash of dried red pepper flakes *and/or* several drops Tabasco sauce, if you like
1 cup shredded low-fat sharp cheddar cheese
1 cup shredded low-fat Monterey Jack cheese
6 6" *or* 7" flour tortillas

1. In a nonstick skillet, brown beef, onions, and green pepper.

2. Add remaining ingredients, except cheeses and tortillas. Bring to a boil.

3. Reduce heat. Cover and simmer 10 minutes.

4. Combine cheeses in a bowl.

5. In slow cooker, layer about ¾ cup beef mixture, one tortilla, and about ¼ cup cheese. Repeat layers until all ingredients are used.

6. Cover. Cook on low 2-3 hours.

—— PER SERVING ——
• 490 calories
  (110 calories from fat)
• 12g total fat
  (4.5g saturated, 0g trans)
• 35mg cholesterol
• 1480mg sodium
• 51g total carbohydrate
  (8g fiber, 6g sugar)
• 43g protein
• 10%DV vitamin A
• 20%DV vitamin C
• 80%DV calcium
• 30%DV iron

Low-Fat Slow-Cooker Barbecue

Martha Hershey
Ronks, PA

Makes 12 sandwich servings

Prep. Time: 30-45 minutes
Cooking Time: 2-3 hours
Ideal slow-cooker size: 3-qt.

1 lb. extra-lean ground beef
2 cups celery, chopped fine
1 cup onions, chopped
1 Tbsp. whipped butter
2 Tbsp. red wine vinegar
1 Tbsp. brown sugar
3 Tbsp. Worcestershire sauce
1 tsp. salt
1 tsp. yellow prepared mustard
1 cup ketchup
2 cups water

1. Brown ground beef, celery, and onions in a nonstick skillet.

2. Combine all ingredients in slow cooker.

3. Cover and cook on low 2-3 hours.

4. Serve in sandwich rolls.

—— PER SERVING ——
• 110 calories
  (45 calories from fat)
• 5g total fat
  (2g saturated, 0g trans)
• 15mg cholesterol
• 540mg sodium
• 8g total carbohydrate
  (0.5g fiber, 3g sugar)
• 8g protein
• 6%DV vitamin A
• 6%DV vitamin C
• 2%DV calcium
• 8%DV iron

To get the best flavor, sauté vegetables or brown meat before placing in cooker to cook.

Connie Johnson, Loudon, NH

Sloppy Beef Sandwiches

Colleen Konetzni
Rio Rancho, NM

Makes 6 servings

Prep. Time: 30 minutes
Cooking Time: 2-3 hours
Ideal slow cooker size: 3- or 4-qt.

1½ lbs. 95% lean ground
   beef
1 onion, chopped
½ cup water
1 jar low-sodium salsa
whole wheat sandwich rolls
2 cups grated fat-free
   cheddar cheese
½ cup chopped lettuce

1. Cook beef and onion in skillet with ½ cup water until meat is no longer pink. Stir with wooden spoon to break up clumps. Drain off drippings.
2. Place beef mixture into slow cooker.
Add salsa.
Mix well.

3. Cover. Cook on low 2-3 hours.
4. Divide sandwich meat among buns and sprinkle with cheese and lettuce.

— PER SERVING —
- 330 calories
  (70 calories from fat)
- 7g total fat
  (3g saturated, 0g trans)
- 70mg cholesterol
- 640mg sodium
- 27g total carbohydrate
  (4g fiber, 5g sugar)
- 38g protein
- 15%DV vitamin A
- 10%DV vitamin C
- 40%DV calcium
- 20%DV iron

Meat Loaf

Jody Moore
Pendleton, IN

Makes 8 servings

Prep. Time: 30 minutes
Cooking Time: 2-5 hours
Ideal slow-cooker size: 3- or 4-qt.

½ lb. extra-lean ground beef
1 lb. lean ground turkey
1 medium-sized onion,
   chopped
2 eggs
⅔ cup dry quick oats
1 envelope dry
   onion soup mix
½-1 tsp. liquid
   smoke
1 tsp. dry mustard
1 cup ketchup,
   divided

1. Fold two strips of tin foil, each long enough to fit from the top of the cooker down inside and up the other side, plus a 2-inch overhang on each side of the cooker—to function as handles for lifting the finished loaf out of the cooker.
2. Mix beef, turkey, and chopped onion together thoroughly.
3. Combine with eggs, oats, dry soup mix, liquid smoke, mustard, and all but 2 Tbsp. of ketchup.
4. Shape into loaf and place in slow cooker sprayed with nonfat cooking spray. Top with remaining ketchup.
5. Cover. Cook on low 4-5 hours or on high 2-3 hours.
6. When finished, pull loaf up gently with foil handles. Place loaf on warm platter. Pull foil handles away. Allow loaf to rest 10 minutes before slicing.

— PER SERVING —
- 210 calories
  (45 calories from fat)
- 5g total fat
  (1.5g saturated,
  0g trans)
- 80mg cholesterol
- 1040mg sodium
- 18g total carbohydrate
  (2g fiber, 5g sugar)
- 23g protein
- 8%DV vitamin A
- 6%DV vitamin C
- 4%DV calcium
- 10%DV iron

Meat Loaf and Mushrooms

Rebecca Meyerkorth
Wamego, KS

Makes 6 servings

Prep. Time: 25 minutes
Cooking Time: 4-5 hours
Ideal slow-cooker size: 3½- or 4-qt.

2 1-oz. slices whole wheat
   bread
½ lb. extra-lean ground beef
¾ lb. fat-free ground turkey
1½ cups mushrooms, sliced
½ cup minced onions
1 tsp. Italian seasoning
¾ tsp. salt
2 eggs
1 clove garlic, minced
3 Tbsp. ketchup
1½ tsp. Dijon mustard
⅛ tsp. ground red pepper

1. Fold two strips of tin
foil, each long enough to fit
from the top of the cooker
down inside and up the other
side, plus a 2-inch overhang
on each side of the cooker—to
function as handles for lifting
the finished loaf out of the
cooker.

2. Process bread slices in
food processor until crumbs
measure 1⅓ cups.

3. Combine bread crumbs,
beef, turkey, mushrooms,
onions, Italian seasoning,
salt, eggs, and garlic in bowl.
Shape into loaf to fit in slow
cooker.

4. Mix together ketchup,
mustard, and pepper. Spread
over top of loaf.

5. Cover. Cook on low 4-5
hours.

6. When finished, pull loaf
up gently with foil handles.
Place loaf on warm platter.
Pull foil handles away. Allow
loaf to rest 10 minutes before
slicing.

—— PER SERVING ——
- 230 calories
  (60 calories from fat)
- 7g total fat
  (2g saturated, 0g trans)
- 100mg cholesterol
- 1190mg sodium
- 15g total carbohydrate
  (2g fiber, 4g sugar)
- 27g protein
- 4%DV vitamin A
- 0%DV vitamin C
- 4%DV calcium
- 15%DV iron

Meat Loaf with a Mexican Touch

Karen Waggoner
Joplin, MO

Makes 6 servings

Prep. Time: 20-30 minutes
Cooking Time: 4 hours
Ideal slow-cooker size: 4-qt.

1¼ lbs. extra-lean ground
   beef
4 cups hash browns, thawed
1 egg, lightly beaten, *or* egg
   substitute
2 Tbsp. dry vegetable soup
   mix
2 Tbsp. low-sodium taco
   seasoning
2 cups fat-free shredded
   cheddar cheese, *divided*

1. Mix together ground
beef, hash browns, egg, soup
mix, taco seasoning, and 1
cup of cheese. Shape into loaf.

2. Line slow cooker with
tin foil, allowing ends of foil
to extend out over edges of
cooker, enough to grab hold of
and to lift the loaf out when
it's finished cooking. Spray
the foil with nonfat cooking
spray.

3. Place loaf in cooker.
Cover. Cook on low 4 hours.

4. Sprinkle with remain-
ing cheese and cover until
melted.

5. Gently lift loaf out, using
tin-foil handles. Allow to rest
10 minutes, then slice and
serve.

—— PER SERVING ——
- 350 calories
  (80 calories from fat)
- 9g total fat
  (3.5g saturated,
  0g trans)
- 70mg cholesterol
- 1040mg sodium
- 32g total carbohydrate
  (4g fiber, 1g sugar)
- 34g protein
- 15%DV vitamin A
- 10%DV vitamin C
- 35%DV calcium
- 15%DV iron

Low-Cal Meat Loaf

Jeanette Oberholtzer
Manheim, PA
Charlotte Shaffer
East Earl, PA
Dorothy VanDeest
Memphis, TN

Makes 6 servings

Prep. Time: 25 minutes
Cooking Time 4-5 hours
Ideal slow-cooker size: 3½-qt.

½ lb. extra-lean ground beef
3 cups shredded cabbage
1 green bell pepper, chopped
½ tsp. salt
1 Tbsp. dried onion flakes
½ tsp. caraway seeds, *optional*

1. Thoroughly combine all ingredients.
2. Shape into a round loaf.
3. Place on rack in slow cooker.
4. Cover. Cook on low 4-5 hours.

—— PER SERVING ——
- 80 calories
  (30 calories from fat)
- 3.5g total fat (1.5g saturated, 0g trans)
- 15mg cholesterol
- 230mg sodium
- 4g total carbohydrate (2g fiber, 2g sugar)
- 9g protein
- 4%DV vitamin A
- 25%DV vitamin C
- 2%DV calcium
- 6%DV iron

Tips:

1. The recipe can be easily doubled if you have a large crowd to feed. Use a 6-quart cooker and cook on high for 4-5 hours or on low 6-7 hours.
2. To add color and flavor, serve with chili sauce or ketchup.

Porcupine Meatballs

Jennifer Dzialonski
Brishton, MI

Makes 5 servings

Prep. Time: 20 minutes
Cooking Time: 4-5 hours
Ideal slow-cooker size: 3½-qt.

¾ lb. extra-lean ground beef, *or* ground turkey
1 cup skim milk
½ cup uncooked long-grain rice
1 medium-sized onion, chopped
1 cup dry bread crumbs
½ tsp. salt
dash of black pepper
10¾-oz. can low-fat, low-sodium cream of mushroom soup
½ cup skim milk

1. Combine meat, 1 cup skim milk, rice, onion, bread crumbs, salt, and pepper in a bowl.
2. Shape into meatballs with an ice cream scoop. Place in slow cooker.
3. Mix together soup and ½ cup milk. Pour over meatballs.
4. Cover. Cook on low 4-5 hours.
5. Serve with mushroom-soup gravy.

—— PER SERVING ——
- 140 calories
  (80 calories from fat)
- 9g total fat (3.5g saturated, 1g trans)
- 30mg cholesterol
- 920mg sodium
- 40g total carbohydrate (1g fiber, 6g sugar)
- 21g protein
- 0%DV vitamin A
- 0%DV vitamin C
- 15%DV calcium
- 20%DV iron

Meatball Stew Topping

Becky Frey
Lebanon, PA

Makes 6 servings

Prep. Time: 30-40 minutes
Cooking Time: 4-5 hours
Ideal slow-cooker size: 3-qt.

1 lb. extra-lean ground beef
1 egg
1 cup bread crumbs
1 medium-sized onion, chopped
¾ tsp. salt
14½-oz. can low-sodium diced tomatoes
10½-oz. can fat-free, low-sodium beef broth
¼ tsp. dried thyme
3 carrots, scrubbed and diced
1 medium-sized onion, chopped
1 rib celery, chopped

1. Combine ground beef, egg, bread crumbs, onion, and salt.
2. Shape into very small meatballs.
3. Brown meatballs in nonstick skillet.
4. Mix remaining ingredients in slow cooker. Spoon in meatballs and stir together gently.
5. Cover. Cook on low 4-5 hours.
6. Serve over potatoes or spaghetti.

—— PER SERVING ——
- 240 calories
  (60 calories from fat)
- 6g total fat
  (2.5g saturated,
  0g trans)
- 45mg cholesterol
- 490mg sodium
- 29g total carbohydrate
  (3g fiber, 5g sugar)
- 17g protein
- 80%DV vitamin A
- 8%DV vitamin C
- 6%DV calcium
- 20%DV iron

Sweet and Sour Meatballs

Alice Miller
Stuarts Draft, VA

Makes 4 servings

Prep. Time: 25 minutes
Cooking Time: 3-4 hours
Ideal slow-cooker size: 4-qt.

1 lb. extra-lean ground
  chuck
½ cup dry bread crumbs
¼ cup fat-free milk
¾ tsp. salt
¼ tsp. black pepper
1 egg, beaten
2 Tbsp. finely chopped
  onions
½ tsp. Worcestershire
  sauce

Sauce:
  ⅓ cup packed brown
    sugar
  2 Tbsp. cornstarch
  13¼-oz. can unsweetened
    pineapple chunks,
    undrained
  ⅓ cup vinegar
  1 Tbsp. soy sauce
  1 green bell pepper,
    chopped
  ⅓ cup water

1. Combine meatball
ingredients. Shape into ¾-1"
balls. Brown in nonstick
skillet. Drain. Place in slow
cooker.

2. Add brown sugar and
cornstarch to skillet. Stir in
remaining ingredients. Heat
to boiling, stirring constantly.
Pour over meatballs.

3. Cover. Cook on low 3-4
hours.

—— PER SERVING ——
- 380 calories
  (110 calories from fat)
- 12g total fat (4.5g
  saturated, 0g trans)
- 90mg cholesterol
- 850mg sodium
- 40g total carbohydrate
  (2g fiber, 28g sugar)
- 28g protein
- 0%DV vitamin A
- 20%DV vitamin C
- 10%DV calcium
- 20%DV iron

Variation:
  If you like pineapples,
use a 20-oz. can of chunks,
instead of the 13¼-oz. can.

Mexican Corn Bread

Jeanne Heyerly
Chenoa, IL

Makes 6 servings

Prep. Time: 20-25 minutes
Cooking Time: 4½-6 hours
Ideal slow-cooker size: 4-qt.

1 lb. extra-lean ground
  beef chuck
16-oz. can cream-style corn
1 cup cornmeal
½ tsp. baking soda
1 tsp. salt
¼ cup oil
1 cup fat-free milk
2 eggs, beaten
½ cup low-sodium taco
  sauce
2 cups shredded fat-free
  cheddar cheese
1 medium-sized onion,
  chopped
1 garlic clove, minced
4-oz. can diced green
  chilies

1. Brown ground chuck in
nonstick skillet.

2. While meat is browning,
combine corn, cornmeal, baking soda, salt, oil, milk, eggs,
and taco sauce. Pour half of
mixture into slow cooker.

2. Layer cheese, onion,
garlic, green chilies, and
ground beef on top of cornmeal mixture. Cover with
remaining cornmeal mixture.

3. Cover. Cook on high 1
hour and on low 3½-4 hours,
or only on low 6 hours.

—— PER SERVING ——
- 360 calories
  (90 calories from fat)
- 10g total fat
  (3g saturated, 0g trans)
- 60mg cholesterol
- 1300mg sodium
- 39g total carbohydrate
  (4g fiber, 6g sugar)
- 29g protein
- 10%DV vitamin A
- 0%DV vitamin C
- 40%DV calcium
- 15%DV iron

African Beef Curry

Rebecca Leichty
Harrisonburg, VA

Makes 6 small servings

Prep. Time: 20 minutes
Cooking Time: 4-5 hours
Ideal slow-cooker size: 3-qt.

1 lb. extra-lean ground
  beef, browned
1 large onion, thinly sliced
1 green bell pepper, diced
1 tomato, peeled and diced
1 apple, peeled, cored, and
  diced
1-2 tsp. curry (*or more to
  taste*)
4 cups prepared rice

1. Spray slow cooker with fat-free cooking spray.
2. Add all ingredients except rice to slow cooker and mix well.
3. Cover and cook on low 4-5 hours.
4. Serve over hot rice.

—— PER SERVING ——
• 340 calories   • 47g total carbohydrate
  (70 calories from fat)   (2g fiber, 6g sugar)
• 7g total fat   • 20g protein
  (3g saturated, 0g trans) • 6%DV vitamin A
• 30mg cholesterol   • 20%DV vitamin C
• 50mg sodium   • 4%DV calcium
     • 20%DV iron

Tips:
1. You can thicken this by stirring in a 6-oz. can of tomato paste in Step 2, if you wish.
2. This is interesting served with a spoonful of lowfat or nonfat "lemon-enhanced" vanilla yogurt on top of each individual dish.

Ground Beef 'n' Biscuits

Karen Waggoner
Joplin, MO

Makes 8 servings

Prep. Time: 20 minutes
Cooking Time: 2½-3½ hours
Ideal slow-cooker size: 6-qt.

1½ lbs. extra-lean ground
  beef
½ cup celery, chopped
½ cup onions, chopped
2 Tbsp. flour
1 tsp. salt
¼ tsp. black pepper
½ tsp. dried oregano
2 8-oz. cans tomato sauce
10-oz. pkg. frozen peas,
  thawed
2 7½-oz. cans refrigerated
  buttermilk biscuits
2 cups fat-free shredded
  cheddar cheese

1. Brown ground beef, celery, and onions in nonstick skillet.
2. Stir in flour, salt, pepper, and oregano.
3. Add tomato sauce and peas.
4. Pour into slow cooker. (A large oval cooker allows the biscuits to be arranged over top. You can also divide the mixture between two round slow cookers and accommodate the biscuits in that way.)
5. Arrange biscuits over top and sprinkle with cheese.
6. Cook uncovered on high 1-1½ hours, then on low for 1½-2 hours, covering for the last 30 minutes.

—— PER SERVING ——
• 370 calories   • 38g total carbohydrate
  (80 calories from fat)   (3g fiber, 5g sugar)
• 9g total fat   • 34g protein
  (3.5g saturated,   • 20%DV vitamin A
  0g trans)   • 10%DV vitamin C
• 35mg cholesterol   • 30%DV calcium
• 1470mg sodium   • 25%DV iron

Hamburger Casserole

Becky Harder
Monument, CO

Makes 6 servings

Prep. Time: 20-25 minutes
Cooking Time: 3-6 hours
Ideal slow-cooker size: 4- or 5-qt.

1½ lbs. extra-lean ground
  beef
½ tsp. salt
¼ tsp. black pepper
2 large potatoes, sliced
2-3 medium-sized carrots,
  sliced
2 cups frozen peas
2 medium-sized onions,
  sliced
2 ribs celery, sliced
10¾-oz. can low-sodium
  tomato soup
soup can of water

1. Brown ground beef in a nonstick skillet over medium heat. Season with salt and pepper.
2. Layer vegetables into slow cooker in order given.
3. Place ground beef on top of celery.
4. Mix tomato soup with water. Pour into slow cooker.

5. Cover. Cook on low 4-6 hours or on high 3-4 hours.

—— PER SERVING ——
- 320 calories
  (100 calories from fat)
- 11g total fat
  (4g saturated, 0g trans)
- 40mg cholesterol
- 360mg sodium
- 28g total carbohydrate
  (5g fiber, 7g sugar)
- 28g protein
- 100%DV vitamin A
- 30%DV vitamin C
- 4%DV calcium
- 25%DV iron

Beef and Noodle Casserole

Delores Scheel
West Fargo, ND

Makes 10 servings

Prep. Time: 20-30 minutes
Cooking Time: 2-3 hours
Ideal slow-cooker size: 4-qt.

1 lb. extra-lean ground
  beef
1 medium-sized onion,
  chopped
1 medium-sized green bell
  pepper, chopped
17-oz. can whole-kernel
  corn, drained
4-oz. can mushroom stems
  and pieces, drained
1 tsp. salt
¼ tsp. black pepper
11-oz. jar salsa
5 cups dry medium egg
  noodles, cooked
28-oz. can low-sodium
  diced tomatoes,
  undrained
1 cup low-fat shredded
  cheddar cheese

1. Brown ground beef and onion in nonstick skillet over medium heat. Transfer to slow cooker.

2. Top with remaining ingredients in order listed.

3. Cover. Cook on low 2-3 hours.

—— PER SERVING ——
- 460 calories
  (100 calories from fat)
- 11g total fat
  (4g saturated, 0g trans)
- 75mg cholesterol
- 1300mg sodium
- 61g total carbohydrate
  (7g fiber, 9g sugar)
- 31g protein
- 15%DV vitamin A
- 30%DV vitamin C
- 25%DV calcium
- 30%DV iron

Beef and Rice Casserole

Colleen Heatwole
Burton, MI

Makes 6 servings

Prep. Time: 20 minutes
Cooking Time: 3-4 hours
Ideal slow-cooker size: 5-qt.

½ lb. extra-lean ground
  beef
1 onion, chopped
1 clove garlic, minced
½ cup green bell pepper,
  cut finely

½ cup celery, diced
1 tsp. dried basil
1 tsp. dried oregano
10¾-oz. can reduced-fat,
  low-sodium cream of
  mushroom soup
1 cup water
4 cups cooked brown rice

1. Brown ground beef, onion, garlic, green pepper, and celery in a nonstick skillet over medium heat. Season with basil and oregano.

2. Combine soup and water in separate bowl.

3. Spray slow cooker with nonfat cooking spray.

4. Layer 2 cups of cooked rice on bottom of slow cooker. Add half of ground beef and half of soup mixture.

5. Repeat layers.

6. Cover. Cook on low 3-4 hours.

—— PER SERVING ——
- 250 calories
  (50 calories from fat)
- 6g total fat
  (2g saturated,
  0.5g trans)
- 15mg cholesterol
- 380mg sodium
- 37g total carbohydrate
  (3g fiber, 2g sugar)
- 12g protein
- 2%DV vitamin A
- 10%DV vitamin C
- 4%DV calcium
- 10%DV iron

If I want to have a hot dish at noon time on Sunday, I bake a casserole on Saturday. Then on Sunday morning I put the prepared food into a slow cooker, turn it on High for 30 minutes, then on Low while I'm at church.

Ruth Hershey, Paradise, PA

China Dish

Lois Stoltzfus
Honey Brook, PA

Makes 6 servings

Prep. Time: 30 minutes
Cooking Time: 4-6 hours
Ideal slow-cooker size: 4-qt.

1½ lbs. extra-lean ground beef
10¾-oz. can cream of chicken soup
10¾-oz. can 98% fat-free cream of mushroom soup
3½ cups water
2 cups celery, chopped
1 cup onions, chopped
1 cup brown rice, uncooked
3 Tbsp. Worcestershire sauce

1. Brown ground beef in a nonstick skillet.
2. Combine all ingredients in slow cooker.
3. Cover. Cook on low 4-6 hours.

—— PER SERVING ——
- 400 calories
  (140 calories from fat)
- 15g total fat
  (6g saturated, 1g trans)
- 45mg cholesterol
- 950mg sodium
- 36g total carbohydrate
  (2g fiber, 3g sugar)
- 28g protein
- 6%DV vitamin A
- 8%DV vitamin C
- 8%DV calcium
- 20%DV iron

Ground Beef Stroganoff

Janie S. Canupp
Millersville, MD

Makes 6 servings

Prep. Time: 30 minutes
Cooking Time: 3 hours
Ideal slow cooker size: 5-qt.

2 lbs. 95% fat-free ground beef
2 medium onions, chopped
2 cloves garlic, minced
4-oz. can sliced mushrooms, drained
1 tsp. salt
¼ tsp. black pepper
1 cup low-sodium, fat-free beef broth, *or* 1 low-sodium bouillon cube dissolved in 1 cup water
3 Tbsp. ketchup
1½ cups fat-free sour cream
¼ cup flour

1. Brown beef in large non-stick skillet. Stir frequently to break up clumps.
2. When meat is no longer pink, add onions, garlic, and mushrooms. Sauté until onion is tender. Put mixture into slow cooker.
3. In a small bowl, mix together salt, pepper, broth, and ketchup. Stir into beef mixture in slow cooker.
4. Cover. Cook on low 2½ hours.
5. Meanwhile, combine sour cream and flour in a small bowl until well blended. Stir into slow cooker.
6. Cover. Cook 30 more minutes, or until Stroganoff is thickened and bubbly.

—— PER SERVING ——
- 290 calories
  (70 calories from fat)
- 8g total fat
  (3.5g saturated, 0g trans)
- 90mg cholesterol
- 690mg sodium
- 20g total carbohydrate
  (1g fiber, 4g sugar)
- 33g protein
- 4%DV vitamin A
- 6%DV vitamin C
- 10%DV calcium
- 20%DV iron

Stuffed Peppers

Mary E. Wheatley
Mashpee, MA

Makes 4 servings

Prep. Time: 20-30 minutes
Cooking Time: 3-5 hours
Ideal slow-cooker size: 5-qt.

1 lb. extra-lean ground beef
4 large green bell peppers, tops removed, cleaned of seeds and cored, but not cut in half
8-oz. can tomato sauce, *divided*
15-oz. can Spanish rice
1 large onion, chopped
½ tsp. salt
¼ tsp. black pepper

1. Combine all ingredients, except peppers and ½ can of tomato sauce.
2. Stuff green peppers full.
3. Stand peppers up in slow cooker. Pour remaining tomato sauce over peppers.
4. Cover. Cook on high 3 hours or on low 4-5 hours.

—— PER SERVING ——
- 340 calories
  (110 calories from fat)
- 12g total fat
  (4.5g saturated,
  0g trans)
- 40mg cholesterol
- 470mg sodium
- 31g total carbohydrate
  (5g fiber, 6g sugar)
- 27g protein
- 30%DV vitamin A
- 150%DV vitamin C
- 6%DV calcium
- 25%DV iron

Tangy Stuffed Green Peppers

Jean Butzer
Batavia, NY

Makes 6 servings

Prep. Time: 25 minutes
Cooking Time: 4-5 hours
Ideal slow-cooker size: 5-qt.

6 green bell peppers
½ lb. extra-lean ground
  beef
¼ cup finely chopped
  onions
1 Tbsp. pimento, chopped
¾ tsp. salt
¼ tsp. black pepper
12-oz. can low-sodium
  whole-kernel corn,
  drained
1 Tbsp. Worcestershire
  sauce
1 tsp. prepared mustard
10¾-oz. can condensed
  low-sodium cream of
  tomato soup

1. Cut a slice off the top of each pepper. Remove core, seeds, and white membrane.
2. In a small bowl, combine beef, onions, pimento, salt, black pepper, and corn.

3. Spoon into peppers. Stand peppers up in slow cooker.
4. Combine Worcestershire sauce, mustard, and tomato soup. Pour over peppers.
5. Cover. Cook on low 4-5 hours.

—— PER SERVING ——
- 170 calories
  (40 calories from fat)
- 4.5g total fat
  (2g saturated, 0g trans)
- 15mg cholesterol
- 650mg sodium
- 24g total carbohydrate
  (4g fiber, 8g sugar)
- 11g protein
- 25%DV vitamin A
- 120%DV vitamin C
- 2%DV calcium
- 15%DV iron

Spaghetti Sauce

Colleen Heatwole
Burton, MI

Makes 20 servings

Prep. Time: 30-35 minutes
Cooking Time: 2½-4½ hours
Ideal slow-cooker size: 1 7-qt.,
* or 2 4-qt. cookers*

1½ lbs. 95 % lean ground
  beef, browned and
  drained
3 onions, coarsely chopped
1 red bell pepper, coarsely
  chopped
1 green pepper coarsely
  chopped
4 cloves garlic, minced
2 28-oz. cans low-sodium
  diced tomatoes
14½-oz. can low-sodium,
  diced tomatoes
2 14½-oz. cans low-sodium,
  fat-free beef broth
2 Tbsp. sugar

2 tsp. dried basil, *or more*
2 tsp. dried oregano, *or*
  more
2 tsp. salt
2 6-oz. cans low sodium
  tomato paste

1. Combine all ingredients except tomato paste in slow cooker.
2. Cook 2 hours on high or 3-4 hours on low. Stir in tomato paste.
3. Cover and cook an additional 30 minutes on low.

—— PER SERVING ——
- 120 calories
  (20 calories from fat)
- 2g total fat
  (1g saturated, 0g trans)
- 20mg cholesterol
- 420mg sodium
- 16g total carbohydrate
  (3g fiber, 8g sugar)
- 10g protein
- 25%DV vitamin A
- 50%DV vitamin C
- 6%DV calcium
- 15%DV iron

Beef Slow-Cooker Pizza

Wilma J. Haberkamp
Fairbank, IA

Makes 8 servings

Prep. Time: 20-30 minutes
Cooking Time: 1-2½ hours
Ideal slow-cooker size: 6-qt.

1 lb. extra-lean ground
beef
2 small onions, chopped
14-oz. can fat-free pizza
sauce
14-oz. can low-fat, low-
sodium spaghetti sauce
1 tsp. garlic powder
1¼ tsp. black pepper
1 tsp. dried oregano
¼ tsp. rubbed sage
12 ozs. dry kluski noodles

1. Brown ground beef and
onions in nonstick skillet.
2. In skillet, or in a large
bowl, mix together browned
meat and onions, pizza sauce,
spaghetti sauce, seasonings,
and herbs.
3. Boil noodles according
to directions on package until
tender. Drain.
4. Layer half of beef sauce
in bottom of cooker. Spoon in
noodles. Top with remaining
beef sauce.
5. Cook on low 1-1½ hours
if ingredients are hot when
placed in cooker. If the sauce
and noodles are at room
temperature or have just been
refrigerated, cook on high
2-2½ hours.

—— PER SERVING ——
• 320 calories
(70 calories from fat)
• 8g total fat
(2.5g saturated,
0g trans)
• 65mg cholesterol
• 610mg sodium
• 42g total carbohydrate
(3g fiber, 6g sugar)
• 20g protein
• 8%DV vitamin A
• 10%DV vitamin C
• 4%DV calcium
• 20%DV iron

Quick Lasagna

Frances Musser
Newmanstown, PA

Makes 6 servings

Prep. Time: 45 minutes
Cooking Time: 2-3 hours
Ideal slow-cooker size: 4-qt.

¼ lb. extra-lean ground
beef
8-oz. pkg. broad egg
noodles
1 cup fat-free cottage
cheese
½ cup shredded low-fat
mozzarella cheese
¼ cup grated Parmesan
cheese
2½ cups spaghetti sauce

1. Brown ground beef in a
nonstick skillet. Set aside.
2. Cook noodles and drain.
Toss noodles with both
cheeses.
3. Mix together browned
beef and spaghetti sauce.
4. Spoon one-third of meat
sauce in bottom of slow
cooker.
5. Layer in half the
noodles.
6. Add a layer of 1 cup
cottage cheese.

7. Add one-third of meat
sauce. Top with remaining
half of noodles. Finish with
the remaining meat sauce.
8. Cover. Cook on low 2-3
hours.

—— PER SERVING ——
• 300 calories
(80 calories from fat)
• 9 total fat (3.5g
saturated, 0g trans)
• 50mg cholesterol
• 590mg sodium
• 33g total carbohydrate
(3g fiber, 6g sugar)
• 21g protein
• 10%DV vitamin A
• 10%DV vitamin C
• 20%DV calcium
• 15%DV iron

Variations:
If you wish, and your
diet permits, add 1 Tbsp.
Italian seasoning, or 1½ tsp.
dried basil and 1½ tsp. dried
oregano, to Step 3.

Pork Main Dishes

Ham and Potatoes

Judy Buller
Bluffton, OH

Makes 8 servings

Prep. Time: 45 minutes
Cooking Time: 4-6 hours
Ideal slow-cooker size: 6-qt.

2 cups carrots, sliced
6 cups raw potatoes, sliced
1 small onion, sliced thin
2-2½ cups lean ham, cubed
3 Tbsp. butter
½ cup flour
3 cups skim milk
¼ tsp. black pepper
½ tsp. parsley
2 Tbsp. Dijon mustard
1 cup shredded, reduced-
   fat cheddar cheese

1. Layer carrots, potatoes, onion, and ham in slow cooker.
2. In a skillet, melt butter. Stir in flour. Gradually add milk. Stir frequently until sauce is smooth and thickened.
3. Add pepper, parsley, mustard, and shredded cheese. Continue heating and stirring until cheese is melted.
4. Pour over vegetables and ham in slow cooker. Push the vegetables down into the sauce, making sure all ingredients are covered as fully as possible.
5. Cover. Cook on low 6 hours, or on high 2 hours and then on low 2 hours.

—— PER SERVING ——
• 380 calories
   (100 calories from fat)
• 11g total fat
   (4g saturated, 1g trans)
• 30mg cholesterol
• 930mg sodium
• 46g total carbohydrate
   (5g fiber, 11g sugar)
• 26g protein
• 200%DV vitamin A
• 30%DV vitamin C
• 30%DV calcium
• 15%DV iron

Try to have vegetable and meat pieces all cut about the same size and thickness. Mary Puskar, Forest Hill, MD

Ham and Scalloped Potatoes

Betty Chalker
Dalhart, TX

Makes 8 servings

Prep. Time: 15-20 minutes
Cooking Time: 4-8 hours
Ideal slow-cooker size: 6-qt.

1½ lbs. 98% fat-free ham,
  cut into 8 pieces
8-10 medium-sized potatoes,
  peeled and thinly sliced
2 onions, peeled and thinly
  sliced
½ tsp. salt
¼ tsp. black pepper, *or*
  more, according to your
  taste
1 cup fat-free grated
  cheddar *or* American
  cheese
10¾-oz. can 98% fat-free
  cream of celery soup
paprika

1. Layer half of ham,
potatoes, and onions in slow
cooker. Sprinkle with half the
salt and pepper, and then half
the grated cheese.
2. Repeat layers.
3. Spoon undiluted soup
over ingredients.
4. Cook on low 6-8 hours
or high 4 hours.

— PER SERVING —
• 310 calories
  (30 calories from fat)
• 3.5g total fat
  (1g saturated, 0g trans)
• 40mg cholesterol
• 1130mg sodium
• 46g total carbohydrate
  (5g fiber, 5g sugar)
• 23g protein
• 6%DV vitamin A
• 30%DV vitamin C
• 20%DV calcium
• 10%DV iron

Creamy Ham Lasagna

Ilene Bontrager
Arlington, KS

Makes 8 servings

Prep. Time: 30-45 minutes
Cooking Time: 3-4 hours
Ideal slow-cooker size: 6-qt.

Ham Gravy:
  ¼ cup onions, chopped
  1 Tbsp. butter
  1 cup flour
  6½ cups skim milk
  3-4 cups turkey ham,
    cubed
  ½-1 tsp. salt
  ½ tsp. black pepper
  4 ozs. fat-free sour cream

Cheese Filling:
  24-oz. tub lowfat cottage
    cheese
  1 egg, beaten

8 10" tortillas, cut in
  2" squares or diamonds,
  or 4 cups cooked noodles

1. Sauté chopped onions in
butter in large saucepan.
2. Add flour and then milk
gradually. Stir until thick and
bubbly. Stir in cubed ham.
3. Add salt, pepper and
sour cream.
4. In a mixing bowl, stir
together cottage cheese and
egg.
5. Layer in slow cooker:
half the ham gravy, then half
the tortilla pieces or cooked
noodles, and then half the
cheese filling. Repeat layers.

6. Cover. Cook on low 3-4
hours.

— PER SERVING —
• 250 calories
  (50 calories from fat)
• 6g total fat
  (3g saturated, 0g trans)
• 65mg cholesterol
• 1220mg sodium
• 25g total carbohydrate
  (0.5g fiber, 12g sugar)
• 25g protein
• 10%DV vitamin A
• 4%DV vitamin C
• 30%DV calcium
• 10%DV iron

Ham-Yam-Apples

Joan Rosenberger
Stephens City, VA

Makes 4 servings

Prep. Time: 15 minutes
Cooking Time: 4-5 hours
Ideal slow-cooker size: 5-qt.

1 slice fully cooked ham
  (about 1 lb.)
29-oz. can sweet potatoes
  or yams, drained
2 apples, thinly sliced
¼ cup light brown sugar
2 Tbsp. orange juice

1. Cube ham.
2. Combine all ingredients
in slow cooker.
3. Cook on low 4-5 hours,
or until apples are tender.

— PER SERVING —
• 460 calories
  (60 calories from fat)
• 7g total fat
  (2g saturated, 0g trans)
• 60mg cholesterol
• 1520mg sodium
• 73g total carbohydrate
  (5g fiber, 57g sugar)
• 28g protein
• 200%DV vitamin A
• 20%DV vitamin C
• 8%DV calcium
• 25%DV iron

Broccoli and Ham Dinner

Delores Scheel
West Fargo, ND

Makes 6 servings

Prep. Time: 15-20 minutes
Cooking Time: 3-4 hours
Ideal slow-cooker size: 4-qt.

10¾-oz. can 98% fat-free cream of mushroom soup
8-oz. jar low-sodium, fat-free cheese spread
1 cup skim milk
1 cup instant rice, uncooked
1 rib celery, chopped
1 small onion, chopped
3 cups cooked ham, cubed
16-oz. pkg. frozen broccoli cuts, thawed and drained

1. In a bowl, mix together cream of mushroom soup, cheese spread, milk, rice, celery, and onion.
2. Stir in ham.
3. Cover. Cook on low 3-4 hours.
4. One hour before serving time, stir in broccoli.

—— PER SERVING ——
· 260 calories
  (70 calories from fat)
· 8g total fat
  (3.5g saturated,
  0g trans)
· 35mg cholesterol
· 1180mg sodium
· 19g total carbohydrate
  (3g fiber, 6g sugar)
· 29g protein
· 20%DV vitamin A
· 30%DV vitamin C
· 25%DV calcium
· 10%DV iron

Ham with Pineapple Sauce

Kayla Snyder
North East, PA

Makes 25 servings

Prep. Time: 20-30 minutes
Cooking Time: 3 hours
Ideal slow cooker size: 5-qt.

40-oz. can crushed pineapple
1 tsp. vinegar
1 Tbsp. lemon juice
½ tsp. salt
2 cups brown sugar
¾ tsp. dry mustard
4 Tbsp. flour
7-8-lb. ham, precooked and sliced in ¼"-thick slices

1. Mix together pineapple, vinegar, lemon juice, salt, brown sugar, mustard, and flour in a saucepan. Bring to boil. Cook, stirring frequently until slightly thickened.
2. Layer several slices of ham into slow cooker. Ladle some of sauce over top. Continue layering until all ham and sauce are stacked in slow cooker.
3. Cover. Cook on high 3 hours, or until heated through.

—— PER SERVING ——
· 260 calories
  (60 calories from fat)
· 7g total fat
  (2.5g saturated,
  0g trans)
· 65mg cholesterol
· 1580mg sodium
· 21g total carbohydrate
  (0g fiber, 18g sugar)
· 27g protein
· 0%DV vitamin A
· 8%DV vitamin C
· 2%DV calcium
· 10%DV iron

Note:
We served this recipe at our wedding, so it is especially special to us.

Ham & Yam Dish

Leona Miller
Millersburg, OH

Makes 8 servings

Prep. Time: 15 minutes
Cooking Time: 1½-4 hours
Ideal slow-cooker size: 4- or 5-qt.

40-oz. can yams in water, drained
1½ lbs. extra-lean smoked ham, cut into bite-sized cubes
20-oz. can unsweetened pineapple chunks, *or* crushed pineapple, in light juice, drained
¼ cup dark brown sugar

1. Spray slow cooker with nonfat cooking spray.
2. Stir all ingredients together gently in the slow cooker.
3. Cook on high 1½-2 hours or on low 3-4 hours.

—— PER SERVING ——
· 320 calories
  (45 calories from fat)
· 5g total fat
  (1.5g saturated,
  0g trans)
· 45mg cholesterol
· 930mg sodium
· 47g total carbohydrate
  (3g fiber, 36g sugar)
· 21g protein
· 300%DV vitamin A
· 10%DV vitamin C
· 6%DV calcium
· 20%DV iron

Chops and Chinese Vegetables

Barbara Walker
Sturgis, SD

Makes 8 servings

Prep. Time: 30 minutes
Cooking Time: 4-5 hours
Ideal slow-cooker size: 3- or 4-qt.

5 pork chops, trimmed of fat and cubed
1-1½ lbs. round steak, cubed
6 cups water
1 rib celery, chopped
1 medium-large onion, chopped
1 can bean sprouts, drained
4 Tbsp. low-sodium soy sauce

1. Brown pork and steak in nonstick skillet. Drain.
2. Combine all ingredients except soy sauce in slow cooker.
3. Cover. Cook on low 4-5 hours.
4. Add soy sauce and thicken with 3 Tbsp. cornstarch mixed with ¼ cup cold water, if desired.
5. Serve over rice or chow mein noodles.

—— PER SERVING ——
• 170 calories
  (60 calories from fat)
• 7g total fat (2.5g saturated, 0g trans)
• 70mg cholesterol
• 320mg sodium
• 2g total carbohydrate
  (0.5g fiber, 1g sugar)
• 24g protein
• 0%DV vitamin A
• 2%DV vitamin C
• 2%DV calcium
• 10%DV iron

Variation:
    If your sodium count allows, you may want to add 1 tsp. salt to Step 2.

Barbecued Pork Steaks

Marcia S. Myer
Manheim, PA

Makes 4 servings

Prep. Time: 15-20 minutes
Cooking Time: 3½-4½ hours
Ideal slow-cooker size: 5-qt.

4 4-oz. pork tenderloin chops, cut ½" thick
1 large onion, sliced
1 large green pepper, sliced
2 tomatoes, sliced
1 Tbsp. instant tapioca
½ cup low-sodium, low-fat barbecue sauce
¼ cup red wine
½ tsp. cumin

1. Brown steaks in nonstick skillet.
2. In slow cooker, arrange slices of onion, green pepper, and tomato.
3. Sprinkle tapioca over vegetables.
4. Place browned pork steaks on top of vegetables.
5. In bowl combine barbecue sauce, wine, and cumin.
6. Pour over meat.
7. Cover. Cook 3½-4½ hours on low.

—— PER SERVING ——
• 270 calories
  (50 calories from fat)
• 6g total fat
  (2g saturated, 0g trans)
• 75mg cholesterol
• 105mg sodium
• 25g total carbohydrate
  (2g fiber, 14g sugar)
• 26g protein
• 6%DV vitamin A
• 80%DV vitamin C
• 4%DV calcium
• 10%DV iron

Barbecued Pork Chops

Loretta Weisz
Aubrun, WA

Makes 6 servings

Prep. Time: 10 minutes
Cooking Time: 5-6 hours
Ideal slow-cooker size: 5-qt.

4 loin pork chops, ¾" thick, trimmed of fat
1 cup ketchup
1 cup hot water
2 Tbsp. vinegar
1 Tbsp. Worcestershire sauce
2 tsp. brown sugar
½ tsp. black pepper
½ tsp. chili powder
½ tsp. paprika

1. Place pork chops in slow cooker.
2. Combine remaining ingredients. Pour over chops.
3. Cover. Cook on high 5-6 hours, or until tender but not dry.
4. Cut chops in half and serve.

—— PER SERVING ——
• 180 calories
  (60 calories from fat)
• 7g total fat
  (2.5g saturated, 0g trans)
• 60mg cholesterol
• 430mg sodium
• 11g total carbohydrate
  (0.5g fiber, 5g sugar)
• 20g protein
• 8%DV vitamin A
• 2%DV vitamin C
• 2%DV calcium
• 8%DV iron

Fresh Tomato Soup, page 162

Green Beans with Dill, page 213

Pork Chops and Potatoes

Sherry H. Kauffman
Minot, ND

Makes 6 servings

Prep. Time: 25 minutes
Cooking Time: 3½-4½ hours
Ideal slow cooker size: 5-qt.

10¾-oz. can low-sodium, low-fat cream of mushroom soup
¼ cup low-sodium, low-fat chicken broth
¼ cup country-style Dijon mustard
1 garlic clove, minced
½ tsp. dried thyme
¼ tsp. salt
¼ tsp. pepper
6 medium red potatoes, sliced
1 medium onion, thinly sliced
6 5-oz. boneless center-cut loin lean pork chops, trimmed of fat

1. In slow cooker, combine soup, broth, mustard, garlic, thyme, salt, and pepper.
2. Stir in potatoes and onion slices.
3. Top with pork chops. Push down into sauce as much as possible.
4. Cover. Cook on low 3½-4½ hours, or until meat and potatoes are tender but not dry.

—— PER SERVING ——
- 400 calories
  (80 calories from fat)
- 9g total fat
  (3.5g saturated,
  0g trans)
- 85mg cholesterol
- 610mg sodium
- 42g total carbohydrate
  (4g fiber, 4g sugar)
- 34g protein
- 0%DV vitamin A
- 40%DV vitamin C
- 8%DV calcium
- 15%DV iron

Fruited Pork Chops

Mrs. Carolyn Baer
Conrath, WI

Makes 6 servings

Prep. Time: 20 minutes
Cooking Time: 3-3¾ hours
Ideal slow-cooker size: 5- or 6-qt.

3 Tbsp. all-purpose flour
1½ tsp. dried oregano
¾ tsp. salt
¼ tsp. garlic powder
¼ tsp. black pepper
6 lean boneless pork loin chops (about 5 ozs. each)
1 Tbsp. olive *or* canola oil
20-oz. can unsweetened pineapple chunks
1 cup water
2 Tbsp. brown sugar
2 Tbsp. dried minced onion
2 Tbsp. tomato paste
¼ cup raisins

1. In a large resealable plastic bag, combine flour, oregano, salt, garlic powder, and pepper.
2. Add pork chops one at a time and shake to coat.
3. Brown pork chops on both sides in a nonstick skillet using canola oil. Transfer browned chops to slow cooker.
4. Drain pineapple, reserving juice. Set pineapple aside.
5. In a mixing bowl, combine ¾ cup reserved pineapple juice, water, brown sugar, dried onion, and tomato paste. Pour over chops.
6. Sprinkle raisins over top.
7. Cook on high 3-3½ hours or until meat is tender and a meat thermometer reads 160°. Stir in reserved pineapple chunks. Cook 10 minutes longer or until heated through.

—— PER SERVING ——
- 280 calories
  (80 calories from fat)
- 9g total fat (2.5g
  saturated, 0g trans)
- 65mg cholesterol
- 350mg sodium
- 28g total carbohydrate
  (2g fiber, 22g sugar)
- 24g protein
- 4%DV vitamin A
- 20%DV vitamin C
- 6%DV calcium
- 10%DV iron

Tips:

1. This is good served over brown rice.
2. If your diet allows, you may want to place 1 tsp. salt (instead of the ¾ tsp.) in coating mixture in Step 1.

Three-Ingredient Sauerkraut Dinner

Esther J. Yoder
Hartville, OH

Makes 8 servings

Prep. Time: 15 minutes
Cooking Time: 4-6 hours
Ideal slow-cooker size: 5-qt.

2 cups low-sodium
  barbecue sauce
1 cup water
2 lbs. thinly sliced lean
  pork chops, trimmed of
  fat
2 lbs. sauerkraut, rinsed

1. Mix together barbecue sauce and water.
2. Combine barbecue sauce, pork chops, and sauerkraut in slow cooker.
3. Cover. Cook on low 4-6 hours, or until chops are tender but not dry.

—— PER SERVING ——
• 300 calories
  (90 calories from fat)
• 11g total fat
  (3.5g saturated,
  0g trans)
• 90mg cholesterol
• 1450mg sodium
• 18g total carbohydrate
  (3g fiber, 12g sugar)
• 32g protein
• 4%DV vitamin A
• 10%DV vitamin C
• 6%DV calcium
• 20%DV iron

Slow-Cooker Pork Tenderloin

Kathy Hertzler
Lancaster, PA

Makes 6 servings

Prep. Time: 5-15 minutes
Cooking Time: 4 hours
Ideal slow-cooker size: 4-qt.

1½-lb. pork tenderloin,
  trimmed of fat and cut
  in half lengthwise
1 cup water
¾ cup red wine
3 Tbsp. light soy sauce
1-oz. envelope dry onion
  soup mix
6 cloves garlic, peeled and
  chopped
freshly ground pepper

1. Place pork tenderloin pieces in slow cooker. Pour water, wine, and soy sauce over pork.
2. Turn pork over in liquid several times to completely moisten.
3. Sprinkle with dry onion soup mix. Top with chopped garlic and pepper.
4. Cover. Cook on low 4 hours.

—— PER SERVING ——
• 160 calories
  (25 calories from fat)
• 3g total fat
  (1g saturated, 0g trans)
• 60mg cholesterol
• 780mg sodium
• 5g total carbohydrate
  (0g fiber, 1g sugar)
• 22g protein
• 0%DV vitamin A
• 2%DV vitamin C
• 2%DV calcium
• 6%DV iron

Tip:
For tasty go-alongs, mix ½ cup uncooked long-grain white rice and ½ cup uncooked brown rice in a microwavable bowl. Stir in 2½ cups water and ½ tsp. salt. Cover. Microwave 5 minutes on high, and then 20 minutes on medium. Place finished pork on a large platter and the finished rice alongside, topped with the au jus from the meat. A green salad goes well with this to make a full meal.

Tasty Pork Tenderloin

Janice Yoskovich
Carmichaels, PA

Makes 8 servings

Prep. Time: 10 minutes
Cooking Time: 4 hours
Ideal slow-cooker size: 4-qt.

1½ lbs. pork tenderloin
12 ozs. chili sauce
16-oz. can jellied cranberry sauce
2 Tbsp. brown sugar
5 cups cooked long-grain enriched rice

1. Place pork tenderloin in slow cooker.
2. Mix together chili sauce, cranberry sauce, and brown sugar. Pour over pork.
3. Cover and cook on low 4 hours, or until cooked through but not dry.
4. Serve over rice.

—— PER SERVING ——
- 360 calories
  (30 calories from fat)
- 3g total fat
  (1g saturated, 0g trans)
- 45mg cholesterol
- 510mg sodium
- 62g total carbohydrate
  (1g fiber, 26g sugar)
- 20g protein
- 2%DV vitamin A
- 4%DV vitamin C
- 2%DV calcium
- 10%DV iron

Pork Loin with Spiced Fruit Sauce

Maricarol Magill
Freehold, NJ

Makes 8 servings

Prep. Time: 25-40 minutes
Cooking Time: 4-6 hours
Ideal slow cooker size: 5- to 6-qt.

8-oz. pkg. dried mixed fruit (including plums and apricots), chopped
¼ cup golden raisins
2 tsp. minced fresh ginger
1 small onion chopped
¼ cup brown sugar
2 Tbsp. cider vinegar
¾ cup water
¼ tsp. ground cinnamon
¼ tsp. curry powder
½ tsp. salt, *divided*
½ tsp. pepper, *divided*
2¼-lb. boneless pork center-cut lean loin roast, trimmed of fat
¾ lb. fresh green beans, ends nipped off
1 Tbsp. Dijon mustard
1 Tbsp. cornstarch
1 Tbsp. cold water

1. In slow cooker, combine dried fruit, raisins, ginger, onion, sugar, vinegar, water, cinnamon, curry powder, and ¼ tsp. each of salt and pepper. Stir.
2. Season pork with remaining ¼ tsp. salt and pepper. Place pork on top of fruit mixture in slow cooker. Cover. Cook on high 2 hours or on low 3 hours.
3. Layer green beans over pork. Cover.
4. Cook for 2 more hours on high or for 3 more hours on low—or until meat is tender and beans are done to your liking.
5. When meat and beans are tender but not dry, remove to separate plates. Cover and keep warm.
6. Stir mustard into sauce in cooker.
7. In a small bowl, mix cornstarch with 1 Tbsp. cold water until smooth. Stir into sauce.
8. Cover. Turn cooker to high and let sauce cook a few minutes until thickened.
9. Slice pork and serve with sauce and green beans.

—— PER SERVING ——
- 290 calories
  (70 calories from fat)
- 8g total fat (2.5g saturated, 0g trans)
- 75mg cholesterol
- 250mg sodium
- 29g total carbohydrate
  (3g fiber, 8g sugar)
- 27g protein
- 15%DV vitamin A
- 6%DV vitamin C
- 4%DV calcium
- 10%DV iron

Note:

We discovered this to be a great Christmas dinner one year when we were remodeling and had limited kitchen facilities. I put the ingredients in the slow cooker, and we played Scrabble all day while it cooked. I served it with microwaved rice pilaf. It was my most stress-free Christmas ever!

Trim as much visible fat from meat as possible before placing it in the slow cooker in order to avoid greasy gravy.
Carolyn Baer, Conrath, WI

Pork and Apricots with Mashed Sweet Potatoes

Carolyn Baer
Conrath, WI

Makes 14 servings

Prep. Time: 35-40 minutes
Cooking Time: 2½-3½ hours
Ideal slow-cooker size: 6-qt.

2½ lbs. sweet potatoes, peeled and cut into ¼"-thick slices
3½-lb. boneless pork tenderloin, trimmed of fat
1 tsp. dried tarragon, crushed
1½ tsp. fennel seed, crushed
3 cloves garlic, minced
1 tsp. salt
1 tsp. pepper
12 ozs. turkey kielbasa, *or* smoked turkey sausage, cut in half lengthwise, then in 2" pieces
14-oz. can low-sodium, nonfat chicken broth
¾ cup apricot nectar, *divided*
½ cup dried apricots
4 tsp. cornstarch

1. Place sweet potato slices in bottom of slow cooker.
2. Combine tarragon, fennel seed, garlic, salt, and pepper in small bowl.
3. Rub spice mix all over pork roast.
4. In large nonstick skillet, brown roast on all sides.
5. Place roast on top of sweet potatoes.
6. Place sausage pieces around roast in cooker.

7. Pour broth and ½ cup apricot nectar over all.
8. Cover and cook 2-3 hours on high.
9. Add dried apricots to cooker. Cover and continue cooking on high 30 more minutes.
10. With slotted spoon, transfer pork, sausage, and apricots to serving platter. Cover and keep warm.
11. Transfer sweet potatoes to large bowl.
12. Mash with potato masher.
13. Strain cooking liquid from cooker into a glass measuring cup.
14. Skim and discard fat.
15. Reserve 2 cups liquid.
16. In a small bowl, whisk together ¼ cup apricot nectar and cornstarch until smooth.
17. In a medium saucepan, combine cooking liquid and cornstarch mixture.
18. Cook and stir over medium heat until thick and bubbly.
19. Cook two minutes longer.
20. Serve sauce with pork and mashed sweet potatoes.

—— **PER SERVING** ——
- 230 calories
  (45 calories from fat)
- 5g total fat (1.5g saturated, 0g trans)
- 75mg cholesterol
- 460mg sodium
- 18g total carbohydrate
  (2g fiber, 7g sugar)
- 26g protein
- 210%DV vitamin A
- 25%DV vitamin C
- 4%DV calcium
- 10%DV iron

Pork Stew

Cyndie Marrara
Port Matilda, PA

Makes 6 servings

Prep. Time: 15 minutes
Cooking Time: 5-7 hours
Ideal slow-cooker size: 4-qt.

2 sweet potatoes *or* yams, peeled and cut in small pieces
10-oz. pkg. frozen corn
10-oz. pkg. frozen Italian beans
1 medium-sized onion, chopped
1½ lbs. lean pork, cut in small pieces
14½-oz. can low-sodium diced tomatoes, undrained
¾ cup water
1 tsp. garlic, chopped
¼ tsp. salt
⅛ tsp. black pepper

1. Combine potatoes, corn, beans, and onion in slow cooker.
2. Place pork on top.
3. Stir together tomatoes, water, garlic, salt, and pepper. Pour over pork.
4. Cover. Cook on low 5-7 hours, or until meat and vegetables are cooked to your liking.

—— **PER SERVING** ——
- 340 calories
  (100 calories from fat)
- 11g total fat
  (4g saturated, 0g trans)
- 105mg cholesterol
- 370mg sodium
- 22g total carbohydrate
  (4g fiber, 10g sugar)
- 36g protein
- 100%DV vitamin A
- 20%DV vitamin C
- 0%DV calcium
- 15%DV iron

Autumn Pork Chops

Jan Mast
Lancaster, PA

Makes 6 servings

Prep. Time: 15-25 minutes
Cooking Time: 3½-5 hours
Ideal slow-cooker size: 5- or 6-qt.

2 medium acorn squash,
   unpeeled
6 4-oz. boneless pork
   tenderloin chops,
   trimmed of fat
½ tsp. salt
¾ cup brown sugar
1 Tbsp. orange juice
½ tsp. grated orange peel
⅛ tsp. ground cloves

1. Cut each squash in half. Remove seeds. Cut each half into 4-5 slices.

2. Arrange 3 or 4 chops in slow cooker. Cover with squash slices. Top with remaining 2 or 3 chops.

3. In a small mixing bowl, combine remaining ingredients and spread over squash slices and chops.

4. Cook on low 3½ hours. Check if chops on bottom of cooker are done. If so, remove from cooker and keep warm. Check remaining chops. If they are not done, place them on bottom of cooker. Cover and continue cooking until tender, up to 1-1½ hours.

5. Serve each chop topped with a slice or two of squash.

—— PER SERVING ——
- 280 calories
  (45 calories from fat)
- 5g total fat
  (2g saturated, 0g trans)
- 75mg cholesterol
- 260mg sodium
- 33g total carbohydrate
  (2g fiber, 21g sugar)
- 26g protein
- 10%DV vitamin A
- 30%DV vitamin C
- 6%DV calcium
- 15%DV iron

Harvest Pork Roast

Dawn Day
Westminster, CA

Makes 8 servings

Prep. Time: 15 minutes
Cooking Time: 4 hours
Ideal slow-cooker size: 4-qt.

2 lbs. pork tenderloin, fat
   trimmed
2 Tbsp. canola oil
3 cups apple juice
3 Granny Smith apples
1 cup fresh cranberries
¾ tsp. salt
½ tsp. black pepper

1. Brown roast on all sides in skillet in canola oil. Place in slow cooker.

2. Add remaining ingredients.

3. Cover. Cook on low 4 hours, or until meat is tender but not dry.

—— PER SERVING ——
- 290 calories
  (80 calories from fat)
- 9g total fat
  (2g saturated, 0g trans)
- 90mg cholesterol
- 290mg sodium
- 19g total carbohydrate
  (2g fiber, 16g sugar)
- 32g protein
- 0%DV vitamin A
- 0%DV vitamin C
- 0%DV calcium
- 8%DV iron

Barbecued Pork

Rhonda L. Burgoon
Collingswood, NJ

Makes 8 servings

Prep. Time: 15 minutes
Cooking Time: 4 hours
Ideal slow-cooker size: 4- or 5-qt.

2 lbs. boneless pork top loin
1½ cups onions, chopped
1 cup diet soda
1 cup low-sodium
   barbecue sauce

1. Place pork in slow cooker. Combine all other ingredients in a bowl and then pour over pork.

2. Cover. Cook on high 4 hours or until meat is very tender.

3. Slice or shred pork. Stir back into sauce.

4. Serve on wheat or multigrain buns.

—— PER SERVING ——
- 200 calories
  (50 calories from fat)
- 6g total fat
  (2g saturated, 0g trans)
- 55mg cholesterol
- 470mg sodium
- 11g total carbohydrate
  (0.5g fiber, 9g sugar)
- 23g protein
- 2%DV vitamin A
- 4%DV vitamin C
- 4%DV calcium
- 4%DV iron

Variation:
If your calorie count allows, you may want to add another ½ cup barbecue sauce to Step 1 to create a juicier sandwich filling.

Ribs with Apples and Kraut

Dede Peterson
Rapid City, SD

Makes 7 servings

Prep. Time: 20-30 minutes
Cooking Time: 3-9 hours
Ideal slow-cooker size: 6-qt.

1½ lbs. pork ribs, trimmed of fat
½ tsp. salt
¼-1½ tsp. black pepper, according to your taste
½ cup water, apple juice, *or* white wine, *optional*
2 16-oz. cans, *or* 1 2-lb. bag, sauerkraut, undrained
3 medium-sized onions, sliced into rings
2 8-oz. cans mushrooms, drained
3 large apples, cored and cut in wedges
⅓ cup brown sugar
½ tsp. celery seed

1. Brown ribs in a nonstick skillet, top and bottom. Season with salt and pepper.

2. Place ribs in slow cooker. Deglaze skillet with ½ cup water, apple juice, or white wine if you wish. Set drippings aside.

3. In large bowl, mix together sauerkraut, onions, mushrooms, apple wedges, brown sugar, and celery seed. Spoon over ribs. Pour any reserved drippings over top.

4. Cook on low 7-9 hours or on high 3-4 hours.

— PER SERVING —
• 250 calories
  (80 calories from fat)
• 9g total fat
  (3.5g saturated, 0g trans)
• 55mg cholesterol
• 590mg sodium
• 25g total carbohydrate
  (5g fiber, 18g sugar)
• 18g protein
• 2%DV vitamin A
• 25%DV vitamin C
• 6%DV calcium
• 15%DV iron

Barbecued Ribs & Sauce

Mary Longenecker
Bethel, PA

Makes 10 servings

Prep. Time: 10-15 minutes
Cooking Time: 8-10 hours
Ideal slow-cooker size: 4-qt.

3 lbs. lean country-style ribs
2½ lbs. sauerkraut, rinsed
2 cups low-sodium barbecue sauce
1 cup water

1. Place ribs on bottom of cooker.

2. Layer sauerkraut over ribs.

3. Mix barbecue sauce and water together. Pour over meat and kraut.

4. Cover. Cook on low 8-10 hours.

— PER SERVING —
• 230 calories
  (80 calories from fat)
• 9g total fat
  (3g saturated, 0g trans)
• 50mg cholesterol
• 1470mg sodium
• 19g total carbohydrate
  (3g fiber, 13g sugar)
• 17g protein
• 4%DV vitamin A
• 20%DV vitamin C
• 6%DV calcium
• 15%DV iron

"Pulled Pork" with Applesauce

Colleen Heatwole
Burton, MI

Makes 12 servings

Prep. Time: 30 minutes
Cooking Time: 10-12 hours
Ideal slow-cooker size: 5- or 6-qt.

3-lb. pork roast, visible fat removed
4 cups unsweetened applesauce
18-oz. low-sodium, low-fat bottle barbecue sauce of your choice

1. Place meat in slow cooker.

2. Spread applesauce over top.

3. Spoon barbecue sauce over top, being careful not to disturb the applesauce.

4. Cover. Cook on low 6-8 hours, or until roast is very tender but not dry.

5. Remove from slow cooker onto platter. Pull apart with forks.

6. Put shredded meat in bowl. Add some of cooking broth so meat is somewhat juicy but not swimming in sauce.

7. Serve on whole wheat buns.

— PER SERVING —
• 230 calories
  (50 calories from fat)
• 6g total fat
  (2g saturated, 0g trans)
• 50mg cholesterol
• 95mg sodium
• 25g total carbohydrate
  (1g fiber, 19g sugar)
• 18g protein
• 2%DV vitamin A
• 2%DV vitamin C
• 2%DV calcium
• 6%DV iron

Tip from Tester:

I cooked rice in the leftover sauce. I mixed some water with it; the proportion of the liquid was about ⅔ roast-pork sauce and ⅓ water. It was delicious rice!

Slow-Cooked Pork Stew

Virginia Graybill
Hershey, PA

Makes 8 servings

Prep. Time: 20-30 minutes
Cooking Time: 4-6 hours
Ideal slow-cooker size: 5-qt.

2 lbs. lean pork loin, cut into 1" cubes
½ lb. baby carrots
3 large potatoes, cut into 1" cubes
2 parsnips, cut into 1" cubes
2 onions, cut into wedges, slices, *or* chopped coarsely
3 garlic cloves, minced
1-2 tsp. ground black pepper, depending on your taste preferences
1 tsp. dried thyme
1 tsp. salt
2½ cups low-sodium canned vegetable juice
2 Tbsp. brown sugar
1 Tbsp. prepared mustard
4 tsp. minute tapioca

1. Place pork in slow cooker.
2. Add carrots, potatoes, parsnips, onions, garlic, pepper, thyme, and salt. Mix together well.
3. In a medium bowl, combine vegetable juice, brown sugar, mustard, and tapioca. Pour over meat and vegetables.
4. Cover. Cook on low 6 hours or on high 4 hours.

—— PER SERVING ——
• 300 calories
  (60 calories from fat)
• 7g total fat
  (2.5g saturated, 0g trans)
• 65mg cholesterol
• 490mg sodium
• 34g total carbohydrate
  (5g fiber, 11g sugar)
• 26g protein
• 60%DV vitamin A
• 30%DV vitamin C
• 8%DV calcium
• 15%DV iron

Sauerkraut and Kielbasa

Colleen Heatwole
Burton, MI

Makes 4 servings

Prep. Time: 5-10 minutes
Cooking Time: 5-6 hours
Ideal slow-cooker size: 4½- or 5-qt.

1½ lbs. fresh *or* canned sauerkraut, drained and rinsed
1 lb. reduced-fat turkey kielbasa, cut in 1" slices

1. Combine sauerkraut and turkey kielbasa in slow cooker.
2. Cover. Cook on low 5-6 hours.
3. Stir before serving.

—— PER SERVING ——
• 190 calories
  (80 calories from fat)
• 9g total fat
  (3g saturated, 0g trans)
• 75mg cholesterol
• 2120mg sodium
• 10g total carbohydrate
  (4g fiber, 3g sugar)
• 19g protein
• 0%DV vitamin A
• 20%DV vitamin C
• 6%DV calcium
• 20%DV iron

Notes:

1. This is delicious served with mashed potatoes.
2. This is a basic recipe. My family prefers this version over more elaborate ones with onions or apples or caraway seeds!

Cabbage with Kielbasa

Millie Schellenburg
Washington, NJ

Makes 8 servings

Prep. Time: 20-30 minutes
Cooking Time: 3-4 hours
Ideal slow-cooker size: 6-qt.

2 cups water
1½ medium-sized heads of
  cabbage, chopped
¾ lb. kielbasa, cut into ½"
  slices
8 medium-sized potatoes,
  cut into chunks
1 onion, sliced

1. Combine all ingredients in slow cooker.

2. Cover. Cook on low 3-4 hours, or until cabbage and potatoes are done to your liking.

—— PER SERVING ——
• 380 calories
  (140 calories from fat)
• 16g total fat
  (6g saturated, 0g trans)
• 30mg cholesterol
• 390mg sodium
• 49g total carbohydrate
  (9g fiber, 8g sugar)
• 13g protein
• 4%DV vitamin A
• 80%DV vitamin C
• 8%DV calcium
• 15%DV iron

Sausage and Cabbage

Melanie Thrower
McPherson, KS

Makes 6 servings

Prep. Time: 15 minutes
Cooking Time: 3-4 hours
Ideal slow-cooker size: 3- or 4-qt.

8 ozs. light smoked sausage
  or kielbasa
1 head cabbage, chopped
2 onions, diced
½ tsp. salt
¼ tsp. black pepper
¼ cup hot water
1 beef bouillon cube

1. Slice sausage into small pieces.

2. Layer cabbage, onions, and sausage in bottom of slow cooker.

3. Add seasonings. Dissolve bouillon cube in water.

4. Cook on high 3-4 hours, or until cabbage is done to your liking.

—— PER SERVING ——
• 130 calories
  (70 calories from fat)
• 7g total fat
  (2.5g saturated,
  0g trans)
• 15mg cholesterol
• 330mg sodium
• 12g total carbohydrate
  (4g fiber, 7g sugar)
• 5g protein
• 4%DV vitamin A
• 40%DV vitamin C
• 8%DV calcium
• 6%DV iron

Sausage Vegetable Stew

Rosann Zeiset
Stevens, PA

Makes 10 servings

Prep. Time: 30 minutes
Cooking Time: 3-10 hours
Ideal slow-cooker size: 5- or 6-qt.

1 lb. sausage (regular,
  turkey, *or* smoked)
4 cups potatoes, cubed
4 cups carrots, sliced
4 cups green beans
28-oz. can tomato sauce
1 tsp. onion powder
¼ *or* ½ tsp. black pepper,
  according to your taste

1. Slice sausage into 1½" pieces. Place in slow cooker.

2. Add vegetables. Pour tomato sauce over top.

3. Sprinkle with onion powder and pepper. Stir.

4. Cook on high 3-4 hours or low 8-10 hours.

—— PER SERVING ——
• 230 calories
  (80 calories from fat)
• 9g total fat
  (3g saturated, 0g trans)
• 15mg cholesterol
• 930mg sodium
• 32g total carbohydrate
  (6g fiber, 9g sugar)
• 8g protein
• 200%DV vitamin A
• 30%DV vitamin C
• 6%DV calcium
• 15%DV iron

Variation:
  If your diet allows, you may want to add ½ tsp. salt to Step 3.

Sausage-Sweet Potato Bake

Betty K. Drescher
Quakertown, PA

Makes 6 servings

Prep. Time: 20 minutes
Cooking Time: 3-7 hours
Ideal slow-cooker size: 4-qt.

½ lb. lean sausage, cut in
    ¼-½" slices
3 medium-sized sweet
    potatoes, peeled and
    sliced thin
4 medium-sized apples,
    peeled and cut in chunks
1 Tbsp. sugar
2 Tbsp. flour
¼ tsp. ground cinnamon
¼ tsp. salt
¼-½ cup water

1. Brown sausage in nonstick skillet. Drain.
2. Layer sweet potatoes, apples, and sausage in slow cooker sprayed with nonfat cooking spray.
3. Combine remaining ingredients. Pour over all.
4. Cover. Cook on low 6-7 hours or on high 3-4 hours.

—— PER SERVING ——
• 230 calories   • 38g total carbohydrate
  (70 calories from fat)   (5g fiber, 22g sugar)
• 7g total fat (2.5g   • 4g protein
  saturated, 0g trans)   • 200%DV vitamin A
• 15mg cholesterol   • 10%DV vitamin C
• 260mg sodium   • 2%DV calcium
                     • 6%DV iron

Tips:
To allow for more even cooking of the ingredients, slice the sweet potatoes thin and cut the apples in thicker chunks. The apples cook soft faster than the potatoes.

Economy One-Dish Supper

Betty Drescher
Quakertown, PA

Makes 6 servings

Prep. Time: 30-45 minutes
Cooking Time: 5-8 hours
Ideal slow-cooker size: 5-qt.

½ lb. lean sausage
1½ cups potatoes, grated or
    cubed
1 cup water
½ tsp. cream of tartar
1 cup raw carrots, grated
    or sliced thin
¼ cup long-grain rice,
    uncooked
1 onion, minced
¼ tsp. salt
¼ tsp. black pepper
¼ tsp. curry powder
3 cups low-sodium
    tomato juice

1. Brown sausage in nonstick skillet. Cut into ¼"-thick slices.
2. Mix water and cream of tartar. Toss with potatoes. Drain.
3. Layer sausage, potatoes, carrots, rice, and onion in slow cooker.
4. Combine salt, pepper, curry powder, and tomato juice. Pour over all.
5. Cover. Cook on low 5-8 hours.

—— PER SERVING ——
• 150 calories   • 18g total carbohydrate
  (60 calories from fat)   (3g fiber, 7g sugar)
• 7g total fat   • 5g protein
  (2.5g saturated,   • 100%DV vitamin A
  0g trans)   • 20%DV vitamin C
• 15mg cholesterol   • 2%DV calcium
• 280mg sodium   • 8%DV iron

Bratwursts

Dede Peterson
Rapid City, SD

Makes 8 servings

Prep. Time: 15-20 minutes
Cooking Time: 4-5 hours
Ideal slow-cooker size: 4-qt.

8 bratwursts
1 large onion, sliced
12-oz. can of beer
1 cup chili sauce
1 Tbsp. Worcestershire
  sauce
1 cup ketchup
2 Tbsp. vinegar
½ tsp. salt
2 Tbsp. brown sugar
1 Tbsp. paprika

1. Boil bratwursts in water in skillet for 10 minutes to remove fat.
2. Drain bratwursts and place in slow cooker.
3. Mix together remaining ingredients in bowl and then pour over meat.
4. Cook on low 4-5 hours.

—— PER SERVING ——

- 160 calories
  (45 calories from fat)
- 5g total fat
  (1.5g saturated,
  0g trans)
- 10mg cholesterol
- 1000mg sodium
- 24g total carbohydrate
  (0.5g fiber, 17g sugar)
- 3g protein
- 20%DV vitamin A
- 10%DV vitamin C
- 2%DV calcium
- 4%DV iron

Bratwurst Stew

Lauren M. Eberhard
Senecca, IL

Makes 8 servings

Prep. Time: 20-25 minutes
Cooking Time: 3-4 hours
Ideal slow-cooker size: 5-qt.

2 10¾-oz. cans fat-free
  chicken broth
4 medium-sized carrots,
  sliced
2 ribs of celery, cut in
  chunks
1 medium-sized onion,
  chopped
1 tsp. dried basil
½ tsp. garlic powder
3 cups chopped cabbage
2 1-lb. cans great northern
  beans, drained
5 fully cooked bratwurst
  links, cut into ½" slices

1. Combine all ingredients in slow cooker.
2. Cook on high 3-4 hours, or until veggies are tender.

—— PER SERVING ——

- 120 calories
  (30 calories from fat)
- 3.5g total fat
  (1g saturated, 0g trans)
- 5mg cholesterol
- 320mg sodium
- 15g total carbohydrate
  (5g fiber, 4g sugar)
- 7g protein
- 150%DV vitamin A
- 10%DV vitamin C
- 6%DV calcium
- 10%DV iron

Tip:
You can eat this as a stew, or over hot corn bread or rice.

Frequently Asked Questions about Slow-Cooker Cooking

Q. Is it okay to begin the slow-cooking process with frozen food?

A. It's not ideal. It takes too long for the frozen food to become hot enough fast enough. That means a food-safety risk.

Bean and Other Main Dishes

Lamb Stew

Dottie Schmidt
Kansas City, MO

Makes 6 servings

Prep. Time: 25 minutes
Cooking Time: 6-8 hours
Ideal slow-cooker size: 6-qt.

2 lbs. lean lamb, cubed
½ tsp. sugar
2 Tbsp. canola oil
1½ tsp. salt
¼ tsp. black pepper
¼ cup flour
2 cups water
¾ cup red cooking wine
¼ tsp. garlic powder
2 tsp. Worcestershire
   sauce
6-8 carrots, sliced
4 small onions, quartered
4 ribs celery, sliced
3 medium-sized potatoes,
   diced

1. Sprinkle lamb with sugar. Brown in oil in skillet.
2. Remove lamb and place in cooker, reserving drippings.
3. Stir salt, pepper, and flour into drippings in skillet until smooth. Stir in water and wine until smooth, stirring loose the meat drippings. Continue cooking and stirring occasionally until broth simmers and thickens.
4. Pour into cooker. Add remaining ingredients and stir until well mixed.
5. Cover. Cook on low 6-8 hours, or until meat and vegetables are tender but not dry or mushy.

— PER SERVING —
• 440 calories
   (130 calories from fat)
• 15g total fat
   (5g saturated, 0g trans)
• 90mg cholesterol
• 940mg sodium
• 39g total carbohydrate
   (7g fiber, 11g sugar)
• 32g protein
• 400%DV vitamin A
• 20%DV vitamin C
• 8%DV calcium
• 25%DV iron

Put your cooker meal together the night before you want to cook it. The following morning put the mixture in the slow cooker, cover, and cook.

Sara Wilson, Blairstown, MO

Lamb Rice

Nanci Keatley
Salem, OR

Makes 8 servings

Prep. Time: 20 minutes
Cooking Time: 6-8 hours
Ideal slow-cooker size: 4-qt.

2 lbs. leg of lamb, shank half
½ cup pine nuts
2 cups long-grain basmati rice, uncooked
4 cups low-sodium, fat-free chicken stock
1 tsp. crushed allspice
1 tsp. salt
1 tsp. pepper

1. Cut lamb into ½" pieces.
2. Brown in nonstick skillet over medium-high heat, just until browned.
3. Add pine nuts to meat.
4. Cook 3-4 minutes.
5. Put all ingredients in slow cooker. Mix well.
6. Cover. Cook 6-8 hours on low, or until rice and meat are tender but not overcooked or dry.

— PER SERVING —
- 390 calories
  (100 calories from fat)
- 11g total fat (2.5g saturated, 0g trans)
- 65mg cholesterol
- 380mg sodium
- 42g total carbohydrate
  (1g fiber, 0g sugar)
- 28g protein
- 0%DV vitamin A
- 0%DV vitamin C
- 2%DV calcium
- 20%DV iron

Note:

I learned to love this dish as I was growing up. We always eat it with dollops of plain yogurt.

New Mexico Pinto Beans

John D. Allen
Rye, CO

Makes 8 servings

Soaking Time: 8 hours or overnight
Prep. Time: 20 minutes
Cooking Time: 6-10 hours
Ideal slow-cooker size: 4- or 5-qt.

2½ cups dried pinto beans
3 qts. water
½ cup lean ham, diced
2 garlic cloves, crushed
1 medium-sized onion, chopped
1 tsp. crushed red chili peppers, *optional*
½ tsp. salt
¼ tsp. black pepper
1 tsp. dried oregano, *optional*
1 tsp. dried thyme, *optional*

1. Sort beans. Discard pebbles, shriveled beans, and floaters. Wash beans under running water. Place in saucepan, cover with 3 quarts water, and soak overnight or for 8 hours.
2. Drain beans and discard soaking water. Pour beans into slow cooker. Cover with fresh water.
3. Add meat, garlic, onions, chili peppers if you wish, salt, and pepper, and other seasonings if you want. Cook on low 6-10 hours, or until beans are soft.

— PER SERVING —
- 90 calories
  (15 calories from fat)
- 1.5g total fat
  (0g saturated, 0g trans)
- 10mg cholesterol
- 380mg sodium
- 12g total carbohydrate
  (4g fiber, 1g sugar)
- 6g protein
- 0%DV vitamin A
- 0%DV vitamin C
- 4%DV calcium
- 8%DV iron

Variation:

If your diet allows, you may want to increase the salt to 1 tsp.

Mexican Pinto Beans

Colleen Heatwole
Burton, MI

Makes 8 servings

Soaking Time: 8 hours or overnight
Prep. Time: 10-15 minutes
Cooking time: 10 hours
Ideal slow-cooker size: 4- or 5-qt.

1 lb. dried pinto beans, soaked overnight in water and drained
4 cups fresh water
1 large onion, chopped
14½-oz. can stewed, *or* diced, tomatoes
2 garlic cloves, minced
2 tsp. chili powder
¼ lb. lean ham, chopped

1. Combine all ingredients in slow cooker.
2. Cover. Cook on high 2 hours. Reduce heat. Cook on low 8 hours.

—— PER SERVING ——
• 230 calories
  (15 calories from fat)
• 1.5g total fat
  (0g saturated, 0g trans)
• 5mg cholesterol
• 320mg sodium
• 40g total carbohydrate
  (15g fiber, 5g sugar)
• 16g protein
• 8%DV vitamin A
• 8%DV vitamin C
• 10%DV calcium
• 20%DV iron

Variations:
1. If your diet allows, you may want to add ½ tsp. salt to Step 1.
2. If you prefer some more zip to your beans, you may serve these with salsa.

Scandinavian Beans

Virginia Bender
Dover, DE

Makes 8 servings

Soaking Time: 8 hours or overnight
Prep. Time: 15 minutes
Cooking Time: 6½-8 hours
Ideal slow-cooker size: 5-qt.

1 lb. dried pinto beans
6 cups water
12 ozs. lean turkey bacon
1 onion, chopped
2-3 garlic cloves, minced
¼ tsp. black pepper
1 tsp. salt
¼ cup molasses
1 cup ketchup
¼ tsp. Tabasco sauce
1 tsp. Worcestershire sauce
½ cup brown sugar
½ cup cider vinegar
¼ tsp. dry mustard

1. Soak beans in 6 cups water in soup pot for 8 hours. Bring beans to boil and cook 1½-2 hours, or until soft. Drain, reserving liquid.
2. Combine all ingredients in slow cooker, using just enough bean liquid to cover everything. Cook on low 5-6 hours.

—— PER SERVING ——
• 270 calories
  (80 calories from fat)
• 9g total fat
  (2.5g saturated, 0g trans)
• 40mg cholesterol
• 1350mg sodium
• 40g total carbohydrate
  (3g fiber, 25g sugar)
• 10g protein
• 0%DV vitamin A
• 0%DV vitamin C
• 8%DV calcium
• 15%DV iron

Anasazi Beans

Melanie Thrower
McPherson, KS

Makes 4 servings

Prep. Time: 5-10 minutes
Cooking Time: 3-4 hours
Ideal slow-cooker size: 3-qt.

2 cups dry anasazi beans, cleaned
4 cups water
1 Tbsp. minced garlic
1 small onion, diced
1 tsp. salt
½ tsp. baking soda

1. Combine all ingredients in slow cooker.
2. Cook on high 3-4 hours.

—— PER SERVING ——
• 320 calories
  (10 calories from fat)
• 1g total fat
  (0g saturated, 0g trans)
• 0mg cholesterol
• 740mg sodium
• 58g total carbohydrate
  (19g fiber, 2g sugar)
• 21g protein
• 0%DV vitamin A
• 0%DV vitamin C
• 15%DV calcium
• 30%DV iron

Tip:
These are a sweet-tasting bean with a texture cooked similar to a pinto bean. You may garnish them with salsa to add spice.

From-Scratch Baked Beans

Wanda Roth
Napoleon, OH

Makes 6 servings

Prep. Time: 5-10 minutes
Cooking Time: 14 hours
Ideal slow-cooker size: 3½- or 4-qt.

2½ cups great northern
    dried beans
4 cups water
1½ cups tomato sauce
½ cup brown sugar
2 tsp. salt
1 small onion, chopped
½ tsp. chili powder

1. Wash and drain dry beans. Combine beans and water in slow cooker. Cook on low 8 hours, or overnight.

2. Stir in remaining ingredients. Cook on low 6 hours. If the beans look too watery as they near the end of their cooking time, you can remove the lid during the last 30-60 minutes.

—— PER SERVING ——
- 350 calories
  (10 calories from fat)
- 1g total fat
  (0g saturated, 0g trans)
- 0mg cholesterol
- 1170mg sodium
- 71g total carbohydrate
  (17g fiber, 26g sugar)
- 18g protein
- 0%DV vitamin A
- 4%DV vitamin C
- 15%DV calcium
- 30%DV iron

New England Baked Beans

Mary Wheatley
Mashpee, MA
Jean Butzer
Batavia, NY

Makes 8 servings

Prep. Time: 20 minutes
Cooking Time: 14-16 hours
Ideal slow-cooker size: 4-qt.

1 lb. dried beans—great
    northern, pea beans, *or*
    navy beans
¼ lb. lean turkey bacon
    slices, diced
1 qt. water
1 tsp. salt
¼-½ tsp. black pepper,
    according to taste
2 Tbsp. brown sugar
½ cup molasses
1 tsp. dry mustard
½ tsp. baking soda
1 onion, coarsely chopped
5 cups water

1. Wash beans and remove any stones or shriveled beans.

2. Meanwhile, simmer turkey bacon in 1 quart water in saucepan for 10 minutes. Drain. Do not reserve liquid.

3. Combine all ingredients in slow cooker.

4. Cook on high until contents come to a boil. Turn to low. Cook 14-16 hours, or until beans are tender.

—— PER SERVING ——
- 300 calories
  (35 calories from fat)
- 3.5g total fat
  (1g saturated, 0g trans)
- 15mg cholesterol
- 570mg sodium
- 54g total carbohydrate
  (12g fiber, 20g sugar)
- 15g protein
- 0%DV vitamin A
- 0%DV vitamin C
- 15%DV calcium
- 25%DV iron

Barbecued Lima Beans

Carol Findling
Princeton, IL

Makes 6 servings

Soaking Time: 8 hours or
  overnight
Prep. Time: 15 minutes
Cooking Time: 8-10 hours
Ideal slow-cooker size: 3½-qt.

1¼ cups dried lima beans
half a medium-sized
    onion, chopped in large
    pieces
½ tsp. salt
½ tsp. dry mustard
1 tsp. cider vinegar
2 Tbsp. molasses
¼ cup chili sauce *or*
    medium salsa
several drops Tabasco
    sauce

1. Place beans in bowl and cover with water. Let beans soak overnight. Drain, reserving 1 cup liquid from beans.

2. Combine all ingredients in slow cooker, including 1 cup bean liquid.

3. Cook on low 8-10 hours.

—— PER SERVING ——
- 180 calories
  (5 calories from fat)
- 0.5g total fat
  (0g saturated, 0g trans)
- 0mg cholesterol
- 330mg sodium
- 35g total carbohydrate
  (9g fiber, 11g sugar)
- 9g protein
- 0%DV vitamin A
- 0%DV vitamin C
- 6%DV calcium
- 15%DV iron

Variation:

The recipe as noted above has almost no fat. For added flavor, and if your diet allows, add ¼ lb. lean ham, smoked, or Cajun turkey, or soy-bacon during the last hour.

Brown-Sugar Barbecued Lima Beans

Hazel L. Propst
Oxford, PA

Makes 10 servings

Soaking Time: 8 hours or overnight
Prep. Time: 20 minutes
Cooking Time: 4½-11 hours
Ideal slow-cooker size: 5-qt.

1½ lbs. dried lima beans
6 cups water
2¼ cups chopped onions
1 cup brown sugar
1½ cups ketchup
13 drops Tabasco sauce
1 cup dark corn syrup
1 Tbsp. salt
4 slices lean turkey bacon, diced

1. Soak washed beans in large soup pot in water overnight. Do not drain.

2. Add onions. Bring to boil. Simmer 30-60 minutes, or until beans are tender. Drain beans, reserving liquid.

3. Combine all ingredients except bean liquid in slow cooker. Mix well. Pour in enough liquid so that beans are barely covered.

4. Cover. Cook on low 10 hours, or on high 4-6 hours. Stir occasionally.

5. If the beans are too soupy as they near the end of their cooking time, remove the lid for the last hour or so of cooking.

—— PER SERVING ——
- 490 calories
  (20 calories from fat)
- 2g total fat
  (0g saturated, 0g trans)
- 5mg cholesterol
- 1270mg sodium
- 108g total carbohydrate
  (15g fiber, 51g sugar)
- 16g protein
- 0%DV vitamin A
- 4%DV vitamin C
- 10%DV calcium
- 30%DV iron

New Orleans Red Beans

Cheri Janzen
Houston, TX

Makes 6 servings

Soaking Time: 1 hour
Prep. Time: 30 minutes
Cooking Time: 8-10 hours
Ideal slow-cooker size: 3½-qt.

2 cups dried kidney beans
5 cups water
¼ lb. lean hot sausage, cut in small pieces
2 onions, chopped

2 cloves garlic, minced
1 tsp. salt

1. Wash beans. Remove any stones or floaters. In saucepan, combine beans and water. Boil 2 minutes. Remove from heat. Soak 1 hour.

2. Brown sausage slowly in nonstick skillet. Add onions, garlic, and salt and sauté until tender.

3. Combine all ingredients, including bean water, in slow cooker.

4. Cover. Cook on low 8-10 hours. During last 20 minutes of cooking, stir frequently and mash lightly with spoon.

5. Serve over hot cooked white rice.

—— PER SERVING ——
- 200 calories
  (110 calories from fat)
- 12g total fat (4.5g saturated, 0g trans)
- 20mg cholesterol
- 870mg sodium
- 17g total carbohydrate
  (4g fiber, 4g sugar)
- 8g protein
- 0%DV vitamin A
- 0%DV vitamin C
- 4%DV calcium
- 8%DV iron

Tip:

Offer salsa as a condiment.

Four Zesty Beans

Ann Van Doren
Lady Lake, FL

Makes 10 servings

Prep. Time: 10-15 minutes
Cooking Time: 2-2½ hours
Ideal slow-cooker size: 4- or 5-qt.

2 15½-oz. cans great northern beans, rinsed and drained
2 15-oz. cans black beans, rinsed and drained
15-oz. can butter beans, rinsed and drained
15-oz. can baked beans, undrained
2 cups salsa
½ cup brown sugar

1. In slow cooker combine northern beans, black beans, butter beans, and baked beans.
2. Stir in salsa and brown sugar.
3. Cover. Cook on low 2-2½ hours.

—— PER SERVING ——
• 300 calories
  (10 calories from fat)
• 1.5g total fat
  (0g saturated,
  0g trans)
• 0mg cholesterol
• 840mg sodium
• 60g total carbohydrate
  (14g fiber, 16g sugar)
• 16g protein
• 10%DV vitamin A
• 8%DV vitamin C
• 10%DV calcium
• 25%DV iron

No-Meat Baked Beans

Esther Becker
Gordonville, PA

Makes 8-10 servings

Soaking Time: 8 hours or overnight
Prep. Time: 10 minutes
Cooking Time: 6½-9½ hours
Ideal slow-cooker size: 3½-qt.

1 lb. dried navy beans
6 cups water
1 small onion, chopped
¾ cup ketchup
½ cup brown sugar
¾ cup water
1 tsp. dry mustard
3 Tbsp. dark molasses
1 tsp. salt

1. Soak beans in water overnight in large soup kettle. Cook beans in water until soft, about 1½ hours. Drain, discarding bean water.
2. Stir together all ingredients in slow cooker. Mix well.

3. Cover. Cook on low 5-8 hours, or until beans are well flavored but not breaking down.

—— PER SERVING ——
• 290 calories
  (10 calories from fat)
• 1g total fat
  (0g saturated, 0g trans)
• 0mg cholesterol
• 580mg sodium
• 60g total carbohydrate
  (14g fiber, 25g sugar)
• 13g protein
• 0%DV vitamin A
• 0%DV vitamin C
• 15%DV calcium
• 30%DV iron

Vegetarian Baked Beans

Janice Muller
Derwood, MD

Makes 5 servings

Prep. Time: 10-15 minutes
Cooking Time: 4-5 hours
Ideal slow cooker size: 4-qt.

1 cup picante sauce
¼ cup molasses
2 Tbsp. packed brown sugar
2 tsp. prepared mustard
1 tsp. onion powder
16-oz. can black beans, rinsed and drained
16-oz. can white beans, rinsed and drained
1 Tbsp. lime juice

1. Mix all ingredients together in slow cooker.
2. Cover. Cook on low 4-5 hours.

— PER SERVING —
- 250 calories
  (5 calories from fat)
- 0.5 total fat
  (0g saturated, 0g trans)
- 0mg cholesterol
- 730mg sodium
- 51g total carbohydrate
  (10g fiber, 17g sugar)
- 12g protein
- 4%DV vitamin A
- 2%DV vitamin C
- 10%DV calcium
- 25%DV iron

Five-Baked Beans

Betty B. Dennison
Grove City, PA

Makes 12 servings

Prep. Time: 20 minutes
Cooking Time: 4-12 hours
Ideal slow-cooker size: 4- or 5-qt.

6 slices turkey bacon
1 cup onions, chopped
1 clove garlic, minced
16-oz. can low-sodium
   lima beans, drained
16-oz. can low-sodium
   beans with tomato
   sauce, undrained
15½-oz. can low-sodium red
   kidney beans, drained
15-oz. can low-sodium
   butter beans, drained
15-oz. can low-sodium
   garbanzo beans, drained
¾ cup ketchup
½ cup unsulfured molasses
¼ cup brown sugar

1 Tbsp. prepared mustard
1 Tbsp. Worcestershire
   sauce
1 onion sliced and cut into
   rings, *optional*

1. In a nonstick skillet, cook bacon until browned.
2. Combine chopped onions, bacon, garlic, lima beans, beans with tomato sauce, kidney beans, butter beans, garbanzo beans, ketchup, molasses, brown sugar, mustard, and Worcestershire sauce in slow cooker.
3. Top with onions if desired.
4. Cover. Cook on low 10-12 hours or high 4-5 hours.

— PER SERVING —
- 200 calories
  (20 calories from fat)
- 2g total fat (0.5g
  saturated, 0g trans)
- 5mg cholesterol
- 600mg sodium
- 40g total carbohydrate
  (7g fiber, 16g sugar)
- 8g protein
- 4%DV vitamin A
- 4%DV vitamin C
- 8%DV calcium
- 20%DV iron

Variation:
   If you prefer less sweet beans, leave out the molasses and add the liquid from all the canned beans.

Six-Bean Barbecued Beans

Gladys Longacre
Susquehanna, PA

Makes 15-18 servings

Prep. Time: 15-20 minutes
Cooking Time: 4-6 hours
Ideal slow-cooker size: 5-qt.

1-lb. can kidney beans,
   drained
1-lb. can pinto beans,
   drained
1-lb. can great northern
   beans, drained
1-lb. can butter beans,
   drained
1-lb. can navy beans,
   drained
1-lb. can pork and beans,
   undrained
¼ cup barbecue sauce
¼ cup prepared mustard
⅓ cup ketchup
1 small onion, chopped
1 small bell pepper,
   chopped
¼ cup sorghum molasses
1 cup brown sugar

1. Mix together all ingredients in slow cooker.
2. Cook on low 4-6 hours.

— PER SERVING —
- 330 calories
  (10 calories from fat)
- 1.5g total fat
  (0g saturated, 0g trans)
- 0mg cholesterol
- 740mg sodium
- 66g total carbohydrate
  (13g fiber, 25g sugar)
- 15g protein
- 0%DV vitamin A
- 10%DV vitamin C
- 15%DV calcium
- 25%DV iron

Since I work full-time, I often put my dinner into the slow cooker to cook until I get home. My three teenagers and umpire/referee husband can all get a hot nutritious meal no matter what time they get home.

Rhonda Burgoon, Collingswood, NJ

Pody Scout Beans

Jody Moore
Pendleton, IN

Makes 15 servings

Prep. Time: 10-15 minutes
Cooking Time: 3 hours
Ideal slow-cooker size: 5- or 6-qt.

1 lb. ground turkey
1 tsp. minced garlic
1 medium-sized onion, chopped
1 cup barbecue sauce
½ cup brown sugar
6 1-lb. cans beans of your choice (pinto, lima, kidney, chili, great northern, and so on), each drained

1. Brown ground turkey in nonstick skillet over medium heat.
2. Combine all ingredients in slow cooker.
3. Cover. Cook on high 3 hours.

—— PER SERVING ——
• 120 calories
(20 calories from fat)
• 2g total fat (0.5g saturated, 0g trans)
• 15mg cholesterol
• 320mg sodium
• 18g total carbohydrate (2g fiber, 12g sugar)
• 8g protein
• 2%DV vitamin A
• 2%DV vitamin C
• 2%DV calcium
• 6%DV iron

Variations:
To add more zest, stir in 4-oz. can chopped green chilies and/or ¼ tsp. dried mustard to Step 2.

Nan's Barbecued Beans

Nan Decker
Albuquerque, NM

Makes 10-12 servings

Prep. Time: 15-20 minutes
Cooking Time: 4-6 hours
Ideal slow-cooker size: 3½-qt.

1 lb. lean ground chuck
1 onion, chopped
5 cups canned baked beans
2 Tbsp. cider vinegar
1 Tbsp. Worcestershire sauce
2 Tbsp. brown sugar
½ cup ketchup

1. Brown ground beef and onion in nonstick skillet. Drain.
2. Combine all ingredients in slow cooker.
3. Cover. Cook on low 4-6 hours.

—— PER SERVING ——
• 260 calories
(50 calories from fat)
• 6g total fat (1.5g saturated, 0g trans)
• 20mg cholesterol
• 670mg sodium
• 35g total carbohydrate (8g fiber, 13g sugar)
• 16g protein
• 10%DV vitamin A
• 0%DV vitamin C
• 6%DV calcium
• 15%DV iron

Smoky Maple Baked Beans

Sharon Miller
Holmesville, OH

Makes 10 servings

Prep. Time: 20 minutes
Cooking Time: 4-6 hours
Ideal slow-cooker size: 3-qt.

half a medium-sized onion, chopped
5 slices turkey bacon, chopped
4 ozs. extra-lean ground beef
16-oz. can vegetarian beans in tomato sauce, undrained
16-oz. can vegetarian baked beans, undrained
16-oz. can red kidney beans, rinsed and drained
½ cup tomato sauce
2 Tbsp. brown sugar
1-2 Tbsp. liquid smoke
½ tsp. maple flavoring

1. Sauté onions and bacon in nonstick skillet sprayed with nonstick cooking spray until onions are tender. Place in slow cooker.
2. Brown beef in nonstick skillet. Place in cooker.
3. Combine all ingredients in slow cooker.
4. Cook on high 4-6 hours. Stir before serving.

—— PER SERVING ——
• 200 calories
(30 calories from fat)
• 3 total fat (1g saturated, 0g trans)
• 10mg cholesterol
• 580mg sodium
• 32g total carbohydrate (8g fiber, 10g sugar)
• 11g protein
• 4%DV vitamin A
• 4%DV vitamin C
• 6%DV calcium
• 15%DV iron

"Lean" Cowboy Beans

John D. Allen
Rye, CO

Makes 8 servings

Prep. Time: 30 minutes
Cooking Time: 1-2 hours
Ideal slow-cooker size: 4-qt.

1 lb. ground turkey
16-oz. can baked beans, undrained
16-oz. can kidney beans, drained
2 cups onions, chopped
¾ cup brown sugar
1 cup ketchup
2 Tbsp. dry mustard
¼ tsp. salt
2 tsp. cider vinegar

1. Brown turkey in nonstick skillet over medium heat.
2. Combine all ingredients in slow cooker sprayed with nonfat cooking spray.
3. Cover. Cook on high 1-2 hours.

— PER SERVING —
• 320 calories
  (50 calories from fat)
• 5g total fat
  (1g saturated, 0g trans)
• 35mg cholesterol
• 880mg sodium
• 53g total carbohydrate
  (7g fiber, 30g sugar)
• 18g protein
• 10%DV vitamin A
• 8%DV vitamin C
• 6%DV calcium
• 15%DV iron

Variations:
For a milder taste, sauté the chopped onions with the turkey in Step 1. You may also decrease the dry mustard to 1 Tbsp., or according to your taste.

Sweet and Sour Beans

Julette Leaman
Harrisonburg, VA

Makes 6-8 servings

Prep. Time: 25 minutes
Cooking Time: 3 hours
Ideal slow-cooker size: 3½- or 4-qt.

5 slices lean turkey bacon
4 medium-sized onions, cut in rings
½ cup brown sugar
1 tsp. dry mustard
½ tsp. salt
¼ cup cider vinegar
1-lb. can green beans, drained
2 1-lb. cans butter beans, drained
1-lb., 11-oz. can pork and beans, undrained

1. Brown bacon in nonstick skillet and cut fine. Drain all but 2 Tbsp. bacon drippings.
2. Stir in onions, brown sugar, mustard, salt, and vinegar. Simmer 20 minutes.
3. Combine all ingredients in slow cooker.
4. Cover. Cook on low 3 hours.

— PER SERVING —
• 400 calories
  (35 calories from fat)
• 4g total fat
  (1g saturated, 0g trans)
• 15mg cholesterol
• 1640mg sodium
• 80g total carbohydrate
  (12g fiber, 48g sugar)
• 14g protein
• 0%DV vitamin A
• 0%DV vitamin C
• 15%DV calcium
• 25%DV iron

Mixed Slow-Cooker Beans

Carol Peachey
Lancaster, PA

Makes 6 servings

Prep. Time: 15-20 minutes
Cooking Time: 4-5 hours
Ideal slow-cooker size: 3½- or 4-qt.

16-oz. can kidney beans, drained
15½-oz. can baked beans, undrained
1 pint home-frozen, *or* 1-lb. pkg. frozen, lima beans
1 pint home-frozen green beans, *or* 1-lb. pkg. frozen green beans
4 slices lean turkey bacon, browned and cut fine
½ cup ketchup
⅓ cup sugar
⅓ cup brown sugar
2 Tbsp. vinegar
½ tsp. salt

1. Combine beans and bacon in slow cooker.
2. Stir together remaining ingredients. Add to beans and mix well.
3. Cover. Cook on low 4-5 hours.

— PER SERVING —
• 360 calories
  (30 calories from fat)
• 3.5g total fat
  (0.5g saturated, 0g trans)
• 10mg cholesterol
• 1100mg sodium
• 71g total carbohydrate
  (12g fiber, 33g sugar)
• 14g protein
• 10%DV vitamin A
• 0%DV vitamin C
• 10%DV calcium
• 20%DV iron

Barbecued Green Beans

Arlene Wengerd
Millersburg, OH

Makes 4-6 servings

Prep. Time: 15 minutes
Cooking Time: 3½-9 hours
Ideal slow-cooker size: 3½-qt.

5 slices lean turkey bacon
¼ cup chopped onions
¾ cup ketchup
⅓ cup brown sugar
3 tsp. Worcestershire sauce
½ tsp. salt
4 cups frozen green beans, thawed

1. Brown bacon in skillet until crisp and then break into pieces. Drain off all but 2 Tbsp. bacon drippings.
2. Sauté onions in reserved bacon drippings.
3. Combine ketchup, brown sugar, Worcestershire sauce, and salt. Stir into bacon and onions.
4. Pour mixture over green beans and mix lightly.
5. Pour into slow cooker and cook on high 3½-4½ hours, or on low 7-9 hours.

—— PER SERVING ——
• 130 calories
  (25 calories from fat)
• 2.5g total fat
  (0.5g saturated,
  0g trans)
• 10mg cholesterol
• 960mg sodium
• 25g total carbohydrate
  (2g fiber, 17g sugar)
• 3g protein
• 0%DV vitamin A
• 0%DV vitamin C
• 4%DV calcium
• 8%DV iron

Mexican Rice & Beans

Jeanne Allen
Rye, CO

Makes 6 servings

Prep. Time: 10-15 minutes
Cooking Time: 6-7 hours
Ideal slow-cooker size: 4-qt.

16-oz. can Mexican-style beans, undrained
16-oz. can crushed tomatoes, undrained
1½ cups converted rice, uncooked
1 large onion, finely chopped
4½-oz. can chopped green chiles, undrained
2 cloves garlic, minced
1½ cups shredded reduced-fat cheese, *divided*

1. Combine all ingredients except ¾ cup cheese in slow cooker sprayed with nonfat cooking spray.
2. Cover. Cook on low 6-7 hours.
3. Sprinkle with remaining cheese 1 hour before serving.

—— PER SERVING ——
• 340 calories
  (25 calories from fat)
• 2.5g total fat
  (1.5g saturated,
  0g trans)
• 5mg cholesterol
• 110mg sodium
• 63g total carbohydrate
  (8g fiber, 3g sugar)
• 18g protein
• 10%DV vitamin A
• 30%DV vitamin C
• 30%DV calcium
• 20%DV iron

Apple Bean Bake

Barbara A. Yoder
Goshen, IN

Makes 10 servings

Prep. Time: 20 minutes
Cooking Time: 2-4 hours
Ideal slow-cooker size: 4-qt.

4 Tbsp. butter
2 large Granny Smith apples, cubed
½ cup brown sugar
¼ cup sugar
½ cup ketchup
1 tsp. cinnamon
1 Tbsp. molasses
1 tsp. salt
24-oz. can great northern beans, undrained
24-oz. can pinto beans, undrained

1. Melt butter in skillet. Add apples and cook until tender.
2. Stir in brown sugar and sugar. Cook until they melt. Stir in ketchup, cinnamon, molasses, and salt.
3. Add beans. Mix well. Pour into slow cooker.
4. Cover. Cook on high 2-4 hours.

—— PER SERVING ——
• 220 calories
  (40 calories from fat)
• 4.5g total fat
  (2.5g saturated,
  0g trans)
• 10mg cholesterol
• 490mg sodium
• 41g total carbohydrate
  (6g fiber, 19g sugar)
• 7g protein
• 0%DV vitamin A
• 0%DV vitamin C
• 8%DV calcium
• 10%DV iron

Ann's Boston Baked Beans

Ann Driscoll
Albuquerque, NM

Makes 20 servings

Prep. Time: 20 minutes
Cooking Time: 6-8 hours
Ideal slow-cooker size: 4- or 5-qt.

1 cup raisins
2 small onions, diced
2 tart apples, diced
1 cup fat-free, low-sodium chili sauce
1 cup chopped lean ham
2 1-lb., 15-oz. cans baked beans, undrained
3 tsp. dry mustard
½ cup sweet pickle relish

1. Mix together all ingredients.
2. Cover. Cook on low 6-8 hours.

—— PER SERVING ——
• 180 calories
  (15 calories from fat)
• 2g total fat
  (0g saturated, 0g trans)
• 10mg cholesterol
• 530mg sodium
• 34g total carbohydrate
  (6g fiber, 18g sugar)
• 7g protein
• 0%DV vitamin A
• 0%DV vitamin C
• 4%DV calcium
• 6%DV iron

Fruity Baked Bean Casserole

Elaine Unruh
Minneapolis, MN

Makes 6-8 servings

Prep. Time: 20 minutes
Cooking Time: 2-3 hours
Ideal slow-cooker size: 4- or 5-qt.

5 slices lean turkey bacon
3 medium-sized onions, chopped
16-oz. can lima beans, drained
16-oz. can kidney beans, drained
2 16-oz. cans baked beans, undrained
15½-oz. can unsweetened pineapple chunks, *or* crushed pineapple, undrained
¼ cup brown sugar
¼ cup cider vinegar
¼ cup molasses
½ cup ketchup
2 Tbsp. prepared mustard
½ tsp. garlic salt
1 green bell pepper, chopped

1. Cook bacon in skillet. Cut fine. Reserve 2 Tbsp. drippings in skillet. Place bacon in slow cooker.
2. Add onions to drippings and sauté until soft. Drain. Add to bacon in slow cooker.
3. Add beans and pineapple to cooker. Mix well.
4. Combine brown sugar, vinegar, molasses, ketchup, mustard, garlic salt, and green pepper. Mix well. Stir into mixture in slow cooker.

5. Cover. Cook on high 2-3 hours.

—— PER SERVING ——
• 370 calories
  (35 calories from fat)
• 3.5g total fat
  (0.5g saturated, 0g trans)
• 10mg cholesterol
• 1080mg sodium
• 71g total carbohydrate
  (14g fiber, 31g sugar)
• 14g protein
• 10%DV vitamin A
• 20%DV vitamin C
• 10%DV calcium
• 20%DV iron

Easy Baked Beans

Alma Weaver
Ephrata, PA

Makes 8 servings

Prep. Time: 15 minutes
Cooking Time: 2 hours
Ideal slow-cooker size: 2½-qt.

2 16-oz. cans baked beans
¼ cup brown sugar
½ tsp. dried mustard
½ cup ketchup
2 small onions, chopped
1 tsp. Worcestershire sauce

1. Combine all ingredients in slow cooker.
2. Cover. Cook on high 2 hours.

—— PER SERVING ——
• 180 calories
  (15 calories from fat)
• 1.5g total fat
  (0g saturated, 0g trans)
• 5mg cholesterol
• 610mg sodium
• 38g total carbohydrate
  (8g fiber, 17g sugar)
• 6g protein
• 10%DV vitamin A
• 2%DV vitamin C
• 6%DV calcium
• 8%DV iron

Variation:
You can reduce the amount of brown sugar without harming the dish, if you prefer a less-sweet outcome.

Creole Black Beans

Joyce Kaut
Rochester, NY

Makes 6-8 servings

Prep. Time: 20-25 minutes
Cooking Time: 4-8 hours
Ideal slow-cooker size: 4-qt.

¾ lb. lean smoked sausage, sliced in ¼" pieces and browned
3 15-oz. cans black beans, drained
1½ cups chopped onions
1½ cups chopped green bell peppers
1½ cups chopped celery
4 garlic cloves, minced
2 tsp. dried thyme
1½ tsp. dried oregano
1½ tsp. black pepper
1 chicken bouillon cube
3 bay leaves
8-oz. can tomato sauce
1 cup water

1. Combine all ingredients in slow cooker.
2. Cover. Cook on low 8 hours or on high 4 hours.
3. Remove bay leaves before serving.

— PER SERVING —
• 250 calories
  (80 calories from fat)
• 9g total fat
  (3g saturated, 0g trans)
• 15mg cholesterol
• 1080mg sodium
• 34g total carbohydrate
  (11g fiber, 6g sugar)
• 13g protein
• 0%DV vitamin A
• 30%DV vitamin C
• 10%DV calcium
• 20%DV iron

Variations:

For a different consistency, you may substitute a 14½-oz.

can of low-sodium stewed tomatoes for the tomato sauce.
    This is tasty served over steamed rice.

Red Beans and Rice

Lavina Hochstedler
Grand Blanc, MI

Makes 8 servings

Prep. Time: 15 minutes
Cooking Time: 5-6 hours
Ideal slow-cooker size: 3½- or 4-qt.

---

1 medium-sized onion, chopped
½ cup green bell peppers, chopped
2 cloves garlic, minced
2 Tbsp. olive oil *or* canola oil
⅓ cup fresh cilantro *or* parsley, minced
3 16-oz. cans red beans, rinsed and drained
¾ cup water
½ tsp. salt
1 tsp. ground cumin
¼ tsp. black pepper

1. In a large skillet, sauté onion, green pepper, and garlic in oil until tender. Or wilt the onion, pepper, and garlic in the microwave for 2 minutes on high.
2. Add cilantro. Stir in beans, water, salt, cumin, and pepper. Transfer to slow cooker.
3. Cover. Cook on low 5-6 hours.

— PER SERVING —
• 320 calories
  (40 calories from fat)
• 4.5g total fat (0.5g
  saturated, 0g trans)
• 0mg cholesterol
• 150mg sodium
• 56g total carbohydrate
  (16g fiber, 4g sugar)
• 14g protein
• 4%DV vitamin A
• 10%DV vitamin C
• 2%DV calcium
• 6%DV iron

Notes:

1. If beans are watery as they near the end of the cooking time, remove the lid for the last hour of cooking.
2. Serve over hot, cooked rice.
3. If diets allow, you can serve the dish with grated cheese for each diner to add to his/her individual serving.

Lentil and Rice Pilaf

Andrea Cunningham
Arlington, KS

Makes 8-10 servings

Prep. Time: 15-20 minutes
Cooking Time: 6-8 hours
Ideal slow-cooker size: 4- or 5-qt.

2-5 large onions, depending on your taste preference
2 Tbsp. olive oil
6 cups water
1¾ cups lentils, sorted, washed, and drained
2 cups brown rice, washed and drained

1. Slice onions into ½" circles. Place in nonstick skillet with olive oil. Sauté over medium heat until onions are golden brown.

2. Remove about 1-onion's-worth from skillet and place on paper towel to drain.

3. Place remaining onions and drippings in slow cooker. Combine with water, lentils, and brown rice.

4. Cover. Cook on low 6-8 hours.

5. Serve hot or cold. Garnish with crisp brown onions.

—— PER SERVING ——
- 350 calories
  (30 calories from fat)
- 3.5g total fat (0.5g saturated, 0g trans)
- 0mg cholesterol
- 15mg sodium
- 66g total carbohydrate
  (16g fiber, 7g sugar)
- 16g protein
- 0%DV vitamin A
- 0%DV vitamin C
- 4%DV calcium
- 25%DV iron

Variations:

1. This is good to dip into with pita triangles. It is also good served as a main dish with a basic green salad topped with herbal vinaigrette dressing.

2. If your diet allows, you may want to add 1 tsp. salt to Step 3.

3. If you like some bite to lentils and rice, add ¼-½ tsp. freshly ground pepper to Step 3.

Pasta with Lentil Sauce

Joy Sutter
Iowa City, IA

Makes 4-6 servings

Prep. Time: 30 minutes
Cooking Time: 3-10 hours
Ideal slow-cooker size: 4- or 5-qt.

½ cup onions, chopped
½ cup carrots, chopped
½ cup celery, chopped
2 cups diced tomatoes in liquid
1 cup tomato sauce
½ cup dried lentils, rinsed and drained
½ tsp. dried oregano
½ tsp. dried basil
½ tsp. garlic powder
¼ tsp. crushed red pepper flakes
4 cups angel-hair pasta, hot, cooked

1. Mix all ingredients except pasta in slow cooker.
2. Cover. Cook on low 8-10 hours, or on high 3-5 hours.
3. Cook pasta according to package directions.
4. Place cooked pasta in large serving bowl and pour lentil sauce over top. Toss to combine.

—— PER SERVING ——
- 230 calories
  (10 calories from fat)
- 1g total fat
  (0g saturated, 0g trans)
- 0mg cholesterol
- 360mg sodium
- 46g total carbohydrate
  (8g fiber, 8g sugar)
- 10g protein
- 50%DV vitamin A
- 15%DV vitamin C
- 6%DV calcium
- 25%DV iron

Carrot Lentil Casserole

Pat Bishop
Bedminster, PA

Makes 6 servings

Prep. Time: 20-30 minutes
Cooking Time: 4-5 hours
Ideal slow-cooker size: 4- or 5-qt.

1 large onion, chopped
1 cup carrots, finely chopped
¾ cup dried lentils
¾ cup brown rice, uncooked
¾ cup low-fat cheese
½ cup green bell pepper, chopped
½ tsp. dried thyme
½ tsp. dried basil
½ tsp. dried oregano
¼ tsp. salt
¼ tsp. sage
¼ tsp. garlic powder
1 cup low-sodium canned tomatoes, undrained
1 cup low-fat, low-sodium chicken broth

1. Combine all ingredients in slow cooker.
2. Cover. Cook on high 4-5 hours.

—— PER SERVING ——
- 230 calories
  (20 calories from fat)
- 2g total fat
  (1g saturated, 0g trans)
- 5mg cholesterol
- 260mg sodium
- 39g total carbohydrate
  (10g fiber, 6g sugar)
- 15g protein
- 80%DV vitamin A
- 20%DV vitamin C
- 20%DV calcium
- 20%DV iron

BBQ Veggie Joes

Andrea Cunningham
Arlington, KS

Makes 10 servings

Prep. Time: 30 minutes
Cooking Time: 8-10 hours
Ideal slow-cooker size: 3-qt.

1 cup dried lentils, rinsed
  and sorted
2 cups water
1½ cups celery, chopped
1½ cups carrots, chopped
1 cup onions, chopped
¾ cup ketchup
2 Tbsp. dark brown sugar
2 Tbsp. Worcestershire
  sauce
2 Tbsp. cider vinegar

1. In a medium saucepan,
combine lentils and water.
Bring to a boil. Reduce
heat. Cover and simmer 10
minutes.
2. Combine celery, carrots,
onions, ketchup, brown sugar,
Worcestershire sauce, and
lentils with water in slow
cooker. Mix well.
3. Cover. Cook on low 8-10
hours, or until lentils are soft.
4. Stir in vinegar just
before serving.
5. Allow ½ cup filling for
each sandwich.

—— PER SERVING ——
• 230 calories   • 45g total carbohydrate
  (20 calories from fat)   (9g fiber, 10g sugar)
• 2.5g total fat   • 10g protein
  (0g saturated, 0g trans) • 100%DV vitamin A
• 0mg cholesterol   • 0%DV vitamin C
• 480mg sodium   • 8%DV calcium
                         • 20%DV iron

Pizza Sloppy Joe— Vegetable Variety

Sue Hamilton
Minooka, IL

Makes 6 servings

Prep. Time: 10 minutes
Cooking Time: 4-5 hours
Ideal slow-cooker size: 4-qt.

1 cup textured vegetable
  protein (T.V.P., soy)
7-oz. can mushrooms,
  undrained
15-oz. can low-sodium
  tomato sauce
14.5-oz. can low-sodium
  Italian diced tomatoes
  with basil, garlic, and
  oregano
½ tsp. fennel seeds
½ tsp. crushed red peppers
1 tsp. Italian seasoning
1 tsp. minced roasted garlic
½ tsp. salt

1. Combine all ingredients
in slow cooker.
2. Cover. Cook on low 4-5
hours.

—— PER SERVING ——
• 90 calories   • 15g total carbohydrate
  (10 calories from fat)   (5g fiber, 7g sugar)
1g total fat   • 9g protein
(0g saturated, 0g trans) • 10%DV vitamin A
0mg cholesterol   • 10%DV vitamin C
1060mg sodium   • 10%DV calcium
                        • 15%DV iron

Cottage Cheese Casserole

Melani Guengerich Novinger
Austin, TX

Makes 6 servings

Prep. Time: 30-45 minutes
Cooking Time: 4-5 hours
Ideal slow-cooker size: 3-qt.

2½ tsp. butter
½ cup fresh mushrooms,
  chopped
½ cup onions, chopped
½ cup celery, chopped
1 clove garlic, minced
½ tsp. dried marjoram
¾ cup low-sodium tomato
  paste
4 cups cooked macaroni
1¼ cups water
2 tsp. salt
1 tsp. sugar
2 cups low-fat, low-sodium
  cottage cheese, *divided*
⅓ cup grated Parmesan
  cheese, *divided*
¼ cup parsley, chopped,
  divided

1. Sauté mushrooms, onions,
celery, and garlic in butter in a
skillet over medium heat.
2. Combine sautéed
vegetables, marjoram, tomato
paste, macaroni, water, salt,
and sugar.
3. Put half of macaroni
mixture in slow cooker.
4. Top with 1 cup cottage
cheese, half of Parmesan
cheese, and parsley.
5. Repeat layers.
6. Cover. Cook on low 4-5
hours.

—— PER SERVING ——

- 270 calories
  (40 calories from fat)
- 4.5g total fat (1.5g
  saturated, 0g trans)
- 5mg cholesterol
- 930mg sodium
- 40g total carbohydrate
  (4g fiber, 6g sugar)
- 18g protein
- 15%DV vitamin A
- 20%DV vitamin C
- 20%DV calcium
- 20%DV iron

Variations:

If you enjoy a tomatoey flavor, and your diet allows, you could add an 8-oz. can of low-sodium tomato sauce to Step 2 and reduce the water to ½ cup.

Tastes-Like-Chili-Rellenos

Roseann Wilson
Albuquerque, NM

Makes 6 servings

Prep. Time: 15 minutes
Cooking Time: 2-3 hours
Ideal slow-cooker size: 4- or 5-qt.

2 4-oz. cans whole green chilies
½ lb. grated fat-free cheddar cheese
½ lb. grated fat-free Monterey Jack cheese
14½-oz. can low-sodium stewed tomatoes
4 eggs
2 Tbsp. flour
¾ cup fat-free evaporated milk

1. Spray sides and bottom of slow cooker with nonfat cooking spray.
2. Cut chilies into strips. Layer chilies and cheeses in slow cooker. Pour in stewed tomatoes.
3. Combine eggs, flour, and milk. Pour into slow cooker.
4. Cover. Cook on high 2-3 hours.

—— PER SERVING ——

- 230 calories
  (40 calories from fat)
- 4.5g total fat
  (1.5g saturated,
  0g trans)
- 135mg cholesterol
- 920mg sodium
- 15g total carbohydrate
  (2g fiber, 9g sugar)
- 28g protein
- 20%DV vitamin A
- 10%DV vitamin C
- 100%DV calcium
- 8%DV iron

Macaroni and Cheddar/Parmesan Cheese

Sherry L. Lapp
Lancaster, PA

Makes 8 servings

Prep. Time: 15 minutes
Cooking Time: 3 hours
Ideal slow-cooker size: 4-qt.

8-oz. pkg. elbow macaroni, cooked al dente
13-oz. can fat-free evaporated milk
1 cup fat-free milk
2 large eggs, slightly beaten
4 cups grated fat-free sharp cheddar cheese, *divided*
¼ tsp. salt
⅛ tsp. white pepper
¼ cup grated fat-free Parmesan cheese

1. Spray inside of cooker with nonfat cooking spray. Then, in cooker, combine lightly cooked macaroni, evaporated milk, milk, eggs, 3 cups cheddar cheese, salt, and pepper.
2. Top with remaining cheddar and Parmesan cheeses.
3. Cover. Cook on low 3 hours.

—— PER SERVING ——

- 190 calories
  (15 calories from fat)
- 1.5g total fat
  (0g saturated, 0g trans)
- 60mg cholesterol
- 740mg sodium
- 17g total carbohydrate
  (0g fiber, 7g sugar)
- 26g protein
- 10%DV vitamin A
- 0%DV vitamin C
- 70%DV calcium
- 2%DV iron

Macaroni and Velveeta Cheese

Lisa F. Good
Harrisonburg, VA

Makes 6 servings

Prep. Time: 10 minutes
Cooking Time: 2-3 hours
Ideal slow-cooker size: 2- or 3-qt.

1½ cups dry macaroni
1 Tbsp. butter
1 tsp. salt
½ lb. Velveeta Light
   cheese, sliced
1 qt. fat-free milk

1. Combine macaroni, butter, and salt.
2. Layer cheese over top.
3. Pour in milk.
4. Cover. Cook on high 2-3 hours, or until macaroni are soft.

—— **PER SERVING** ——
- 270 calories
  (80 calories from fat)
- 9g total fat
  (5g saturated,
  1.5g trans)
- 30mg cholesterol
- 1070mg sodium
- 32g total carbohydrate
  (0g fiber, 12g sugar)
- 16g protein
- 0%DV vitamin A
- 0%DV vitamin C
- 35%DV calcium
- 2%DV iron

Lasagna

Rosemarie Fitzgerald
Gibsonia, PA

Makes 8 servings

Prep. Time: 15-20 minutes
Cooking Time: 5 hours
Ideal slow-cooker size: 4- or 5-qt.

4½ cups fat-free, low-sodium meatless spaghetti sauce
½ cup water
16-oz. container fat-free ricotta cheese
2 cups shredded part-skim mozzarella cheese, *divided*
¾ cup grated Parmesan cheese, *divided*
1 egg
2 tsp. minced garlic
1 tsp. Italian seasoning
8-oz. box no-cook lasagna noodles

1. Mix spaghetti sauce and ½ cup water in bowl.
2. In separate bowl, mix ricotta, 1½ cups mozzarella cheese, ½ cup Parmesan cheese, egg, garlic, and seasoning.
3. Spread ¼ of sauce mixture in bottom of slow cooker. Top with ⅓ of noodles, breaking if needed to fit.
4. Spread with ⅓ of cheese mixture, making sure noodles are covered.
5. Repeat layers twice more.
6. Spread with remaining sauce.
7. Cover. Cook on low 5 hours.

8. Sprinkle with remaining cheeses. Cover. Let stand 10 minutes to allow cheeses to melt.

—— **PER SERVING** ——
- 360 calories
  (90 calories from fat)
- 10g total fat
  (4.5g saturated,
  0g trans)
- 40mg cholesterol
- 870mg sodium
- 39g total carbohydrate
  (6g fiber, 10g sugar)
- 25g protein
- 0%DV vitamin A
- 0%DV vitamin C
- 50%DV calcium
- 10%DV iron

Garden-Fresh Chili Sauce

Dianna Milhizer
Brighton, MI

Makes 4 quarts, or 16 servings

Prep. Time: 1-1½ hours
Cooking Time: 4 hours
Ideal slow-cooker size: 6-qt.

1½ cups tomato juice
12 dried red (hot chili) peppers, chopped, *or* enough to make 2 cups-worth
4 qts. fresh tomatoes, peeled and chopped
2 cups onions, chopped
2 cups red sweet peppers, chopped
1 tsp. ground ginger
1 tsp. ground nutmeg
1 tsp. whole cloves
1 bay leaf
2 tsp. ground cinnamon
2 tsp. salt
4 cups white vinegar
1 tsp. whole peppercorns

1. In a saucepan, bring 1½ cups tomato juice to a boil. Place dried peppers in hot juice and allow to steep and soften for 5 minutes. Cover your hands with plastic gloves. Remove stems from dried peppers, and then purée peppers in food processor.

2. Combine all ingredients in large slow cooker.

3. Cover. Cook on high 4 hours.

4. Remove bay leaf.

5. Freeze or can in pint jars.

—— PER SERVING ——
- 80 calories
  (5 calories from fat)
- 1g total fat
  (0g saturated, 0g trans)
- 0mg cholesterol
- 310mg sodium
- 16g total carbohydrate
  (3g fiber, 7g sugar)
- 2g protein
- 40%DV vitamin A
- 100%DV vitamin C
- 2%DV calcium
- 6%DV iron

Tips:

1. If you prefer a smoother sauce, purée it in a blender.

2. This is an excellent side dish for Mexican recipes and can be used as a flavoring when cooking pork, chicken, or beef. A little bit goes a long way! You may reduce the amount of chili peppers but then the sauce isn't as pungent. It makes a great last-minute, end-of-the-garden-season use for your tomatoes and peppers.

Marinara Sauce
Dorothy VanDeest
Memphis, TN

Makes 12 servings

Prep. Time: 20-25 minutes
Cooking Time: 7-9 hours
Ideal slow-cooker size: 4-qt.

2 28-oz. cans low-sodium whole tomatoes
1 onion, finely chopped
2 carrots, pared and finely chopped
1 clove garlic, chopped
2 Tbsp. vegetable oil
1 Tbsp. brown sugar
½ tsp. salt

1. Purée tomatoes in blender or food processor.

2. In a skillet, sauté onions, carrots, and garlic in oil until tender. Do not brown.

3. Combine all ingredients in slow cooker. Stir well.

4. Cover. Cook on low 6-8 hours.

5. Remove cover. Stir well.

6. Cook on high uncovered for 1 hour for a thicker marinara sauce.

—— PER SERVING ——
- 50 calories
  (25 calories from fat)
- 2.5g total fat
  (0g saturated, 0g trans)
- 0mg cholesterol
- 15mg sodium
- 8g total carbohydrate
  (2g fiber, 4g sugar)
- 1g protein
- 50%DV vitamin A
- 20%DV vitamin C
- 4%DV calcium
- 4%DV iron

Tip:
You can make this in advance of needing it and then freeze it in handy serving-size containers.

Slimmed-Down Pasta Sauce
Dolores Kratz
Souderton, PA

Makes 3½ cups sauce, or 4 servings

Prep. Time: 15 minutes
Cooking Time: 2-4 hours
Ideal slow-cooker size: 3-qt.

24-oz. can low-sodium tomato juice
6-oz. can tomato paste
½ cup carrots, grated
2 large cloves, mashed
1 tsp. dried oregano leaves, crushed
1 tsp. onion salt
1 medium bay leaf
dash of pepper

1. Combine all ingredients in slow cooker.

2. Cover. Cook on low 2-4 hours.

3. Remove bay leaf

4. Serve over your favorite pasta.

—— PER SERVING ——
- 80 calories
  (0 calories from fat)
- 0g total fat
  (0g saturated, 0g trans)
- 0mg cholesterol
- 510mg sodium
- 18g total carbohydrate
  (4g fiber, 8g sugar)
- 3g protein
- 100%DV vitamin A
- 60%DV vitamin C
- 4%DV calcium
- 10%DV iron

Delicious Spaghetti Sauce

Andrea Cunningham
Arlington, KS

Makes 8 servings

Prep. Time: 20-45 minutes
Cooking Time: 6½-8½ hours
Ideal slow-cooker size: 4-qt.

2 tsp. olive oil
1 medium-sized onion,
  finely chopped
6 cloves garlic, minced
56-oz. can low-sodium
  crushed tomatoes, *or* 7
  cups fresh, peeled, diced
  tomatoes
6-oz. can low-sodium
  tomato paste
2 tsp. dried basil
½ tsp. dried oregano
1 tsp. salt
½ tsp. black pepper
1 Tbsp. sugar
2 Tbsp. fresh parsley,
  chopped

1. Heat oil in saucepan
over medium heat. Add onion
and garlic. Sauté until onion
becomes very soft (about 10
minutes).

2. Combine all ingredients
except parsley in slow cooker.

3. Cover. Cook on low 6-8
hours.

4. Add parsley. Cook an
additional 30 minutes.

5. Serve over cooked
noodles.

---— PER SERVING —---
- 110 calories
  (15 calories from fat)
- 2g total fat
  (0g saturated, 0g trans)
- 0mg cholesterol
- 570mg sodium
- 22g total carbohydrate
  (5g fiber, 3g sugar)
- 4g protein
- 30%DV vitamin A
- 20%DV vitamin C
- 10%DV calcium
- 20%DV iron

Lentil Tacos

Judy Buller
Bluffton, OH

Makes 6 servings

Prep. Time: 20 minutes
Cooking Time: 3-6 hours
Ideal slow-cooker size: 4-qt.

¾ cup onions, finely
  chopped
⅛ tsp. garlic powder
1 tsp. canola oil
½ lb. dry lentils, picked
  clean of stones and
  floaters
1 Tbsp. chili powder
2 tsp. ground cumin
1 tsp. dried oregano
2 cups fat-free, low-sodium
  chicken broth
1 cup salsa
12 taco shells
shredded lettuce
tomatoes, chopped
shredded, reduced-fat
  cheddar cheese
fat-free sour cream
taco sauce

1. Sprinkle garlic powder
over onions and sauté in oil
in skillet until tender. Add
lentils and spices. Cook and
stir 1 minute.

2. Place lentil mixture and
broth in slow cooker.

3. Cover. Cook on low 3
hours for somewhat-crunchy
lentils, or on low 6 hours for
soft lentils.

4. Add salsa.

5. Spoon about ¼ cup into
each taco shell. Top with your
choice of lettuce, tomatoes,
cheese, sour cream, and taco
sauce.

---— PER SERVING —---
- 340 calories
  (100 calories from fat)
- 11g total fat (3.5g
  saturated, 2g trans)
- 15mg cholesterol
- 600mg sodium
- 42g total carbohydrate
  (5g fiber, 12g sugar)
- 19g protein
- 40%DV vitamin A
- 20%DV vitamin C
- 50%DV calcium
- 15%DV iron

Tip:
  This mixture is also tasty
served over rice.

Vegetable Sloppy Joes

Darla Sathre
Baxter, MN

Makes 8 servings

Prep. Time: 45 minutes
Cooking Time: 4-5 hours
Ideal slow-cooker size: 3- or 4-qt.

1 onion
1 green bell pepper
4 cloves garlic
2 carrots
8-oz. pkg. tempeh (we like 5-grain)
2 Tbsp. olive oil
1 envelope dry onion soup mix
¼ tsp. ground cumin
16-oz. can pinto beans, drained
16-oz. can fat-free refried beans
½ cup barbecue sauce

1. Dice the onion, green pepper, garlic, carrots, and tempeh. Sauté briefly in olive oil in skillet.

2. Combine with onion soup mix, cumin, beans, and barbecue sauce in slow cooker. You may want to slightly mash the pinto beans.

3. Cook on low 4-5 hours.

4. Serve on buns. Open-faced is less sloppy!

—— PER SERVING ——
- 340 calories
  (70 calories from fat)
- 8g total fat
  (1g saturated, 0g trans)
- 0mg cholesterol
- 890mg sodium
- 56g total carbohydrate
  (12g fiber, 9g sugar)
- 16g protein
- 50%DV vitamin A
- 20%DV vitamin C
- 10%DV calcium
- 25%DV iron

Variations:

You may want to increase the cumin to ½ tsp., if you prefer more bite.

You may serve this over pasta or rice, or just-as-is as a side dish.

Vegetable-Stuffed Peppers

Shirley Hinh
Wayland, IA

Makes 8 servings

Prep. Time: 20 minutes
Cooking Time: 6-8 hours
Ideal slow-cooker size: 6-qt., (large enough so that all peppers sit on the bottom of the cooker)

4 large green, red, *or* yellow bell peppers
½ cup quick-cooking rice
¼ cup minced onions
¼ cup black olives, sliced
2 tsp. lite soy sauce
¼ tsp. black pepper
1 clove garlic, minced
28-oz. can low-sodium whole tomatoes
6-oz. can low-sodium tomato paste
15¼-oz. can corn *or* kidney beans, drained

1. Cut tops off peppers (reserve) and remove seeds. Stand peppers up in slow cooker.

2. Mix remaining ingredients in a bowl. Stuff peppers. (You'll have leftover filling.)

3. Place pepper tops back on peppers. Pour remaining ingredients over the stuffed peppers and work down in between the peppers.

4. Cover. Cook on low 6-8 hours, or until the peppers are done to your liking.

5. If you prefer, you may add ½ cup tomato juice if recipe is too dry.

6. Cut peppers in half and serve.

—— PER SERVING ——
- 100 calories
  (20 calories from fat)
- 2g total fat
  (0g saturated,
  0g trans)
- 0mg cholesterol
- 420mg sodium
- 22g total carbohydrate
  (3g fiber, 6g sugar)
- 3g protein
- 10%DV vitamin A
- 60%DV vitamin C
- 4%DV calcium
- 8%DV iron

Fruit and Vegetable Curry

Melani Guengerich Novinger
Austin, TX

Makes 6 servings

Prep. Time: 30 minutes
Cooking Time: 3-8 hours
Ideal slow-cooker size: 4-qt.

4 onions, coarsely chopped
2 Tbsp. vegetable oil
2 cloves garlic, minced
1 tsp. gingerroot, grated
1½ Tbsp. ground cumin
½ tsp. cayenne pepper
1½ Tbsp. ground coriander
¼ tsp. ground cardamom
¼ tsp. ground cloves
1 tsp. ground turmeric
2 medium-sized zucchini,
    quartered lengthwise
    and sliced
¾ cup water
1 cup green beans, cut
2 firm, tart apples, cored
    and cubed
half a red bell pepper,
    chopped
1 cup dried apricots,
    chopped
½ cup currants *or* raisins
½ cup apricot conserve
    (*or smashed halves and
    juice*)

1. In skillet sauté onions in oil for 10 minutes. Stir in garlic, gingerroot, and spices. Continue to sauté, stirring constantly for about 3 minutes.

2. Transfer to slow cooker. Add zucchini, water, green beans, apples, red bell pepper, and dried apricots.

3. Cover. Cook on high 3-4 hours or on low 6-8 hours.

4. Stir in raisins and apricot conserve just before serving.

—— PER SERVING ——
• 300 calories
  (50 calories from fat)
• 6g total fat
  (1g saturated, 0g trans)
• 0mg cholesterol
• 20mg sodium
• 63g total carbohydrate
  (7g fiber, 48g sugar)
• 4g protein
• 20%DV vitamin A
• 30%DV vitamin C
• 8%DV calcium
• 15%DV iron

Tips:
This is tasty served over brown rice and topped with peanuts and chopped or sliced bananas.

Surprise Stuffed Peppers

Dorothy VanDeest
Memphis, TN

Makes 4 servings

Prep. Time: 20-25 minutes
Cooking Time: 6-8 hours
*Ideal slow-cooker size: 5-qt.,
(large enough so that all peppers
sit on the bottom of the cooker*

2 cups low-sodium tomato
    juice
6-oz. can tomato paste
2 7-oz. cans chunk-style
    tuna, drained and rinsed
2 Tbsp. dried onion flakes
2 Tbsp. dried veggie flakes
¼ tsp. garlic powder
4 medium-sized green bell
    peppers, tops removed
    and seeded

1. Mix tomato juice and tomato paste, reserving 1 cup.

2. Mix remaining tomato-juice mixture with tuna, onion flakes, veggie flakes, and garlic powder.

3. Fill peppers equally with mixture. Place upright in slow cooker.

4. Pour the reserved 1 cup tomato-juice mixture over peppers.

5. Cover. Cook on low 6-8 hours, or until peppers are done to your liking.

—— PER SERVING ——
• 220 calories
  (5 calories from fat)
• 0.5g total fat
  (0g saturated, 0g trans)
• 60mg cholesterol
• 460mg sodium
• 23g total carbohydrate
  (5g fiber, 9g sugar)
• 30g protein
• 20%DV vitamin A
• 200%DV vitamin C
• 4%DV calcium
• 10%DV iron

Seafood Main Dishes

Tex-Mex Luau

Dorothy VanDeest
Memphis, TN

Makes 6 servings

Prep. Time: 20 minutes
Cooking Time: 2-3 hours
Ideal slow-cooker size: 3- or 4-qt.

1½ lbs. frozen firm-textured
   fish fillets, thawed
2 onions, thinly sliced
2 lemons, *divided*
2 Tbsp. butter, melted
2 tsp. salt
1 bay leaf
4 whole peppercorns
1 cup water

1. Cut fillets into serving
portions.
2. Combine onion slices
and 1 sliced lemon in butter,
along with salt, bay leaf, and
peppercorns. Pour into slow
cooker.
3. Place fillets on top of onion
and lemon slices. Add water.

4. Cover. Cook on high 2-3
hours or until fish is flaky.
5. Before serving, carefully
remove fish fillets with
slotted spoon. Place on
heatproof plate.
6. Sprinkle with juice of
half of the second lemon.
Garnish with remaining
lemon slices.
7. Serve hot with Avocado
Sauce (next), if desired. Or
chill and serve cold, also with
Avocado Sauce, if you wish.

—— PER SERVING ——
- 160 calories
  (50 calories from fat)
- 5g total fat
  (2.5g saturated, 0g
  trans)
- 65mg cholesterol
- 870mg sodium

- 7g total carbohydrate
  (2g fiber, 3g sugar)
- 22g protein
- 4%DV vitamin A
- 20%DV vitamin C
- 6%DV calcium
- 4%DV iron

Avocado Sauce

Prep. Time: 10 minutes

7½ ozs. frozen low-fat
   avocado dip, thawed
½ cup fat-free sour cream
2 Tbsp. lemon juice
half a small onion, finely
   chopped

Combine all ingredients.
Mix well.

123

Herbed Flounder

Dorothy VanDeest
Memphis, TX

Makes 6 servings

Prep. Time: 10 minutes
Cooking Time: 2-3 hours
Ideal slow-cooker size: 6-qt.

2 lbs. flounder fillets (fresh
  or frozen)
½ tsp. salt
¾ cup chicken broth
2 Tbsp. lemon juice
2 Tbsp. dried chives
2 Tbsp. dried minced onion
½-1 tsp. leaf marjoram
4 Tbsp. fresh parsley,
  chopped

1. Wipe fish as dry as possible. Cut fish into portions to fit slow cooker.
2. Combine broth and lemon juice. Stir in remaining ingredients.
3. Place a meat rack in the slow cooker. Lay fish on rack. Pour liquid mixture over each portion.
4. Sprinkle with salt.
5. Cover. Cook on high 2-3 hours, or until fish is flaky.

——— PER SERVING ———
- 160 calories
  (20 calories from fat)
- 2.5g total fat
  (0.5 saturated,
  0g trans)
- 75mg cholesterol
- 2590mg sodium
- 5g total carbohydrate
  (0.5g fiber, 2g sugar)
- 29g protein
- 8%DV vitamin A
- 10%DV vitamin C
- 6%DV calcium
- 4%DV iron

Fish Feast

Anne Townsend
Albuquerque, NM

Makes 8 servings

Prep. Time: 20 minutes
Cooking Time: 2-3 hours
Ideal slow-cooker size: 6-qt.

3 lbs. red snapper fillets
1 Tbsp. garlic, minced
1 large onion, sliced
1 green bell pepper, cut in
  1" pieces
2 unpeeled zucchini, sliced
14-oz. can low-sodium
  diced tomatoes
½ tsp. dried basil
½ tsp. dried oregano
¼ tsp. salt
¼ tsp. black pepper
¼ cup dry white wine *or*
  white grape juice

1. Rinse snapper and pat dry. Place in slow cooker sprayed with nonfat cooking spray.
2. Mix remaining ingredients together and pour over fish.
3. Cover. Cook on high 2-3 hours, being careful not to overcook the fish.

——— PER SERVING ———
- 200 calories
  (25 calories from fat)
- 2.5g total fat (0.5g
  saturated, 0g trans)
- 65mg cholesterol
- 260mg sodium
- 7g total carbohydrate
  (2g fiber, 3g sugar)
- 36g protein
- 4%DV vitamin A
- 20%DV vitamin C
- 8%DV calcium
- 6%DV iron

Variation:
1. Red snapper can be pricey. You may substitute a sturdy white fish.

---

2. Serve in a bowl; the Feast is juicy. Or serve as a topping for rice.

Crockpot Oyster Stew

Judy Miles
Centreville, MD

Makes 8 servings

Prep. Time: 15 minutes
Cooking Time: 3½-4½ hours
Ideal slow-cooker size: 3-qt.

2 qts. 2% milk
3 Tbsp. butter
2 pints fresh oysters
1½ tsp. salt
2 tsp. Worcestershire sauce

1. Heat milk on high in covered slow cooker 1½ hours.
2. In a saucepan, melt butter. Add oysters with liquid. Simmer on low until edges of oysters curl.
3. Add salt and Worcestershire sauce to oysters. Combine with hot milk in slow cooker.
4. Cover. Cook on low 2-3 hours, stirring occasionally.

——— PER SERVING ———
- 240 calories
  (110 calories from fat)
- 12g total fat
  (7g saturated, 0g trans)
- 95mg cholesterol
- 830mg sodium
- 17g total carbohydrate
  (0g fiber, 12g sugar)
- 17g protein
- 10%DV vitamin A
- 0%DV vitamin C
- 35%DV calcium
- 45%DV iron

Oyster and Potato Filling

Jane Geigley
Honey Brook, PA

Makes 3-4 servings

Prep. Time: 10 minutes if mashed potatoes are already prepared; 50 minutes if you need to make the mashed potatoes
Cooking Time: 1½-3 hours
Ideal slow cooker size: 3-qt.

1 small onion, minced
½ cup celery, diced
¾ tsp. butter, melted
2 cups very moist mashed potatoes (mashed only with fat-free milk)
¼ cup Egg Beaters
1 Tbsp. minced parsley
1 tsp. salt
dash of black pepper
1 qt. stale whole wheat bread, cubed
1 doz. oysters with liquid

1. Sauté onion and celery in butter in skillet.
2. Blend together mashed potatoes and Egg Beaters in slow cooker. Pour in sautéed onions and celery. Mix together well.
3. Stir in parsley, salt, pepper, bread cubes, and oysters with their liquid.
4. Cover cooker.
5. Cook on high 1½ hours, or on low 3 hours.

— PER SERVING —
• 270 calories
 (25 calories from fat)
• 3g total fat
 (1g saturated, 0g trans)
• 15mg cholesterol
• 930mg sodium
• 45g total carbohydrate
 (8g fiber, 4g sugar)
• 12g protein
• 8%DV vitamin A
• 15%DV vitamin C
• 8%DV calcium
• 20%DV iron

Spaghetti Sauce with Crab

Dawn Day
Westminster, CA

Makes 4-6 servings

Prep. Time: 20 minutes
Cooking Time: 3-4 hours
Ideal slow-cooker size: 2- or 3-qt.

1 medium-sized onion, chopped
½ lb. fresh mushrooms, sliced
2 12-oz. cans low-sodium tomato sauce, *or* 1 12-oz. can low-sodium tomato sauce and 1 12-oz. can low-sodium chopped tomatoes
6-oz. can tomato paste
½ tsp. garlic powder
½ tsp. dried basil
½ tsp. dried oregano
½ tsp. salt
1 lb. crabmeat
16 ozs. angel-hair pasta, cooked

1. Sauté onions and mushrooms in nonstick skillet over low heat. When wilted, place in slow cooker.
2. Add tomato sauce, tomato paste, and seasonings.

Stir in crab.
3. Cover. Cook on low 3-4 hours.
4. Serve over angel-hair pasta.

— PER SERVING —
• 550 calories
 (45 calories from fat)
• 5g total fat
 (0g saturated, 0g trans)
• 80mg cholesterol
• 1710mg sodium
• 88g total carbohydrate
 (9g fiber, 12g sugar)
• 42g protein
• 20%DV vitamin A
• 30%DV vitamin C
• 15%DV calcium
• 35%DV iron

Simple Tuna Delight

Karen Waggoner
Joplin, MO

Makes 3 servings

Prep. Time: 5-10 minutes
Cooking Time: 1½ hours
Ideal slow-cooker size: 2-qt.

1¾ cups frozen vegetables
12-oz. can water-packed tuna, drained
10¾-oz. can low-sodium condensed cream of chicken *or* celery soup

1. Combine all ingredients in slow cooker.
2. Cover. Cook on high 1½ hours, stirring occasionally.
3. Serve over hot cooked rice or noodles.

— PER SERVING —
• 290 calories
 (60 calories from fat)
• 7g total fat
 (2g saturated, 0g trans)
• 40mg cholesterol
• 1220mg sodium
• 21g total carbohydrate
 (5g fiber, 4g sugar)
• 35g protein
• 80%DV vitamin A
• 6%DV vitamin C
• 6%DV calcium
• 15%DV iron

Slow-Cooker Shrimp Marinara

Judy Miles
Centreville, MD

Makes 6 servings

Prep. Time: 10-15 minutes
Cooking Time: 3¼-4¼ hours
Ideal slow-cooker size: 3½-qt.

16-oz. can low-sodium
tomatoes, cut up
2 Tbsp. minced parsley
1 clove garlic, minced
½ tsp. dried basil
½ tsp. salt
¼ tsp. black pepper
1 tsp. dried oregano
6-oz. can tomato paste
½ tsp. seasoned salt
1 lb. shrimp, cooked and
shelled
3 cups cooked spaghetti
grated Parmesan cheese

1. Combine tomatoes,
parsley, garlic, basil, salt, pepper, oregano, tomato paste, and
seasoned salt in slow cooker.
2. Cover. Cook on low 3-4
hours.
3. Stir shrimp into sauce.
4. Cover. Cook on high
10-15 minutes.
5. Serve over cooked
spaghetti. Top with Parmesan
cheese.

—— PER SERVING ——
• 210 calories
  (15 calories from fat)
• 1.5g total fat
  (0g saturated, 0g trans)
• 145mg cholesterol
• 720mg sodium
• 29g total carbohydrate
  (4g fiber, 4g sugar)
• 21g protein
• 10%DV vitamin A
• 10%DV vitamin C
• 10%DV calcium
• 25%DV iron

Company Casserole

Vera Schmucker
Goshen, IN

Makes 6 servings

Prep. Time: 15-25 minutes
Cooking Time: 2-6 hours
Ideal slow-cooker size: 4- or 5-qt.

1¼ cups uncooked rice
2 Tbsp. butter, melted
3 cups fat-free, low-sodium
chicken broth
1 cup water
3 cups cut-up, cooked
skinless chicken breast
2 4-oz. cans sliced
mushrooms, drained
⅓ cup light soy sauce
12-oz. pkg. shelled frozen
shrimp, thawed
8 green onions, chopped,
2 Tbsp. reserved
⅔ cup slivered almonds

1. Combine rice and butter
in slow cooker. Stir to coat
rice well.
2. Add remaining ingredi-
ents except shrimp, almonds
and 2 Tbsp. green onions.
3. Cover. Cook on low 5-6
hours or on high 2-3 hours,
until rice is tender.
4. Fifteen minutes before
the end of cooking time, stir
in shrimp.
5. Sprinkle almonds and
green onions over top before
serving.

—— PER SERVING ——
• 410 calories
  (130 calories from fat)
• 15g total fat (3.5g
  saturated, 0g trans)
• 150mg cholesterol
• 850mg sodium
• 26g total carbohydrate
  (5g fiber, 10g sugar)
• 42g protein
• 0%DV vitamin A
• 10%DV vitamin C
• 15%DV calcium
• 25%DV iron

Salmon Cheese Casserole

Wanda S. Curtin
Bradenton, FL

Makes 6 servings

Prep. Time: 10 minutes
Cooking Time: 2½-3½ hours
Ideal slow-cooker size: 2-qt.

14¾-oz. can salmon with
liquid
4-oz. can mushrooms,
drained
1½ cups bread crumbs
⅓ cup Egg Beaters
1 cup grated fat-free cheese
1 Tbsp. lemon juice
1 Tbsp. minced onion

1. Flake fish in bowl,
removing bones. Stir in
remaining ingredients. Pour
into lightly greased slow
cooker.
2. Cover. Cook on low
2½-3½ hours.

—— PER SERVING ——
• 150 calories
  (40 calories from fat)
• 4g total fat
  (1g saturated, 0g trans)
• 70mg cholesterol
• 650mg sodium
• 9g total carbohydrate
  (1g fiber, 1g sugar)
• 19g protein
• 0%DV vitamin A
• 0%DV vitamin C
• 20%DV calcium
• 6%DV iron

Shrimp Jambalaya

Karen Ashworth
Duenweg, MO

Makes 8 servings

Prep. Time: 45 minutes
Cooking Time: 2¼ hours
Ideal slow-cooker size: 5-qt.

2 Tbsp. butter
2 medium-sized onions, chopped
2 green bell peppers, chopped
3 ribs celery, chopped
1 cup chopped, cooked lean ham
2 garlic cloves, chopped
1½ cups uncooked minute rice
1½ cups fat-free low-sodium beef broth
28-oz. can low-sodium chopped tomatoes
2 Tbsp. chopped parsley, fresh *or* dried
1 tsp. dried basil
½ tsp. dried thyme
¼ tsp. black pepper
⅛ tsp. cayenne pepper
1 lb. shelled, deveined, medium-sized shrimp
1 Tbsp. chopped parsley for garnish

1. One-half hour before assembling recipe, melt butter in slow cooker set on high. Add onions, peppers, celery, ham, and garlic. Cook 30 minutes.

2. Add rice. Cover and cook 15 minutes.

3. Add broth, tomatoes, 2 Tbsp. parsley, and remaining seasonings. Cover and cook on high 1 hour.

4. Add shrimp. Cook on high 30 minutes, or until liquid is absorbed.

5. Garnish with 1 Tbsp. parsley.

—— PER SERVING ——
• 160 calories
  (35 calories from fat)
• 4g total fat
  (1g saturated, 0g trans)
• 15mg cholesterol
• 350mg sodium
• 23g total carbohydrate
  (3g fiber, 5g sugar)
• 9g protein
• 10%DV vitamin A
• 30%DV vitamin C
• 8%DV calcium
• 6%DV iron

Variation:
If you wish, and your diet allows, you may want to add ½ tsp. salt to Step 3.

Jambalaya

Mary Ann Lefever
Lancaster, PA

Makes 10 servings

Prep. Time: 30 minutes
Cooking Time: 2-3 hours
Ideal slow-cooker size: 4- to 5-qt.

1 lb. hot, *or* mild, Italian turkey sausage, removed from casings
½ cup chopped celery
1 cup chopped onion
½ cup chopped green bell pepper
1 tsp. minced garlic
16-oz. can low-sodium diced tomatoes
12-oz. can low-sodium, nonfat chicken broth
6-oz. can low-sodium tomato juice
½ cup long-grain rice, uncooked
¼ tsp. black pepper
14 drops hot pepper sauce, *or* to taste, *optional*
1 lb. boneless, skinless chicken breasts, cooked, and cut into small pieces, *or* 2 cups leftover cooked turkey
½ lb. uncooked medium shrimp, peeled

1. Brown sausage in nonstick skillet with celery and onions, breaking up sausage as it cooks until no longer pink.

2. Spoon meat, celery, and onion into slow cooker.

3. Add green pepper, garlic, tomatoes, broth, tomato juice, rice, pepper, and hot sauce if you wish to cooker. Stir together well.

4. Cover. Cook on low 2-3 hours, or until rice has cooked tender.

5. Five minutes before end of cooking time, stir in cooked chicken and shrimp.

6. Cover and cook 5 more minutes.

—— PER SERVING ——
• 210 calories
  (60 calories from fat)
• 6g total fat
  (2g saturated, 0g trans)
• 85mg cholesterol
• 440mg sodium
• 15g total carbohydrate
  (2g fiber, 3g sugar)
• 23g protein
• 10%DV vitamin A
• 30%DV vitamin C
• 4%DV calcium
• 15%DV iron

Tip:
Serve with plenty of cooked rice.

Tuna Casserole

Dorothy VanDeest
Memphis, TN

Makes 6 servings

Prep. Time: 15 minutes
Cooking Time: 2-6 hours
Ideal slow-cooker size: 3-qt.

2 6-oz. cans tuna, water-packed, rinsed and drained
1½ cups cooked macaroni
½ cup onions, finely chopped
¼ cup green bell peppers, finely chopped
4-oz. can sliced mushrooms, drained
10-oz. pkg. frozen cauliflower, partially thawed
½ cup low sodium, fat-free chicken broth

1. Combine all ingredients in slow cooker. Stir well.
2. Cover. Cook on low 4-6 hours or on high 2-3 hours.

—— PER SERVING ——
- 210 calories
  (20 calories from fat)
- 2.5g total fat (0.5g saturated, 0g trans)
- 35mg cholesterol
- 1940mg sodium
- 16g total carbohydrate
  (3g fiber, 4g sugar)
- 32g protein
- 4%DV vitamin A
- 20%DV vitamin C
- 4%DV calcium
- 15%DV iron

Variation:
If you like some zest, and your diet allows, you may want to add ½-1 tsp. seasoning salt to Step 1.

Tuna Noodle Casserole

Kathryn Yoder
Minot, ND

Makes 8 servings

Prep. Time: 25 minutes
Cooking Time: 3-4 hours
Ideal slow-cooker size: 5-qt.

2 cups nonfat powdered milk
4 Tbsp. cornstarch
2 Tbsp. onion flakes
4 Tbsp. low-sodium chicken bouillon granules
½ tsp. dried thyme
1 Tbsp. dried parsley
¼ tsp. black pepper
4 cups cold water
2 6-oz. cans water-packed tuna, drained
4-oz. can sliced mushrooms, drained
6-oz. can sliced water chestnuts, drained
16-oz. pkg. frozen mixed vegetables, thawed
8-oz. pkg. wide noodles, cooked al dente and drained
½ cup toasted sliced almonds

1. Mix powdered milk, cornstarch, onion flakes, bouillon, dried herbs, and pepper in large saucepan.
2. Add water. Cook over medium heat until thickened, stirring frequently.
3. Add tuna, mushrooms, water chestnuts, and vegetables. Pour into slow cooker sprayed with nonfat cooking spray.
4. Cover. Cook on low 3-4 hours.
5. Fifteen minutes before end of cooking time, stir in noodles.
6. Sprinkle almonds over casserole.

—— PER SERVING ——
- 470 calories
  (50 calories from fat)
- 6g total fat
  (1g saturated, 0g trans)
- 50mg cholesterol
- 1110mg sodium
- 67g total carbohydrate
  (5g fiber, 32g sugar)
- 39g protein
- 40%DV vitamin A
- 10%DV vitamin C
- 80%DV calcium
- 15%DV iron

Frequently Asked Questions about Slow-Cooker Cooking

Q. Fresh herbs or dried herbs?

A. It's your choice. But you get maximum flavor if you treat them differently.

Mix *dried* herbs into the dish *before* you cook it.

Add *fresh* herbs *after* the dish has finished cooking, just before you serve it.

Soups, Stews, and Chilis

Mixed Vegetables Beef Soup

Judi Manos
West Islip, NY

Makes 6-8 servings

Prep. Time: 25-30 minutes
Cooking Time: 4-6 hours
Ideal slow-cooker size: 4-qt.

1 lb. boneless round steak,
  well trimmed of fat and
  cut into ½" cubes
14½-oz. can diced
  tomatoes, undrained
3 cups water
2 medium-sized potatoes,
  peeled and cubed
2 medium-sized onions,
  diced
3 ribs celery, sliced
2 carrots, sliced
3 beef bouillon cubes
½ tsp. dried basil
½ tsp. dried oregano
½ tsp. salt
¼ tsp. black pepper
1½ cups frozen mixed
  vegetables

1. Combine all ingredients,
except mixed vegetables, in
slow cooker.
2. Cover. Cook on high 3-4
hours.
3. Add vegetables.
4. Cover. Cook on high 1-2
hours.

—— PER SERVING ——
- 220 calories
  (35 calories from fat)
- 4g total fat
  (1.5g saturated,
  0g trans)
- 45mg cholesterol
- 770mg sodium
- 28g total Carbohydrate
  (6g fiber, 8g sugar)
- 19g protein
- 100%DV vitamin A
- 20%DV vitamin C
- 10%DV calcium
- 20%DV iron

When I want to warm rolls to go with a slow-cooker
stew, I wrap them in foil and lay them on top of the stew
until they're warm.
Donna Barnitz, Jenks, OK

Sirloin No-Bean Chili

Dawn Day
Westminster, CA

Makes 10 servings

Prep. Time: 15 minutes
Cooking Time: 6-8 hours
Ideal slow-cooker size: 3-qt.

1 lb. sirloin steak, trimmed
   of fat
2 Tbsp. canola oil
2 large onions, chopped
16-oz. can low-sodium
   chopped tomatoes
8-oz. can low-sodium
   tomato paste
1½ cups low-sodium, low-
   fat beef broth
½ tsp. salt
¼ tsp. black pepper

1. Cube steak into 1"
pieces. Brown pieces in a
skillet in oil.
2. Combine all ingredients
in slow cooker.
3. Cover. Cook on low 6-8
hours, or until meat is tender
but not dry.

—— PER SERVING ——
• 120 calories   • 8g total carbohydrate
   (45 calories from fat)   (2g fiber, 3g sugar)
• 5g total fat   • 11g protein
   (1g saturated, 0g trans) • 15%DV vitamin A
• 30mg cholesterol   • 10%DV vitamin C
• 290mg sodium   • 4%DV calcium
                            • 10%DV iron

Variations:
1. If you want a zestier
dish, and if your diet allows,
you may want to add 2 tsp.
chili powder and/or 1 tsp.
ground cumin to Step 2.

2. This works well served
over rice and topped with
low-fat cheddar cheese.

Hearty Vegetable Soup

Betty B. Dennison
Grove City, PA

Makes 8 servings

Prep. Time: 30 minutes
Cooking Time: 7-7½ hours
Ideal slow-cooker size: 5-qt.

1-1½ lbs. beef chuck, well
   trimmed of fat and cut
   in ½" cubes
2 Tbsp. shortening
1 tsp. salt
¼ tsp. black pepper
3 cups potatoes, cubed
2 cups carrots, sliced
2 cups low-sodium stewed
   tomatoes
½ cup celery, chopped
½ cup onions, diced
½ cup frozen corn
½ cup frozen cut green
   beans
½ cup frozen peas

1. Brown meat in shorten-
ing in skillet. Add salt and
pepper.
2. Place meat, potatoes,
carrots, stewed tomatoes,
celery, onions, corn, and
green beans in slow cooker
(everything but the peas).
3. Add enough water to
cover all ingredients.
4. Cover. Simmer 20
minutes.

5. Cook on low 6½ to 7
hours.
6. One-half hour before end
of cooking time, stir in peas.

—— PER SERVING ——
• 210 calories   • 22g total carbohydrate
   (60 calories from fat)   (5g fiber, 7g sugar)
• 7g total fat   • 15g protein
   (2g saturated, 1g trans) • 100%DV vitamin A
• 35mg cholesterol   • 20%DV vitamin C
• 350mg sodium   • 4%DV calcium
                            • 15%DV iron

Variation:
For a thicker soup, and if
your diet allows, coat cubed
meat with 2 Tbsp. flour
before browning.

Vegetable Beef Barley Soup

Mary Rogers
Waseca, MN

Makes 12 servings

Prep. Time: 20 minutes
Cooking Time: 4-5 hours
Ideal slow-cooker size: 5- or 6-qt.

1 lb. lean stewing meat,
   cut into bite-sized pieces
½ cup onions, chopped
½ cup cut green beans,
   fresh *or* frozen
½ cup corn, fresh *or* frozen
4 cups fat-free, low-sodium
   beef broth
2 14½-oz. cans low-sodium
   stewed tomatoes
12-oz. can low-sodium V8
   juice
⅔ cup pearl barley,
   uncooked
1 cup water

1. Combine all ingredients in slow cooker.

2. Cover. Cook on high 4-5 hours, until vegetables are cooked to your liking.

—— PER SERVING ——

- 130 calories
  (20 calories from fat)
- 2g total fat
  (0.5g saturated,
  0g trans)
- 25mg cholesterol
- 65mg sodium

- 15g total carbohydrate
  (4g fiber, 5g sugar)
- 12g protein
- 4%DV vitamin A
- 10%DV vitamin C
- 4%DV calcium
- 10%DV iron

Many Vegetables Beef Soup

Doris Perkins
Mashpee, MA

Makes 8 servings

Prep. Time: 25 minutes
Cooking Time: 4-6 hours
Ideal slow-cooker size: 4-qt.

1 lb. extra-lean ground
  beef
14½-oz. can low-sodium,
  stewed tomatoes
10¾-oz. can low-sodium
  tomato soup
1 onion, chopped
2 cups water
15½-oz. can garbanzos,
  drained
15¼-oz. can corn, drained
14½-oz. can sliced carrots,
  drained
1 cup potatoes, diced
1 cup celery, chopped
½ tsp. salt
¼ tsp. black pepper
chopped garlic to taste,
  optional

1. Sauté ground beef in nonstick skillet.

2. Combine all ingredients in slow cooker.

3. Cook on low 4-6 hours, or until vegetables are as tender as you like them.

—— PER SERVING ——

- 220 calories
  (50 calories from fat)
- 6g total fat
  (2g saturated, 0g trans)
- 20mg cholesterol
- 590mg sodium

- 28g total carbohydrate
  (5g fiber, 7g sugar)
- 15g protein
- 100%DV vitamin A
- 20%DV vitamin C
- 8%DV calcium
- 15%DV iron

Variations:

1. You may use green beans and turnips, or any other combination of vegetables you wish.

2. If your diet allows, you may want to top individual servings with a spoonful of low-fat grated cheddar cheese.

Beef Barley Lentil Soup

Janie Steele
Moore, OK

Makes 10 servings

Prep. Time: 25-30 minutes
Cooking Time: 7-8 hours
Ideal slow-cooker size: 5- or 6-qt.

1 lb. extra-lean ground
  beef
1 medium-sized onion,
  chopped
2 cups potatoes, cubed
1 cup celery, chopped
1 cup carrots, diced
1 cup dry lentils, rinsed

½ cup medium-sized pearl
  barley
8 cups water
2 tsp. beef bouillon granules
½ tsp. salt
½ tsp. lemon pepper
  seasoning
2 14½-oz. cans low-sodium
  stewed tomatoes,
  undrained

1. Brown ground beef with onions in nonstick skillet. Drain.

2. Combine all ingredients except tomatoes in slow cooker.

3. Cook on low 6 hours, or until tender.

4. Add tomatoes. Cook on low 1-2 more hours.

—— PER SERVING ——

- 250 calories
  (40 calories from fat)
- 4.5g total fat (1.5g
  saturated, 0g trans)
- 15mg cholesterol
- 680mg sodium

- 35g total carbohydrate
  (9g fiber, 7g sugar)
- 17g protein
- 60%DV vitamin A
- 40%DV vitamin C
- 6%DV calcium
- 25%DV iron

Variations:

For added zest, you may want to increase lemon pepper seasoning to 1 tsp. You may also want to add ½ tsp. dried basil and ½ tsp. dried thyme to Step 2.

Hamburger Soup

Betty Moore
Plano, IL

Makes 6 servings

Prep. Time: 25 minutes
Cooking Time: 5¼-6¼ hours
Ideal slow-cooker size: 4-qt.

1 lb. extra-lean ground
  beef
¼ tsp. black pepper
¼ tsp. dried oregano
¼ tsp. seasoned salt
1 envelope dry onion soup
  mix
3 cups hot water
8-oz. can tomato sauce
1 Tbsp. low-sodium soy
  sauce
1 cup carrots, sliced
1 cup celery, sliced
1 cup macaroni, cooked
¼ cup grated Parmesan
  cheese

1. Combine all ingredients
except macaroni and Parmesan cheese in slow cooker.
2. Cook on low 5-6 hours.
3. Turn to high. Add
macaroni and Parmesan
cheese.
4. Cook another 15-20
minutes.

—— PER SERVING ——
• 160 calories
  (60 calories from fat)
• 6g total fat
  (2.5g saturated,
  0g trans)
• 25mg cholesterol
• 440mg sodium
• 12g total carbohydrate
  (2g fiber, 4g sugar)
• 15g protein
• 120%DV vitamin A
• 10%DV vitamin C
• 6%DV calcium
• 10%DV iron

Meatball-Potato-Carrot Stew

Barbara Hershey
Lititz, PA

Makes 10 servings

Prep. Time: 1 hour (includes pre-
paring and baking meatballs)
Cooking Time: 4-5 hours
Ideal slow-cooker size: 4- to 6-qt.

Meatballs
  1 lb. 95% lean ground
    beef
  ½ cup Egg Beaters
  ¼ cup chopped onion
  ⅔ cup dried bread
    crumbs
  ½ cup fat-free milk
  ¾ tsp. salt
  ¼ tsp. pepper
  1 tsp. Dijon mustard
  2 tsp. Worcestershire
    sauce

6 medium potatoes,
  unpeeled if you wish,
  and diced fine
1 large onion, sliced
8 medium carrots, sliced
4 cups low-sodium, fat-free
  vegetable juice
1 tsp. dried basil
1 tsp. dried oregano
½ tsp. salt
½ tsp. pepper

1. In a bowl, thoroughly
mix meatball ingredients
together. Form into 1" balls.
2. Place meatballs on
lightly greased jelly-roll pan.
Bake at 400° for 20 minutes.
3. Meanwhile, to make
stew, prepare potatoes, onion,
and carrots. Place in slow
cooker.
4. When finished baking,
remove meatballs from pan.
Blot dry with paper towels to
remove excess fat.
5. Place meatballs on top of
vegetables in slow cooker.
6. In large bowl, combine
vegetable juice and seasonings. Pour over meatballs and
vegetables in slow cooker.
7. Cover cooker. Cook on
high 4 to 5 hours, or until
vegetables are tender.

—— PER SERVING ——
• 210 calories
  (25 calories from fat)
• 3g total fat
  (1g saturated, 0g trans)
• 25mg cholesterol
• 520mg sodium
• 33g total carbohydrate
  (4g fiber, 9g sugar)
• 14g protein
• 200%DV vitamin A
• 80%DV vitamin C
• 8%DV calcium
• 15%DV iron

Tip:
If you will be gone more
hours than the time required
to cook the slow-cooker dish
that you want to make, you
can cook that recipe in your
slow cooker overnight on
low. I've done this many
times. In the morning I put
the slow-cooker insert, now
full of the cooked food, into
the refrigerator. When I get
home, I reheat the food in my
microwave.

Beef Goulash Vegetable Soup

Betty Moore
Plano, IL

Makes 6 servings

Prep. Time: 20 minutes
Cooking Time: 5-6 hours
Ideal slow-cooker size: 4-qt.

1 lb. extra-lean ground beef
1 large onion, diced
2 ribs celery, chopped
8-oz. can no-salt-added
   tomato sauce
3 14½-oz. cans fat-free beef
   broth
10-oz. pkg. frozen green
   beans
1½ tsp. chili powder
1 tsp. paprika
½ tsp. black pepper
1½ cups flat wide noodles,
   cooked

1. Sauté ground beef, onions, and celery in nonstick skillet until meat is browned and vegetables are crisp-tender. Transfer to slow cooker.

2. Add tomato sauce, broth, green beans, chili powder, paprika, and black pepper. Mix together.

3. Cook on low 5-6 hours.

4. Add noodles 15 minutes before serving.

—— PER SERVING ——
• 240 calories
   (70 calories from fat)
• 8g total fat
   (3g saturated, 0g trans)
• 40mg cholesterol
• 270mg sodium
• 19g total carbohydrate
   (3g fiber, 5g sugar)
• 23g protein
• 15%DV vitamin A
• 10%DV vitamin C
• 4%DV calcium
• 20%DV iron

Tip:
To eliminate a step, add 1 cup uncooked noodles to cooker 1 hour before serving.

Stick-to-Your-Ribs Veggie Soup

Judy Govotsos
Frederick, MD

Makes 12 servings

Prep. Time: 30 minutes
Cooking Time: 4-5 hours
Ideal slow-cooker size: 5- or 6-qt.

1 lb. 95% lean ground beef
2 cups onion, chopped
2 cups celery, chopped
2 1-lb. pkgs. frozen
   vegetables of your choice
2 14½-oz. cans low-sodium
   Italian-style stewed
   tomatoes, undrained
1 tsp. black pepper
2 low-sodium beef
   bouillon cubes
½ lb. shredded
   cabbage
2 medium potatoes,
   unpeeled and
   chopped very fine
6 cups water, *or* more if
   needed

1. Brown ground beef in nonstick skillet over medium-high heat. Add onion and celery to skillet and sauté until tender.

2. Place frozen vegetables, tomatoes, pepper, bouillon cubes, cabbage, and potatoes in slow cooker. Mix together well.

3. Stir in browned beef mixture.

4. Cover. Cook on low 4 to 5 hours, or until vegetables are done to your liking.

—— PER SERVING ——
• 160 calories
   (20 calories from fat)
• 2g total fat
   (1g saturated, 0g trans)
• 20mg cholesterol
• 75mg sodium
• 23g total carbohydrate
   (4g fiber, 8g sugar)
• 11g protein
• 35%DV vitamin A
• 40%DV vitamin C
• 6%DV calcium
• 15%DV iron

Note:
This soup tastes great even as leftovers.

Vegetable Beef Soup with Salsa

Annabelle Unternahrer
Shipshewana, IN

Makes 8 servings

Prep. Time: 15-20 minutes
Cooking time: 4-8 hours
Ideal slow-cooker size: 4-qt.

1 lb. extra-lean ground beef
4 cups water
1 lb. potatoes, pared and chopped
1 medium-sized onion, chopped
2 4-oz. cans mushroom pieces, drained
1 envelope dry low-sodium onion soup mix
16-oz. jar low-sodium chunky salsa
2 medium-sized carrots, chopped

1. Brown ground beef in nonstick skillet.
2. Combine all ingredients in slow cooker.
3. Cover. Cook on low 8 hours or on high 4 hours.

—— PER SERVING ——
• 200 calories   • 22g total carbohydrate
(50 calories from fat)   (3g fiber, 5g sugar)
• 5g total fat   • 14g protein
(2g saturated, 0g trans) • 80%DV vitamin A
• 20mg cholesterol   • 10%DV vitamin C
• 1230mg sodium   • 4%DV calcium
   • 10%DV iron

Burger Soup

Barbara Jean Fabel
Wausau, WI

Makes 8 servings

Prep. Time: 20-25 minutes
Cooking Time: 6-8 hours
Ideal slow-cooker size: 4- or 5-qt.

2 lbs. extra-lean ground beef
5 cups water
1 medium-sized onion, chopped
14½-oz. can diced tomatoes
½ cup celery, chopped
3 Yukon gold potatoes, cubed
½ cup carrots, chopped
½ cup frozen corn, thawed
¼ tsp. salt
¼ tsp. freshly ground pepper
½ tsp. dried basil
½ cup frozen peas, thawed

1. Brown beef in nonstick skillet.
2. Combine all ingredients in slow cooker, except peas.
3. Cover. Cook on low 6-8 hours.
4. One-half hour before serving, stir in peas.

—— PER SERVING ——
• 290 calories   • 22g total carbohydrate
(90 calories from fat)   (4g fiber, 4g sugar)
• 11g total fat   • 26g protein
(4g saturated, 0g trans) • 40%DV vitamin A
• 40mg cholesterol   • 30%DV vitamin C
• 190mg sodium   • 4%DV calcium
   • 20%DV iron

Variation:
If your diet permits, you may want to increase the salt to 1 tsp.

Taco Soup

Marla Folkerts
Holland, OH

Makes 6 servings

Prep. Time: 20 minutes
Cooking Time: 4-6 hours
Ideal slow-cooker size: 3½- or 4-qt.

Soup:
1 lb. extra-lean ground beef *or* ground turkey
1 medium-sized onion, chopped
1 medium-sized green bell pepper, chopped
1 envelope dry reduced-sodium taco seasoning
½ cup water
4 cups reduced-sodium vegetable juice
1 cup chunky salsa

Toppings:
¾ cup shredded lettuce
6 Tbsp. fresh tomato, chopped
6 Tbsp. reduced-fat cheddar cheese, shredded
¼ cup green onions *or* chives, chopped
¼ cup fat-free sour cream *or* fat-free plain yogurt
baked tortilla *or* corn chips

1. Brown meat with onion in nonstick skillet. Drain.
2. Combine all soup ingredients in slow cooker.
3. Cover. Cook on low 4-6 hours.
4. Serve with your choice of toppings.

Turkey Rosemary Veggie Soup

Willard E. Roth
Elkhart, IN

Makes 8 servings

Prep. Time: 30 minutes
Cooking Time: 8 hours
Ideal slow-cooker size: 6-qt.

1 lb. 99% fat-free ground
  turkey
3 parsley stalks with
  leaves, sliced
3 scallions, chopped
3 medium carrots,
  unpeeled, sliced
3 medium potatoes,
  unpeeled, sliced
3 celery ribs with leaves
3 small onions, sliced
1-lb. can whole-kernel corn
  with juice
1-lb. can green beans with
  juice
1-lb. can low-sodium diced
  Italian-style tomatoes
3 cans water
3 packets dry Herb-Ox
  vegetable broth
1 Tbsp. crushed rosemary,
  fresh *or* dry

1. Brown turkey with
parsley and scallions in
nonstick skillet. Drain. Pour
into slow cooker sprayed with
nonfat cooking spray.

2. Add vegetables, water,
dry vegetable broth, and
rosemary.

3. Cover. Cook on low 8
hours, or until vegetables are
done to your liking.

Tips:

This is tasty served topped
with a dollop of nonfat yogurt
and corn bread on the side.

Ground Turkey Soup

Betty K. Drescher
Quakertown, PA

Makes 12 servings

Prep. Time: 20-30 minutes
Cooking Time: 8-9 hours
Ideal slow-cooker size: 5- or 6-qt.

1 lb. 99% fat-free ground
  turkey
1 cup onions, chopped
1 clove garlic, minced
15-oz. can kidney beans,
  drained
1 cup carrots, sliced
1 cup celery, sliced

¼ cup long-grain rice,
  uncooked
1 qt. low-sodium diced
  Italian tomatoes
2 cups fresh *or* frozen
  green beans
1 tsp. parsley flakes
half a green bell pepper,
  chopped
1 tsp. salt
⅛ tsp. black pepper
1 Tbsp. Worcestershire
  sauce
1 bay leaf
3 cups water

1. Brown turkey in a large
nonstick skillet.
2. Combine with remaining
ingredients in slow cooker.
3. Cover. Cook on low 8-9
hours.

In recipes calling for rice, don't use minute or quick-cooking rice.
Mary Puskar, Forest Hill, MD

Stew in a Snap

Janice Yoskovich
Carmichaels, PA

Makes 6 servings

Prep. Time: 15-20 minutes
Cooking Time: 5-6 hours
Ideal slow-cooker size: 4-qt.

2 cups water
2 potatoes, diced
1 envelope dry onion soup mix
16-oz. pkg. mixed frozen vegetables
1 lb. ground turkey
4 slices bacon, diced and browned to a crisp
¼ tsp. black pepper
2 cloves garlic, minced
1 Tbsp. sugar
1 Tbsp. flour
28-oz. can chopped stewed tomatoes

1. Combine all ingredients in slow cooker.
2. Cook on high 3 hours; then turn to low for 2-3 hours, or until vegetables are done to your liking.

—— PER SERVING ——
• 280 calories
 (70 calories from fat)
• 7g total fat
 (2g saturated, 0g trans)
• 45mg cholesterol
• 280mg sodium
• 34g total carbohydrate
 (7g fiber, 8g sugar)
• 21g protein
• 50%DV vitamin A
• 30%DV vitamin C
• 8%DV calcium
• 25%DV iron

To make your own cream of mushroom or celery soup, please turn to pages 264-265.

Turkey Meatball Soup

Mary Ann Lefever
Lancaster, PA

Makes 8 servings

Prep. Time: 30 minutes
Cooking Time: 8 hours
Ideal slow cooker size: 5- or 6-qt.

4-5 large carrots, chopped
10 cups low-sodium, nonfat chicken broth
¾ lb. escarole, washed and cut into bite-size pieces
¾ lb. 95% fat-free ground turkey, uncooked
1 medium onion, chopped
½ cup Egg Beaters
½ cup Italian bread crumbs
½ cup freshly grated fat-free Parmesan cheese, plus more for serving
1 tsp. salt
¼ tsp. pepper

1. In slow cooker, combine carrots and chicken broth.
2. Stir in escarole.
3. Cover. Cook on low 4 hours.
4. Combine turkey, onion, Egg Beaters, bread crumbs, ½ cup Parmesan cheese, salt, and pepper in good-sized bowl. Mix well and shape into ¾" balls. Drop carefully into soup.
5. Cover cooker. Cook on low 4 more hours, or just until meatballs and vegetables are cooked through.
6. Serve hot, sprinkled with extra Parmesan cheese.

—— PER SERVING ——
• 170 calories
 (30 calories from fat)
• 3g total fat
 (1g saturated, 0g trans)
• 30mg cholesterol
• 740mg sodium
• 16g total carbohydrate
 (3g fiber, 3g sugar)
• 18g protein
• 140%DV vitamin A
• 10%DV vitamin C
• 10%DV calcium
• 15%DV iron

Variation:
If you wish, you can substitute 3 cups cut-up, cooked turkey for the ground turkey meatballs.

Meatball Mushroom Soup

Nanci Keatley
Salem, OR

Makes 8 servings

Prep. Time: 30 minutes
Cooking Time: 3-6 hours
Ideal slow-cooker size: 3½-qt.

½ lb. ground turkey
½ tsp. garlic powder
½ tsp. onion powder
¼ tsp. black pepper
1 large egg
1 Tbsp. olive oil
1 cup carrots, sliced
2 cloves garlic, crushed
2 cups fresh mushrooms, sliced
10¾-oz. can low-fat, *or* fat-free, low-sodium beef broth
10¾-oz. can 98% fat-free cream of mushroom soup

2 Tbsp. tomato paste
Parmesan cheese for
  garnish
fresh parsley for garnish

1. In a small bowl mix together ground turkey and seasonings. Add egg, stirring until well blended. Form into small meatballs.

2. Heat olive oil in skillet. Brown meatballs. Drain well.

3. Transfer meatballs to slow cooker. Add remaining ingredients, except Parmesan cheese and parsley.

4. Cover. Cook on low 5-6 hours or on high 3 hours.

——— PER SERVING ———
- 100 calories
  (45 calories from fat)
- 5g total fat
  (1g saturated, 0g trans)
- 25mg cholesterol
- 290mg sodium
- 7g total carbohydrate
  (0.5g fiber, 2g sugar)
- 8g protein
- 80%DV vitamin A
- 4%DV vitamin C
- 2%DV calcium
- 4%DV iron

Cheeseburger Soup

Nanci Keatley
Salem, OR

Makes 6 servings

Prep. Time: 25 minutes
Cooking Time: 6 hours
Ideal slow-cooker size: 4-qt.

1 lb. ground turkey
1 cup onions, chopped
½ cup green bell peppers, chopped
2 ribs celery, chopped
20-oz. can low-fat, low-sodium beef broth
1 cup nonfat milk
2 cups water
2 Tbsp. flour
8 ozs. low-fat cheddar cheese, grated

1. Brown turkey in nonstick skillet. Spoon into slow cooker.

2. Add vegetables to slow cooker.

3. Heat broth, milk, and water in skillet. Sprinkle flour over liquid. Stir until smooth. Let boil for 3 minutes.

4. Pour into slow cooker.

5. Cover. Cook on low 4 hours. Then add cheese and cook another 2 hours.

——— PER SERVING ———
- 240 calories
  (100 calories from fat)
- 11g total fat
  (3.5g saturated,
  0g trans)
- 70mg cholesterol
- 140mg sodium
- 8g total carbohydrate
  (1g fiber, 5g sugar)
- 26g protein
- 6%DV vitamin A
- 10%DV vitamin C
- 35%DV calcium
- 8%DV iron

Rice & Bean Soup

Sharon Easter
Yuba City, CA

Makes 6 servings

Prep. Time: 10 minutes
Cooking Time: 3½ hours
Ideal slow-cooker size: 5-qt.

⅓ lb. loose Italian turkey sausage, hot *or* sweet
2 32-oz. boxes low-sodium, fat-free chicken, *or* vegetable, broth
28-oz. can low-sodium diced tomatoes
½ tsp. salt
¼ tsp. pepper
½ tsp. dried oregano
1 cup long-grain rice, uncooked
15-oz. can white beans, rinsed and drained
1 cup diced celery
4 carrots, sliced

1. Brown sausage in nonstick skillet.

2. Put all ingredients in slow cooker. Stir until well blended.

3. Cover. Cook on low 2 hours. Stir Soup.

4. Cover and cook an additional 1½-2 hours on low, or until vegetables and rice are tender, but not mushy.

——— PER SERVING ———
- 320 calories
  (30 calories from fat)
- 3g total fat
  (1g saturated, 0g trans)
- 15mg cholesterol
- 790mg sodium
- 57g total carbohydrate
  (8g fiber, 7g sugar)
- 17g protein
- 160%DV vitamin A
- 30%DV vitamin C
- 15%DV calcium
- 35%DV iron

Turkey-Zucchini Soup

Wilma J. Haberkamp
Fairbank, IA

Makes 8 servings

Prep. Time: 20 minutes
Cooking Time: 2½-3½ hours
Ideal slow-cooker size: 4-qt.

8- *or* 10-oz. pkg. frozen
   green beans
2 cups zucchini, thinly
   sliced
2 cups turkey, cooked and
   chopped
8-oz. can tomato sauce
½ cup onions, chopped
1 Tbsp. instant chicken
   bouillon granules
1 tsp. Worcestershire sauce
¼ tsp. salt
½ tsp. dried savory, crushed
dash of black pepper
4 cups water
3 ozs. light cream cheese,
   softened

1. Thaw green beans. If
you're in a hurry, place them
in a strainer and run hot
water over them.
2. Combine beans, zucchini,
turkey, tomato sauce, onions,
bouillon, Worcestershire sauce,
salt, savory, black pepper, and
water in slow cooker.
3. Cook on high 2-3 hours.
4. Blend 1 cup hot soup with
cream cheese. Return to slow
cooker and stir well. Cook
until hot, about 20 minutes.

— PER SERVING —
- 110calories
  (35 calories from fat)
- 3.5g total fat
  (2g saturated, 0g trans)
- 30mg cholesterol
- 470mg sodium
- 7g total carbohydrate
  (2g fiber, 4g sugar)
- 13g protein
- 10%DV vitamin A
- 10%DV vitamin C
- 4%DV calcium
- 8%DV iron

Turkey Mushroom Soup

Lois Stoltzfus
Honey Brook, PA

Makes 6-8 servings

Prep. Time: 20-30 minutes
Cooking Time: 6-9 hours
Ideal slow cooker size: 4-qt.

2 cups cooked turkey
2 qts. low-sodium, fat-free
   turkey, *or* chicken, broth
   (add water if necessary to
   reach 2 qts.)
2 cups carrots, chopped
1 cup celery, chopped
2 cups potatoes, cubed
1 small onion, chopped
1 cup long-grain rice,
   uncooked
½ tsp. garlic salt
¼ tsp. pepper
1 tsp. dried parsley
10¾-oz. low-sodium, low-fat
   cream of mushroom soup

1. Place all ingredients
except cream of mushroom
soup in slow cooker.
2. Cover. Cook on low 6-9
hours, or until potatoes and
rice are as tender as you like
them.

3. Add cream of mushroom
soup during last hour of
cooking time.

— PER SERVING —
- 230 calories
  (15 calories from fat)
- 2g total fat (0.5g
  saturated, 0g trans)
- 35mg cholesterol
- 360mg sodium
- 35g total carbohydrate
  (3g fiber, 3g sugar)
- 16g protein
- 100%DV vitamin A
- 15%DV vitamin C
- 6%DV calcium
- 15%DV iron

Note:

   This recipe, with some
changes, comes from an old
cookbook first published in
1950. The quote at the end of
the recipe said, "A grand end
to a noble bird!"

Turkey Green Chili Chowder

Colleen Konetzni
Rio Rancho, NM

Makes 12 servings

Prep. Time: 45 minutes
Cooking Time: 6 hours
Ideal slow cooker size: 6-qt.

1 cup chopped celery
1 cup chopped onion
1½ Tbsp. butter
3 cups chopped cooked
   turkey
4 cups low-sodium, fat-free
   turkey, *or* chicken, broth
4 potatoes, peeled *or*
   unpeeled, and cubed
½ cup green chilies, chopped
½ cup cubed low-sodium,
   fat-free cheese, your choice
2 cans creamed corn
2 cups fat-free milk

1. In a skillet, sauté celery and onion in butter until vegetables soften and begin to brown.

2. Place sautéed vegetables, turkey, broth, potatoes, chilies, cheese, corn, and milk in slow cooker.

3. Cover. Cook on low 6 hours, or until potatoes are soft.

4. If you wish, mash the Soup a few times with a potato masher to make it thicker.

5. Turn slow cooker to low until time to serve.

—— PER SERVING ——

- 190 calories
  (25 calories from fat)
- 3g total fat
  (1g saturated, 0g trans)
- 40mg cholesterol
- 340mg sodium
- 25g total carbohydrate
  (2g fiber, 6g sugar)
- 16g protein
- 6%DV vitamin A
- 45%DV vitamin C
- 10%DV calcium
- 8%DV iron

Turkey Frame Soup

Joyce Zuercher
Hesston, KS

Makes 8 servings

Prep. Time: 40 minutes, if turkey and broth are already prepared
Cooking Time: 3¼-4½ hours
Ideal slow cooker size: 6-qt.

3 cups cooked and cut-up turkey*
3 qts. low-sodium, nonfat turkey broth
1 onion, diced
½ tsp. salt, *or* to taste
16-oz. can low-sodium chopped tomatoes
1 Tbsp. low-sodium chicken bouillon granules
1 tsp. dried thyme
⅛ tsp. pepper
1½ tsp. dried oregano
4 cups chopped fresh vegetables – any combination of sliced celery, carrots, onions, rutabaga, broccoli, cauliflower, mushrooms, and more
1½ cups uncooked noodles

1. Place turkey, broth, onion, salt, tomatoes, bouillon granules, thyme, pepper, oregano, and vegetables into slow cooker. Stir.

2. Cover. Cook on low 3-4 hours, or until vegetables are nearly done.

3. Fifteen to 30 minutes before serving time, stir in noodles. Cover. Cook on low. If noodles are thin and small, they'll cook in 15 minutes or less. If heavier, they may need 30 minutes to become tender.

4. Stir well before serving.

—— PER SERVING ——

- 180 calories
  (20 calories from fat)
- 2g total fat
  (0.5g saturated, 0g trans)
- 55mg cholesterol
- 400mg sodium
- 17g total carbohydrate
  (3g fiber, 4g sugar)
- 22g protein
- 50%DV vitamin A
- 30%DV vitamin C
- 6%DV calcium
- 20%DV iron

* If you've got a big turkey frame, and you know it's got some good meaty morsels on it, here's what to do. Break it up enough to fit into your Dutch oven. Add 3 quarts water, 1 onion, quartered, and 2 tsp. salt. Cover, and simmer 1½ hours. Remove turkey bones from Dutch oven and allow to cool. Then debone and chop meat coarsely. Discard bones and skin. Strain broth. Begin with Step 1 above!

139

Turkey Soup

Mary Rogers
Waseca, MN

Makes 12 servings

Prep. Time: 15-20 minutes
Cooking Time: 6-8 hours
Ideal slow-cooker size: 5-qt.

1 cup macaroni, uncooked
4 cups water
4 10¾-oz. cans fat-free,
 low-sodium chicken
 broth
2 ribs celery, sliced
2 large carrots, sliced
1 cup onions, chopped
2 cloves garlic, mashed
1 tsp. salt
½ tsp. black pepper
4 cups cooked turkey,
 chopped

1. Combine all ingredients
except turkey in slow cooker.
2. Cover. Cook on low 6-8
hours. Add turkey 1 hour
before end of cooking time.

—— PER SERVING ——
• 140 calories
 (25 calories from fat)
• 2.5g total fat
 (1g saturated, 0g trans)
• 35mg cholesterol
• 310mg sodium
• 9g total carbohydrate
 (0.5g fiber, 2g sugar)
• 18g protein
• 40%DV vitamin A
• 0%DV vitamin C
• 4%DV calcium
• 10%DV iron

Variations:

Experiment by adding
more vegetables, such as
zucchini, corn, and chopped
tomatoes, to Step 1, or
halfway through the cooking
process so that they don't
cook too soft.

Chicken Vegetable Soup

Barbara Walker
Sturgis, SD
Sheridy Steele
Ardmore, OK

Makes 6 servings

Prep. Time: 15 minutes
Cooking Time: 3-4 hours
Ideal slow-cooker size: 4-qt.

28-oz. can low-sodium diced
 tomatoes, undrained
2 cups low-sodium, reduced-
 fat chicken broth
1 cup frozen corn
2 ribs celery, chopped
6-oz. can tomato paste
¼ cup dry lentils, rinsed
1 Tbsp. sugar
1 Tbsp. Worcestershire
 sauce
2 tsp. dried parsley flakes
1 tsp. dried marjoram
2 cups cooked chicken
 breast, cubed

1. Combine all ingredients
in slow cooker except chicken.
2. Cover. Cook on low 3-4
hours. Stir in chicken one hour
before end of cooking time.

—— PER SERVING ——
• 190 calories
 (20 calories from fat)
• 2g total fat
 (0g saturated, 0g trans)
• 35mg cholesterol
• 520mg sodium
• 24g total carbohydrate
 (6g fiber, 7g sugar)
• 21g protein
• 20%DV vitamin A
• 20%DV vitamin C
• 10%DV calcium
• 20%DV iron

Apple Chicken Stew

Lorraine Pflederer
Goshen, IN

Makes 8 servings

Prep. Time: 30-40 minutes
Cooking Time: 4-5 hours
Ideal slow cooker size: 5-qt.

4 medium potatoes, cubed
4 medium carrots, cut
 ¼"-thick slices
1 medium red onion,
 halved and sliced
1 celery rib, thinly sliced
1 tsp. salt
¾ tsp. dried thyme
½ tsp. pepper
¼-½ tsp. caraway seeds
2 lbs. boneless, skinless
 chicken breasts, cubed
 and uncooked
2 Tbsp. olive oil
1 large tart apple, peeled
 and cubed
1¼ cups apple cider, *or*
 juice
1 Tbsp. cider vinegar
1 bay leaf
minced fresh parsley

1. Layer potatoes, carrots,
onion, and celery into slow
cooker.
2. In a small bowl, com-
bine salt, thyme, pepper, and
caraway seeds. Sprinkle half
over vegetables.
3. In a skillet, sauté
chicken in oil just until
lightly browned. Drain off
drippings.
4. Transfer chicken to slow
cooker. Top with cubed apple.

5. In another small bowl, combine apple cider and vinegar. Pour over chicken and apple.

6. Sprinkle with remaining salt mixture. Lay bay leaf on top.

7. Cover. Cook on high 4-5 hours, or until vegetables are tender and chicken juices run clear.

8. Discard bay leaf. Stir before serving.

9. Sprinkle individual serving bowls with parsley.

—— PER SERVING ——

- 290 calories
  (60 calories from fat)
- 6g total fat
  (1.5g saturated,
  0g trans)
- 65mg cholesterol
- 390mg sodium
- 32g total carbohydrate
  (4g fiber, 10g sugar)
- 26g protein
- 100%DV vitamin A
- 25%DV vitamin C
- 4%DV calcium
- 10%DV iron

Weney's Chicken & Vegetable Stew

Becky Frey
Lebanon, PA

Makes 8 servings
Ideal slow-cooker size: 4-qt.

To make this Stew from scratch, you'll need two days. On Day One you'll cook the chicken for 6-8 hours. On Day Two, you'll add the vegetables to the chicken broth and the deboned chicken and allow the Stew to cook 7-8 hours.

You can reduce the cooking to a total of 7-8 hours by using a deboned rotisserie chicken, chicken you've already cooked (and may have in the freezer), or canned chicken. And you can use boxed or canned chicken broth from the grocery store if you don't have your own.

If you choose to use already-prepared chicken and broth, begin with "On the next day" below, Step 2.

4 chicken legs *or* thighs, skinned
2 carrots, diced
4-6 medium-sized potatoes, diced
2-3 garlic cloves, minced
half a medium-sized head of cabbage, cut in chunks
1 green bell pepper, coarsely chopped
1 medium-sized onion, coarsely chopped
14½-oz. can low-sodium diced tomatoes (*or* fresh tomatoes in season)
1 tsp. ground coriander
1 tsp. ground annatto
½ tsp. salt
¼ tsp. black pepper

The day before serving the Stew:
1. Place chicken in slow cooker, sprinkle lightly with salt, and cover with water.

2. Cover. Cook on low 6-8 hours, or until tender.

3. Remove chicken from bones and reserve.

4. Strain and chill broth.

On the next day:
1. Remove fat from broth.

2. Place broth, deboned chicken, vegetables, and seasonings into slow cooker.

3. Cover. Cook on low 7-8 hours or until vegetables are tender.

—— PER SERVING ——

- 430 calories
  (130 calories from fat)
- 14g total fat
  (4g saturated, 0g trans)
- 90mg cholesterol
- 310mg sodium
- 50g total carbohydrate
  (9g fiber, 8g sugar)
- 27g protein
- 100%DV vitamin A
- 100%DV vitamin C
- 15%DV calcium
- 20%DV iron

Note:
Our dear friend Weney (from Puerto Rico) worked on our farm for many years. On cool fall evenings he would share this delicious stew with us. He didn't use a recipe so this is my best effort to recreate his stew.

Chicken Stew

Carol Eberly
Harrisonburg, VA

Makes 5 servings

Prep. Time: 25-30 minutes
Cooking Time: 6-8 hours
Ideal slow-cooker size: 4 qt.

1 lb. uncooked boneless, skinless chicken breasts, cubed
14½ oz.-can low-sodium, Italian diced tomatoes, undrained
2 potatoes, peeled and cubed
5 carrots, chopped
3 celery ribs, chopped
1 onion, chopped
2 4-oz. cans mushroom stems and pieces, drained
3 chicken bouillon cubes
2 tsp. sugar
½ tsp. dried basil
½ tsp. dill weed
1 tsp. chili powder
¼ tsp. black pepper
1 Tbsp. cornstarch
1 cup water

1. Combine all ingredients except cornstarch and water in slow cooker.
2. Combine water and cornstarch. Stir into slow cooker.
3. Cover. Cook on low 6-8 hours or until vegetables are tender.

— PER SERVING —
- 300 calories
  (35 calories from fat)
- 4g total fat
  (1g saturated, 0g trans)
- 75mg cholesterol
- 840mg sodium
- 33g total carbohydrate
  (6g fiber, 10g sugar)
- 33g protein
- 200%DV vitamin A
- 30%DV vitamin C
- 8%DV calcium
- 15%DV iron

Chicken Borscht

Jeanne Heyerly
Chenoa, IL

Makes 8 servings

Prep. Time: 25-30 minutes
Cooking Time: 6-8 hours
Ideal slow-cooker size: 5- or 6-qt.

1 qt. low-fat, low-sodium chicken broth
3 medium-sized potatoes, cubed
3 carrots, sliced
2 ribs celery, sliced
half a medium-sized head of cabbage, chopped
2 cups frozen corn
2 cups green beans
1 medium-sized onion, chopped
1 clove garlic, minced
2 cups low-sodium tomato juice
2 cups skinless chicken, cooked and diced *or* shredded
½ tsp. salt
¼ tsp. black pepper

1. Combine chicken broth, potatoes, carrots, celery, cabbage, corn, green beans, onions, garlic, and tomato juice in slow cooker.

---

2. Cover. Cook on low 6-8 hours, or until vegetables are as tender as you like.
3. Add chicken, salt, and pepper ½-1 hour before serving.

— PER SERVING —
- 230 calories
  (15 calories from fat)
- 2g total fat
  (0g saturated, 0g trans)
- 25mg cholesterol
- 300mg sodium
- 37g total carbohydrate
  (7g fiber, 10g sugar)
- 19g protein
- 100%DV vitamin A
- 80%DV vitamin C
- 10%DV calcium
- 20%DV iron

Roasted Chicken Noodle Soup

Janie Steele
Moore, OK

Makes 8 servings

Prep. Time: 30 minutes
Cooking Time: 5½-6½ hours
Ideal slow-cooker size: 5-qt.

1 cup onions, chopped
1 cup carrots, chopped
1 cup celery, chopped
1 clove garlic, minced
2 tsp. olive, *or* canola, oil
1 tsp. flour
½ tsp. dried oregano
½ tsp. dried thyme
¼ tsp. poultry seasoning
6 cups fat-free chicken broth
4 cups diced potatoes
1 tsp. salt
2 cups skinless roasted chicken, diced
2 cups uncooked wide noodles
1 cup fat-free evaporated milk

1. Brown onions, carrots, celery, and garlic in oil in skillet.

2. Stir in flour, oregano, thyme, and poultry seasoning and blend well. Pour into slow cooker.

3. Mix in broth, potatoes, and salt.

4. Cook on low 5-6 hours, or until potatoes are soft.

5. Add chicken, noodles, and milk. Cook until noodles are tender. Do not bring to a boil after milk is added.

——— PER SERVING ———
- 280 calories
  (35 calories from fat)
- 4g total fat
  (1g saturated, 0g trans)
- 65mg cholesterol
- 520mg sodium
- 31g total carbohydrate
  (3g fiber, 7g sugar)
- 28g protein
- 60%DV vitamin A
- 20%DV vitamin C
- 15%DV calcium
- 20%DV iron

Chicken Noodle Soup with Vegetables

Bernice A. Esau
North Newton, KS

Makes 6 servings

Prep. Time: 25-30 minutes
Cooking Time: 5-7 hours
Ideal slow-cooker size: 4- or 5-qt.

2 onions, chopped
2 cups carrots, sliced
2 cups celery, sliced
10-oz. pkg. frozen peas,
  optional
2 tsp. salt, *optional*
¼ tsp. black pepper
½ tsp. dried basil
¼ tsp. dried thyme
3 Tbsp. dry parsley flakes
4 cups water
2½-3-lb. chicken, cut-up
1 cup uncooked thin
  noodles

1. Place all ingredients in slow cooker, except chicken and noodles.

2. Remove skin and any fat from chicken pieces. Then place chicken in cooker, on top of rest of ingredients.

3. Cover. Cook on high 4-6 hours.

4. One hour before serving, remove chicken. Cool slightly. Cut meat from bones.

5. Return meat to cooker. Add noodles.

6. Cover. Cook on high 1 more hour.

——— PER SERVING ———
- 440 calories
  (70 calories from fat)
- 8g total fat
  (2g saturated, 0g trans)
- 175mg cholesterol
- 1030mg sodium
- 25g total carbohydrate
  (6g fiber, 8g sugar)
- 64g protein
- 200%DV vitamin A
- 20%DV vitamin C
- 8%DV calcium
- 25%DV iron

Alternate directions:

1. Place chicken in cooker. Cover ⅔ of it with water and cook 4 hours on high.

2. Remove chicken. Cool. Cut meat from bone.

3. Add some ice cubes to cooker broth. When cooled, remove fat.

4. Add all ingredients, except noodles.

5. Cover. Cook on high 2-3 hours.

6. Add noodles 1 hour before serving or place cooked noodles in individual bowls and serve chicken soup over noodles.

Chicken Soup in a Pot

Robin Schrock
Millersburg, OH

Makes 4 servings

Prep. Time: 15-20 minutes
Cooking Time: 3 hours
Ideal slow-cooker size: 3½-qt.

4 cups fat-free, low-sodium chicken broth
3 medium-sized carrots, diced
2 celery ribs, diced
1 chicken breast, cooked and cubed
½ cup uncooked noodles

1. Pour chicken broth into slow cooker. Add carrots and celery.
2. Cover. Cook on low 2 hours, or until carrots are nearly tender.
3. Add chicken and noodles.
4. Cover. Cook on low 1 hour.

── PER SERVING ──
- 100 calories
  (10 calories from fat)
- 1g total fat
  (0g saturated, 0g trans)
- 20mg cholesterol
- 220mg sodium
- 8g total carbohydrate
  (2g fiber, 3g sugar)
- 14g prOtein, 200%DV vitamin A
- 0%DV vitamin C
- 4%DV calcium
- 15%DV iron

Chicken Chowder

Sara Puskar
Abingdon, MD

Makes 4 servings

Prep. Time: 20 minutes
Cooking Time: 3¼-4¼ hours
Ideal slow-cooker size: 3½-qt.

½ cup shredded carrots
1 cup skim milk
½ cup low-sodium chicken broth
¼ tsp. black pepper
1 cup onions, chopped
1 potato, peeled and cut into ½" chunks
½ lb. uncooked boneless, skinless chicken breast cut into 1" cubes
2 15-oz. cans cream-style corn
½ cup dried potato flakes
½ cup shredded low-fat cheddar cheese

1. Combine all ingredients except potato flakes and cheese in slow cooker.
2. Cover. Cook on low 3-4 hours, or until potatoes are tender and chicken is thoroughly cooked.
3. Add potato flakes and stir well to combine.
4. Cook on high, uncovered, 5-10 minutes, or until chowder has thickened and dried potato flakes have dissolved.
5. Top each serving with cheese.

── PER SERVING ──
- 380 calories
  (40 calories from fat)
- 4g total fat (1.5g saturated, 0g trans)
- 50mg cholesterol
- 720mg sodium
- 61g total carbohydrate
  (5g fiber, 14g sugar)
- 30g protein
- 80%DV vitamin A
- 20%DV vitamin C
- 20%DV calcium
- 15%DV iron

Variations:
For more zest, and if your diet allows, you may want to add ½ tsp. salt to Step 1. You may also want to add ½ tsp. dried thyme to Step 1.

Spicy Chicken Rice Soup

Karen Waggoner
Joplin, MO

Makes 6 servings

Prep. Time: 25-30 minutes
Cooking Time: 3½ hours
Ideal slow-cooker size: 3½- or 4-qt.

4 cups low-fat, low-sodium chicken broth
2 cups chicken, cooked and cubed
2 celery ribs, chopped
2 medium-sized carrots, chopped
1 medium-sized green bell pepper, chopped
1 medium-sized onion, chopped
¾ cup long-grain rice, uncooked
¼ cup fresh parsley *or* cilantro, minced
½ tsp. salt
½ tsp. black pepper
½ tsp. dried oregano

¼ tsp. ground cumin
¼ tsp. crushed red pepper flakes, *optional*

1. Combine all ingredients in slow cooker.
2. Cover. Cook on high until boiling point, about 2 hours.
3. Turn down to low for 1½ hours, or just until rice and vegetables are tender.

—— PER SERVING ——
- 160 calories
  (15 calories from fat)
- 2g total fat
  (0g saturated, 0g trans)
- 35mg cholesterol
- 360mg sodium
- 14g total carbohydrate
  (2g fiber, 3g sugar)
- 19g protein
- 100%DV vitamin A
- 20%DV vitamin C
- 4%DV calcium
- 15%DV iron

Chicken Mushroom Stew

Bernice A. Esau
North Newton, KS

Carol Sherwood
Batavia, NY

Makes 6 servings

Prep. Time: 25 minutes
Cooking Time: 4 hours
Ideal slow-cooker size: 3½- or 4-qt.

6 boneless, skinless chicken breast halves (about 1½ lbs.), uncooked
2 Tbsp. cooking oil, *divided*
8 ozs. sliced fresh mushrooms
1 medium-sized onion, diced
3 cups diced zucchini

1 cup diced green bell peppers
4 garlic cloves, diced
3 medium-sized tomatoes, diced
6-oz. can tomato paste
¾ cup water
2 tsp. salt, *optional*
1 tsp. dried thyme
1 tsp. dried oregano
1 tsp. dried marjoram
1 tsp. dried basil

1. Cut chicken into 1-inch cubes. Brown in 1 Tbsp. oil in a large skillet. Transfer to slow cooker, reserving drippings.
2. In same skillet, sauté mushrooms, onions, zucchini, green peppers, and garlic in drippings, and remaining 1 Tbsp. oil if needed, until crisp-tender. Place in slow cooker.
3. Add tomatoes, tomato paste, water, and seasonings.
4. Cover. Cook on low 4 hours, or until vegetables are tender.

—— PER SERVING ——
- 260 calories
  (80 calories from fat)
- 8g total fat (1.5g
  saturated, 0g trans)
- 75mg cholesterol
- 880mg sodium
- 18g total carbohydrate
  (5g fiber, 5g sugar)
- 31g protein
- 30%DV vitamin A
- 40%DV vitamin C
- 6%DV calcium
- 20%DV iron

Tip:
This is also good served over rice.

Chicken Wild Rice Soup

Karen Ceneviva
Seymour, CT

Makes 8 servings

Prep. Time: 15 minutes
Cooking Time: 3-7 hours
Ideal slow-cooker size: 3½-qt.

½ cup wild rice, uncooked
½ cup long-grain rice, uncooked
1 tsp. vegetable oil
1 lb. boneless, skinless chicken breasts, uncooked, and cut into ¾" cubes
5¼ cups low-sodium, fat-free chicken broth
1 cup celery (about 2 ribs), chopped in ½" thick pieces
1 medium onion, chopped
2 tsp. dried thyme leaves
¼ tsp. red pepper flakes

1. Mix wild and white rice with oil in slow cooker.
2. Cover. Cook on high 15 minutes.
3. Add chicken, broth, vegetables, and seasonings.
4. Cover. Cook 3-4 hours on high, or 6-7 hours on low.

—— PER SERVING ——
- 170 calories
  (20 calories from fat)
- 2g total fat
  (0.5g saturated,
  0g trans)
- 30mg cholesterol
- 90mg sodium
- 21g total carbohydrate
  (1g fiber, 1g sugar)
- 16g protein
- 2%DV vitamin A
- 4%DV vitamin C
- 2%DV calcium
- 10%DV iron

Chicken Rice Soup

Michelle Steffen
Harrisonburg, VA

Makes 14 servings

Prep. Time: 20-30 minutes
Cooking Time: 4-5 hours
Ideal slow-cooker size: 6-qt.

3 quarts hot water
1 medium onion, finely
　chopped
2-3 celery ribs, finely
　chopped
2 sprigs fresh parsley,
　finely chopped
1 clove garlic, crushed
2 tsp. salt
½ cup carrots, thinly sliced
4 large skinless chicken
　legs and thighs
½ cup fresh parsley,
　chopped
3 cups hot cooked rice

1. Combine water, onion, celery, 2 sprigs parsley, garlic, salt, carrots, and chicken in slow cooker.
2. Cover. Cook on high 4-5 hours.

3. Remove chicken when tender and debone.
4. Stir cut-up chicken back into soup. Add ½ cup fresh chopped parsley
5. To serve, ladle soup into bowls. Add a rounded tablespoonful of hot cooked rice to each bowl.

—— PER SERVING ——
• 80 calories
　(5 calories from fat)
• 1g total fat
　(0g saturated, 0g trans)
• 15mg cholesterol
• 530mg sodium
• 11g total carbohydrate
　(0.5g fiber, 1g sugar)
• 7g protein
• 20%DV vitamin A
• 0%DV vitamin C
• 2%DV calcium
• 4%DV iron

Tip:

If you want to eliminate washing another pan, add 1 cup raw long grain rice to the slow-cooker mixture after the chicken has cooked 3-4 hours. Cook on high another hour.

When chicken and rice are tender, remove chicken and debone. Continue with Step 5.

Colorful Chicken Stew

Sharon Miller
Holmesville, OH

Makes 10 servings

Prep. Time: 25-30 minutes
Cooking Time: 6-8 hours
Ideal slow-cooker size: 5- or 6-qt.

1 lb. boneless, skinless
　chicken breasts,
　uncooked and cubed
14½-oz. can diced Italian
　tomatoes, undrained
2 medium-sized potatoes,
　peeled and cubed into
　½" pieces
4 large carrots, diced
3 celery ribs, diced
1 large onion, chopped
1 medium-sized green bell
　pepper, chopped
8-oz. can mushroom
　pieces, drained
2 tsp. chicken bouillon
　granules
1 pkg. Splenda
1 tsp. chili powder
¼ tsp. black pepper
1 Tbsp. cornstarch
2 cups cold water

1. Combine first 12 ingredients (through the black pepper) in a large slow cooker.
2. Mix together cornstarch and cold water. Add to slow cooker.
3. Cook on low 6-8 hours, or until vegetables are tender.

—— PER SERVING ——
- 120 calories
  (15 calories from fat)
- 1.5g total fat
  (0g saturated, 0g trans)
- 25mg cholesterol
- 330mg sodium
- 16g total carbohydrate
  (3g fiber, 4g sugar)
- 11g protein
- 100%DV vitamin A
- 25%DV vitamin C
- 6%DV calcium
- 6%DV iron

Barley and Chicken Soup

Millie Schellenburg
Washington, NJ

Makes 5 servings

Prep. Time: 15-20 minutes
Cooking Time: 4½-6½ hours
Ideal slow-cooker size: 5- or 6-qt.

½ lb. dry barley
1 small chicken
fresh celery, as desired
parsley, as desired
basil, as desired
carrots as desired

1. Combine all ingredients in slow cooker. Cover with water.
2. Cover. Cook on low 4-6 hours.
3. Remove chicken from bones. Discard skin. Return chicken to soup. Continue cooking until barley is soft.

—— PER SERVING ——
- 310 calories
  (50 calories from fat)
- 6g total fat
  (1.5g saturated,
  0g trans)
- 55mg cholesterol
- 95mg sodium
- 41g total carbohydrate
  (11g fiber, 4g sugar)
- 26g protein
- 200%DV vitamin A
- 10%DV vitamin C
- 15%DV calcium
- 30%DV iron

Chicken, Vegetables, and Dumplings

Colleen Heatwole
Burton, MI

Makes 8 servings

Prep. Time: 45 minutes
Cooking Time: 4¼-6¼ hours
Ideal slow-cooker size: 4-qt.

Soup:
  4 cups cubed cooked chicken
  6 cups fat-free, low-sodium chicken broth
  1 Tbsp. fresh parsley, *or* 1½ tsp. dry parsley flakes
  1 cup onions, chopped
  1 cup celery, chopped
  6 cups diced potatoes
  1 cup green beans
  1 cup carrots
  1 cup peas, *optional*

Dumplings: (*optional***)**
  2 cups flour (half white and half whole wheat)
  1 tsp. salt
  4 tsp. baking powder
  1 egg, beaten
  2 Tbsp. olive oil
  ⅔ cup skim milk

1. Combine all soup ingredients, except peas.
2. Cover. Cook on low 4-6 hours.
3. Transfer to large soup kettle with lid. Add peas, if desired. Bring to a boil. Reduce to simmer.
4. To make Dumplings, combine flour, salt, and

baking powder in a large bowl.
5. In a separate bowl, combine egg, olive oil, and milk until smooth. Add to flour mixture.
6. Drop by large table-spoonsful on top of simmering broth until the dumplings cover the surface of the soup.
7. Cover. Simmer without lifting the lid for 18 minutes.

—— PER SERVING ——
- 400 calories
  (60 calories from fat)
- 7g total fat (1.5g
  saturated, 0g trans)
- 80mg cholesterol
- 510mg sodium
- 51g total carbohydrate
  (5g fiber, 5g sugar)
- 32g protein
- 50%DV vitamin A
- 20%DV vitamin C
- 20%DV calcium
- 30%DV iron

Note:
   I use this recipe a lot. I adapted it from a potpie recipe which needs to be baked in the oven. I like to make this because the soup can cook in the slow cooker while we're at church. When I get home, I transfer it to a soup kettle and make the dumplings while others set the table.
   The dish is good served with applesauce or fruit salad.

Chicken Clam Chowder

Irene Klaeger
Inverness, FL

Makes 10 servings

Prep. Time: 25-30 minutes
Cooking Time: 3-6 hours
Ideal slow-cooker size: 4-qt.

6 slices lean turkey bacon, diced
¼ lb. lean ham, cubed
2 cups chopped onions
2 cups diced celery
½ tsp. salt
¼ tsp. black pepper
2 cups diced potatoes
2 cups cooked, diced, lean chicken
4 cups fat-free, low-sodium clam juice, *or* 2 cans clams with juice
1-lb. can whole-kernel corn with liquid
¾ cup flour
4 cups fat-free milk
4 cups shredded fat-free cheddar, *or* Jack, cheese
½ cup fat-free evaporated milk
2 Tbsp. fresh parsley

1. Sauté bacon, ham, onions, and celery in nonstick skillet until bacon is crisp and onions and celery are limp. Add salt and pepper.
2. Combine all ingredients in slow cooker except flour, milk, cheese, evaporated milk, and parsley.
3. Cover. Cook on low 4-5 hours or on high 2-3 hours.
4. Whisk flour into milk.

Stir into soup, along with cheese, evaporated milk, and parsley. Cook one more hour on low.

— PER SERVING —
• 250 calories
  (35 calories from fat)
• 3.5g total fat
  (1g saturated, 0g trans)
• 45mg cholesterol
• 880mg sodium
• 23g total carbohydrate
  (3g fiber, 9g sugar)
• 31g protein
• 10%DV vitamin A
• 10%DV vitamin C
• 50%DV calcium
• 10%DV iron

San-Antonio-Style Tortilla Soup

Rashell Harris
Wichita, KS

Makes 9-10 servings

Prep. Time: 20 minutes
Cooking Time: 4-8 hours
Ideal slow-cooker size: 5-qt.

1 Tbsp. olive oil
1 onion, chopped
2 garlic cloves, minced
2 tsp. ground cumin
2 14½-oz. cans fat-free chicken broth
2 15-oz. cans stewed tomatoes
1 Tbsp. jalapeño pepper, minced (remove seeds to reduce heat)
¼ tsp. black pepper
4-5 cups (about 1½ lbs.) boneless, skinless chicken breasts, uncooked and cubed
2 cups water

1. Combine all ingredients in slow cooker.

2. Cover. Cook on low 6-8 hours or on high 4-6 hours.

— PER SERVING —
• 320 calories
  (50 calories from fat)
• 6g total fat
  (2g saturated, 0g trans)
• 30mg cholesterol
• 390mg sodium
• 44g total carbohydrate
  (5g fiber, 7g sugar)
• 22g protein
• 10%DV vitamin A
• 10%DV vitamin C
• 30%DV calcium
• 15%DV iron

Variations:

1. If you like, and your diet permits, you may want to add a 17-oz. can of whole-kernel corn, drained, to Step 1, for an additional Southwest touch to your dish.
2. Use the following garnishes if you wish, and if your diet allows:
  2 cups shredded low-fat cheese
  fat-free sour cream
  cilantro
  1 bag baked tortilla chips, crushed

Wild Rice Soup

Joyce Shackelford
Green Bay, WI

Makes 8 servings

Prep. Time: 25 minutes
Cooking Time: 3-4 hours
Ideal slow-cooker size: 4-qt.

2 Tbsp. butter
½ cup dry wild rice
6 cups fat-free, low-sodium chicken stock
½ cup onions, minced
½ cup celery, minced
½ lb. winter squash, peeled, seeded, cut in ½" cubes
2 cups chicken, chopped and cooked
½ cup browned, slivered almonds

1. Melt butter in small skillet. Add rice and sauté 10 minutes over low heat. Transfer to slow cooker.
2. Add all remaining ingredients except chicken and almonds.
3. Cover. Cook on low 3-4 hours, or until vegetables are cooked to your liking. One hour before serving stir in chicken.
4. Top with browned slivered almonds just before serving.

— PER SERVING —
• 310 calories
  (70 calories from fat)
• 8g total fat
  (4g saturated, 0g trans)
• 70mg cholesterol
• 320mg sodium
• 25g total carbohydrate
  (3g fiber, 3g sugar)
• 33g protein
• 2%DV vitamin A
• 2%DV vitamin C
• 8%DV calcium
• 25%DV iron

Wild Rice and Lentil Soup

Maryann Markano
Wilmington, DE

Makes 8-10 servings

Soaking Time: 6-8 hours or overnight
Prep. Time: 10 minutes
Cooking Time: 5-8 hours
Ideal slow-cooker size: 3½- or 4-qt.

½ cup dried lentils, sorted, rinsed and drained
3 cups water
6-oz. pkg. long-grain and wild rice blend, with spice packet
14-oz. can vegetable broth
10-oz. pkg. frozen mixed vegetables
1 cup skim milk
½ cup reduced-fat mild cheddar cheese, shredded

1. Cover lentils with water and soak overnight or for 6-8 hours. Drain and discard soaking water.
2. Put all ingredients into slow cooker, including 3 cups fresh water. Mix well.
3. Cook on low 5-8 hours, or until vegetables are done to your liking.

— PER SERVING —
• 240 calories
  (25 calories from fat)
• 2.5g total fat
  (1.5g saturated, 0g trans)
• 5mg cholesterol
• 280mg sodium
• 42g total carbohydrate
  (7g fiber, 5g sugar)
• 13g protein
• 30%DV vitamin A
• 10%DV vitamin C
• 15%DV calcium
• 15%DV iron

Tip:
It may be necessary to add more water if the soup seems too thick.

Cheesy Menudo

Eileen Eash
Carlsbad, NM

Makes 8 servings

Prep. Time: 10 minutes
Cooking Time: 4 hours
Ideal slow-cooker size: 3½-qt.

3 16-oz. cans white or yellow hominy, undrained
4-oz. can chopped green chilies
½ lb. Velveeta Light cheese, diced
1 tsp. garlic salt
½ tsp. black pepper
fresh cilantro, *or* parsley, chopped
2 cups cooked chicken, *or* lean beef, chopped

1. Combine all ingredients in slow cooker. Stir well.
2. Cover. Cook on low 4 hours.

— PER SERVING —
• 240 calories
  (50 calories from fat)
• 6g total fat
  (2.5g saturated, 1g trans)
• 40mg cholesterol
• 1000mg sodium
• 28g total carbohydrate
  (5g fiber, 3g sugar)
• 18g protein
• 6%DV vitamin A
• 2%DV vitamin C
• 20%DV calcium
• 8%DV iron

Green Bean Soup

Carla Koslowsky
Hillsboro, KS

Makes 4 servings

Ideal slow-cooker size: 4-qt.

This recipe requires two main "events" in its preparation. First you cook the ham hock itself before making the Green Bean Soup. You can prepare the ham hock in the slow cooker by covering it with water, and then cooking it on low for 5 hours, or until the meat is tender and falling off the bone.

When you've cooked the ham and deboned it, and you have a rich, flavorful broth, you're ready for the second main "event." For this you'll need about 10-15 minutes of Prep Time to do Step 1 below. And you'll need 4-5 hours of additional Cooking Time.

1 ham hock, cooked, cooled, deboned, and fat removed—with cooking broth reserved and skimmed of fat
2 potatoes, peeled and cubed
½ cup onions, chopped
1 sprig dill weed
16-oz. pkg. green beans
ham broth and water to equal 6 cups
½ tsp. salt
¼ tsp. black pepper
½ cup milk

1. Combine all ingredients except milk in slow cooker.
2. Cover. Cook on low 4-5 hours, or until vegetables are tender.
3. Add milk just before serving.

—— PER SERVING ——
• 160 calories
  (30 calories from fat)
• 3g total fat
  (1g saturated, 0g trans)
• 15mg cholesterol
• 660mg sodium
• 26g total carbohydrate
  (5g fiber, 5g sugar)
• 8g protein
• 0%DV vitamin A
• 30%DV vitamin C
• 8%DV calcium
• 10%DV iron

Red and Green Bean Soup

Carol Duree
Salina, KS

Makes 8 servings

Prep. Time: 15 minutes
Cooking Time: 6¼-8¼ hours
Ideal slow cooker size: 4-qt.

1 lb. dry navy beans
6 cups boiling water
1 cup sliced carrots
½ cup chopped onion
¾ lb. smoked dark turkey meat
salt and pepper to taste, *optional*
2 cups chopped kale, spinach, *or* chard
½ cup roasted red peppers, chopped
low-fat Parmesan cheese, grated, *optional*

1. Rinse beans; then place in slow cooker.
2. Add all other ingredients except kale, red peppers, and cheese.
3. Cover. Cook on low 6-8 hours, or until beans are tender but not mushy.
4. Ten minutes before serving, add kale and peppers.

Cover and continue to cook 10 more minutes.
5. If you wish, sprinkle Parmesan cheese on top of individual servings.

—— PER SERVING ——
• 270 calories
  (30 calories from fat)
• 3g total fat
  (0.5g saturated, 0g trans)
• 30mg cholesterol
• 500mg sodium
• 38g total carbohydrate
  (15g fiber, 2g sugar)
• 24g protein
• 110%DV vitamin A
• 50%DV vitamin C
• 15%DV calcium
• 25%DV iron

Healthy Bean Soup

Karen Ceneviva
Seymour, CT

Makes 10 servings

Prep. Time: 20-30 minutes
Cooking Time: 6¼-7¼ hours
Ideal slow-cooker size: 5-qt.

1½ cups dry great northern beans
3 cups parsnips, chopped
2 cups carrots, chopped
1 cup onion, chopped
2 gloves garlic, minced
5 cups water
¾ lb. smoked dark turkey meat
1½ tsp. salt
½ tsp. pepper
⅛-¼ tsp. hot sauce

1. Wash dried beans. Place beans in large stockpot. Cover with water.
2. Bring to a boil. Turn off heat. Allow beans to sit for 10 minutes.
3. Drain off water. Place beans in slow cooker.

4. Add parsnips, carrots, onion, and garlic to slow cooker.

5. Add water, turkey, salt, pepper, and hot sauce to slow cooker. Stir well.

6. Cover. Cook on low 6-7 hours, or until vegetables and meat are tender.

7. Remove meat from cooker and allow to cool enough to handle.

8. Cut meat into bite-size pieces and return to slow cooker. Heat through.

—— PER SERVING ——

- 180 calories (20 calories from fat)
- 2g total fat (0.5g saturated, 0g trans)
- 25mg cholesterol
- 870mg sodium
- 25g total carbohydrate (7g fiber, 3g sugar)
- 17g protein
- 80%DV vitamin A
- 15%DV vitamin C
- 8%DV calcium
- 15%DV iron

Ham and Split Pea Soup

Mary C. Casey
Scranton, PA

Makes 6-8 servings

Prep. Time: 25-30 minutes
Cooking Time: 6-8 hours
Ideal slow-cooker size: 5-qt.

2 cups cooked ham, diced
1 bay leaf
16-oz. pkg. dried split peas
2 ribs celery, sliced
1 small onion, chopped
¼-½ tsp. black pepper, according to your taste preference

½ tsp. salt
¼-½ tsp. dried marjoram, according to your taste preference
½ cup carrots, shredded
2 10¾-oz. cans reduced-sodium, low-fat chicken broth
5 cups water
1 cup potatoes, cooked and diced, *optional*

1. Combine all ingredients in slow cooker.

2. Cover. Cook on low 6-8 hours, or until peas are tender.

3. To thicken, remove 4 cups of soup after potatoes have been added and purée in blender.

4. Return to soup. Stir.

—— PER SERVING ——

- 330 calories (30 calories from fat)
- 3.5g total fat (1g saturated, 0g trans)
- 25mg cholesterol
- 850mg sodium
- 48g total carbohydrate (17g fiber, 8g sugar)
- 29g protein
- 50%DV vitamin A
- 10%DV vitamin C
- 6%DV calcium
- 25%DV iron

Hearty Split Pea Soup

Beatrice Orgish
Richardson, TX

Makes 9 servings

Prep. Time: 20 minutes
Cooking Time: 4-5 hours
Ideal slow-cooker size: 4-qt.

1-lb. pkg. dried split peas
2 cups fully cooked lean ham, diced
1 cup diced carrots
1 medium-sized onion, chopped
2 cloves garlic, minced
2 bay leaves
½ tsp. salt
½ tsp. black pepper
5 cups boiling water
1 cup hot skim milk

1. Layer first 9 ingredients in slow cooker in order listed.

2. Cover. Cook on high 4-5 hours.

3. Stir in milk.

4. Discard bay leaves before serving.

—— PER SERVING ——

- 230 calories (30 calories from fat)
- 3.5g total fat (1g saturated, 0g trans)
- 30mg cholesterol
- 470mg sodium
- 30g total carbohydrate (11g fiber, 7g sugar)
- 20g protein
- 50%DV vitamin A
- 0%DV vitamin C
- 6%DV calcium
- 10%DV iron

Variation:

If you prefer a thinner soup, you may want to increase the milk to 1½-2 cups.

Ham 'n' Cheese Soup

Janie Steele
Moore, OK

Makes 7 servings

Prep. Time: 30 minutes
Cooking Time: 4¼-6¼ hours
Ideal slow-cooker size: 3½- or 4-qt.

2 cups potatoes, cubed (you decide whether to peel or not)
1½ cups water
1½ cups cooked ham, cubed
1 large onion, chopped
3 Tbsp. butter
3 Tbsp. flour
¼ tsp. black pepper
3 cups fat-free milk
6 ozs. low-fat shredded cheese
1 cup frozen broccoli, thawed and chopped

1. Combine all ingredients except cheese and broccoli in slow cooker.
2. Cook on low 4-6 hours.
3. Add cheese and broccoli. Stir well. Cook an additional 15 minutes, or until cheese is melted and broccoli is warm.

—— PER SERVING ——
• 250 calories • 22g total carbohydrate
  (80 calories from fat) (3g fiber, 7g sugar)
• 9g total fat • 19g protein
  (5g saturated, 0g trans) • 10%DV vitamin A
• 35mg cholesterol • 20%DV vitamin C
• 650mg sodium • 25%DV calcium
  • 8%DV iron

Tips:
You may wilt the onion in the microwave, or sauté it in a nonstick skillet, so that it is

soft and its flavor well blended when the soup is served. You may also cook the broccoli lightly in the microwave if you want to make sure it is tender when served.

Pork and Vegetable Soup

Kristi See
Weskan, KS

Makes 6 servings

Prep. Time: 30-45 minutes
Cooking Time: 3-8 hours
Ideal slow-cooker size: 3- or 4-qt.

1 lb. lean uncooked pork, *or* chicken, cut in ½" cubes
2 medium-sized carrots, cut in julienne strips
4 medium-sized green onions, chopped
1 clove garlic, finely chopped
3-4 Tbsp. low-sodium soy sauce, according to your taste preference
½ tsp. finely chopped gingerroot
⅛ tsp. black pepper
10¾-oz. can fat-free, reduced-sodium beef broth
1 cup fresh mushrooms, sliced
1 cup bean sprouts

1. Cook meat in large non-stick skillet over medium heat 8-10 minutes. Stir occasionally.
2. Mix meat and remaining ingredients, except mushrooms and bean sprouts, in slow cooker.

3. Cover. Cook on low 5-7 hours or on high 2-3 hours.
4. Stir in mushrooms and bean sprouts.
5. Cover. Cook on low 1 hour.

—— PER SERVING ——
• 230 calories • 12g total carbohydrate
  (70 calories from fat) (3g fiber, 7g sugar)
• 8g total fat • 28g protein
  (2.5g saturated, • 80%DV vitamin A
  0g trans) • 10%DV vitamin C
• 70mg cholesterol • 4%DV calcium
• 430mg sodium • 10%DV iron

Creamy Pork Stew

Betty Moore
Plano, IL

Makes 8 servings

Prep. Time: 25-30 minutes
Cooking Time: 6-8 hours
Ideal slow-cooker size: 5-qt.

2 lbs. ground pork
2 10¾-oz. cans 98% fat-free cream of mushroom soup
2 14½-oz. cans green beans with liquid
4 potatoes, diced
4 carrots, chopped
2 small onions, diced
2 10¾-oz. cans condensed vegetarian vegetable soup
2 soup cans of water
3 ribs celery, chopped
½ tsp. salt
¼ tsp. black pepper
¼ tsp. garlic powder
½ tsp. dried marjoram

1. Brown ground pork in a nonstick skillet.

2. Combine all ingredients in slow cooker.

3. Cook on low 6-8 hours.

—— PER SERVING ——

• 490 calories
(170 calories from fat)
• 19g total fat
(7g saturated, 1g trans)
• 80mg cholesterol
• 1910mg sodium

• 48g total carbohydrate
(9g fiber, 12g sugar)
• 28g protein
• 200%DV vitamin A
• 20%DV vitamin C
• 10%DV calcium
• 25%DV iron

Variations:

1. Add a can of diced tomatoes to Step 2 if you wish.

2. This recipe goes well with homemade bread.

Irish Stew

Rebecca Leichty
Harrisonburg, VA

Makes 8 servings

Prep. Time: 20 minutes
Cooking Time: 5-6 hours
Ideal slow-cooker size: 4- or 5-qt.

2 lbs. boneless lamb, cubed
1½ tsp. salt
¼ tsp. black pepper
2 medium-sized carrots, sliced
1 large onion, diced
3 medium-sized potatoes, diced
1 bay leaf
2 cups water
¼ cup dry small pearl tapioca
1 can small, tender peas

1. Grease slow cooker with fat-free cooking spray.

2. Place cubed lamb in bottom of slow cooker. Season with salt and pepper.

3. Add carrots, onion, potatoes, and bay leaf.

4. Stir in water and tapioca.

5. Cover and cook on high 1 hour. Turn down to low and cook 4-5 hours.

6. Add peas for last 30 minutes of cooking.

7. Remove bay leaf before serving.

—— PER SERVING ——

• 280 calories
(70 calories from fat)
• 8g total fat
(3g saturated, 1g trans)
• 65mg cholesterol
• 580mg sodium

• 27g total carbohydrate
(6g fiber, 5g sugar)
• 25g protein
• 80%DV vitamin A
• 20%DV vitamin C
• 4%DV calcium
• 20%DV iron

Tip:

For increased flavor, you may want to divide ½ tsp. Mrs. Dash seasoning among the layers of vegetables in Step 3.

Shrimp Chowder

Kristi See
Weskan, KS
Karen Waggoner
Joplin, MO

Makes 8 servings

Prep. Time: 20-25 minutes
Cooking Time: 3¼-4¼ hours
Ideal slow-cooker size: 5- or 6-qt.

1 lb. red potatoes cubed
2½ cups fat-free, reduced-sodium chicken broth
3 celery ribs, chopped

8 green onions, chopped
1½ lbs. medium-sized shrimp, uncooked, peeled, and deveined
½ cup sweet red bell peppers, chopped
1½ cups fat-free milk
¼ cup all-purpose flour
½ cup fat-free evaporated milk
2 Tbsp. fresh parsley, minced
½ tsp. paprika
½ tsp. Worcestershire sauce
⅛ tsp. cayenne pepper
⅛ tsp. black pepper

1. Combine potatoes, broth, celery, onions, and red bell peppers in slow cooker.

2. Cover. Cook on low 3-4 hours, or until vegetables are done to your liking.

3. Stir in 1½ cups milk and gently mash vegetables with potato masher. Leave some small chunks of potato.

4. Stir in shrimp.

5. Combine flour and evaporated milk. Mix until smooth. Gradually stir into soup mixture.

6. Cook and stir uncovered on high until thickened.

—— PER SERVING ——

• 230 calories
(15 calories from fat)
• 2g total fat
(0g saturated, 0g trans)
• 130mg cholesterol
• 240mg sodium

• 28g total carbohydrate
(4g fiber, 12g sugar)
• 25g protein
• 15%DV vitamin A
• 30%DV vitamin C
• 20%DV calcium
• 20%DV iron

Tip:

This chowder is even better the next day after the flavors have melded overnight.

Corn and Shrimp Chowder

Naomi E. Fast
Hesston, KS

Makes 6 servings

Prep. Time: 20 minutes
Cooking Time: 3-4 hours
Ideal slow-cooker size: 3½-qt.

3 slices lean turkey bacon, diced
1 cup chopped onions
2 cups diced, unpeeled red potatoes
2 10-oz. pkgs. frozen corn
1 tsp. Worcestershire sauce
½ tsp. paprika
½ tsp. salt
⅛ tsp. black pepper
2 cups water
2 Tbsp. butter
2 6-oz. cans shrimp, drained
12-oz. can fat-free evaporated milk
chopped chives

1. Brown bacon in nonstick skillet until lightly crisp. Add onions to drippings and sauté until transparent. Using slotted spoon, transfer bacon and onions to slow cooker.

2. Add remaining ingredients to cooker except shrimp, milk, and chives.

3. Cover. Cook on low 3-4 hours, adding shrimp, milk, and chives 30 minutes before end of cooking time.

—— PER SERVING ——
- 310 calories
  (70 calories from fat)
- 7g total fat
  (3g saturated, 0g trans)
- 115mg cholesterol
- 480mg sodium
- 41g total carbohydrate
  (4g fiber, 11g sugar)
- 23g protein
- 10%DV vitamin A
- 20%DV vitamin C
- 25%DV calcium
- 15%DV iron

Note:
I learned to make this recipe in a 7th-grade home economics class. It made an impression on my father who liked seafood very much. The recipe calls only for canned shrimp, but I often increase its taste appeal with extra cooked shrimp.

Creamy Salmon Chowder

Diane Shetler
Hyde Park, MA

Makes 5 servings

Prep. Time: 15-20 minutes
Cooking Time: 3¾-8¼ hours
Ideal slow-cooker size: 3½-qt.

2 cups fat-free chicken broth
2 cups water
10-oz. pkg. frozen corn
1 cup celery, chopped
½ cup onions, chopped
¾ cup dry wheat berries
8-oz. pkg. fat-free cream cheese, cut into cubes
16-oz. can salmon, drained, skin and bones removed, and fish coarsely flaked
1 Tbsp. dill weed

1. Combine chicken broth, water, corn, celery, onions, and wheat berries in slow cooker.

2. Cover. Cook on low 6-8 hours or on high 3½-4 hours.

3. Turn cooker to high. Add cheese, stirring until melted.

4. Stir in salmon and dill.

5. Cover. Cook 10 minutes longer.

—— PER SERVING ——
- 350 calories
  (60 calories from fat)
- 7g total fat
  (2g saturated, 0g trans)
- 40mg cholesterol
- 790mg sodium
- 42g total carbohydrate
  (6g fiber, 3g sugar)
- 34g protein
- 10%DV vitamin A
- 10%DV vitamin C
- 35%DV calcium
- 15%DV iron

Vegetable Salmon Chowder

Esther J. Yoder
Hartville, OH

Makes 8 servings

Prep. Time: 25-30 minutes
Cooking Time: 3-4 hours
Ideal slow-cooker size: 3½-qt.

1½ cups potatoes, cubed
1 cup celery, diced
½ cup onions, diced
2 Tbsp. fresh parsley, *or*
   1 Tbsp. dried parsley
½ tsp. salt
¼ tsp. black pepper
water to cover
16-oz. can pink salmon
4 cups skim milk
2 tsp. lemon juice
2 Tbsp. red bell peppers,
   finely cut
2 Tbsp. carrots, finely
   shredded
½ cup instant potatoes

1. Combine cubed potatoes, celery, onions, parsley, salt, pepper, and water to cover in slow cooker.
2. Cook on high 2-3 hours, or until soft. Add a bit more water if needed.
3. Add salmon, milk, lemon juice, red peppers, carrots, and instant potatoes.
4. Heat 1 hour more until very hot.

—— PER SERVING ——
• 140 calories
   (20 calories from fat)
• 2g total fat
   (0g saturated, 0g trans)
• 30mg cholesterol
• 115mg sodium
• 15g total carbohydrate
   (1g fiber, 7g sugar)
• 16g protein
• 10%DV vitamin A
• 10%DV vitamin C
• 15%DV calcium
• 4%DV iron

Variations:
1. If you enjoy garlic, add a tablespoon or two of it, minced, to Step 1.
2. If you like a thicker chowder, and your diet allows, increase the instant potatoes in Step 3 to ¾-1 cup.

Smoked Salmon Corn Chowder

Sandra Haverstraw
Hummelstown, PA

Makes 8-10 servings

Prep. Time: 30 minutes
Cooking Time: 3½-4½ hours
Ideal slow cooker size: 5- or 6-qt.

1 large onion, chopped
½ cup chopped celery
⅓ cup chopped red bell
   pepper
2 tsp. butter
3 cups peeled, cubed
   potatoes, cooked
2 cups low-sodium, fat-free
   chicken broth
15-oz. can creamed corn
16-oz. bag frozen corn
½ tsp. ground black pepper
2 tsp. dried dill weed
2 oz. smoked salmon,
   chopped
1 cup fat-free milk
1 cup shredded low-fat
   cheddar cheese
½ tsp. hot pepper sauce,
   optional
1 cup fat-free sour cream,
   optional

1. In medium skillet, sauté onion, celery, and red bell pepper in butter until soft.
2. Mix sautéed vegetables, cooked potatoes, chicken broth, creamed corn, frozen corn, pepper, dill, and smoked salmon in slow cooker.
3. Cover. Cook on low 3-4 hours.
4. Add milk and cheese, and hot pepper sauce and sour cream if you wish, to Chowder in slow cooker.
5. Cover and continue cooking 25-30 minutes, or until cheese has melted and chowder is fully heated.

—— PER SERVING ——
• 180 calories
   (25 calories from fat)
• 3g total fat
   (1g saturated, 0g trans)
• 15mg cholesterol
• 220mg sodium
• 30g total carbohydrate
   (3g fiber, 6g sugar)
• 10g protein
• 10%DV vitamin A
• 25%DV vitamin C
• 10%DV calcium
• 4%DV iron

If your recipe turns out to have too much liquid, remove the cover and use the High setting for about 45 minutes.
Esther Porter, Minneapolis, MN

Manhattan Clam Chowder

Joyce Slaymaker
Strasburg, PA
Louise Stackhouse
Benton, PA

Makes 8 servings

Prep. Time: 30 minutes
Cooking Time: 4-5 hours
Ideal slow-cooker size: 3½-qt.

¼ lb. lean turkey bacon, diced and browned
1 large onion, chopped
2 carrots, thinly sliced
3 ribs celery, sliced
1 Tbsp. dried parsley flakes
1-lb. 12-oz. can low-sodium tomatoes
½ tsp. salt
2 whole peppercorns
1 bay leaf
1½ tsp. dried crushed thyme
3 medium-sized potatoes, cubed
3 8-oz. cans clams with liquid

1. Combine all ingredients, except clams, in slow cooker.
2. Cover. Cook on low 4-5 hours, or until vegetables are done to your liking.
3. Twenty minutes before end of cooking time, stir in clams

—— PER SERVING ——
• 260 calories
  (45 calories from fat)
• 5g total fat
  (1g saturated, 0g trans)
• 70mg cholesterol
• 710mg sodium
• 27g total carbohydrate
  (4g fiber, 5g sugar)
• 27g protein
• 80%DV vitamin A
• 40%DV vitamin C
• 20%DV calcium
• 100%DV iron

Tasty Clam Chowder

Jean H. Robinson
Cinnaminson, NJ

Makes 8 servings

Prep. Time: 30 minutes
Cooking Time: 2½ hours
Ideal slow-cooker size: 5-qt.

2 1-lb. cans low-fat, low-sodium chicken broth
3 large potatoes, peeled and diced finely
2 large onions, chopped finely
1-lb. can creamed corn
1 carrot, chopped finely
1 dozen littleneck clams, *or* 3 6-oz. cans minced clams
2 cups low-fat milk
¼ tsp. black pepper
¼ tsp. salt
2 Tbsp. fresh parsley, chopped
6 slices bacon, well cooked, drained and crumbled, *optional*

1. Pour broth into slow cooker.
2. Add potatoes, onions, creamed corn, and carrot.
3. Cover. Cook on high 1 hour. Stir. Cook on high another hour.
4. Using a potato masher, mash potatoes coarsely to thicken soup.
5. Add clams, milk, black pepper, salt, and parsley.
6. Cover. Cook on high 20 minutes.
7. Garnish with crumbled bacon, if desired.

—— PER SERVING ——
• 210 calories
  (30 calories from fat)
• 3.5g total fat (1.5g saturated, 0g trans)
• 15mg cholesterol
• 660mg sodium
• 33g total carbohydrate
  (3g fiber, 8g sugar)
• 14g protein
• 40%DV vitamin A
• 20%DV vitamin C
• 10%DV calcium
• 15%DV iron

Variation:

If your diet permits, you may want to increase the salt to ½ tsp.

Hot & Sour Soup

Judy Govotsos
Frederick, MD

Makes 4 servings

Prep. Time: 20 minutes
Cooking Time: 4½-6 hours
Ideal slow-cooker size: 3½-qt.

4 cups fat-free, low-sodium chicken broth
8-oz. can sliced bamboo shoots, drained
1 carrot, julienned
8-oz. can water chestnuts, drained and sliced
3 Tbsp. quick-cooking tapioca
6-oz. can sliced mushrooms, drained
1 Tbsp. vinegar, *or* rice wine vinegar
1 Tbsp. light soy sauce
1 tsp. sugar
¼ tsp. black pepper
¼-½ tsp. red pepper flakes, according to your taste preference
8-oz. pkg. frozen, peeled, and deveined shrimp, *optional*
4 ozs. firm tofu, drained and cubed
1 egg, beaten

1. Combine all ingredients, except shrimp, tofu, and egg in slow cooker.
2. Cover. Cook on low 3¾-5 hours.
3. Add shrimp and tofu.
4. Cover. Cook 45-60 minutes.
5. Pour egg into the soup in a thin stream. Stir the soup gently until the egg forms fine shreds instead of clumps.

— PER SERVING —
• 240 calories   • 24g total carbohydrate
  (45 calories from fat)   (4g fiber, 4g sugar)
• 5g total fat   • 26g protein
  (1g saturated, 0g trans) • 80%DV vitamin A
• 135mg cholesterol   • 0%DV vitamin C
• 600mg sodium   • 25%DV calcium
     • 30%DV iron

Variation:
You may want to stir in ½ tsp. garlic salt, if your diet permits, in Step 1.

Egg Drop Soup

Shirley Unternahrer Hinh
Wayland, IA

Makes 8 servings

Prep. Time: 30 minutes
Cooking Time: 1 hour
Ideal slow-cooker size: 3½-qt.

2 14½-oz. cans fat-free, low-sodium chicken broth
1 qt. water
2 Tbsp. fish sauce
¼ tsp. salt
4 Tbsp. cornstarch
1 cup cold water
2 eggs, beaten
1 chopped green onion
¼ tsp. black pepper

1. Combine broth and water in large saucepan.
2. Add fish sauce and salt. Bring to boil.
3. Mix cornstarch into cold water until smooth. Add to soup. Bring to boil while stirring. Remove from heat.
4. Pour beaten eggs into thickened broth, but do not stir. Instead, pull fork through soup with 2 strokes.
5. Transfer to slow cooker. Add green onions and pepper and pull through soup with fork.
6. Cover. Cook on low 1 hour. Keep warm in cooker.
7. Eat plain or with rice.

— PER SERVING —
• 50 calories   • 5g total carbohydrate
  (10 calories from fat)   (0g fiber, 1g sugar)
• 1g total fat   • 4g protein
  (0g saturated, 0g trans) • 0%DV vitamin A
• 45mg cholesterol   • 0%DV vitamin C
• 510mg sodium   • 0%DV calcium
     • 6%DV iron

Note:
One day when the kids were sledding, I surprised them with something other than hot cocoa when they came in. "Mmmmm," was all I heard, and, "This tastes great!" "You're the best, Mom!" They finished all the egg drop soup and wondered if I'd make more.

Greek Lentil Soup

Andrea Cunningham
Arlington, KS

Makes 8 servings

Prep. Time: 15-20 minutes
Cooking Time: 6½-8½ hours
Ideal slow-cooker size: 3½-qt.

1½ cups dried lentils
1½ qts. water
1 medium-sized onion,
  chopped
1 carrot, peeled and grated
1 rib celery, chopped
3 Tbsp. olive oil
1 bay leaf
2 cloves garlic, minced
1 tsp. salt
½ tsp. dried oregano
1 cube low-sodium beef
  bouillon
½ cup tomato sauce
3 Tbsp. red wine vinegar

1. Place lentils and water in slow cooker.
2. In large skillet, sauté onion, carrot, and celery in oil until limp and glazed. Add to slow cooker.
3. Add bay leaf, garlic, salt, oregano, and bouillon cube to cooker.
4. Cover. Cook on low 6-8 hours.
5. Add tomato sauce and vinegar. Stir well.
6. Cover. Cook on high 30 minutes to blend flavors. Remove bay leaf before serving.

—— PER SERVING ——
• 180 calories
  (50 calories from fat)
• 6g total fat
  (1g saturated, 0g trans)
• 0mg cholesterol
• 470mg sodium
• 25g total carbohydrate
  (9g fiber, 4g sugar)
• 10g protein
• 20%DV vitamin A
• 0%DV vitamin C
• 4%DV calcium
• 20%DV iron

Variations:
If you prefer a little more zing, you may want to increase the dried oregano to 1 tsp. and add ½-1 tsp. ground cumin in Step 3.

Sweet Potato Lentil Stew

Mrs. Carolyn Baer
Conrath, WI

Makes 6 servings

Prep. Time: 30 minutes
Cooking 5-6 hours
Ideal slow-cooker size: 4-qt.

4 cups fat-free vegetable
  broth
3 cups (about 1¼ lbs.)
  sweet potatoes, peeled
  and cubed
1½ cups lentils, rinsed
3 medium-sized carrots,
  cut into ½" pieces
1 medium-sized onion,
  chopped
4 garlic cloves, minced
½ tsp. ground cumin
¼ tsp. ground ginger
¼ tsp. cayenne pepper
¼ cup minced fresh
  cilantro *or* parsley
¼ tsp. salt

1. Combine first nine ingredients in slow cooker.
2. Cook on low 5-6 hours or just until vegetables are tender.
3. Stir in cilantro and salt just before serving.

—— PER SERVING ——
• 280 calories
  (5 calories from fat)
• 1g total fat
  (0g saturated, 0g trans)
• 0mg cholesterol
• 580mg sodium
• 54g total carbohydrate
  (19g fiber, 12g sugar)
• 16g protein
• 300%DV vitamin A
• 25%DV vitamin C
• 8%DV calcium
• 30%DV iron

Variations:
For added flavor, you may want to increase cumin to ¾-1 tsp. and ginger to ½ tsp. And if your diet allows, you may also stir in ⅓ cup raisins, ¼ cup chopped nuts, and ¼ cup grated coconut just before serving.

Lentil-Tomato Stew

Marci Baum
Annville, PA

Makes 8 servings

Prep. Time: 20 minutes
Cooking Time: 4-12 hours
Ideal slow-cooker size: 6-qt.

3 cups water
28-oz. can low-sodium
  peeled Italian tomatoes,
  undrained
6-oz. can low-sodium
  tomato paste
½ cup dry red wine
¾ tsp. dried basil
¾ tsp. dried thyme

½ tsp. crushed red pepper
1 lb. dried lentils, rinsed
and drained with any
stones removed
1 large onion, chopped
4 medium-sized carrots,
cut in ½" rounds
4 medium-sized celery
ribs, cut into ½" slices
3 garlic cloves, minced
1 tsp. salt
fresh basil *or* parsley,
chopped, for garnish

1. Combine water, tomatoes
with juice, tomato paste,
red wine, basil, thyme, and
crushed red pepper in slow
cooker.
2. Break-up tomatoes with
a wooden spoon and stir to
blend them and the paste into
the mixture.
3. Add lentils, onion,
carrots, celery, and garlic.
4. Cover. Cook on low
10-12 hours or on high 4-5
hours.
5. Stir in salt.
6. Serve in bowls sprinkled
with chopped basil or parsley.

— PER SERVING —
- 250 calories
  (10 calories from fat)
- 1g total fat
  (0g saturated, 0g trans)
- 0mg cholesterol
- 530mg sodium
- 44g total carbohydrate
  (16g fiber, 7g sugar)
- 17g protein
- 20%DV vitamin A
- 20%DV vitamin C
- 8%DV calcium
- 40%DV iron

Lentil Soup with Ham

Rhonda L. Burgoon
Collingswood, NJ

Makes 8 servings

Prep. Time: 30 minutes
Cooking Time: 7-9 hours
Ideal slow-cooker size: 4-qt.

1 cup onions, chopped
3 cloves garlic, minced
5 cups fat-free, low-sodium
chicken broth
1 cup dried lentils
½ cup carrots, chopped
2 bay leaves
3 cups Swiss chard, chopped
1½ cups potatoes, chopped
1 cup ham, chopped
14½-oz. can low-sodium
diced tomatoes
1 tsp. dried basil
½ tsp. dried thyme
½ tsp. black pepper
3 Tbsp. fresh parsley,
chopped

1. Combine all ingredients
except fresh parsley in slow
cooker.
2. Cover. Cook on low 7-9
hours.
3. Stir in fresh parsley and
serve.

— PER SERVING —
- 200 calories
  (30 calories from fat)
- 3.5g total fat
  (1g saturated, 0g trans)
- 15mg cholesterol
- 290mg sodium
- 25g total carbohydrate
  (10g fiber, 5g sugar)
- 17g protein
- 50%DV vitamin A
- 20%DV vitamin C
- 8%DV calcium
- 25%DV iron

"Mom's Favorite" Vegetable Soup

Wendy McPhillips
Wichita, KS

Makes 5 servings

Prep. Time: 20 minutes
Cooking Time: 6-8 hours
Ideal slow-cooker size: 4-qt.

½ cup dry pearl barley
14½-oz. can low-sodium
diced tomatoes
1 cup frozen corn
1 cup frozen peas
4 carrots, peeled and sliced
1 cup frozen green beans
water to cover
5 cubes low-sodium beef
bouillon
5 cubes low-sodium
chicken bouillon
½ tsp. salt
½ tsp. black pepper
½ tsp. dried basil
1 tsp. fresh thyme
½ tsp. fresh dill
1 tsp. fresh parsley

1. Combine all ingredients
in slow cooker, except fresh
herbs.
2. Cover. Cook on low 6-8
hours, or until barley and
vegetables are tender.
3. Just before serving, stir in
fresh thyme, dill, and parsley.

— PER SERVING —
- 190 calories
  (10 calories from fat)
- 1.5g total fat
  (0g saturated, 0g trans)
- 0mg cholesterol
- 2340mg sodium
- 40g total carbohydrate
  (9g fiber, 10g sugar)
- 7g protein
- 200%DV vitamin A
- 20%DV vitamin C
- 10%DV calcium
- 10%DV iron

Vegetable Minestrone

Marcia S. Myer
Manheim, PA

Makes 12 servings

Prep. Time: 20 minutes
Cooking Time: 6¼-8¼ hours
Ideal slow-cooker size: 5-qt.

4 cups low-fat, low-sodium chicken broth
4 cups low-sodium tomato juice
1 Tbsp. dried basil
1 tsp. salt
½ tsp. dried oregano
¼ tsp. black pepper
2 medium-sized carrots, sliced
2 ribs celery, chopped
1 medium-sized onion, chopped
1 cup fresh mushrooms, sliced
2 cloves garlic, crushed
28-oz. can low-sodium diced tomatoes
1½ cups uncooked rotini pasta

1. Combine all ingredients except pasta in slow cooker.
2. Cover. Cook on low 6-8 hours.
3. Add pasta.
4. Cover. Cook on high 15-20 minutes.

—— PER SERVING ——
• 70 calories
  (0 calories from fat)
• 0g total fat
  (0g saturated, 0g trans)
• 0mg cholesterol
• 520mg sodium
• 13g total carbohydrate
  (3g fiber, 6g sugar)
• 5g protein
• 50%DV vitamin A
• 20%DV vitamin C
• 8%DV calcium
• 10%DV iron

Variations:
1. Sprinkle each serving with fat-free Parmesan cheese if you like.
2. If your diet allows, you may want to increase the salt to 2 tsp.

Naturally Colorful Vegetable Soup

Darla Sathre
Baxter, MN

Makes 8 servings

Prep. Time: 20-30 minutes
Cooking Time: 4-6 hours
Ideal slow cooker size: 4-qt.

15-oz. can low-sodium whole-kernel corn, undrained
16-oz. can kidney beans, undrained
14½-oz. can low-sodium diced tomatoes with juice
15-oz. can low-sodium tomato sauce
½ lb. baby carrots, halved lengthwise
1 onion, chopped
6 cloves garlic, thinly sliced
2 tsp. Italian seasoning
1 tsp. dried marjoram
1 tsp. dried basil
2 cups frozen peas

1. Put all ingredients except peas into slow cooker. Stir well.
2. Cover. Cook on high 1-2 hours. Then cook on low 3-4 hours, or until carrots and onions are as tender as you like them.
3. Twenty minutes before end of cooking time stir in peas.

—— PER SERVING ——
• 180 calories
  (10 calories from fat)
• 1g total fat
  (0g saturated, 0g trans)
• 0mg cholesterol
• 290mg sodium
• 36g total carbohydrate
  (8g fiber, 11g sugar)
• 8g protein
• 110%DV vitamin A
• 35%DV vitamin C
• 8%DV calcium
• 15%DV iron

Adirondack Soup

Joanne Kennedy
Plattsburgh, NY

Makes 12 servings

Prep. Time: 20-30 minutes
Cooking Time: 7 hours
Ideal slow-cooker size: 6-qt.

2 qts. low-sodium stewed
    tomatoes
3 1-lb. cans low-sodium
    vegetable broth
3 cups water
5 large carrots, chopped
1 large onion, chopped
4 celery ribs, chopped
2 tsp. dried basil
1 tsp. dried parsley
1 tsp. black pepper
2 dashes Tabasco sauce
3 cups frozen mixed
    vegetables, thawed

1. Combine all ingredients
except frozen vegetables in
slow cooker.
2. Cover. Cook 6 hours on
low.
3. Add vegetables.
4. Cover. Cook 1 hour more
on low.

—— PER SERVING ——
• 110 calories   • 24g total carbohydrate
  (0 calories from fat)   (7g fiber, 13g sugar)
• 0g total fat   • 4g protein
  (0g saturated, 0g trans) • 150%DV vitamin A
• 0mg cholesterol   • 20%DV vitamin C
• 450mg sodium   • 10%DV calcium
                        • 15%DV iron

Tomato Green Bean Soup

Colleen Heatwole
Burton, MI

Makes 8 servings

Prep. Time: 30 minutes
Cooking Time: 6-8 hours
Ideal slow-cooker size: 4-qt.

1 cup onions, chopped
1 cup carrots, chopped
6 cups low-fat, reduced-
    sodium chicken broth
1 lb. fresh green beans, cut
    in 1" pieces
1 clove garlic, minced
3 cups fresh tomatoes,
    diced
1 tsp. dried basil
½ tsp. salt
¼ tsp. black pepper

1. Combine all ingredients
in slow cooker.
2. Cover. Cook on low 6-8
hours.

—— PER SERVING ——
• 70 calories   • 10g total carbohydrate
  (0 calories from fat)   (4g fiber, 6g sugar)
• 0g total fat   • 6g protein
  (0g saturated, 0g trans) • 80%DV vitamin A
• 0mg cholesterol   • 10%DV vitamin C
• 290mg sodium   • 6%DV calcium
                        • 10%DV iron

Tips:

This recipe is best with
fresh green beans and
tomatoes, but if they are
not in season you may use
canned tomatoes and canned
or frozen green beans—or
corn. Remember, of course,
that canned vegetables are
likely to include salt.

Quick-to-Mix Vegetable Soup

Cyndie Marrara
Port Matilda, PA

Makes 4 servings

Prep. Time: 10 minutes
Cooking Time: 3-6 hours
Ideal slow-cooker size: 2-qt.

2 cups frozen vegetables of
    your choice, thawed
¾ cup fat-free, low-sodium
    beef gravy
16-oz. can diced tomatoes
¼ cup dry red wine
½ cup diced onions
1 tsp. garlic, crushed
¼ tsp. black pepper
½ cup water

1. Combine all ingredients
in slow cooker.
2. Cover. Cook on high 3
hours or on low 5-6 hours.

—— PER SERVING ——
• 130 calories   • 26g total carbohydrate
  (5 calories from fat)   (6g fiber, 4g sugar)
• 0.5g total fat   • 5g protein
  (0g saturated, 0g trans) • 80%DV vitamin A
• 5mg cholesterol   • 10%DV vitamin C
• 600mg sodium   • 10%DV calcium
                        • 8%DV iron

Variation:

If your diet permits, you
may want to add ¼-½ tsp. salt
to Step 1.

Quick & Healthy Vegetable Soup

Dawn Day
Westminster, CA

Makes 8 servings

Prep. Time: 20 minutes
Cooking Time: 4-7 hours
Ideal slow-cooker size: 4-qt.

4 cups vegetable, *or* chicken, broth
1 cup frozen corn
½ cup carrots, chopped
½ cup green beans
12-oz. can chopped tomatoes
½ cup onions, chopped
2 cloves garlic, minced
½ tsp. dried thyme
½ tsp. dried basil
¼ tsp. lemon pepper
1 cup zucchini, cubed
1 cup broccoli, chopped
½ cup frozen peas

1. Combine all ingredients except zucchini, broccoli, and peas in slow cooker.
2. Cover. Cook on low 6 hours or on high 3 hours.
3. Stir in zucchini and broccoli. Cook an additional 45 minutes on high.
4. Stir in peas. Cook an additional 15 minutes on high.

—— PER SERVING ——
• 70 calories
(0 calories from fat)
• 0g total fat
(0g saturated, 0g trans)
• 0mg cholesterol
• 470mg sodium
• 14g total carbohydrate
(3g fiber, 6g sugar)
• 3g protein
• 80%DV vitamin A
• 20%DV vitamin C
• 6%DV calcium
• 6%DV iron

Fresh Tomato Soup

Rebecca Leichty
Harrisonburg, VA

Makes 6 servings

Prep. Time: 20-25 minutes
Cooking Time: 3-4 hours
Ideal slow-cooker size: 3½- or 4-qt.

5 cups ripe tomatoes, diced (your choice about whether or not to peel them)
1 Tbsp. tomato paste
4 cups salt-free chicken broth
1 carrot, grated
1 onion, minced
1 Tbsp. garlic, minced
1 tsp. dried basil
pepper to taste
2 Tbsp. lemon juice
1 bay leaf

1. Combine all ingredients in a slow cooker.
2. Cook on low for 3-4 hours. Stir once while cooking.
3. Remove bay leaf before serving.

—— PER SERVING ——
• 80 calories
(5 calories from fat)
• 0.5g total fat
(0g saturated, 0g trans)
• 0mg cholesterol
• 135mg sodium
• 14g total carbohydrate
(3g fiber, 7g sugar)
• 6g protein
• 40%DV vitamin A
• 40%DV vitamin C
• 4%DV calcium
• 15%DV iron

Variation:

To thicken the soup slightly, and if your diet allows, you may want to add a full 6-oz. can of tomato paste instead of just 1 Tbsp.

Mexican Tomato-Corn Soup

Jeanne Heyerly
Chenoa, IL

Makes 8 servings

Prep. Time: 25 minutes
Cooking Time: 4-5 hours
Ideal slow-cooker size: 4-qt.

1 medium-sized onion, diced
1 medium-sized green bell pepper, diced
1 clove garlic, minced
1 cup carrots, diced
14½-oz. can low-sodium diced Italian tomatoes
2½ cups low-sodium tomato juice
1 qt. low-fat, low-sodium chicken broth
3 cups corn, frozen and thawed, *or* canned
4-oz. can chopped chilies, undrained
1 tsp. chili powder
1½ tsp. ground cumin
dash cayenne powder

1. Combine all ingredients in slow cooker.
2. Cover. Cook on low 4-5 hours.

—— PER SERVING ——
• 100 calories
(10 calories from fat)
• 1g total fat
(0g saturated, 0g trans)
• 0mg cholesterol
• 115mg sodium
• 20g total carbohydrate
(4g fiber, 9g sugar)
• 6g protein
• 50%DV vitamin A
• 30%DV vitamin C
• 4%DV calcium
• 10%DV iron

Tips:

Garnish individual servings with cilantro leaves, corn or tortilla chips, and/or low-fat shredded sharp cheddar cheese, if your diet permits.

Fresh or Frozen Corn Chowder

Janie Steele
Moore, OK

Makes 7 servings

Prep. Time: 30-35 minutes
Cooking Time: 5¼-6½ hours
Ideal slow-cooker size: 3½- or 4-qt.

4 large ears of corn, cut off cob, *or* 1-lb. bag frozen whole-kernel corn, thawed
1 large onion, chopped
1 celery rib, chopped
1 Tbsp. butter
1½ cups potatoes, cubed
1 cup water
2 tsp. chicken bouillon granules
¼ tsp. dried thyme
¼ tsp. pepper
6 Tbsp. flour
3 cups fat-free milk

1. Combine all ingredients in slow cooker except flour and milk.
2. Cook on low 5-6 hours, or until potatoes are tender.
3. Mix flour and milk until smooth. Stir into corn chowder slowly until thickened. Cook 15-30 minutes more.

— PER SERVING —
- 180 calories (25 calories from fat)
- 2.5g total fat (1.5g saturated, 0g trans)
- 5mg cholesterol
- 190mg sodium
- 34g total carbohydrate (3g fiber, 10g sugar)
- 8g protein
- 8%DV vitamin A
- 10%DV vitamin C
- 15%DV calcium
- 6%DV iron

Variation:

If your diet permits, you may want to add ½ tsp. salt to Step 1.

Corn Chowder

Mary Rogers
Waseca, MN

Makes 12 servings

Prep. Time: 30-35 minutes
Cooking Time: 2 hours
Ideal slow-cooker size: 4-qt.

½ lb. lean turkey bacon
4 cups diced potatoes
2 cups chopped onions
2 cups fat-free sour cream
1½ cups fat-free milk
2 10¾-oz. cans fat-free, low-sodium cream of chicken soup
2 15¼-oz. cans fat-free, low-sodium whole-kernel corn, undrained

1. Cut bacon into 1" pieces. Cook for 5 minutes in large nonstick skillet, doing it in two batches so all the pieces brown.
2. Add potatoes and onions and a bit of water to skillet. Cook 15-20 minutes, until vegetables are tender, stirring occasionally. Drain. Transfer to slow cooker.

3. Combine sour cream, milk, chicken soup, and corn. Place in slow cooker.
4. Cover. Cook on low 2 hours.

— PER SERVING —
- 260 calories (70 calories from fat)
- 8 total fat (2.5g saturated, 0g trans)
- 25mg cholesterol
- 840mg sodium
- 37g total carbohydrate (3g fiber, 10g sugar)
- 11g protein
- 2%DV vitamin A
- 20%DV vitamin C
- 15%DV calcium
- 10%DV iron

Tips:

If you'll be gone for most of the day, you may want to use a different procedure from the one above. After Step 1, place bacon, potatoes, onions, 2 inches of water, the 2 cans of soup and the 2 cans of corn into the slow cooker. Cook on low 6-8 hours, or until the vegetables are done to your liking. Thirty minutes before serving, stir in sour cream and milk and continue cooking on low. Serve when soup is heated through and steaming.

Double Corn and Cheddar Chowder

Maryann Markano
Wilmington, DE

Makes 6 servings

Prep. Time: 25 minutes
Cooking Time: 4½ hours
Ideal slow-cooker size: 4-qt.

1 Tbsp. butter
1 cup onions, chopped
2 Tbsp. all-purpose flour
2½ cups fat-free, reduced-sodium chicken broth
16-oz. can creamed corn
1 cup frozen corn
½ cup red bell peppers, finely chopped
½ tsp. hot pepper sauce
¾ cup shredded, reduced-fat, sharp cheddar cheese
freshly ground pepper to taste, *optional*

1. In saucepan on top of stove, melt butter. Stir in onions and sauté until wilted. Stir in flour. When well mixed, whisk in chicken broth. Stir frequently over medium heat until broth is thickened.

2. Pour into slow cooker. Mix in remaining ingredients except cheese and pepper.

3. Cook on low 4½ hours. About an hour before the end of cooking time, stir in cheese until melted and well blended and pepper.

—— PER SERVING ——
- 200 calories
  (60 calories from fat)
- 7g total fat
  (4g saturated, 0g trans)
- 20mg cholesterol
- 530mg sodium
- 25g total carbohydrate
  (2g fiber, 5g sugar)
- 12g protein
- 20%DV vitamin A
- 20%DV vitamin C
- 20%DV calcium
- 8%DV iron

Variation:

You may also add a cup of cooked white or brown rice during the last hour if you like.

Potato Cheddar-Cheese Soup

Marla Folkerts
Holland, OH

Makes 4 servings

Prep. Time: 25 minutes
Cooking Time: 4-9 hours
Ideal slow-cooker size: 4-qt.

6-10 potatoes, peeled and cubed
½ cup fat-free, low-sodium vegetable broth
1 cup water
1 large onion, finely chopped
½ tsp. garlic powder
⅛ tsp. white pepper
2 cups fat-free milk, heated
1 cup shredded fat-free sharp, *or* extra sharp, cheddar cheese
paprika

1. Place potatoes, broth, water, onions, and garlic powder in slow cooker.

2. Cover. Cook on low 7-9 hours, or on high 4-6 hours.

3. Mash potatoes, leaving them a bit lumpy. Stir in pepper and milk a little at a time. Add cheese. Cook until cheese has melted, about 5 minutes. Add more milk if you'd like a thinner or creamier soup.

4. Garnish each serving with paprika.

—— PER SERVING ——
- 510 calories
  (5 calories from fat)
- 0.5g total fat
  (0g saturated,
  0g trans)
- 5mg cholesterol
- 450mg sodium
- 104g total
  carbohydrate (12g
  fiber, 12g sugar)
- 24g protein
- 10%DV vitamin A
- 60%DV vitamin C
- 50%DV calcium
- 25%DV iron

164

Cream Cheese Potato Soup

Jean H. Robinson
Cinnaminson, NJ

Makes 6 servings

Prep. Time: 20-25 minutes
Cooking Time: 3-4 hours
Ideal slow-cooker size: 3½-qt.

3 cups water
1 cup ham, diced
5 medium-sized potatoes, diced fine
8-oz. pkg. fat-free cream cheese, cubed
half an onion, chopped
1 tsp. garlic salt
½ tsp. black pepper
½ tsp. dill weed

1. Combine all ingredients in slow cooker.
2. Cover. Cook on high 3-4 hours, stirring occasionally, until potatoes are as soft as you like them.
3. Turn to low until ready to serve.

— PER SERVING —
• 220 calories
  (25 calories from fat)
• 3g total fat
  (1g saturated, 0g trans)
• 25mg cholesterol
• 400mg sodium
• 34g total carbohydrate
  (4g fiber, 2g sugar)
• 16g protein
• 0%DV vitamin A
• 30%DV vitamin C
• 10%DV calcium
• 10%DV iron

Cream of Potato Soup

Dale Peterson
Rapid City, SD

Makes 8 servings

Prep. Time: 25 minutes
Cooking Time: 7-9 hours
Ideal slow-cooker size: 6- or 7-qt.

4 cups water
1 cup flour
6 large potatoes, peeled and cubed
1 large onion, chopped
2 large carrots, chopped
½ cup celery, diced
2 leeks, chopped
4 Tbsp. butter
4 chicken bouillon cubes
1 Tbsp. fresh, *or* dried, parsley
1 Tbsp. fresh, *or* dried, chives
1 tsp. garlic powder
1 tsp. lemon pepper seasoning
13-oz. can evaporated skim milk
4 ozs. fat-free sour cream
8 ozs. low-fat, low-sodium cheese spread

1. Mix flour and water together in slow cooker.
2. Stir in all remaining ingredients except evaporated milk, sour cream, and cheese spread.
3. Cook on low 7-9 hours.
4. Add evaporated milk, sour cream, and cheese spread during last hour.
5. When cheese is melted, soup is ready to eat.

— PER SERVING —
• 360 calories
  (80 calories from fat)
• 9g total fat
  (5g saturated, 0g trans)
• 30mg cholesterol
• 810mg sodium
• 56g total carbohydrate
  (5g fiber, 12g sugar)
• 17g protein
• 80%DV vitamin A
• 30%DV vitamin C
• 40%DV calcium
• 15%DV iron

Potato Soup

Colleen Heatwole
Burton, MI

Makes 6 servings

Prep. Time: 20-25 minutes
Cooking Time: 3-9 hours
Ideal slow-cooker size: 3½-qt.

6 potatoes, peeled and cubed
2 onions, chopped
1 medium-sized carrot, sliced
1 rib celery, sliced
4 cubes low-sodium chicken, *or* vegetable, bouillon
4 cups water
1 Tbsp. parsley flakes
¼ tsp. black pepper
½ tsp. salt, *optional*
13-oz. can fat-free evaporated milk

1. Combine all ingredients, except evaporated milk in slow cooker.
2. Cover. Cook on high 3-4 hours or low 7-9 hours.
3. Stir in evaporated milk during last hour.

— PER SERVING —
• 240 calories
  (5 calories from fat)
• 0.5g total fat
  (0g saturated, 0g trans)
• 5mg cholesterol
• 1090mg sodium
• 50g total Carbohydrate
  (6g fiber, 12g sugar)
• 10g protein
• 50%DV vitamin A
• 40%DV vitamin C
• 20%DV calcium
• 10%DV iron

Snowmobile Soup

Jane Geigley
Honey Brook, PA

Makes 6 servings

Prep. Time: 20 minutes
Cooking Time: 3-4 hours
Ideal slow-cooker size: 4- to 6-qt.

⅓ lb. 95% lean ground beef
1 small onion, chopped
5 large potatoes, julienned,
   skins on
16-oz. can low-sodium,
   low-fat cream of
   mushroom soup
1 soup can fat-free milk
1 lb. shredded fat-free
   cheddar cheese
¾ tsp. salt
¼ tsp. pepper

1. Brown beef in skillet.
Stir frequently to break up
clumps. When meat is no
longer pink, drain and place
in slow cooker.
2. Sauté onion in drippings
in skillet until softened.
3. Stir onions, potatoes,
soup, milk, cheese, salt, and
pepper into meat in slow
cooker.
4. Cover. Cook on high 3-4
hours, or until potatoes are as
soft as you like them.

—— PER SERVING ——
• 430 calories
  (25 calories from fat)
• 2.5g total fat
  (1g saturated, 0g trans)
• 30mg cholesterol
• 1380mg sodium
• 62g total carbohydrate
  (5g fiber, 6g sugar)
• 36g protein
• 25%DV vitamin A
• 30%DV vitamin C
• 80%DV calcium
• 8%DV iron

Swiss Cheese
and Veggie Soup

Sharon Miller
Holmesville, OH

Makes 4 servings

Prep. Time: 15 minutes
Cooking Time: 5-6 hours
Ideal slow-cooker size: 3½-qt.

2¼ cups frozen California-
   blend vegetables
   (broccoli, carrots, and
   cauliflower), thawed
½ cup onions, chopped
½ cup water
½ tsp. chicken bouillon
   granules
1 cup skim milk
3 ozs. shredded fat-free
   Swiss cheese

1. Combine vegetables,
onions, water, and bouillon in
slow cooker.
2. Cook on low 5-6 hours,
or until vegetables are tender.
3. Pour all ingredients into
blender or food processor.
Add milk. Process until
smooth, or chunky smooth,
whichever you prefer.
4. Serve, topped with
shredded cheese.

—— PER SERVING ——
• 100 calories
  (0 calories from fat)
• 0g total fat
  (0g saturated, 0g trans)
• 5mg cholesterol
• 290mg sodium
• 11g total carbohydrate
  (3g fiber, 8g sugar)
• 11g protein
• 40%DV vitamin A
• 30%DV vitamin C
• 40%DV calcium
• 4%DV iron

Variation:
   If you want, and your diet
permits, you may like to add
½ tsp. salt to Step 1.

Broccoli Soup

Betty B. Dennison
Grove City, PA

Makes 5 servings

Prep. Time: 15-20 minutes
Cooking Time: 1½-2½ hours
Ideal slow-cooker size: 4-qt.

2-3 lbs. fresh broccoli
1 Tbsp. butter
water to cover
2 cups skim milk
½ cup Velveeta Light cheese,
   cut into small cubes

1. Chop broccoli. Remove
any tough stalks and discard.
2. Place chopped broccoli,
butter, and water to cover in
slow cooker.
3. Cover. Cook on high 1-2
hours.
4. Add skim milk. Cook an
additional 15 minutes.
5. Stir in ½ cup Velveeta
Light cheese and continue
cooking until cheese is melted
into soup.

—— PER SERVING ——
• 160 calories
  (35 calories from fat)
• 4g total fat
  (2g saturated, 1g trans)
• 10mg cholesterol
• 490mg sodium
• 22g total carbohydrate
  (8g fiber, 12g sugar)
• 16g protein
• 100%DV vitamin A
• 200%DV vitamin C
• 40%DV calcium
• 15%DV iron

Cream of Broccoli and Mushroom Soup

Leona Miller
Millersburg, OH

Makes 12 servings

Prep. Time: 20 minutes
Cooking Time: 3½-8 hours
Ideal slow-cooker size: 5- or 6-qt.

8 ozs. fresh mushrooms, sliced
2 lbs. fresh broccoli
3 10¾-oz. cans 98% fat-free cream of broccoli soup
½ tsp. dried thyme leaves, crushed, *optional*
3 bay leaves, *optional*
1 pint fat-free half-and-half
4 ozs. extra-lean smoked ham, chopped
¼ tsp. black pepper

1. Combine all ingredients in slow cooker.
2. Cook on low 4-5 hours or on high 2-3 hours.
3. Remove bay leaves before serving.

—— PER SERVING ——

• 110 calories
  (25 calories from fat)
• 2.5g total fat
  (1g saturated, 0g trans)
• 10mg cholesterol
• 580mg sodium
• 16g total carbohydrate
  (3g fiber, 6g sugar)
• 7g protein
• 30%DV vitamin A
• 40%DV vitamin C
• 10%DV calcium
• 6%DV iron

Broccoli and Cauliflower Soup

Wafi Brandt
Manheim, PA

Makes 6 servings

Prep. Time: 30 minutes
Cooking Time: 2¼-2½ hours
Ideal slow cooker size: 3-qt.

16-oz. bag frozen broccoli and cauliflower, thawed
1½ Tbsp. butter
½ Tbsp. dried onion
2 cups water
2 low-sodium chicken bouillon cubes
4 Tbsp. flour
2 cups fat-free milk, *divided*
½ tsp. Worcestershire sauce
½ tsp. salt
1 cup grated fat-free cheddar cheese
chopped chives
parsley

1. Put broccoli and cauliflower, butter, onion, water, and bouillon cubes in slow cooker.
2. Cover. Cook on high 2 hours.
3. When broccoli and cauliflower are soft, mix flour and 1 cup milk together in a jar with a tight-fitting lid. Cover jar and shake vigorously until flour dissolves and mixture is smooth.
4. Pour milk mixture into vegetables and stir. The soup will soon thicken.
5. Then stir in Worcestershire sauce, salt, and cheese.
6. When cheese is melted, stir in last cup of milk. Allow to heat through before serving, about 15-30 minutes.
7. Sprinkle chives and parsley over top of each individual serving bowl.

—— PER SERVING ——

• 130 calories
  (30 calories from fat)
• 3g total fat
  (2g saturated, 0g trans)
• 15mg cholesterol
• 480mg sodium
• 13g total carbohydrate
  (2g fiber, 6g sugar)
• 10g protein
• 10%DV vitamin A
• 40%DV vitamin C
• 30%DV calcium
• 4%DV iron

167

Broccoli, Potato, and Cheese Soup

Ruth Shank
Gridley, IL

Makes 6 servings

Prep. Time: 20-25 minutes
Cooking Time: 3-4 hours
Ideal slow-cooker size: 3-qt.

2 cups cubed *or* diced
   potatoes
3 Tbsp. chopped onions
10-oz. pkg. frozen broccoli
   cuts, thawed
2 Tbsp. butter, melted
1 Tbsp. flour
1 cup cubed Velveeta Light
   cheese
½ tsp. salt
¼ tsp. black pepper
5½ cups fat-free milk

1. Cook potatoes and
onions in boiling water in
saucepan until potatoes are
crisp-tender. Drain. Place in
slow cooker.

2. Add remaining ingredi-
ents. Stir together.

3. Cover. Cook on low 3-4
hours.

—— PER SERVING ——
- 230 calories
  (70 calories from fat)
- 7g total fat (4.5g
  saturated, 1g trans)
- 25mg cholesterol
- 780mg sodium
- 27g total carbohydrate
  (3g fiber, 15g sugar)
- 16g protein
- 10%DV vitamin A
- 25%DV vitamin C
- 40%DV calcium
- 6%DV iron

Variation:

   If you prefer a thicker
soup, and your diet allows,
you may want to increase the
flour to 3 Tbsp.

Carrot Ginger Soup

Jean Harris Robinson
Pemberton, NJ

Makes 8-10 servings

Prep. Time: 30 minutes
Cooking Time: 3¼-4¼ hours
Ideal slow cooker size: 4-qt.

1 Tbsp. olive oil
3 lbs. carrots, peeled and
   thinly sliced
2 Tbsp. chopped gingerroot
2 Tbsp. minced green
   onion
3 ribs celery, chopped
49½-oz. can low-
   sodium, fat-free
   chicken broth
1 tsp. kosher salt
1 tsp. ground
   pepper
2 Tbsp. honey
1 cup fat-free
   half-and-half

1. Pour olive oil into slow
cooker. Swirl to cover bottom
of cooker.

2. Add carrots, ginger,
onion, and celery.

3. Pour in broth. Add salt,
pepper, and honey. Stir to
mix all ingredients well.

4. Cover. Cook on high 3-4
hours, or until carrots are soft.

5. Pulse with an immersion
blender to purée.

6. Stir in half-and-half.
Heat Soup 15-20 minutes until
heated through, but don't let it
boil. Serve immediately.

—— PER SERVING ——
- 110 calories
  (20 calories from fat)
- 2g total fat
  (0g saturated, 0g trans)
- 0mg cholesterol
- 380mg sodium
- 20g total carbohydrate
  (4g fiber, 11g sugar)
- 3g protein
- 460%DV vitamin A
- 15%DV vitamin C
- 8%DV calcium
- 4%DV iron

Note:

   I was first introduced to
this Soup at one of my quilt
guild's regular meetings. Even
the professed carrot-haters
loved it.

Barley-Mushroom Soup

Janie Steele
Moore, OK

Makes 8 servings

Prep. Time: 25-30 minutes
Cooking Time: 7-8 hours
Ideal slow-cooker size: 5-qt.

6 cups fresh mushrooms, sliced
2 large onions, chopped
3 cloves garlic, minced
1 cup celery, chopped
1 cup carrots, chopped
5 cups water, *divided*
¼ cup dry quick-cooking pearl barley
4 cups low-sodium beef broth
4 tsp. Worcestershire sauce
1-1½ tsp. salt, *optional*
1½ tsp. dried basil
1½ tsp. dried parsley flakes
1 tsp. dill weed
1½ tsp. dried oregano
½ tsp. salt-free seasoning blend
½ tsp. dried thyme
½ tsp. garlic powder

1. Combine all ingredients in slow cooker.
2. Cook on low 4-5 hours, or until vegetables and barley are done to your liking.

—— PER SERVING ——
• 320 calories
  (10 calories from fat)
• 1g total fat
  (0g saturated, 0g trans)
• 0mg cholesterol
• 310mg sodium
• 69g total carbohydrate
  (14g fiber, 5g sugar)
• 12g protein
• 30%DV vitamin A
• 2%DV vitamin C
• 6%DV calcium
• 20%DV iron

Barley Cabbage Soup

Betty K. Drescher
Quakertown, PA

Makes 8 servings

Prep. Time: 20 minutes
Cooking Time: 4-10 hours
Ideal slow-cooker size: 3½- or 4-qt.

¼ cup dry pearl barley
6 cups fat-free, low-sodium meat, *or* vegetable, broth
1 cup onions, chopped
3-4 cups green cabbage, finely chopped
¼ cup fresh parsley, chopped
½ tsp. celery salt
½ tsp. salt
⅛ tsp. black pepper
1 Tbsp. minute tapioca

1. Combine all ingredients in slow cooker.
2. Cover. Cook on low 8-10 hours or on high 4-5 hours.

—— PER SERVING ——
• 60 calories
  (0 calories from fat)
• 0g total fat
  (0g saturated, 0g trans)
• 0mg cholesterol
• 300mg sodium
• 10g total carbohydrate
  (2g fiber, 2g sugar)
• 5g protein
• 0%DV vitamin A
• 10%DV vitamin C
• 2%DV calcium
• 4%DV iron

Cabbage Sausage Soup

Karen Waggoner
Joplin, MO

Makes 8 servings

Prep. Time: 20-25 minutes
Cooking Time: 5¼-6¼ hours
Ideal slow-cooker size: 5-qt.

4 cups low-fat, low-sodium chicken broth
1 medium-sized head of cabbage, chopped
2 medium-sized onions, chopped
½ lb. fully cooked smoked turkey sausage, halved lengthwise and sliced
½ cup all-purpose flour
¼ tsp. black pepper
1 cup skim milk

1. Combine chicken broth, cabbage, onions, and sausage in slow cooker.
2. Cover. Cook on high 5-6 hours, or until cabbage is tender.
3. Mix flour and black pepper in bowl.
4. Gradually add milk, stirring until smooth.
5. Gradually stir into hot soup.
6. Cook, stirring occasionally for about 15 minutes, until soup is thickened. Serve.

—— PER SERVING ——
• 210 calories
  (100 calories from fat)
• 11g total fat
  (4g saturated, 0g trans)
• 20mg cholesterol
• 790mg sodium
• 17g total carbohydrate
  (3g fiber, 7g sugar)
• 11g protein
• 4%DV vitamin A
• 30%DV vitamin C
• 10%DV calcium
• 15%DV iron

Cabbage Veggie Soup

Judy Govotsos
Frederick, MD

Makes 8 servings

Prep. Time: 25 minutes
Cooking Time: 2¾-7 hours
Ideal slow-cooker size: 5-qt.

1 cup carrots, sliced
1 cup onions, diced
4 garlic cloves, chopped
6 cups fat-free low-sodium chicken broth
3-4 cups shredded cabbage (*or* cole slow mix ready-cut)
1 cup green beans, fresh, canned, *or* frozen and thawed
2 Tbsp. tomato paste
1-1½ tsp. dried basil
¼-½ tsp. dried oregano
½ tsp. salt
1 very small zucchini, diced
1 very small yellow squash, diced

1. Combine all ingredients in slow cooker, except zucchini and squash.
2. Cover. Cook on low 5-6 hours or on high 2-3 hours.
3. Add zucchini and squash.
4. Cover. Cook on low 45 minutes to 1 hour.

— PER SERVING —
- 60 calories
  (0 calories from fat)
- 0g total fat
  (0g saturated, 0g trans)
- 0mg cholesterol
- 290mg sodium
- 8g total carbohydrate
  (3g fiber, 4g sugar)
- 6g protein
- 80%DV vitamin A
- 20%DV vitamin C
- 6%DV calcium
- 10%DV iron

Sausage White Bean Soup

Christie Anne Detamore-Hunsberger
Harrisonburg, VA

Makes 8 servings

Prep. Time: 30-45 minutes
Cooking Time: 3 hours
Ideal slow-cooker size: 4-qt.

⅓ lb. Italian turkey sausage, sweet *or* hot, cut in ½"-thick slices
½ cup water, *or* more
1 large onion, diced
2 cloves garlic, minced
5 carrots, grated
3 stalks celery, chopped
2-2½ qts. low-sodium, fat-free chicken broth
3-4 tsp. low-sodium chicken bouillon granules
1 tsp. vegetable seasoning blend, your choice, but without salt
½ tsp. dried oregano
¼ tsp. pepper
3 15-oz. cans white beans, rinsed and drained
3 cups frozen spinach, thawed
2 Tbsp. parsley

1. Brown sausage in skillet in ½ cup water over medium to high heat. Cover. Check and stir after 10 minutes or so to make sure sausage isn't cooking dry and burning. Add more water if needed and continue stirring until browned on all sides.
2. Remove sausage to slow cooker, reserving drippings.
3. Sauté onion, garlic, carrots, and celery in drippings in skillet until tender. Place vegetables in slow cooker.
4. Add chicken broth and granules, all seasonings, and beans. Stir well.
5. Cook on low 3 hours.
6. Squeeze excess liquid out of thawed spinach. Add to slow cooker for last 20-30 minutes of cooking time.
7. Garnish with parsley.

— PER SERVING —
- 260 calories
  (25 calories from fat)
- 2.5g total fat
  (1g saturated, 0g trans)
- 10mg cholesterol
- 660mg sodium
- 39g total carbohydrate
  (10g fiber, 5g sugar)
- 19g protein
- 190%DV vitamin A
- 15%DV vitamin C
- 20%DV calcium
- 35%DV iron

I find that adding ¼-½ cup of a burgundy or Chablis wine to most soup and stew recipes brings out the flavor of the other seasonings.
Joyce Kant, Rochester, NY

Soup to Get Thin On

Jean H. Robinson
Cinnaminson, NJ

Makes 20+ servings

Prep. Time: 30-40
Cooking Time: 6-8 hours
Ideal slow-cooker size: 7-qt., or
2 4-qt. cookers

3 48-oz. cans low-fat, low-sodium chicken broth
2 medium-sized onions, chopped
5 celery ribs, chopped
5 parsnips, chopped
1 head (8 cups) cabbage, shredded
4 bell peppers, red *or* green, chopped
8 ozs. mushrooms, chopped
10-oz. pkg. frozen chopped spinach, thawed
10-oz. pkg. frozen broccoli florets, thawed
10-oz. pkg. frozen cauliflower, thawed
2-3 pieces chopped gingerroot
14½-oz. can crushed tomatoes
1 Tbsp. black pepper
1 Tbsp. salt

1. Combine all ingredients in slow cooker.
2. Cover. Cook on low 6-8 hours.

—— PER SERVING ——
• 90 calories
  (0 calories from fat)
• 0g total fat
  (0g saturated, 0g trans)
• 0mg cholesterol
• 660mg sodium
• 16g total carbohydrate
  (15g fiber, 5g sugar)
• 7g protein
• 20%DV vitamin A
• 40%DV vitamin C
• 8%DV calcium
• 15%DV iron

Low-Calorie Soup

Cindy Kiestynick
Glen Lyon, PA

Makes 14 servings

Prep. Time: 20-25 minutes
Cooking Time: 4-5 hours
Ideal slow-cooker size: 4- or 5-qt.

2 cups carrots, thinly sliced
2 cups celery, thinly sliced
2 cups cabbage, chopped
8-oz. pkg. frozen green beans, thawed
1 onion, chopped
28-oz. can diced tomatoes
3 envelopes dry low-sodium beef-flavored soup mix
3 Tbsp. Worcestershire sauce
½ tsp. salt
¼ tsp. black pepper
water to cover

1. Combine all ingredients in slow cooker.
2. Cover. Cook on high 4-5 hours.

—— PER SERVING ——
• 80 calories
  (0 calories from fat)
• 0g total fat
  (0g saturated, 0g trans)
• 0mg cholesterol
• 630mg sodium
• 17g total carbohydrate
  (4g fiber, 5g sugar)
• 2g protein
• 100%DV vitamin A
• 10%DV vitamin C
• 8%DV calcium
• 6%DV iron

Variation:
If you like, stir in a handful or two of baby spinach just before serving.

Survival Soup

Betty B. Dennison
Grove City, PA

Makes 10 servings

Prep. Time: 25 minutes
Cooking Time: 6-8 hours
Ideal slow-cooker size: 5-qt.

3 cups cabbage, cut up
1 cup carrots, cut up
½ cup celery, cut up
1 large onion, diced
1-lb. can French-style green beans, drained
4 cups water
2 beef bouillon cubes
12-oz. can low-sodium tomato juice
½ tsp. salt
¼-½ tsp. black pepper, according to your taste preference

1. Combine cabbage, carrots, celery, onion, and green beans in slow cooker.
2. Heat water to boiling in saucepan. Stir in bouillon cubes. When dissolved, pour over vegetables.
3. Add tomato juice, salt, and pepper.
4. Cover. Cook on low 6-8 hours, or until vegetables are done as you like them.

—— PER SERVING ——
• 30 calories
  (0 calories from fat)
• 0g total fat
  (0g saturated, 0g trans)
• 0mg cholesterol
• 410mg sodium
• 7g total carbohydrate
  (2g fiber, 4g sugar)
• 1g protein
• 60%DV vitamin A
• 20%DV vitamin C
• 4%DV calcium
• 4%DV iron

Pumpkin Soup

Jane Meiser
Harrisonburg, VA

Makes 6 servings

Prep. Time: 20 minutes
Cooking Time: 3-4 hours
Ideal slow-cooker size: 3½-qt.

¼ cup green bell pepper, chopped
1 small onion, finely chopped
2 cups low-sodium chicken stock, *or* broth, fat removed
2 cups pumpkin purée
2 cups skim milk
⅛ tsp. dried thyme
¼ tsp. ground nutmeg
½ tsp. salt
2 Tbsp. cornstarch
¼ cup cold water
1 tsp. fresh parsley, chopped

1. Combine all ingredients except cornstarch, cold water, and fresh parsley in slow cooker. Mix well.
2. Cover. Cook on low 3-4 hours.
3. During the last hour add cornstarch mixed with water and stir until soup thickens.
4. Just before serving, stir in fresh parsley.

—— PER SERVING ——
• 70 calories
  (0 calories from fat)
• 0g total fat
  (0g saturated, 0g trans)
• 0mg cholesterol
• 300mg sodium
• 12g total carbohydrate
  (1g fiber, 8g sugar)
• 6g protein
• 15%DV vitamin A
• 10%DV vitamin C
• 10%DV calcium
• 6%DV iron

Cream of Pumpkin Soup

Nanci Keatley
Salem, OR

Makes 4-6 servings

Prep. Time: 10-15 minutes
Cooking Time: 3-4 hours
Ideal slow cooker size: 4-qt.

1 Tbsp. butter, melted
1 large onion, diced fine
32-oz. box vegetable stock
16-oz. can solid-pack pumpkin
1 tsp. salt
¼ tsp. cinnamon
¼ tsp. freshly ground nutmeg
⅛ tsp. ginger
⅛ tsp. cloves
⅛ tsp. cardamom
¼ tsp. freshly ground pepper
1½ cups low-fat half-and-half
1 cup heavy cream
chopped chives

1. Mix butter and onion in slow cooker.
2. Add stock, pumpkin, salt, and other seasonings. Mix well.
3. Cover. Cook on low 2-3 hours.
4. Add half-and-half and cream.
5. Cover. Cook on low 1 hour, or until heated through.
6. Garnish individual serving bowls with chives.

—— PER SERVING ——
• 90 calories
  (25 calories from fat)
• 3g total fat
  (1g saturated, 0g trans)
• 5mg cholesterol
• 320mg sodium
• 14g total carbohydrate
  (3g fiber, 7g sugar)
• 3g protein
• 170%DV vitamin A
• 4%DV vitamin C
• 10%DV calcium
• 4%DV iron

Sweet Potato Soup

Janie Steele
Moore, OK

Makes 4 servings

Prep. Time: 1¼-1½ hours
Cooking Time: 1 hour
Ideal slow-cooker size: 4-qt.

3 large sweet potatoes, baked, peeled, and cubed
1½ cups low-sodium, fat-free chicken broth, *divided*
1 Tbsp. butter
1 Tbsp. flour
¼ tsp. ground ginger
1 cup fat-free evaporated milk
1 Tbsp. pecans, chopped, *optional*

1. Combine cooked sweet potatoes and ¾ cup broth in blender. Blend on high until mixture is smooth.
2. Place butter, flour, and ginger in slow cooker. Turn cooker to high and add milk gradually.
3. Cook, stirring frequently, until thickened.
4. Add sweet potato mixture from blender. Add

remaining chicken broth. Stir until smooth.

5. Cover. Cook on high until heated through, about 1 hour.

6. Garnish each individual serving with a scattering of pecans if you wish.

—— PER SERVING ——
- 210 calories
  (30 calories from fat)
- 3g total fat
  (2g saturated, 0g trans)
- 10mg cholesterol
- 170mg sodium
- 37g total carbohydrate
  (5g fiber, 16g sugar)
- 9g protein
- 530%DV vitamin A
- 45%DV vitamin C
- 25%DV calcium
- 8%DV iron

Onion Soup

Rosemarie Fitzgerald
Gibsonia, PA

Makes 8 servings

Prep. Time: 20-25 minutes
Cooking Time: 6-8 hours
Ideal slow-cooker size: 3½-qt.

3 medium-sized onions, thinly sliced
2 Tbsp. butter
2 Tbsp. vegetable oil
1 tsp. salt
1 Tbsp. sugar
2 Tbsp. flour
1 qt. fat-free, low-sodium vegetable broth
½ cup dry white wine
slices of French bread
½ cup grated fat-free Swiss, or Parmesan, cheese

1. Sauté onions in butter and oil in covered skillet until soft.

2. Uncover. Add salt and sugar. Cook 15 minutes.

3. Stir in flour. Cook 3 more minutes.

4. Combine onions, broth, and wine in slow cooker.

5. Cover. Cook on low 6-8 hours.

6. Toast bread. Sprinkle with grated cheese and then broil.

7. Dish soup into individual bowls; then float a slice of broiled bread on top of each serving of soup.

—— PER SERVING ——
- 360 calories
  (50 calories from fat)
- 6g total fat
  (2.5g saturated, 0.5g trans)
- 10mg cholesterol
- 1320mg sodium
- 61g total carbohydrate
  (4g fiber, 7g sugar)
- 11g protein
- 0%DV vitamin A
- 0%DV vitamin C
- 15%DV calcium
- 15%DV iron

Pizza in a Bowl

Laurie Sylvester
Ridgely, MD

Makes 6 servings

Prep. Time: 20 minutes
Cooking Time: 5-6 hours
Ideal slow-cooker size: 3½-qt.

26-oz. jar fat-free, low-sodium marinara sauce
14½-oz. can low-sodium diced tomatoes
4 ozs. low-fat pepperoni, diced *or* sliced
1½ cups fresh mushrooms, sliced
1 large bell pepper, diced
1 large red onion, chopped
1 cup water
1 Tbsp. Italian seasoning
1 cup dry macaroni
low-fat shredded mozzarella cheese

1. Combine all ingredients, except cheese, in cooker.

2. Cover. Cook on low 5-6 hours.

3. Ladle into soup bowls. Sprinkle with cheese.

—— PER SERVING ——
- 280 calories
  (100 calories from fat)
- 12g total fat
  (3.5g saturated, 0g trans)
- 15mg cholesterol
- 1270mg sodium
- 34g total carbohydrate
  (5g fiber, 12g sugar)
- 11g protein
- 10%DV vitamin A
- 30%DV vitamin C
- 10%DV calcium
- 15%DV iron

Chicken Stock for Soup (or other uses)

Stacy Schmucker Stoltzfus
Enola, PA

Makes 3+ quarts

Prep. Time: 15 minutes
Cooking Time: 4-6 hours
Ideal slow-cooker size: 6-qt.

3 lbs. chicken backs and
  necks, *or* whole chicken
3 qts. cold water
4 ribs celery, chopped
  coarsely
6 carrots, unpeeled, sliced
  thick
2 onions, peeled and
  quartered
8 peppercorns

1. Rinse chicken. Place in slow cooker. Add water and vegetables.
2. Cover. Cook on high 4-6 hours.

3. Remove chicken and vegetables from broth.
4. When broth has cooled slightly, place in refrigerator to cool completely. Remove fat and any foam when chilled.
5. The stock is ready for soup. Freeze it in 1-cup containers.
6. Use the cooked chicken and vegetables for soup or stews.

—— PER SERVING ——
• 220 calories
  (45 calories from fat)
• 5g total fat
  (1g saturated, 0g trans)
• 110mg cholesterol
• 170mg sodium
• 8g total carbohydrate
  (2g fiber, 5g sugar)
• 36g protein
• 200%DV vitamin A
• 10%DV vitamin C
• 6%DV calcium
• 10%DV iron

Tip from Tester:

I made a chicken noodle soup with a portion of the stock just to see how it turned out. It was probably the best chicken noodle soup I've ever made! I did discover that the flavor of the stock was enhanced by adding salt.

Veggie Stock

Char Hagner
Montague, MI

Makes 6 cups

Prep. Time: 15-20 minutes
Cooking Time: 4-10 hours
Ideal slow-cooker size: 4-qt.

2 tomatoes, chopped
2 onions, cut up
4 carrots, cut up
1 stalk celery, cut up
1 potato, cut up
6 garlic cloves
dash of salt
½ tsp. dried thyme
1 bay leaf
6 cups water

1. Combine tomatoes, onions, carrots, celery, potato, garlic, salt, thyme, bay leaf, and water.
2. Cover. Cook on low 8-10 hours or on high 4-5 hours.
3. Strain stock through large sieve. Discard solids.
4. Freeze until needed (up to 3 months). Use for soups or stews.

—— PER SERVING ——
• 70 calories
  (0 calories from fat)
• 0g total fat
  (0g saturated, 0g trans)
• 0mg cholesterol
• 75mg sodium
• 15g total carbohydrate
  (3g fiber, 5g sugar)
• 2g protein
• 100%DV vitamin A
• 10%DV vitamin C
• 4%DV calcium
• 6%DV iron

6-Can Soup

Mrs. Audrey L. Kneer
Williamsfield, IL

Makes 8 servings

Prep. Time: 10 minutes
Cooking Time: 3-4 hours
Ideal slow-cooker size: 3½- or 4-qt.

10¾-oz. can low-sodium
    tomato soup
15-oz. can whole-kernel
    corn, drained
15-oz. can mixed
    vegetables, drained
15-oz. can chili beans,
    undrained
14½-oz. can low-sodium
    diced tomatoes,
    undrained
14½-oz. can low-sodium,
    reduced-fat chicken
    broth

1. Combine all ingredients
in slow cooker.
2. Cover. Cook on low 3-4
hours.

—— PER SERVING ——
• 140 calories   • 27g total carbohydrate
  (15 calories from fat)   (6g fiber, 3g sugar)
• 1.5g total fat   • 7g protein
  (0g saturated, 0g trans) • 50%DV vitamin A
• 0mg cholesterol   • 20%DV vitamin C
• 610mg sodium   • 6%DV calcium
                      • 10%DV iron

15-Bean Soup

Eileen Eash
Carlsbad, NM

Makes 10 servings

Soaking Time: 8 hours or
    overnight
Prep. Time: 15 minutes
Cooking Time: 9-12 hours
Ideal slow-cooker size: 6-qt.

1 lb. dry 15-bean mixture
2 qts. water
2 cups lean ham, chopped
1 cup onions, chopped
2 cups canned, low-sodium
    diced tomatoes
1 tsp. chili powder
2 Tbsp. lemon juice
2 cloves garlic, chopped
    finely
1 tsp. salt
½ tsp. black pepper

1. Cover beans with water
in stockpot. Soak 8 hours or
overnight. Drain.
2. Mix beans, fresh 2
quarts water, and ham in
slow cooker.
3. Cover. Cook on low 8-10
hours.
4. Add remaining ingredients.
5. Cook on high another
1 hour or on low another 2
hours.

—— PER SERVING ——
• 210 calories   • 33g total carbohydrate
  (20 calories from fat)   (9g fiber, 7g sugar)
• 2.5g total fat   • 14g protein
  (0.5g saturated,   • 10%DV vitamin A
  0g trans)   • 10%DV vitamin C
• 10mg cholesterol   • 5%DV calcium
• 1740mg sodium   • 20%DV iron

Steak Chili

Jenny R. Unternahrer
Wayland, IA

Makes 4 servings

Prep. Time: 20-25 minutes
Cooking Time: 6-8 hours
Ideal slow-cooker size: 3½-qt.

16-oz. can kidney beans,
    drained
14½-oz. can low-sodium
    diced tomatoes
1 lb. lean top round steak,
    trimmed of fat and cubed
half a medium-sized
    onion, diced
one-third green bell
    pepper, diced
1 clove garlic, minced
½ Tbsp. chili powder
¼ tsp. black pepper
½ tsp. salt
15-oz. can low-sodium
    tomato sauce
several drops Tabasco
    sauce, *optional*

1. Combine all ingredients
in slow cooker. Stir.
2. Cover. Cook on low 6-8
hours, or until meat is tender
but not dry.

—— PER SERVING ——
• 300 calories   • 32g total carbohydrate
  (60 calories from fat)   (8g fiber, 9g sugar)
• 6g total fat   • 31g protein
  (2g saturated, 0g trans) • 20%DV vitamin A
• 70mg cholesterol   • 30%DV vitamin C
• 1660mg sodium   • 10%DV calcium
                      • 30%DV iron

Variation:
    If you'd like some more zip,
add a 4-oz. can of chopped
green chilies, undrained, to
Step 1.

Chipotle Chili

Karen Ceneviva
Seymour, CT

Makes 9 servings

Prep. Time: 10-15 minutes
Cooking Time: 3-8 hours
Ideal slow-cooker size: 3½-qt.

16-oz. jar low-sodium
　chipotle chunky salsa
1 cup water
2 tsp. chili powder
1 large onion, chopped
1 lb. stewing beef,
　trimmed of fat and cut
　into ½" pieces
19-oz. can red kidney beans,
　rinsed and drained

1. Stir all ingredients
together in slow cooker.
2. Cover. Cook on high 3-4
hours, or on low 6-8 hours,
until beef is fork-tender.

—— PER SERVING ——
- 150 calories　　　　　• 14g total carbohydrate
　(30 calories from fat)　　(5g fiber, 2g sugar)
- 3g total fat　　　　　• 16g protein
　(1g saturated, 1g trans)　• 8%DV vitamin A
- 30mg cholesterol　　　• 15%DV vitamin C
- 480mg sodium　　　　• 2%DV calcium
　　　　　　　　　　　• 15%DV iron

Slow-Cooked Chili

Bernice A. Esau
North Newton, KS
Carol Sherwood
Batavia, NY

Makes 10 servings

Prep. Time: 15-20 minutes
Cooking Time: 3-8 hours
Ideal slow-cooker size: 5-qt.

2 lbs. extra-lean ground
　beef
2 16-oz. cans kidney beans,
　rinsed and drained
2 14½-oz. cans low-sodium
　diced tomatoes, undrained
8-oz. can low-sodium
　tomato sauce
2 medium-sized onions,
　chopped
1 green bell pepper, chopped
2 garlic cloves, minced
2 Tbsp. chili powder
2 tsp. salt, *optional*
1 tsp. black pepper
shredded low-fat cheddar
　cheese, *optional*

1. Brown beef in nonstick
skillet (or microwave strainer).
2. Place in slow cooker.
3. Add all ingredients,
except cheese.
4. Cover. Cook on high 3-4
hours or on low 6-8 hours.
5. Garnish individual servings with cheese if desired.

—— PER SERVING ——
- 270 calories　　　　　• 22g total carbohydrate
　(80 calories from fat)　　(6g fiber, 6g sugar)
- 9g total fat　(3.5g　　• 25g protein
　saturated, 0g trans)　　• 25%DV vitamin A
- 35mg cholesterol　　　• 20%DV vitamin C
- 1220mg sodium　　　　• 10%DV calcium
　　　　　　　　　　　• 20%DV iron

Tip:
　Serve as a soup, or as a
topping for rice or potatoes.

Chili Con Carne Supreme

Jane Geigley
Honey Brook, PA

Makes 8 servings

Prep. Time: 30-35 minutes
Cooking Time: 2 hours
Ideal slow cooker size: 4-qt.

1½ lbs. 95% lean ground
　beef
1 Tbsp. olive oil
2 garlic cloves, minced,
　optional
2 medium onions, chopped
1 green bell pepper, chopped
3 low-sodium beef bouillon
　cubes
1 cup boiling water
1½ tsp. salt
2 Tbsp. chili powder
1 tsp. ground cumin
2 tsp. dried oregano
¼ tsp. ground cinnamon
⅛ tsp. cayenne pepper
2 16-oz. cans low-sodium
　tomatoes with liquid
2 15½-oz. cans kidney
　beans, undrained

*Browning the meat, onions, and vegetables before putting
them in the cooker improves their flavor, but this extra step
can be skipped in most recipes. The flavor will still be good.*
Dorothy M. Van Deest, Memphis, TN

1. Brown ground beef in large skillet in oil. Stir frequently to break up clumps. When no longer pink, reserve drippings. Spoon meat into slow cooker.

2. In skillet drippings, sauté garlic, onions, and green peppers over low heat until onions are tender. Spoon veggies into slow cooker.

3. Dissolve bouillon cubes in boiling water. Pour into slow cooker.

4. Add rest of ingredients to slow cooker. Stir together until well mixed.

5. Cover. Cook on low 2 hours.

—— PER SERVING ——

- 280 calories
  (60 calories from fat)
- 6g total fat
  (2g saturated, 0g trans)
- 45mg cholesterol
- 790mg sodium
- 31g total carbohydrate
  (8g fiber, 7g sugar)
- 25g protein
- 30%DV vitamin A
- 50%DV vitamin C
- 10%DV calcium
- 30%DV iron

Brown-Sugar Chili

Alma Weaver
Ephrata, PA

Makes 8 servings

Prep. Time: 20 minutes
Cooking Time: 2 hours
Ideal slow-cooker size: 3½-qt.

1 lb. extra-lean ground beef
1 medium-sized onion, chopped
½ cup brown sugar
2 Tbsp. prepared mustard
2 14-oz. cans kidney beans, drained
1 pint low-sodium tomato juice
½ tsp. salt
¼ tsp. black pepper
1 tsp. chili powder

1. Brown lean ground beef and onion in nonstick skillet over medium heat. Stir brown sugar and mustard into meat.

2. Combine all ingredients in slow cooker.

3. Cover. Cook on high 2 hours. If it's convenient, stir several times during cooking.

—— PER SERVING ——

- 240 calories
  (50 calories from fat)
- 6g total fat
  (2g saturated, 0g trans)
- 20mg cholesterol
- 590mg sodium
- 32g total carbohydrate
  (4g fiber, 18g sugar)
- 17g protein
- 6%DV vitamin A
- 10%DV vitamin C
- 6%DV calcium
- 20%DV iron

Classic Beef Chili

Esther S. Martin
Ephrata, PA

Makes 6 servings

Prep. Time: 20 minutes
Cooking Time: 2-3 hours
Ideal slow-cooker size: 4-qt.

1 lb. extra-lean ground beef
2 cloves garlic, chopped fine
2 Tbsp. chili powder
1 tsp. ground cumin
28-oz. can crushed tomatoes
15-oz. can red kidney beans, rinsed and drained
1 onion, chopped
4-oz. can diced chilies, undrained
2 Tbsp. tomato paste
fresh oregano sprigs for garnish

1. In large nonstick skillet, brown beef and garlic over medium heat. Stir to break up meat. Add chili powder and cumin. Stir to combine.

2. Mix together tomatoes, beans, onion, chilies, and tomato paste in slow cooker. Add beef mixture and mix thoroughly.

3. Cook on high 2-3 hours, or until flavors are well blended.

4. Garnish with oregano to serve.

—— PER SERVING ——

- 280 calories
  (70 calories from fat)
- 8g total fat
  (3g saturated, 0g trans)
- 30mg cholesterol
- 300mg sodium
- 30g total carbohydrate
  (11g fiber, 3g sugar)
- 24g protein
- 40%DV vitamin A
- 20%DV vitamin C
- 8%DV calcium
- 20%DV iron

Chili Bake

Michele Rubola
Selden, NY

Makes 6 servings

Prep. Time: 20 minutes
Cooking Time: 3-4 hours
Ideal slow-cooker size: 4-qt.

3 turkey bacon slices
½ lb. extra-lean ground
　round
15½-oz. can lima beans,
　undrained
15-oz. can pork and beans,
　undrained
15-oz. can red kidney
　beans, drained
½ cup ketchup
½ cup barbecue sauce
¼ cup firmly packed
　brown sugar
1 tsp. dry mustard

1. Brown bacon until crisp
in nonstick skillet. Cut fine
and set aside.
2. Cook beef in nonstick
skillet over medium heat
until beef is brown, stirring to
crumble beef.
3. Combine all ingredients
in slow cooker. Stir well.
4. Cover and cook on high
1 hour; then reduce to low
and cook 2-3 hours.

—— PER SERVING ——
• 380 calories　　• 59g total carbohydrate
　(60 calories from fat)　(11g fiber, 24g sugar)
• 7g total fat　　• 22g protein
　(2g saturated, 0g trans) • 10%DV vitamin A
• 25mg cholesterol　• 10%DV vitamin C
• 1200mg sodium　• 10%DV calcium
　　　　　　　　• 25%DV iron

Mexico Casserole

Janie Steele
Moore, OK

Makes 8 servings

Prep. Time: 15-20 minutes
Cooking Time: 3½-5 hours
Ideal slow-cooker size: 4- or 5-qt.

1 lb. extra-lean ground beef
1 medium-sized onion,
　chopped
1 small green bell pepper,
　chopped
16-oz. can kidney beans,
　rinsed and drained
14½ oz.-can diced
　tomatoes, undrained
8-oz. can tomato sauce
¼ cup water
1 envelope reduced-sodium
　taco seasoning
1 Tbsp. chili powder
1⅓ cups instant rice,
　uncooked
1 cup low-fat cheddar cheese

1. Brown ground beef and
onion in nonstick skillet.
2. Combine all ingredients
in slow cooker except rice
and cheese.
3. Cook on low 3-4 hours.
4. Stir in rice, cover, and
cook until tender, about 30-60
minutes.
5. Sprinkle with cheese.
Cover and cook until cheese
is melted. Serve.

—— PER SERVING ——
• 270 calories　　• 32g total carbohydrate
　(60 calories from fat)　(5g fiber, 3g sugar)
• 7g total fat　　• 21g protein
　(3g saturated, 0g trans) • 25%DV vitamin A
• 25mg cholesterol　• 20%DV vitamin C
• 820mg sodium　• 15%DV calcium
　　　　　　　　• 20%DV iron

Many-Beans Chili

Rosann Zeiset
Stevens, PA

Makes 12 servings

Prep. Time: 20 minutes
Cooking Time: 4-5 hours
Ideal slow-cooker size: 4-qt.

½ lb. lean hamburger, *or*
　ground turkey
½ lb. loose sausage
1 onion, chopped
15-oz. can kidney beans, *or*
　chili beans, undrained
15-oz. can ranch-style
　beans, undrained
15-oz. can pinto beans,
　undrained
14½-oz. can stewed
　tomatoes, undrained
15-oz. can tomato sauce
1 envelope dry chili
　seasoning mix
3 Tbsp. brown sugar
3 Tbsp. chili powder

1. Brown hamburger,
sausage, and onion together in
nonstick skillet.
2. Combine all ingredients
in large slow cooker. Mix well.
3. Cook on low 4-5 hours.

—— PER SERVING ——
• 240 calories　　• 34g total carbohydrate
　(60 calories from fat)　(8g fiber, 11g sugar)
• 7g total fat　　• 14g protein
　(2g saturated, 0g trans) • 35%DV vitamin A
• 15mg cholesterol　• 10%DV vitamin C
• 1570mg sodium　• 8%DV calcium
　　　　　　　　• 25%DV iron

Chilly-Chili

Alix Nancy Botsford
Seminole, OK

Makes 6 servings

Soaking Time: 4-6 hours
Freezing Time: 4 hours
Prep. Time: 25 minutes
Cooking Time: 3-11 hours
Ideal slow-cooker size: 4½- or 5-qt.

2 cups assorted dried beans
1 tsp. salt
1 lb. fat-free ground turkey
1 large onion, chopped
2 tsp. minced garlic
2 Tbsp. olive oil
2 celery ribs, chopped
1 green bell pepper, diced
1 tsp. salt
10-oz. can tomatoes and green chilies, undrained
28-oz. can diced tomatoes, undrained

1. A day—or a week—before you want to serve and eat Chilly-Chili, sort, wash, and cover beans with water for 4-6 hours. Drain.
2. Place in plastic resealable bag. Place in freezer and freeze until solid.
3. On the day you want to serve the chili, place frozen beans in slow cooker. Cover with fresh water. Add 1 tsp. salt (this will keep the beans firm).
4. Cover. Cook on high 2-3 hours, or until you can crush a bean with a fork.
5. Drain, reserving 1-2 cups liquid.
6. In a skillet, brown turkey, onion, and garlic in oil.

7. Add celery, green pepper, and 1 tsp. salt. Continue cooking until vegetables begin to soften. Add both kinds of tomatoes and pour into beans in slow cooker.
8. Add as much bean liquid as you can fit in your slow cooker.
9. Cover. Cook on low 1-8 hours, whatever fits your schedule for the day.

—— PER SERVING ——
- 380 calories
  (60 calories from fat)
- 6g total fat
  (1g saturated, 0g trans)
- 30mg cholesterol
- 1390mg sodium
- 50g total carbohydrate
  (18g fiber, 10g sugar)
- 34g protein
- 10%DV vitamin A
- 30%DV vitamin C
- 20%DV calcium
- 35%DV iron

4-Bean Turkey Chili

Dawn Day
Westminster, CA

Makes 10 servings

Prep. Time: 30 minutes
Cooking Time: 4-5 hours
Ideal slow-cooker size: 4-qt.

1 lb. ground turkey, browned in nonstick skillet and drained
1 large onion, chopped
6-oz. can low-sodium tomato paste

2 Tbsp. chili powder
12-oz. can chili beans, undrained
12-oz. can kidney beans, undrained
12-oz. can black beans, undrained
12-oz. can pinto beans, undrained
12-oz. can low-sodium tomatoes with juice

1. Combine browned ground turkey, onion, and tomato paste in slow cooker.
2. Add chili powder, beans, and tomatoes. Mix well.
3. Cover. Cook on low 4-5 hours.
4. Serve with grated low-fat cheddar cheese.
5. Sprinkle individual servings with fresh parsley, if you wish.

—— PER SERVING: ——
- 190 calories
  (15 calories from fat)
- 2g total fat
  (0g saturated, 0g trans)
- 20mg cholesterol
- 610mg sodium
- 27g total carbohydrate
  (8g fiber, 3g sugar)
- 19g protein
- 20%DV vitamin A
- 10%DV vitamin C
- 8%DV calcium
- 15%DV iron

Fill the cooker no more than two-thirds full and no less than half-full.
Rachel Kauffman, Alto, MI

Hot Chili

Kristen Allen
Houston, TX

Makes 8 servings

Prep. Time: 15-20 minutes
Cooking Time: 4-5 hours
Ideal slow-cooker size: 5-qt.

2 lbs. 99% fat-free ground
  turkey
2 medium-sized onions,
  diced
2 garlic cloves, minced
1 green bell pepper, diced
⅔ Tbsp. chili powder
1 tsp. salt
1 tsp. black pepper
1 tsp. ground cumin
16-oz. can low-sodium
  stewed, *or* diced, tomatoes
2 12-oz. cans low-sodium
  tomato sauce
2 16-oz. cans Mexican chili
  beans

1. Brown turkey with onions,
garlic, and green pepper in a
nonstick skillet. Drain.
2. Combine all ingredients
in slow cooker.
3. Cover. Cook on low 4-5
hours.

—— PER SERVING ——
• 320 calories
  (40 calories from fat)
• 4.5g total fat
  (1g saturated, 0g trans)
• 45mg cholesterol
• 1400mg sodium
• 36g total carbohydrate
  (12g fiber, 8g sugar)
• 37g protein
• 80%DV vitamin A
• 30%DV vitamin C
• 8%DV calcium
• 30%DV iron

Garden Chili

Stacy Schmucker Stoltzfus
Enola, PA

Makes 10 servings

Prep. Time: 45 minutes
Cooking Time: 6-8 hours
Ideal slow-cooker size: 3½- or 4-qt.

¾ lb. onions, chopped
1 tsp. garlic, minced
1 Tbsp. olive oil
¾ cup celery, chopped
1 large carrot, peeled and
  thinly sliced
1 large green bell pepper,
  chopped
1 small zucchini, sliced
¼ lb. fresh mushrooms,
  sliced
1¼ cups water
14-oz. can kidney beans,
  drained
14-oz. can low-sodium
  diced tomatoes with
  juice
1 tsp. lemon juice
⅛ tsp. dried oregano
1 tsp. ground cumin
1 tsp. chili powder
1 tsp. salt
1 tsp. black
  pepper

1. Sauté onions and garlic
in olive oil in large skillet
over medium heat until
tender.
2. Add remaining fresh
veggies. Sauté 2-3 minutes.
Transfer to slow cooker.
3. Add remaining ingredi-
ents.
4. Cover. Cook on low 6-8
hours.

—— PER SERVING ——
• 80 calories
  (15 calories from fat)
• 2g total fat
  (0g saturated, 0g trans)
• 0mg cholesterol
• 500mg sodium
• 14g total carbohydrate
  (4g fiber, 5g sugar)
• 4g protein
• 30%DV vitamin A
• 20%DV vitamin C
• 6%DV calcium
• 6%DV iron

Tip:
  This is good served over
rice.

Vegetarian Chili with Mushrooms

Leona Yoder
Hartville, OH

Makes 8 servings

Soaking Time: 1 hour
Prep. Time: 30-45 minutes
Cooking Time: 6-8 hours
Ideal slow-cooker size: 4-qt.

1 cup dried pinto, *or* kidney, beans
3 cups water
1 Tbsp. vegetable oil
2 cups onions, chopped
1 green bell pepper, seeded and chopped
2 heaping cups fresh mushrooms, sliced (about 10 ozs.)
1 cup carrots, thinly sliced
2 cups fresh, *or* canned, unsalted tomatoes, chopped
6-oz. can unsalted tomato paste
¾ cup water
2 Tbsp. chili powder
1 large dried bay leaf
1 Tbsp. vinegar
1-2 tsp. garlic, finely minced

1. Place beans and 3 cups water in saucepan. Bring to boil and cook 2 minutes. Do not drain. Let sit 1 hour.

2. Pour beans and water into slow cooker. If water does not cover beans, add additional water to cover them.

3. Cover cooker. Cook on high 2 hours.

4. Heat oil in skillet. Add onions and green pepper. Cook until onions are transparent. Drain. Add to slow cooker.

5. Add remaining ingredients.

6. Cover. Cook on low 4-6 hours.

7. Remove bay leaf before serving.

8. Serve over brown rice or potatoes.

—— PER SERVING ——
- 100 calories (25 calories from fat)
- 2.5g total fat (0g saturated, 0g trans)
- 0mg cholesterol
- 170mg sodium
- 19g total carbohydrate (5g fiber, 6g sugar)
- 4g protein
- 180%DV vitamin A
- 20%DV vitamin C
- 4%DV calcium
- 10%DV iron

Variations:

1. Add the onions and green peppers to the cooker without cooking them in the skillet if you like.

2. If your diet allows, you may want to add 1 tsp. salt to Step 5. You can also increase the amount of chili powder and add ¼-½ tsp. black pepper.

Vegetable Chili

Janie Steele
Moore, OK

Makes 7 servings

Prep. Time: 25-30 minutes
Cooking Time: 6-8 hours
Ideal slow-cooker size: 4-qt.

1½ cups chopped onions
¾ cup chopped red bell pepper
¾ cup chopped green bell pepper
14½-oz. can fat-free, low-sodium vegetable broth
2 10-oz. cans diced tomatoes and green chilies, undrained
½ cup salsa
1 Tbsp. chili powder
1 tsp. ground cumin
¾ tsp. garlic powder
15-oz. can pinto beans, rinsed and drained
1 cup fresh, *or* frozen, corn
1 cup fat-free shredded cheddar cheese

1. Turn slow cooker on high.

2. Combine all ingredients except cheese in slow cooker.

3. Cover. Turn cooker to low and cook 6-8 hours.

4. Garnish with cheese when serving.

—— PER SERVING ——
- 160 calories (10 calories from fat)
- 1g total fat (0g saturated, 0g trans)
- 5mg cholesterol
- 850mg sodium
- 28g total carbohydrate (7g fiber, 8g sugar)
- 11g protein
- 40%DV vitamin A
- 40%DV vitamin C
- 25%DV calcium
- 10%DV iron

Liquids don't boil down in a slow cooker. At the end of the cooking time, remove the cover, set dial on High and allow the liquid to evaporate, if the dish is soup-ier than you want.

John D. Allen, Rye, CO

Hearty Veggie Chili

Nanci Keatley
Salem, OR

Makes 6 servings

Prep. Time: 20-25 minutes
Cooking Time: 6-8 hours
Ideal slow-cooker size: 4- or 5-qt.

1 Tbsp. olive oil
1 onion, chopped
1 carrot, thinly sliced
1 green bell pepper,
   chopped
8 ozs. fresh, *or* canned,
   mushrooms, sliced
1 small zucchini, sliced *or*
   cubed
12 black olives, *optional*
4 large garlic cloves,
   minced
28-oz. can low-sodium
   tomatoes, undrained
2 cups nonfat low-sodium
   tomato sauce
4-oz. can chopped green
   chilies
4 cups cooked kidney beans
2-3 Tbsp. chili powder,
   depending on your taste
   preference
1 Tbsp. dried oregano
2 tsp. ground cumin
2 tsp. paprika
1 Tbsp. white wine vinegar

1. Sauté onion in olive oil
in skillet.
2. Place in slow cooker.
3. Add remaining ingredi-
ents. Mix well.
4. Cover. Cook on low 6-8
hours.

— PER SERVING —
• 270 calories
  (40 calories from fat)
• 4g total fat
  (0.5g saturated,
  0g trans)
• 0mg cholesterol
• 1570mg sodium
• 48g total carbohydrate
  (13g fiber, 12g sugar)
• 14g protein
• 100%DV vitamin A
• 30%DV vitamin C
• 20%DV calcium
• 30%DV iron

Norma's Vegetarian Chili

Kathy Hertzler
Lancaster, PA

Makes 8-10 servings

Prep. Time: 25 minutes
Cooking Time: 8½ hours
Ideal slow-cooker size: 5-qt.

2 Tbsp. oil
2 cups minced celery
1½ cups chopped green
   bell peppers
1 cup minced onions
4 garlic cloves, minced
5½ cups low-sodium
   stewed tomatoes
2 1-lb. cans kidney beans,
   undrained
1½-2 cups raisins
¼ cup wine vinegar
1 Tbsp. chopped parsley
2 tsp. salt
1½ tsp. dried oregano
1½ tsp. ground cumin
¼ tsp. black pepper
¼ tsp. Tabasco sauce

1 bay leaf
¾ cup raw cashews
1 cup grated fat-free cheese

1. Combine all ingredients
except cashews and cheese in
slow cooker.
2. Cover. Simmer on low
8 hours. Add cashews and
simmer 30 minutes.
3. Garnish individual
servings with grated cheese.

— PER SERVING —
• 340 calories
  (80 calories from fat)
• 9g total fat
  (1.5g saturated,
  0g trans)
• 0mg cholesterol
• 1080mg sodium
• 55g total carbohydrate
  (8g fiber, 28g sugar)
• 12g protein
• 0%DV vitamin A
• 30%DV vitamin C
• 10%DV calcium
• 25%DV iron

In place of ground meat in a recipe, use vegetarian burgers. Cut them up, and you won't need to brown the meat.
Sue Hamilton, Minooka, IL

Vegetarian Chili Soup

Rosemarie Fitzgerald
Gibsonia, PA

Makes 8 servings

Prep. Time 20-30 minutes
Cooking Time: 4-9½ hours
Ideal slow-cooker size: 5-qt.

1 large onion, chopped
1 Tbsp. butter
1 clove garlic, finely
  chopped
2 tsp. chili powder
½ tsp. dried oregano,
  crumbled
2 14½-oz. cans vegetable
  broth
14½-oz. can no-salt-
  added stewed, *or* diced,
  tomatoes
5 cups water
½ tsp. salt
¼ tsp. black pepper
¾ lb. fresh kale
⅓ cup white long-grain
  rice, uncooked
19-oz. can cannellini
  beans, drained and
  rinsed

1. Sauté onion in skillet in butter until tender.

2. Add garlic, chili powder, and oregano. Cook 30 seconds. Pour into slow cooker.

3. Add remaining ingredients except kale, rice, and beans.

4. Cover. Cook on low 7 hours or on high 3-4 hours.

5. Cut kale stalks into small pieces and chop leaves coarsely.

6. Add to soup with rice and beans.

7. Cover. Cook on high 1-2½ hours more, or until rice is tender and kale is done to your liking.

—— PER SERVING ——
• 120 calories   • 24g total carbohydrate
  (15 calories from fat)   (6g fiber, 6g sugar)
• 1.5g total fat   • 6g protein
  (0g saturated, 0g trans) • 80%DV vitamin A
• 0mg cholesterol   • 20%DV vitamin C
• 790mg sodium   • 10%DV calcium
               • 15%DV iron

Vegetarian Chili with Corn

Jennifer Dzialowski
Brunton, MI

Makes 8-10 servings

Prep. Time: 20 minutes
Cooking Time: 2-5 hours
Ideal slow-cooker size: 6-qt.

2 15-oz. cans diced
  tomatoes, undrained
2 15-oz. cans kidney beans,
  drained
15-oz. can garbanzo beans,
  drained
15-oz. can corn, drained
1 bell pepper, chopped
½ cup, *or more*, onions,
  chopped
6 cups low-sodium tomato
  juice
2 Tbsp. minced garlic
½ tsp. ground cumin
½ tsp. dried oregano
¼-½ tsp. black pepper,
  according to taste
1-3 tsp. chili powder,
  according to your taste
  preference
1 cup Textured Vegetarian
  Protein (T.V.P.)

1. Place tomatoes, kidney beans, garbanzo beans, corn, bell pepper, and onions in slow cooker.

2. Add tomato juice, garlic, cumin, oregano, black pepper, and chili powder. Top with Textured Vegetable Protein.

3. Cover. Cook on low 4-5 hours or on high 2 hours.

—— PER SERVING ——
• 270 calories   • 52g total carbohydrate
  (15 calories from fat)   (12g fiber, 15g sugar)
• 2g total fat   • 17g protein
  (0g saturated, 0g trans) • 30%DV vitamin A
• 0mg cholesterol   • 80%DV vitamin C
• 900mg sodium   • 15%DV calcium
               • 30%DV iron

Variation:

If your sodium intake allows, you may want to add 1 tsp. salt to Step 2.

Beans and Tomato Chili

Joleen Albrecht
Gladstone, MI

Makes 10 servings

Prep. Time: 10-15 minutes
Cooking Time: 2-4 hours
Ideal slow-cooker size: 5-qt.

15½-oz. can kidney beans, rinsed and drained
19-oz. can black bean soup
15½-oz. can garbanzo beans, rinsed and drained
16-oz. can vegetarian baked beans
15-oz. can whole-kernel corn, drained
14½-oz. can low-sodium chopped tomatoes
1 green bell pepper, chopped
1 onion, chopped
2 ribs celery, chopped
2 cloves garlic, chopped
1 Tbsp. chili powder
1 Tbsp. dried oregano
1 Tbsp. dried parsley
1 Tbsp. dried basil
1½ tsp. Tabasco, *optional*
fat-free sour cream, *optional*
low-fat shredded cheddar cheese, *optional*
baked tortilla chips, *optional*

1. Combine all beans, soup, and all vegetables in slow cooker.
2. Stir in all seasonings. (Do not add sour cream, shredded cheese, or tortilla chips.)
3. Cover. Cook on high 2-3 hours, or on low 4 hours.

4. If you wish, garnish individual servings of chili with sour cream, shredded cheese, and tortilla chips.

—— PER SERVING ——
• 210 calories
  (15 calories from fat)
• 2g total fat
  (0g saturated, 0g trans)
• 0mg cholesterol
• 610mg sodium
• 41g total carbohydrate
  (10g fiber, 10g sugar)
• 11g protein
• 35%DV vitamin A
• 35%DV vitamin C
• 10%DV calcium
• 20%DV iron

Wintertime-Vegetables Chili

Maricarol Magill
Freehold, NJ

Makes 6 servings

Prep. Time: 30 minutes
Cooking Time: 6-8 hours
Ideal slow-cooker size: 6-qt.

1 medium-sized butternut squash, peeled and cubed
2 medium-sized carrots, peeled and diced

1 medium-sized onion, diced
1-4 Tbsp. chili powder, depending upon how hot you like your chili
2 14-oz. cans diced low-sodium tomatoes
4-oz. can chopped mild green chilies
½ tsp. salt
1 cup fat-free, low-sodium vegetable broth
2 16-oz. cans black beans, drained and rinsed
⅓ cup fat-free sour cream

1. In slow cooker, layer all ingredients in order given—except sour cream.
2. Cover. Cook on low 6-8 hours, or until vegetables are tender.
3. Stir before serving.
4. Top individual servings with dollops of sour cream.

—— PER SERVING ——
• 200 calories
  (10 calories from fat)
• 1g total fat
  (0g saturated, 0g trans)
• 0mg cholesterol
• 1310mg sodium
• 40g total carbohydrate
  (13g fiber, 9g sugar)
• 11g protein
• 100%DV vitamin A
• 20%DV vitamin C
• 20%DV calcium
• 15%DV iron

Chili-Chili Bang-Bang

Vera Schmucker
Goshen, IN

Makes 8 servings

Prep. Time: 30-35 minutes
Cooking Time: 4 hours
Ideal slow-cooker size: 5-qt.

1¼ cups onions, coarsely
    chopped
1 cup red bell peppers,
    chopped
1 cup green bell peppes,
    chopped
¾ cup celery, chopped
¾ cup carrots, chopped
3 cloves garlic, minced
1 Tbsp. chili powder
1½ cups quartered fresh
    mushrooms
1 cup zucchini, cubed
28-oz. can low-sodium
    diced tomatoes
28-oz. can black beans,
    drained and rinsed
15-oz. can chickpeas,
    drained and rinsed
11-oz. can kernel corn,
    undrained
1 Tbsp. ground cumin
1½ tsp. dried oregano
1½ tsp. dried basil
½ tsp. cayenne pepper

1. Combine all ingredients
in slow cooker.
2. Cover. Cook on high
4 hours, stirring occasionally.

—— PER SERVING ——
• 230 calories
  (20 calories from fat)
• 2g total fat
  (0g saturated, 0g trans)
• 0mg cholesterol
• 890mg sodium
• 48g total carbohydrate
  (13g fiber, 10g sugar)
• 12g protein
• 100%DV vitamin A
• 60%DV vitamin C
• 15%DV calcium
• 20%DV iron

Hearty Bean and Vegetable Stew

Jeanette Oberholtzer
Manheim, PA

Makes 12 servings

*Soaking Time: 8 hours or
overnight*
Prep. Time: 25-30 minutes
Cooking Time: 8-9 hours
Ideal slow-cooker size: 5-qt.

1 lb. dry beans, assorted
2 cups fat-free vegetable
    broth
½ cup white wine
⅓ cup soy sauce
⅓ cup apple, *or* pineapple,
    juice, unsweetened
vegetable stock, *or* water
½ cup celery, diced
½ cup parsnips, diced
½ cup carrots, diced
½ cup mushrooms, sliced
1 onion, sliced
1 tsp. dried basil
1 tsp. parsley flakes
1 bay leaf
3 cloves garlic, minced

1 tsp. black pepper
1 cup rice, *or* pasta, cooked

1. Sort and rinse beans
and soak overnight in water.
Drain. Place in slow cooker.
2. Add vegetable juice,
wine, soy sauce, and apple or
pineapple juice.
3. Cover with vegetable
stock or water.
4. Cover. Cook on high 2
hours.
5. Add vegetables, herbs,
and spices.
6. Cover cooker. Cook on
low 5-6 hours, or until carrots
and parsnips are tender.
7. Add cooked rice or pasta.
8. Cover. Cook 1 hour more
on low.

—— PER SERVING ——
• 180 calories
  (5 calories from fat)
• 0.5g total fat
  (0g saturated, 0g trans)
• 0mg cholesterol
• 370mg sodium
• 34g total carbohydrate
  (9g fiber, 6g sugar)
• 10g protein
• 35%DV vitamin A
• 10%DV vitamin C
• 6%DV calcium
• 20%DV iron

Tip:
Use 3 or 4 kinds of beans
such as black, kidney, pinto,
baby lima, lentils, or split
peas.

*Don't peek. It takes 15-20 minutes for the cooker to
regain lost steam and return to the right temperature.*

Janet V. Yocum, Elizabethtown, PA

185

Mexican Rice and Bean Soup

Esther J. Mast
East Petersburg, PA

Makes 6 servings

Prep. Time: 15-20 minutes
Cooking Time: 6 hours
Ideal slow-cooker size: 4-qt.

½ cup chopped onions
⅓ cup chopped green bell
 peppers
1 garlic clove, minced
1 Tbsp. oil
4-oz. pkg. sliced, *or* chipped,
 dried beef
18-oz. can low-sodium
 tomato juice
15½-oz. can red kidney
 beans, undrained
1½ cups water
½ cup long-grain rice,
 uncooked
1 tsp. paprika
½-1 tsp. chili powder
½ tsp. salt
dash of black pepper

1. Cook onions, green peppers, and garlic in oil in skillet until vegetables are tender but not brown. Transfer to slow cooker.
2. Tear beef into small pieces and add to slow cooker.
3. Add remaining ingredients. Mix well.
4. Cover. Cook on low 6 hours. Stir before serving.

PER SERVING

- 190 calories
 (30 calories from fat)
- 3.5g total fat (0.5g
 saturated, 0g trans)
- 10mg cholesterol
- 1110mg sodium
- 30g total carbohydrate
 (6g fiber, 5g sugar)
- 11g protein
- 10%DV vitamin A
- 20%DV vitamin C
- 4%DV calcium
- 20%DV iron

Note:

 This is a recipe I fixed often when our sons were growing up. We have all enjoyed it in any season of the year.

Beef 'n' Black Bean Soup

Deborah Santiago
Lancaster, PA

Makes 10 servings (2½ quarts)

Prep. Time: 20-25 minutes
Cooking Time: 6-7 hours
Ideal slow-cooker size: 4- or 5-qt.

1 lb. extra-lean ground beef
2 14½-oz. cans fat-free, low-
 sodium chicken broth
14½-oz. can low-sodium,
 diced tomatoes,
 undrained
8 green onions, thinly sliced
3 medium carrots, thinly
 sliced
2 celery ribs, thinly sliced
2 garlic cloves, minced
1 Tbsp. sugar
1½ tsp. dried basil
½ tsp. salt
½ tsp. dried oregano
½ tsp. ground cumin
½ tsp. chili powder
2 15-oz. cans black beans,
 rinsed and drained
1½ cups cooked rice

1. In a nonstick skillet over medium heat, cook beef until no longer pink. Drain.
2. Place beef in slow cooker.
3. Add remaining ingredients except black beans and rice.
4. Cover. Cook on high 1 hour.
5. Reduce to low. Cook 4-5 hours, or until vegetables are tender.
6. Add beans and rice.
7. Cook 1 hour longer on low, or until heated through.

PER SERVING

- 200 calories
 (40 calories from fat)
- 4.5g total fat (1.5g
 saturated, 0g trans)
- 15mg cholesterol
- 640mg sodium
- 23g total carbohydrate
 (6g fiber, 4g sugar)
- 17g protein
- 6%DV vitamin A
- 10%DV vitamin C
- 8%DV calcium
- 20%DV iron

Variation:

 If you enjoy tomatoes, you can brighten the flavor by adding a second 14½-oz. can of diced tomatoes, undrained.

Caribbean-Style Black Bean Soup

Sheryl Shenk
Harrisonburg, VA

Makes 8 servings

Soaking Time: 8 hours or overnight
Prep. Time: 15-20 minutes
Cooking Time: 4-10 hours
Ideal slow-cooker size: 4-qt.

1 lb. dried black beans, washed and stones removed
3 onions, chopped
1 green bell pepper, chopped
4 cloves garlic, minced
1 lean ham hock, *or* ¾ cup lean cubed ham
1 Tbsp. oil
1 Tbsp. ground cumin
1-2 tsp. dried oregano, according to your taste preference
¼-1 tsp. dried thyme, depending upon how much you like thyme
1 tsp. salt
½ tsp. black pepper

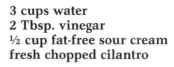

3 cups water
2 Tbsp. vinegar
½ cup fat-free sour cream
fresh chopped cilantro

1. Soak beans overnight in 4 quarts water. Drain.
2. Combine soaked beans, onions, green pepper, garlic, ham or ham hock, oil, cumin, oregano, thyme, salt, pepper, and 3 cups fresh water. Stir well.
3. Cover. Cook on low 8-10 hours, or on high 4-5 hours.
4. For a thick soup, remove half of cooked bean mixture and purée until smooth in blender or mash with potato masher. Return to cooker. If you like a soup-ier soup, leave as is.
5. Add vinegar and stir well. If you used a ham hock, debone the ham, cut into bite-sized pieces, and return to soup.
6. Serve soup in bowls with a dollop of sour cream in the middle of each individual serving, topped with fresh cilantro.

—— PER SERVING ——
• 100 calories (30 calories from fat)
• 3g total fat (0.5g saturated, 0g trans)
• 5mg cholesterol
• 880mg sodium
• 14g total carbohydrate (4g fiber, 4g sugar)
• 5g protein
• 0%DV vitamin A
• 10%DV vitamin C
• 6%DV calcium
• 8%DV iron

Black Bean and Corn Soup

Joy Sutter
Iowa City, IA

Makes 6-8 servings

Prep. Time: 15 minutes
Cooking Time: 5-6 hours
Ideal slow-cooker size: 3½- or 4-qt.

2 15-oz. cans black beans, drained and rinsed
14½-oz. can low-sodium Mexican stewed tomatoes, undrained
14½-oz. can diced low-sodium tomatoes, undrained
11-oz. can whole-kernel corn, drained
4 green onions, sliced
2-3 Tbsp. chili powder
1 tsp. ground cumin
½ tsp. dried minced garlic

1. Combine all ingredients in slow cooker.
2. Cover. Cook on high 5-6 hours.

—— PER SERVING ——
• 170 calories (10 calories from fat)
• 1.5g total fat (0g saturated, 0g trans)
• 0mg cholesterol
• 790mg sodium
• 35g total carbohydrate (10g fiber, 9g sugar)
• 9g protein
• 10%DV vitamin A
• 10%DV vitamin C
• 10%DV calcium
• 15%DV iron

Variations:
1. For a varied taste, use 2 cloves fresh garlic, minced, instead of dried garlic.
2. To include more vegetables, add 1 large rib celery, sliced thin, and 1 small green bell pepper, chopped.

Mexican Black Bean Soup

Becky Harder
Monument, CO

Makes 8 servings

Prep. Time: 15 minutes
Cooking Time: 6-8 hours
Ideal slow-cooker size: 4-qt.

28-oz. can fat-free low-
   sodium chicken broth
1 cup onions, chopped
2 tsp. minced garlic
3 cups fat-free black beans
2 tsp. chili powder
¾ tsp. ground cumin
28-oz. can Mexican
   tomatoes with green
   chilies *or* jalapeños
¾ tsp. lemon juice
fat-free sour cream
1 bunch green onions

1. Combine all ingredients
except green onions and sour
cream in slow cooker.
2. Cover. Cook on low 6-8
hours.
3. Top each individual
serving with sliced green
onions sprinkled over a
spoonful of sour cream.

—— PER SERVING ——
- 130 calories
  (10 calories from fat)
- 1g total fat
  (0g saturated, 0g trans)
- 0mg cholesterol
- 830mg sodium
- 24g total carbohydrate
  (7g fiber, 4g sugar)
- 10g protein
- 10%DV vitamin A
- 4%DV vitamin C
- 10%DV calcium
- 15%DV iron

Slow-Cooker Black Bean Chili

Mary Seielstad
Sparks, NV

Makes 8 servings

Prep. Time: 25 minutes
Cooking Time: 6-8 hours
Ideal slow-cooker size: 3½- or 4-qt.

1 lb. lean pork tenderloin,
   cut into 1" chunks
16-oz. jar low-sodium,
   thick, chunky salsa
3 15-oz. cans black beans,
   rinsed and drained
½ cup fat-free, low-sodium
   chicken broth
1 medium-sized red bell
   pepper, chopped
1 medium-sized onion,
   chopped
1 tsp. ground cumin
2-3 tsp. chili powder
1-1½ tsp. dried oregano
¼ cup fat-free sour cream

1. Combine all ingredients
except sour cream in slow
cooker.
2. Cover. Cook on low 6-8
hours, or until pork is tender.
3. Garnish individual
servings with sour cream.

—— PER SERVING ——
- 250 calories
  (30 calories from fat)
- 3.5g total fat
  (1g saturated, 0g trans)
- 40mg cholesterol
- 1050mg sodium
- 34g total carbohydrate
  (10g fiber, 7g sugar)
- 24g protein
- 10%DV vitamin A
- 20%DV vitamin C
- 8%DV calcium
- 20%DV iron

Tip:
   This is good served over
brown rice.

Sausage and Black Bean Stew

John D. Allen
Rye, CO

Makes 6 servings

Prep. Time: 20 minutes
Cooking Time: 5½-7½ hours
Ideal slow-cooker size: 6-qt.

3 15-oz. cans black beans,
   drained and rinsed
14½-oz. can fat-free,
   reduced-sodium chicken
   broth
1 cup celery, sliced
2 4-oz. cans green chilies,
   chopped
3 cloves garlic, minced
1½ tsp. dried oregano
¾ tsp. coriander, ground
½ tsp. ground cumin
¼ tsp. ground red pepper
   (not cayenne)
1 lb. link turkey sausage,
   thinly sliced and cooked

1. Combine all ingredients
in slow cooker except sausage.
2. Cover. Cook on low 5-7
hours.
3. Remove 1½ cups of bean
mixture and purée in blender.
Return to slow cooker.
4. Add sliced sausage.
5. Cover. Cook on low 30
minutes.

—— PER SERVING ——
- 310 calories
  (80 calories from fat)
- 9g total fat
  (2g saturated, 0g trans)
- 55mg cholesterol
- 1580mg sodium
- 36g total carbohydrate
  (13g fiber, 2g sugar)
- 28g protein
- 2%DV vitamin A
- 2%DV vitamin C
- 15%DV calcium
- 25%DV iron

Lentil and Rice Pilaf, page 114

Macaroni and Cheddar/Parmesan Cheese, page 117

Variation:

If your diet permits, you may want to add ¾ tsp. salt to Step 1.

Turkey Chili with Black Beans

Susan Tjon
Austin, TX

Makes 5 servings

Prep. Time: 45 minutes
Cooking Time: 4-5 hours
Ideal slow-cooker size: 4- or 5-qt.

1 lb. uncooked ground turkey breast
1 large onion, finely chopped
1 green bell pepper, chopped
14-oz. can fat-free, reduced-sodium chicken broth
2 tsp. chili powder, *or* more, according to your preference
½ tsp. ground all-spice
¼ tsp. ground cinnamon
¼ tsp. paprika
15-oz. can black beans, rinsed and drained
14-oz. can tomato puree
2 tsp. cider vinegar

1. Spray skillet with fat-free cooking spray. Brown turkey with onion and green pepper, breaking up the turkey and cooking until the meat is no longer pink.
2. Combine all ingredients in slow cooker.
3. Cook on low 4-5 hours.

—— **PER SERVING** ——
- 280 calories
  (80 calories from fat)
- 9g total fat
  (2g saturated, 0g trans)
- 70mg cholesterol
- 560mg sodium
- 25g total carbohydrate
  (8g fiber, 8g sugar)
- 25g protein
- 20%DV vitamin A
- 60%DV vitamin C
- 8%DV calcium
- 25%DV iron

Tip:

I brown my turkey the night before so I only need to combine the ingredients in my slow cooker in the morning.

Black Bean Chili

Rashell Harris
Wichita, KS

Makes 6 servings

Soaking Time: 8 hours or overnight
Prep. Time: 20-25 minutes
Cooking Time: 6-10 hours
Ideal slow-cooker size: 6-qt.

2 cups black beans, dried
6 cups water
1 bunch cilantro, chopped
1-2 Tbsp. ground cumin
1 Tbsp. dried oregano
1 tsp. paprika
½ tsp. cayenne pepper
2 tsp. olive oil
1 large onion, chopped
1 bell pepper, diced
2 cloves garlic, minced
1 pkg. dry Herb-Ox vegetable broth
1½ cups tomatoes, chopped
½ tsp. salt
¼ cup green onions, chopped
additional cilantro

1. Rinse beans. Place in stockpot and cover with water. Soak beans overnight. Drain and rinse before mixing with other ingredients and placing in slow cooker.
2. Place all ingredients (including 6 cups fresh water) except tomatoes, salt, green onions, and additional cilantro in slow cooker.
3. Cover. Cook on low 8-10 hours or high 6-8 hours.
4. Add tomatoes and salt. Place in bowls. Garnish with onions and additional cilantro.

—— **PER SERVING** ——
- 270 calories
  (30 calories from fat)
- 3g total fat
  (0g saturated, 0g trans)
- 0mg cholesterol
- 180mg sodium
- 48g total carbohydrate
  (12g fiber, 12g sugar)
- 15g protein
- 10%DV vitamin A
- 25%DV vitamin C
- 10%DV calcium
- 25%DV iron

Tips:

1. Serve with corn bread if desired.
2. If diets allow, you may top individual servings with a dollop of lowfat sour cream and a spoonful of grated low-fat cheddar cheese.

Cabbage Bean Soup

Joy Sutter
Iowa City, IA

Makes 24 servings

Prep. Time: 20-25 minutes
Cooking Time: 3-10 hours
Ideal slow-cooker size: 2 6-qt. cookers

16-oz. can kidney beans, drained
15-oz. can black beans, drained
1 cup onions, chopped
4 cups fat-free beef broth
4 cups crushed canned tomatoes
2-3 cups carrots, chopped
1 cup celery, chopped
1 cup tomato sauce
11 cups cabbage, shredded
4 cups frozen mixed vegetables
¼ cup fresh parsley, chopped
1½ tsp. dried basil
4 cups water (*or more*), according to the consistency you prefer

1. Combine all ingredients in slow cooker.
2. Cook on high 3-5 hours or low 8-10 hours.

—— PER SERVING ——
• 160 calories
  (5 calories from fat)
• 1g total fat
  (0g saturated, 0g trans)
• 0mg cholesterol
• 510mg sodium
• 32g total carbohydrate
  (10g fiber, 9g sugar)
• 10g protein
• 200%DV vitamin A
• 30%DV vitamin C
• 10%DV calcium
• 15%DV iron

Football Bean Serve

Dianna R. Milhizer
Brighton, MI

Makes 12 servings

Prep. Time: 20-25 minutes
Cooking Time: 6-8 hours
Ideal slow-cooker size: 4-qt.

1 lb. ground turkey
1 cup minced onions
2 cups diced celery
2 cups diced carrots
2 15-oz. cans kidney beans, drained and rinsed
2 15-oz. cans pinto beans, drained and rinsed
2 15-oz. cans diced tomatoes
2 cups water
1 Tbsp. garlic powder
1 Tbsp. parsley flakes
1 Tbsp. dried oregano
1 Tbsp. cumin powder
1 Tbsp. salt

1. Brown turkey with onions in nonstick skillet over medium heat. Add celery and carrots and cook until just wilted. Place in slow cooker.
2. Add remaining ingredients. Stir to combine.
3. Cover. Cook on low 6-8 hours.
4. Serve over brown rice. If you wish, sprinkle baked tortilla chips over top.

—— PER SERVING ——
• 200 calories
  (15 calories from fat)
• 1.5g total fat
  (0g saturated, 0g trans)
• 15mg cholesterol
• 1280mg sodium
• 29g total carbohydrate
  (8g fiber, 6g sugar)
• 18g protein
• 100%DV vitamin A
• 10%DV vitamin C
• 10%DV calcium
• 20%DV iron

Tips:
1. This is a perfect dish to serve after an afternoon of football games.
2. This is a high-fiber meal. I usually cook dried beans from scratch the night before making the soup. You can adjust the spices, adding more or less to suit your taste.
3. If you start with dried beans, you can cook them whenever it's convenient for you and keep them in the freezer until you need them. You can then use them for soups or stews or purée them for tacos or sandwiches.

Minestrone Soup

Kathy Moyer
Ottsville, PA

Makes 12 servings

Prep. Time: 25 minutes
Cooking Time: 6 hours
Ideal slow-cooker size: 4-qt.

1 lb. extra-lean ground beef
1 large onion, chopped
1 clove garlic, minced
2 15½-oz. cans low-sodium stewed tomatoes
15-oz. can kidney beans, drained
10-oz. pkg. frozen corn
2 ribs celery, sliced
2 small zucchini, sliced
1 cup uncooked macaroni
2½ cups hot water
2 beef bouillon cubes
½ tsp. salt
2 tsp. Italian seasoning

1. Brown ground beef in nonstick skillet.

2. Combine browned ground beef, onion, garlic, stewed tomatoes, kidney beans, corn, celery, zucchini, and macaroni in slow cooker.

3. Dissolve bouillon cubes in hot water. Combine with salt and Italian seasoning. Add to slow cooker.

4. Cover. Cook on low 6 hours.

—— PER SERVING ——
- 180 calories (35 calories from fat)
- 4g total fat (1.5g saturated, 0g trans)
- 15mg cholesterol
- 430mg sodium
- 24g total carbohydrate (4g fiber, 6g sugar)
- 13g protein
- 4%DV vitamin A
- 10%DV vitamin C
- 4%DV calcium
- 15%DV iron

Mexican Bean Soup

Andrea Cunningham
Arlington, KS

Makes 8 servings

Prep. Time: 10 minutes
Cooking Time: 8½-10½ hours
Ideal slow-cooker size: 4- or 5-qt.

¾ cup dried pinto beans, rinsed
¾ cup dried kidney beans, rinsed
2 Tbsp. dried onion flakes
2 Tbsp. dried parsley flakes
1 Tbsp. chili powder
2 tsp. ground cumin
1 tsp. dried oregano
6 chicken bouillon cubes
½ cup brown rice, uncooked
8 cups water
1 cup uncooked small-cut pasta

1. Combine all ingredients except pasta in slow cooker.
2. Cover. Cook on low 8-10 hours.
3. Add pasta.
4. Cover. Cook on high 30 minutes.

—— PER SERVING ——
- 120 calories (10 calories from fat)
- 1g total fat (0g saturated, 0g trans)
- 0mg cholesterol
- 1070mg sodium
- 24g total carbohydrate (3g fiber, 2g sugar)
- 5g protein
- 0%DV vitamin A
- 0%DV vitamin C
- 4%DV calcium
- 8%DV iron

Tip:
This makes a good gift. Put dried beans into a 1-quart jar with lid. Put flavor packet ingredients in a sandwich-size plastic bag. Seal bag with tie or ribbon. Do the same with the pasta. Place in the jar with the beans. Attach the cooking directions to the outside of the jar. You're ready to give a healthy, nutritious gift.

Taco Twist Soup

Janie Steele
Moore, OK

Makes 6-8 servings

Prep. Time: 15-20 minutes
Cooking Time: 4-6 hours
Ideal slow-cooker size: 3- or 4-qt.

1 medium-sized onion, chopped
2 garlic cloves, minced
2 Tbsp. canola, *or* olive, oil
3 cups reduced-sodium beef broth, *or* vegetable, broth
15-oz. can black beans, rinsed and drained
14½-oz. can diced tomatoes, undrained
1½ cups picante sauce
1 cup spiral pasta, uncooked
1 small green bell pepper, chopped
2 tsp. chili powder
1 tsp. ground cumin
½ cup shredded reduced-fat cheese
fat-free sour cream, *optional*

1. Sauté onions and garlic in oil in skillet.
2. Combine all ingredients except cheese and sour cream in slow cooker.
3. Cook on low 4-6 hours, or just until pasta is tender.
4. Add cheese and sour cream as desired when serving.

—— PER SERVING ——
- 220 calories (60 calories from fat)
- 6g total fat (1g saturated, 0g trans)
- 0mg cholesterol
- 1060mg sodium
- 31g total carbohydrate (6g fiber, 6g sugar)
- 11g protein
- 10%DV vitamin A
- 20%DV vitamin C
- 10%DV calcium
- 10%DV iron

Tip:
An alternative method is to cook the pasta in 3 cups broth on top of the stove in a saucepan, and then add it (along with the broth in which it cooked) during the last 15 minutes of the Soup's cooking time. That would allow the Soup to cook longer without risking mushy noodles, if that better fits your schedule.

Taco Corn Soup

Sara Kinsinger
Stuarts Draft, VA

Makes 6 servings

Prep. Time: 20 minutes
Cooking Time: 4 hours
Ideal slow-cooker size: 6-qt.

1 large onion, chopped
1 lb. extra-lean ground beef
1 envelope dry taco
  seasoning
16-oz. can kidney beans,
  drained
16-oz. can corn, drained
2 qts. tomato juice
¼ cup sugar
½ tsp. salt
¼-½ tsp. black pepper,
  according to taste
7 ozs. baked corn chips,
  optional
reduced fat grated cheese,
  optional
fat-free sour cream,
  optional

1. Brown hamburger and
chopped onion in nonstick
skillet. Drain.
2. Combine ground beef,
onions, taco seasoning,
kidney beans, corn,
tomato juice, sugar,
salt, and pepper in
slow cooker.
3. Cook on low
4 hours or until
heated through.

— PER SERVING —
• 650 calories
  (210 calories from fat)
• 23g total fat
  (7g saturated, 0g trans)
• 40mg cholesterol
• 2200mg sodium
• 81g total carbohydrate
  (9g fiber, 25g sugar)
• 32g protein
• 40%DV vitamin A
• 40%DV vitamin C
• 30%DV calcium
• 30%DV iron

Note:
If you prefer a less juicy
stew, remove the lid during
the last hour of cooking.

Note from tester:
Our son, Quincy, who
would prefer to live on bread
and chocolate alone, initially
turned up his nose in disgust
at the Soup. I explained that I
wanted him to try this recipe
and give his opinion because
that's why I had made the
Soup. So…3 good-sized servings later…we determined it
was a rave review.

Southwest Chicken and White Bean Soup

Karen Ceneviva
Seymour, CT

Makes 6 servings

Prep. Time: 15 minutes
Cooking Time: 2-4 hours
Ideal slow-cooker size: 3½-qt.

1 lb. boneless, skinless
  chicken breasts, cut into
  1" cubes
1¾ cups low-sodium, fat-
  free chicken broth
1 cup low-sodium chunky
  salsa
3 cloves garlic, minced
2 Tbsp. cumin
15½-oz. can small white
  beans, drained and
  rinsed
1 cup frozen corn
1 large onion, chopped

1. Brown chicken on all
sides in 10" nonstick skillet
over medium to high heat.
Stir frequently to prevent
sticking.
2. Mix broth, salsa, garlic,
cumin, beans, corn, and
onion in slow cooker. Add
chicken. Stir well.
3. Cover. Cook 2 hours on
high or 4 hours on low.

— PER SERVING —
• 200 calories
  (25 calories from fat)
• 2.5g total fat
  (0.5g saturated,
  0g trans)
• 40mg cholesterol
• 190mg sodium
• 22g total carbohydrate
  (5g fiber, 2g sugar)
• 22g protein
• 4%DV vitamin A
• 15%DV vitamin C
• 8%DV calcium
• 20%DV iron

Oh! Good! Soup!

Alix Nancy Botsford
Seminole, OK

Makes 10 servings

Soaking Time: 2-6 hours
Prep. Time: 20-25 minutes
Cooking Time: 3-6 hours
Ideal slow-cooker size: 5-qt.

2 cups mixed, dried beans
2½ qts. water
1 large onion, chopped
1 garlic clove, minced
28-oz. can low-sodium
   diced tomatoes
½ cup red bell pepper,
   chopped
½ cup celery, chopped
juice of 1 lemon
1 tsp. salt
1 tsp. black pepper
several drops Tabasco
   sauce, according to your
   taste preference
1 cup brown rice, uncooked
1 cup assorted small pasta,
   cooked

1. Sort and wash beans.
Cover with water. Soak 2-6
hours. Drain.
2. Place beans in slow
cooker. Add 2½ quarts fresh
water.
3. Cover. Cook on high
2 hours.
4. Add all remaining
ingredients except pasta.
5. Add enough water so all
ingredients are covered.
6. Cover. Cook on high
3 hours or on low 6 hours.

7. Add pasta just before
serving.

—— PER SERVING ——
• 210 calories
  (10 calories from fat)
• 1g total fat
  (0g saturated, 0g trans)
• 5mg cholesterol
• 470mg sodium
• 41g total carbohydrate
  (11g fiber, 6g sugar)
• 11g protein
• 10%DV vitamin A
• 20%DV vitamin C
• 10%DV calcium
• 20%DV iron

Tip:
   When using pasta for other
dishes, always reserve a
small handful in a reclosable
bag. That way you will have
a variety of shapes for this
soup.

Navy Bean Vegetable Soup

Lavina Hochstedler
Grand Blanc, MI

Makes 12 servings

Prep. Time: 25 minutes
Cooking Time: 9-10 hours
Ideal slow-cooker size: 6-qt.

4 medium-sized carrots,
   thinly sliced
2 celery ribs, chopped
1 medium-sized onion,
   chopped
2 cups fully cooked
   ham cubes, trimmed
   of fat
1½ cups dried navy beans
1.68-oz. pkg. dry vegetable
   soup mix
1 envelope dry onion soup
   mix
1 bay leaf

½ tsp. black pepper
8 cups water
1 tsp. salt, *optional*

1. Combine all ingredients
in slow cooker.
2. Cover. Cook on low 9-10
hours.
3. Discard bay leaf before
serving.

—— PER SERVING ——
• 160 calories
  (20 calories from fat)
• 2.5g total fat
  (1g saturated, 0g trans)
• 20mg cholesterol
• 520mg sodium
• 22g total carbohydrate
  (8g fiber, 4g sugar)
• 14g protein
• 100%DV vitamin A
• 0%DV vitamin C
• 6%DV calcium
• 15%DV iron

Variation:
   If you like the taste, and
your diet allows, you may
want to substitute smoked
turkey sausage or kielbasa in
place of the ham.

193

Black Bean and Butternut Chicken Chili

Colleen Heatwole
Burton, MI

Makes 12 servings

Prep. Time: 20 minutes
Cooking Time: 4-5 hours
Ideal slow-cooker size: 5-qt.

1 medium onion, chopped
1 medium red bell sweet
  pepper, chopped
3 cloves garlic, minced
1 tsp. olive oil
3 cups low-sodium, fat-free
  chicken broth
2 15-oz. can black beans,
  rinsed and drained
2½ cups cooked chicken, *or*
  turkey, cubed
3 cups butternut squash,
  peeled and cubed
14½-oz. can crushed
  tomatoes
2 tsp. dried parsley flakes
1½ tsp. dried oregano

1½ tsp. cumin
1 tsp. chili powder
½ tsp. salt

1. In large skillet, sauté onion, red pepper, and garlic in olive oil until tender. Stir frequently to prevent sticking.
2. Combine sautéed ingredients with all other ingredients in slow cooker.
3. Cover. Cook on low 4-5 hours, or until vegetables are done to your liking.

—— PER SERVING ——
- 150 calories
  (25 calories from fat)
- 3g total fat
  (0.5g saturated,
  0g trans)
- 20mg cholesterol
- 300mg sodium
- 19g total carbohydrate
  (6g fiber, 1g sugar)
- 13g protein
- 80%DV vitamin A
- 35%DV vitamin C
- 6%DV calcium
- 15%DV iron

Gourmet White Chili

Rashell Harris
Wichita, KS

Makes 8 servings

Soaking Time: 8 hours or
* overnight*
Prep. Time: 20-30 minutes
Cooking Time: 4-10 hours
Ideal slow-cooker size: 5-qt.

1 lb. dried great northern
  white beans
1 Tbsp. olive oil
2 medium-sized onions,
  chopped
4 cloves garlic, minced
8-oz. can chopped green
  chilies
2 tsp. ground cumin
2 tsp. dried oregano
¼ tsp. ground cloves
¼ tsp cayenne pepper
2 lbs. boneless, skinless,
  chicken breasts, cubed
  and uncooked
6 cups low-fat, low-sodium
  chicken broth
2 cups grated low-fat, *or*
  fat-free, cheese, *divided*
1 tsp. salt
½ tsp. black pepper

Garnishes:
  1 cup fat-free sour cream
  1 cup salsa
  ½ cup cilantro

1. Cover beans with water and soak overnight. Drain, discarding soaking water.
2. In skillet, sauté onions in olive oil until clear. Add garlic, green chilies, cumin,

oregano, cloves, and cayenne. Sauté 2 minutes more. (This step may be skipped if you are pressed for time.)

3. Place all ingredients in slow cooker except cheese and garnishes.

4. Cover. Cook on low 8-10 hours or on high 4-6 hours.

5. Add 1 cup of cheese. Stir until melted.

6. Serve in bowls topped with garnishes and remaining cheese.

— PER SERVING —
- 510 calories
  (70 calories from fat)
- 8g total fat
  (3g saturated, 0g trans)
- 95mg cholesterol
- 770mg sodium
- 46g total carbohydrate
  (11g fiber, 11g sugar)
- 60g protein
- 10%DV vitamin A
- 10%DV vitamin C
- 50%DV calcium
- 50%DV iron

Chicken Barley Chili

Colleen Heatwole
Burton, MI

Makes 12 servings

Prep. Time: 20 minutes
Cooking Time: 6-8 hours
Ideal slow-cooker size: 6-qt.

2 14½-oz. cans low-sodium tomatoes
16-oz. jar low-sodium salsa
1 cup quick-cooking barley, uncooked
3 cups water
14½-oz. can low-sodium, fat-free chicken broth

15½-oz. can black beans, rinsed and drained
3 cups cooked chicken, *or* turkey, cubed
15¼-oz. can whole-kernel corn, undrained
1-3 tsp. chili powder, depending on how hot you like your chili
1 tsp. cumin
fat-free sour cream, *optional*
low-fat shredded cheese, *optional*

1. Combine all ingredients except sour cream and cheese in slow cooker.

2. Cover. Cook on low 6-8 hours, or until barley is tender.

3. Serve in individual soup bowls topped with sour cream and shredded cheese if you wish.

— PER SERVING —
- 200 calories
  (25 calories from fat)
- 3g total fat
  (0.5g saturated, 0g trans)
- 25mg cholesterol
- 300mg sodium
- 27g total carbohydrate
  (6g fiber, 4g sugar)
- 15g protein
- 15%DV vitamin A
- 25%DV vitamin C
- 4%DV calcium
- 15%DV iron

Healthy Chicken Chili

Dawn Day
Westminster, CA

Makes 10 servings

Prep. Time: 30-45 minutes
Cooking Time: 4-5 hours
Ideal slow-cooker size: 6-qt.

3 cups chicken, cooked and cubed
1 large onion, chopped
12-oz. can low-sodium chopped tomatoes
6-oz. can low-sodium tomato paste
3 12-oz. cans low-sodium chili beans, undrained
3 Tbsp. chili powder
1 cup frozen corn

1. Combine all ingredients in slow cooker. Stir well.

2. Cover. Cook on low 4-5 hours.

3. Serve with low-fat grated cheese.

— PER SERVING —
- 250 calories
  (35 calories from fat)
- 4g total fat
  (1g saturated, 0g trans)
- 60mg cholesterol
- 560mg sodium
- 26g total carbohydrate
  (7g fiber, 2g sugar)
- 28g protein
- 30%DV vitamin A
- 10%DV vitamin C
- 6%DV calcium
- 15%DV iron

Most slow cookers perform best when more than half full.
Dorothy M. Van Deest, Memphis, TN

Chicken Chili with Pesto

Marilyn Mowry
Irving, TX

Makes 4 servings

Prep. Time: 25-30 minutes
Cooking Time: 6-8 hours
Ideal slow-cooker size: 5-qt.

¾ lb. boneless, skinless chicken breasts, cut into bite-sized pieces, uncooked
2 tsp. vegetable oil, *optional*
¾ cup onion, finely chopped
1½ cups carrots, finely chopped
¾ cup red bell pepper, finely chopped
¾ cup celery, sliced thin
¼ cup canned chopped green chilies
¾ tsp. dried oregano
½ tsp. ground cumin
¼ tsp. salt
⅛ tsp. black pepper
16-oz. can cannellini beans *or* other white beans, rinsed and drained
14½-oz. can fat-free, low-sodium chicken broth
3 Tbsp. classic pesto sauce (recipe at right)

1. Sauté chicken in a nonstick skillet, or in a traditional skillet with oil.
2. Combine all ingredients except pesto sauce in slow cooker.
3. Cook on low 6-8 hours.
4. Stir in pesto just before serving.

---— PER SERVING ---—
• 370 calories (110 calories from fat)
• 12 total fat (2.5g saturated, 0g trans)
• 50mg cholesterol
• 820mg sodium
• 36g total carbohydrate (9g fiber, 10g sugar)
• 29g protein
• 200%DV vitamin A
• 40%DV vitamin C
• 15%DV calcium
• 20%DV iron

Pesto

Makes ¾ cup

Prep. Time: 5-10 minutes

2 Tbsp. walnuts, *or* pine nuts, coarsely chopped
2 garlic cloves, peeled
3 Tbsp. extra-virgin olive oil
4 cups fresh basil leaves (about 4 ozs.)
½ cup grated Parmesan cheese
¼ tsp. salt

1. Mince nuts and garlic in food processor.
2. Add oil, and pulse 3 times.
3. Add basil, cheese, and salt. Process until finely minced, scraping sides of bowl.

Taco Chicken Soup

Colleen Heatwole
Burton, MI

Janie Steele
Moore, OK

Makes 4-6 servings

Prep. Time: 10-20 minutes
Cooking Time: 4-6 hours
Ideal slow-cooker size: 4- or 5-qt.

1 envelope dry reduced-sodium taco seasoning
32-oz. can low-sodium V8 juice
16-oz. jar salsa
15-oz. can black beans, drained
1 cup frozen corn
1 cup frozen peas
2 whole chicken breasts, cooked and shredded

1. Combine all ingredients except corn, peas, and chicken in slow cooker.
2. Cover. Cook on low 4-6 hours. Add remaining vegetables and chicken 1 hour before serving.

---— PER SERVING ---—
• 210 calories (15 calories from fat)
• 2g total fat (0g saturated, 0g trans)
• 25mg cholesterol
• 970mg sodium
• 35g total carbohydrate (8g fiber, 9g sugar)
• 17g protein
• 40%DV vitamin A
• 40%DV vitamin C
• 8%DV calcium
• 20%DV iron

Variation:
Garnish individual servings with chopped fresh cilantro, and, if diets allow, with chunks of avocado.

Chicken Tortilla Soup

Becky Harder
Monument, CO

Makes 8 servings

Prep. Time: 10 minutes
Cooking Time: 8 hours
Ideal slow-cooker size: 4- or 5-qt.

4 uncooked boneless, skinless chicken breast halves
2 15-oz. cans black beans, undrained
2 15-oz. cans low-sodium Mexican stewed tomatoes, *or* Rotel tomatoes
1 cup low-sodium salsa (mild, medium, *or* hot, whichever you prefer)
4-oz. can chopped green chilies, undrained
14½-oz. can low-sodium tomato sauce
baked tortilla chips
2 cups grated fat-free cheese

1. Combine all ingredients except chips and cheese in large slow cooker.
2. Cover. Cook on low 8 hours.
3. Just before serving, remove chicken breasts and slice into bite-sized pieces. Stir into soup.
4. To serve, put a handful of chips in each individual soup bowl. Ladle soup over chips. Top with cheese.

— PER SERVING —
· 330 calories (20 calories from fat)
· 2.5g total fat (0g saturated, 0g trans)
· 35mg cholesterol
· 1760mg sodium
· 55g total carbohydrate (10g fiber, 15g sugar)
· 28g protein
· 10%DV vitamin A
· 15%DV vitamin C
· 10%DV calcium
· 15%DV iron

Southwest Corn Soup

Susan Tjon
Austin, TX

Makes 6 servings

Prep. Time: 15-20 minutes
Cooking Time: 4 hours
Ideal slow-cooker size: 5-qt.

2 4-oz. cans chopped green chilies, undrained
2 small zucchini, cut into bite-sized pieces
1 medium-sized onion, thinly sliced
3 cloves garlic, minced
1 tsp. ground cumin
3 14½-oz. cans fat-free, sodium-reduced chicken broth
1½-2 cups shredded, cooked turkey
15-oz. can chickpeas, *or* black beans, rinsed and drained
10-oz. pkg. frozen corn
1 tsp. dried oregano
½ cup chopped cilantro

1. Combine all ingredients in slow cooker.
2. Cook on low 4 hours.

— PER SERVING —
· 240 calories (40 calories from fat)
· 4.5g total fat (1g saturated, 0g trans)
· 25mg cholesterol
· 520mg sodium
· 31g total carbohydrate (7g fiber, 5g sugar)
· 21g protein
· 6%DV vitamin A
· 20%DV vitamin C
· 10%DV calcium
· 20%DV iron

Variation:

For a twist on the Soup's flavor and consistency, substitute 1 14½-oz. can low-sodium diced tomatoes for one of the cans of chicken broth.

Taco Bean Soup

Karen Waggoner
Joplin, MO

Makes 12 servings

Prep. Time: 15-20 minutes
Cooking Time: 1½ hours
Ideal slow-cooker size: 6-qt.

¾ lb. lean pork sausage
1 lb. extra-lean ground
   beef
1 envelope dry low-sodium
   taco seasoning
4 cups water
2 16-oz. cans kidney beans,
   rinsed and drained
2 14½-oz. cans low-sodium
   stewed tomatoes
2 14½-oz. cans diced
   Mexican tomatoes with
   juice
16-oz. jar chunky salsa

1. Cook sausage and beef in nonstick skillet over medium heat until no longer pink. Spoon into slow cooker.
2. Add taco seasoning and mix well.
3. Stir in water, beans, tomatoes, and salsa.
4. Cover. Cook on high 1 hour.
5. Uncover. Cook another 30 minutes on high. Stir occasionally. Serve.

— PER SERVING —
• 320 calories
  (130 calories from fat)
• 14g total fat
  (5g saturated, 0g trans)
• 40mg cholesterol
• 1830mg sodium
• 27g total carbohydrate
  (7g fiber, 8g sugar)
• 20g protein
• 20%DV vitamin A
• 10%DV vitamin C
• 10%DV calcium
• 20%DV iron

Tip:

If your diet allows, you may want to garnish individual servings with low-fat sour cream, shredded low-fat cheddar cheese, and a sprinkling of sliced ripe olives.

Bean and Ham Soup

Dolores Kratz
Souderton, PA

Makes 10 servings

Soaking Time: 8 hours or
*   overnight*
Prep. Time: 25 minutes
Cooking Time: 9-11 hours
Ideal slow-cooker size: 7-qt., or
*   2 4-qt. cookers*

1 lb. mixed dried beans
ham bone from half a ham
   butt
1½ cups ham, cubed
1 large onion, chopped
¾ cup celery, chopped
¾ cup carrots, sliced *or*
   chopped
15-oz. can low-sodium
   diced tomatoes
2 Tbsp. parsley, chopped
1 cup low-sodium tomato
   juice
5 cups water
2 Tbsp. Worcestershire sauce
1 bay leaf
1 tsp. prepared mustard

½ tsp. chili powder
juice of 1 lemon
1 tsp. salt
½ tsp. black pepper

1. Place beans in saucepan. Cover with water and soak overnight. Drain.
2. Cover beans with fresh water and cook in saucepan 30 minutes uncovered. Drain again. Discard water.
3. Combine beans with remaining ingredients in slow cooker.
4. Cover. Cook on low 9-11 hours.
5. Remove bay leaf and ham bone before serving.

— PER SERVING —
• 220 calories
  (30 calories from fat)
• 3g total fat (0.5g
  saturated, 0g trans)
• 20mg cholesterol
• 200mg sodium
• 34g total carbohydrate
  (11g fiber, 7g sugar)
• 17g protein
• 50%DV vitamin A
• 10%DV vitamin C
• 10%DV calcium
• 25%DV iron

Tip:

I chop the vegetables and mix the other ingredients together in the evening, and then refrigerate them overnight. I have less work in the morning. A wonderful aroma greets the family as they come home for the evening meal. And it's healthy, too!

Cube meat while partially frozen for easier cutting.
Eleanor Glick, Bird-In-Hand, PA

Cassoulet Chowder

Miriam Friesen
Staunton, VA

Makes 8 servings

Soaking Time: 4-8 hours or overnight
Prep. Time: 2 hours
Cooking Time: 4-10 hours
Ideal slow-cooker size: 3½- or 4-qt.

1¼ cups dry pinto beans
4 cups water
½ lb. lean sausage, cut in ¼" slices, cooked and drained
2 cups cubed cooked lean chicken
2 cups cubed cooked lean ham
1½ cups sliced carrots
8-oz. can low-sodium tomato sauce
¾ cup dry red wine
½ cup chopped onions
½ tsp. garlic powder
1 bay leaf

1. Combine beans and water in large saucepan. Bring to boil. Reduce heat and simmer, covered, 1½ hours. Refrigerate beans and liquid 4-8 hours.

2. Combine all ingredients in slow cooker.

3. Cover. Cook on low 8-10 hours or on high 4 hours. If the chowder seems too thin, remove lid during last 30 minutes of cooking time to allow it to thicken.

4. Remove bay leaf before serving.

— PER SERVING —
- 200 calories
  (70 calories from fat)
- 8g total fat
  (2.5g saturated, 0g trans)
- 55mg cholesterol
- 360mg sodium
- 10g total carbohydrate
  (2g fiber, 3g sugar)
- 20g protein
- 80%DV vitamin A
- 0%DV vitamin C
- 4%DV calcium
- 8%DV iron

Navy Bean and Bacon Chowder

Ruth A. Feister
Narvon, PA

Makes 6 servings

Soaking Time: 8 hours or overnight
Prep. Time: 20 minutes
Cooking Time: 7-9 hours
Ideal slow-cooker size: 4-qt.

1½ cups dried navy beans
2 cups cold water
5 slices lean turkey bacon, cooked and crumbled
2 medium-sized carrots, sliced
1 rib celery, sliced
1 medium onion, chopped
1 tsp. dried Italian seasoning
⅛ tsp. black pepper
2, *or 3*, bay leaves, *optional*
46-oz. can fat-free, low-sodium chicken broth
1 cup fat-free milk

1. Soak beans in 2 cups cold water for 8 hours.

2. After beans have soaked, drain, if necessary, and place in slow cooker.

3. Add all remaining ingredients, except milk, to slow cooker.

4. Cover. Cook on low 7-9 hours, or until beans are crisp-tender.

5. Place 2 cups cooked bean mixture into blender. Process until smooth. Return to slow cooker.

6. Add milk. Cover and heat on high 10 minutes.

— PER SERVING —
- 260 calories
  (30 calories from fat)
- 3g total fat
  (1g saturated, 0g trans)
- 10mg cholesterol
- 400mg sodium
- 38g total carbohydrate
  (14g fiber, 8g sugar)
- 21g protein
- 80%DV vitamin A
- 0%DV vitamin C
- 15%DV calcium
- 30%DV iron

Variation:
If you like a zippier soup, you may want to add 1 tsp. ground cumin to Step 3.

Salsa Soup

Esther J. Yoder
Hartville, OH

Makes 10 servings

Prep. Time: 15 minutes
Cooking Time: 3-8 hours
Ideal slow-cooker size: 4-qt.

1 lb. mild sausage, sliced
1 qt. white navy beans, undrained
2 cups mild, *or* medium, salsa
4 cups fat-free chicken broth

1. Brown sausage in skillet and drain well.
2. Combine all ingredients in slow cooker.
3. Cook on low 6-8 hours or high 3-4 hours.

—— PER SERVING ——
• 240 calories
  (80 calories from fat)
• 9g total fat
  (3g saturated, 0g trans)
• 15mg cholesterol
• 480mg sodium
• 27g total carbohydrate
  (6g fiber, 5g sugar)
• 14g protein
• 6%DV vitamin A
• 6%DV vitamin C
• 10%DV calcium
• 25%DV iron

Tips:
1. If you like a thickened soup, mix ¼ cup cornstarch with ¼ cup water. Remove 1 cup hot soup broth from cooker about 15 minutes before end of cooking time. Whisk together with cornstarch mixture. When smooth, stir back into soup in cooker and stir until thickened.
2. This can be served over rice, in addition to serving it as a soup.

Black-Eyed Peas

Wendy McPhillips
Wichita, KS

Makes 4-5 servings

Prep. Time: 5-10 minutes
Cooking Time: 6-8 hours
Ideal slow-cooker size: 5-qt.

1-lb. pkg. dried black-eyed peas
1½ cups ham, diced
6 cups water
½ tsp. salt
¼ tsp. black pepper

1. Combine all ingredients in slow cooker.
2. Cover. Cook on low 6-8 hours.

—— PER SERVING ——
• 160 calories
  (40 calories from fat)
• 4g total fat (1.5g saturated, 0g trans)
• 40mg cholesterol
• 270mg sodium
• 14g total carbohydrate
  (3g fiber, 0g sugar)
• 17g protein
• 0%DV vitamin A
• 0%DV vitamin C
• 2%DV calcium
• 10%DV iron

Variations:
1. If you want a zestier dish, and if your diet allows, consider adding 2 4-oz. cans diced green chilies, a pinch of red pepper flakes, or several drops Tabasco sauce to Step 1.
2. This is good served with corn bread.

Black-Eyed Pea Chili

Lena Mae Janes
Lane, KS

Makes 10 servings

Prep. Time: 20-30 minutes
Cooking Time: 2 hours
Ideal slow-cooker size: 5- or 6-qt.

¾ lb. loose turkey sausage
1 medium onion, chopped
½ cup celery chopped
4 15-oz. cans black-eyed peas, undrained
14-oz. can low-sodium diced tomatoes, undrained
10-oz. can low-sodium diced tomatoes with green chilies, undrained
2 Tbsp. chili powder

1. Cook sausage in skillet until no longer pink, stirring frequently. Drain sausage on paper towel.
2. Add onion and celery to skillet. Cook until translucent, stirring frequently.
3. Place peas, tomatoes, tomatoes with green chilies, cooked onions and celery, sausage, and chili powder in slow cooker. Stir well.
4. Cover. Cook on high until all ingredients are hot, about an hour. Then turn cooker to low and cook 1 more hour.

—— PER SERVING ——
- 220 calories
  (25 calories from fat)
- 3g total fat
  (0.5g saturated,
  0g trans)
- 25mg cholesterol
- 850mg sodium
- 33g total carbohydrate
  (7g fiber, 3g sugar)
- 15g protein
- 25%DV vitamin A
- 20%DV vitamin C
- 6%DV calcium
- 20%DV iron

Turkey Sausage Stew

Sheridy Steele
Ardmore, OK

Makes 6 servings

Prep. Time: 25-30 minutes
Cooking Time: 4-6 hours
Ideal slow-cooker size: 3½- or 4-qt.

½ lb. turkey sausage,
    removed from casing
1 large onion, chopped
2 garlic cloves, minced
¾ cup carrots, chopped
1 fennel bulb, chopped
½ cup celery, chopped
10¾-oz. can fat-free,
    reduced-sodium chicken
    broth
3 medium tomatoes, peeled,
    seeded, and chopped
1 tsp. dried basil
1 tsp. dried oregano
¼ tsp. salt
15-oz. can navy beans,
    drained and rinsed
1 cup uncooked shell pasta
½ cup lowfat Parmesan
    cheese

1. In nonstick skillet, brown turkey sausage, onion, and garlic. Drain well.

2. Combine all ingredients except pasta and cheese in slow cooker.

3. Cook on low 4-6 hours.

4. One hour before end of cooking time, stir in pasta.

5. Sprinkle with cheese to serve.

—— PER SERVING ——
- 280 calories
  (60 calories from fat)
- 7 total fat
  (2.5g saturated,
  0g trans)
- 35mg cholesterol
- 930mg sodium
- 36g total carbohydrate
  (7g fiber, 6g sugar)
- 20g protein
- 80%DV vitamin A
- 20%DV vitamin C
- 20%DV calcium
- 20%DV iron

White Bean and Barley Soup

Sharon Miller
Holmesville, OH

Makes 12 servings

Prep. Time: 25 minutes
Cooking Time: 8-10 hours
Ideal slow-cooker size: 6-qt.

1 large onion, chopped
2 garlic cloves, minced
1 Tbsp. olive, *or* canola, oil
2 24-oz. cans great
    northern beans (*or* equal
    amount prepared from
    dried beans), undrained
4 cups no-fat, low-sodium
    chicken broth
4 cups water
2 large carrots, chunked
2 medium-sized green,
    or red, bell peppers,
    chunked
2 celery ribs, chunked
½ cup quick-cooking
    barley
¼ cup fresh parsley,
    chopped
2 bay leaves
½ tsp. dried thyme
¼ tsp. black pepper
28-oz. can diced tomatoes,
    undrained

1. Sauté onion and garlic in oil in skillet until just wilted.

2. Combine all ingredients in slow cooker.

3. Cook on low 8-10 hours.

4. Discard bay leaves before serving.

—— PER SERVING ——
- 210 calories
  (15 calories from fat)
- 2g total fat
  (0g saturated, 0g trans)
- 0mg cholesterol
- 260mg sodium
- 36g total carbohydrate
  (9g fiber, 6g sugar)
- 12g protein
- 50%DV vitamin A
- 20%DV vitamin C
- 15%DV calcium
- 20%DV iron

Variations:

1. If you wish, use pearl barley instead of quick-cooking, but cook it until nearly soft on the stove and add it halfway through the cooking cycle.

2. If you want, and your diet allows, you may want to add ½-¾ tsp. salt in Step 2.

White Bean Fennel Soup

Janie Steele
Moore, OK

Makes 6 servings

Prep. Time: 20-30 minutes
Cooking Time: 1-3 hours
Ideal slow-cooker size: 5-qt.

1 Tbsp. olive, *or* canola, oil
1 large onion, chopped
1 small fennel bulb, sliced thin
5 cups fat-free chicken broth
15-oz. can white kidney, *or* cannellini, beans, rinsed and drained
14½-oz. can diced tomatoes, undrained
1 tsp. dried thyme
¼ tsp. black pepper
1 bay leaf
3 cups chopped fresh spinach

1. Sauté onions and fennel in oil in skillet until brown.
2. Combine onions, fennel, broth, beans, tomatoes, thyme, pepper, and bay leaf.
3. Cook on low 2-3 hours, or on high 1 hour, until fennel and onions are tender.
4. Remove bay leaf.
5. Add spinach about 10 minutes before serving.

—— PER SERVING ——
• 160 calories
 (25 calories from fat)
• 3g total fat
 (0g saturated, 0g trans)
• 0mg cholesterol
• 690mg sodium
• 22g total carbohydrate
 (8g fiber, 4g sugar)
• 13g protein
• 100%DV vitamin A
• 40%DV vitamin C
• 20%DV calcium
• 35%DV iron

Great Northern Bean Soup

Alice Miller
Stuarts Draft, VA

Makes 6 servings

Prep. Time: 15-20 minutes
Cooking Time: 3 hours
Ideal slow cooker size: 3-qt.

2 1-lb. cans great northern beans, rinsed and drained
1-lb. can low-sodium diced, tomatoes, including juice
1 Tbsp. brown sugar
½ cup green bell peppers, chopped
½ cup red bell peppers, chopped

1. Put beans, tomatoes, and brown sugar into slow cooker. Stir until well mixed.
2. Cover. Cook on high 2½ hours.
3. Stir chopped red and green peppers into Soup.
4. Cover. Cook on high 30 more minutes.

—— PER SERVING ——
• 160 calories
 (5 calories from fat)
• 0.5g total fat
 (0g saturated, 0g trans)
• 0mg cholesterol
• 350mg sodium
• 32g total carbohydrate
 (9g fiber, 4g sugar)
• 10g protein
• 25%DV vitamin A
• 60%DV vitamin C
• 10%DV calcium
• 20%DV iron

Fresh vegetables take longer to cook than meats, because, in a slow cooker, liquid simmers rather than boils. Remember this if you've adapted range-top recipes to slow cooking.

Beatrice Orgish, Richardson, TX

Vegetables

Vegetable Medley

Deborah Santiago
Lancaster, PA

Judi Manos
West Islip, NY

Makes 8 servings

Prep. Time: 25 minutes
Cooking Time: 5-6 hours
Ideal slow-cooker size: 4-qt.

4 cups potatoes, diced and
　peeled
1½ cups frozen whole-
　kernel corn
4 medium-sized tomatoes,
　seeded and diced
1 cup carrots, sliced
½ cup onions, chopped
¾ tsp. salt
½ tsp. sugar
¾ tsp. dill weed
¼ tsp. black pepper
½ tsp. dried basil
¼ tsp. dried rosemary

1. Combine all ingredients in slow cooker.

2. Cover. Cook on low 5-6 hours, or until vegetables are tender.

—— **PER SERVING** ——

- 120 calories
  (5 calories from fat)
- 0.5g total fat
  (0g saturated, 0g trans)
- 0mg cholesterol
- 240mg sodium
- 27g total carbohydrate
  (4g fiber, 5g sugar)
- 4g protein
- 80%DV vitamin A
- 20%DV vitamin C
- 2%DV calcium
- 6%DV iron

If you're having guests, and those dinners that require last-minute attention drive you crazy, do your side-dish vegetables in your small slow cooker. They won't demand any of your attention until they're ready to be served.

Vegetables with Pasta

Donna Lantgen
Rapid City, SD

Makes 4-5 servings

Prep. Time: 20-25 minutes
Cooking Time: 6 hours
Ideal slow-cooker size: 3½- or 4-qt.

2 cups chopped zucchini
½ cup cherry tomatoes, cut in half
half green, *or* red, bell pepper, sliced
half medium-sized onion, sliced
½ cup fresh mushrooms, sliced
4 cloves garlic, minced
1 Tbsp. olive oil
1 Tbsp. Italian seasoning
8-oz. can tomato sauce

1. Combine all ingredients in slow cooker.
2. Cook on low 4-5 hours or until vegetables are tender.

———— PER SERVING ————
• 80 calories   • 12g total carbohydrate
(25 calories from fat)   (2g fiber, 6g sugar)
• 3g total fat   • 4g protein
(0g saturated, 0g trans)   • 20%DV vitamin A
• 0mg cholesterol   • 30%DV vitamin C
• 580mg sodium   • 2%DV calcium
   • 6%DV iron

Tips:
Serve with your favorite cooked pasta and top with grated low-fat Parmesan or mozzarella cheese if you wish.

Vegetable Rice Casserole

Esther Martin
Ephrata, PA

Makes 8 servings

Prep. Time: 25 minutes
Cooking Time: 3-4 hours
Ideal slow-cooker size: 6-qt.

¼ cup uncooked long-grain rice
1 lb. zucchini, sliced
1 lb. yellow summer squash, sliced
1 large onion, sliced
1 Tbsp. dried basil, *divided*
1 medium-sized green bell pepper, julienned
4 celery ribs with leaves, chopped
2 large tomatoes, sliced
¼ cup packed brown sugar
½ tsp. salt
¼ tsp. black pepper
2 Tbsp. olive oil

1. Spread rice in slow cooker that has been coated with fat-free cooking spray.
2. Layer in zucchini, yellow squash, onion, and half the basil.
3. Top with green pepper, celery, and tomatoes.
4. Combine brown sugar, salt, and pepper. Sprinkle over vegetables. Drizzle with oil.
5. Cover. Cook on high 3-4 hours, or until vegetables reach the degree of "doneness" you prefer.
6. Sprinkle with remaining basil when finished.

———— PER SERVING ————
• 100 calories   • 16g total carbohydrate
(35 calories from fat)   (3g fiber, 11g sugar)
• 4g total fat (0.5g   • 2g protein
saturated, 0g trans)   • 10%DV vitamin A
• 0mg cholesterol   • 30%DV vitamin C
• 170mg sodium   • 4%DV calcium
   • 6%DV iron

Variations:
1. If your diet allows, and if you prefer a less juicy dish, increase the amount of rice to ½ cup.
2. If you want to use fresh basil instead of dried, stir in 3 Tbsp. just before serving the dish.

"Stir-Fry" Veggies

Shari and Dale Mast
Harrisonburg, VA

Makes 8 servings

Prep. Time: 30 minutes
Cooking Time: 4-10 hours
Ideal slow-cooker size: 6-qt.

16-oz. bag baby carrots
4 ribs celery, chunked
1 medium-sized onion, diced
14½-oz. can low-sodium Italian-style stewed tomatoes
½ tsp. dried basil
½ tsp. dried oregano
½ tsp. salt
1 large red, *or* yellow, bell pepper, diced
1 small head cabbage, cut up
1 lb. raw broccoli, cut up

1. Combine carrots, celery, onion, tomatoes, basil, oregano, and salt in slow cooker.

2. Cover. Cook on high 3-4 hours or on low 6-8 hours, stirring occasionally.

3. Stir in pepper, cabbage, and broccoli.

4. Cook 1 hour more on high, or 2 hours more on low, stirring occasionally. You may need to add a little water if there is not liquid left on the veggies.

—— PER SERVING ——
- 90 calories
  (10 calories from fat)
- 1g total fat
  (0g saturated, 0g trans)
- 0mg cholesterol
- 220mg sodium
- 19g total carbohydrate
  (7g fiber, 10g sugar)
- 4g protein
- 200%DV vitamin A
- 100%DV vitamin C
- 10%DV calcium
- 15%DV iron

Tip:
Serve this as a side dish, or as a main dish over hot cooked rice, garnished with Parmesan cheese.

Tofu and Vegetables
Donna Lantgen
Rapid City, SD

Makes 6 servings

Prep. Time: 25-30 minutes
Cooking Time: 6 hours
Ideal slow-cooker size: 4- or 5-qt.

16 ozs. firm tofu, drained and crumbled
½ cup onion, chopped
½ cup celery, chopped
2 cups bok choy, chopped
2 cups napa cabbage, chopped
½ cup pea pods, cut in half

1. Combine all ingredients in slow cooker.

2. Cook on low 6 hours.

—— PER SERVING ——
- 60 calories
  (25 calories from fat)
- 3g total fat
  (0g saturated, 0g trans)
- 0mg cholesterol
- 25mg sodium
- 4g total carbohydrate
  (1g fiber, 2g sugar)
- 6g protein
- 10%DV vitamin A
- 10%DV vitamin C
- 10%DV calcium
- 8%DV iron

Tip:
I like to serve this with soy sauce on a bed of rice.

Vegetable Casserole
Eileen Eash
Carlsbad, NM

Makes 12 servings

Prep. Time: 25-30 minutes
Cooking Time: 6-7 hours
Ideal slow-cooker size: 5- or 6-qt.

2 cups low-sodium stewed tomatoes with juice
2 cups carrots, sliced
2 cups onions, diced
2 cups celery, chopped
¾ cup green bell pepper, chopped
2 Tbsp. minute tapioca
2 tsp. seasoned salt
1 cup cabbage, shredded
½ tsp. black pepper
2 cups fresh green beans

1. Combine all ingredients except beans in slightly greased slow cooker.

2. Cover. Cook on low 4-5 hours.

3. Add beans.

4. Cook an additional 2 hours.

—— PER SERVING ——
- 50 calories
  (0 calories from fat)
- 0g total fat
  (0g saturated, 0g trans)
- 0mg cholesterol
- 290mg sodium
- 11g total carbohydrate
  (3g fiber, 6g sugar)
- 2g protein
- 80%DV vitamin A
- 20%DV vitamin C
- 4%DV calcium
- 6%DV iron

Cut up vegetables for your slow-cooker dish the night before and place them in ziplock bags in the refrigerator. This cuts down on preparation time in the morning.

Tracy Supcoe, Barclay, MD

Chinese Vegetables

Rebecca Leichty
Harrisonburg, VA

Makes 6 servings

Prep. Time: 15-20 minutes
Cooking Time: 3-6 hours
Ideal slow-cooker size: 5- or 6-qt.

1 bunch celery, sliced on diagonal
1 large onion, sliced
1-lb. can bean sprouts, drained
12-oz. pkg. chop-suey vegetables
8-oz. can water chestnuts, drained
2 4-oz. cans sliced mushrooms, drained
1 Tbsp. sugar
3 Tbsp. low-sodium soy sauce
¾ cup water
¼ tsp. black pepper, *or* to taste

1. Spray slow cooker with fat-free cooking spray.
2. Combine all ingredients in slow cooker.
3. Cover. Cook on low 3-6 hours, depending upon how soft or crunchy you like your vegetables.

—— PER SERVING ——
• 120 calories
  (0 calories from fat)
• 0g total fat
  (0g saturated, 0g trans)
• 0mg cholesterol
• 135mg sodium
• 28g total carbohydrate
  (5g fiber, 5g sugar)
• 4g protein
• 4%DV vitamin A
• 40%DV vitamin C
• 8%DV calcium
• 8%DV iron

Lemon Red Potatoes

Joyce Shackelford
Green Bay, WI

Makes 6 servings

Prep. Time: 15-20 minutes
Cooking Time: 2½-3 hours
Ideal slow-cooker size: 4-qt.

1½ lbs. medium-sized red potatoes
¼ cup water
2 Tbsp. butter, melted
1 Tbsp. lemon juice
3 Tbsp. fresh chives, snipped
chopped fresh parsley
1 tsp. salt
½ tsp. black pepper

1. Cut a strip of peel from around the middle of each potato. Place potatoes and water in slow cooker.
2. Cover. Cook on high 2½-3 hours.
3. Drain.
4. Combine butter, lemon juice, chives, and parsley. Pour over potatoes. Toss to coat.
5. Season with salt and pepper.

—— PER SERVING ——
• 120 calories
  (35 calories from fat)
• 4g total fat
  (2.5g saturated, 0g trans)
• 10mg cholesterol
• 400mg sodium
• 18g total carbohydrate
  (2g fiber, 1g sugar)
• 2g protein
• 0%DV vitamin A
• 20%DV vitamin C
• 2%DV calcium
• 6%DV iron

Saucy Scalloped Potatoes

Sue Pennington
Bridgewater, VA

Makes 6 servings

Prep. Time: 20 minutes
Cooking Time: 7-9 hours
Ideal slow-cooker size: 3½- or 4-qt.

4 cups peeled, thinly sliced potatoes
10¾-oz. can fat-free, low-sodium cream of celery, *or* mushroom, soup
12-oz. can fat-free evaporated milk
1 large onion, sliced
½ tsp. salt
¼ tsp. black pepper
1½ cups chopped fully cooked, lean ham

1. Combine potatoes, soup, evaporated milk, onion, salt, and pepper in slow cooker. Mix well.
2. Cover. Cook on high 1 hour. Stir in ham. Reduce to low. Cook 6-8 hours, or until potatoes are tender. Stir well before serving.

—— PER SERVING ——
• 230 calories
  (40 calories from fat)
• 4.5g total fat
  (1.5g saturated, 0g trans)
• 35mg cholesterol
• 630mg sodium
• 29g total carbohydrate
  (3g fiber, 9g sugar)
• 17g protein
• 0%DV vitamin A
• 10%DV vitamin C
• 20%DV calcium
• 8%DV iron

To make your own cream of mushroom or celery soup, please turn to pages 264-265.

Garlicky Potatoes

Donna Lantgen
Rapid City, SD

Makes 6 servings

Prep. Time: 15- 20 minutes
Cooking Time: 5-6 hours
Ideal slow-cooker size: 3½-qt.

6 potatoes, peeled and cubed
6 garlic cloves, minced
¼ cup dried onion, *or* one medium onion, chopped
2 Tbsp. olive oil

1. Combine all ingredients in slow cooker.

2. Cook on low 5-6 hours, or until potatoes are soft but not turning brown.

—— PER SERVING ——
• 220 calories
  (40 calories from fat)
• 4.5 total fat (0.5g saturated, 0g trans)
• 0mg cholesterol
• 15mg sodium
• 40g total carbohydrate (5g fiber, 3g sugar)
• 5g protein
• 0%DV vitamin A
• 30%DV vitamin C
• 4%DV calcium
• 10%DV iron

Variations:

For added flavor, stir in ¼ tsp. dill weed and/or ¼ tsp. dried basil as part of Step 1.

Rustic Potatoes au Gratin

Nancy Savage
Factoryville, PA

Makes 6 servings

Prep. Time: 30 minutes
Cooking Time: 6-8 hours
Ideal slow-cooker size: 5-qt.

½ cup skim milk
10¾-oz. can light condensed cheddar cheese soup
8-oz. pkg. fat-free cream cheese, softened
1 clove garlic, minced
¼ tsp. ground nutmeg
¼ tsp. black pepper
2 lbs. baking potatoes (about 7) cut into ¼"-thick slices
1 small onion, thinly sliced
paprika

1. Heat milk in small saucepan over medium heat until small bubbles form around edge of pan. Remove from heat.

2. Add soup, cream cheese, garlic, nutmeg, and pepper to pan. Stir until smooth.

3. Spray inside of slow cooker with nonfat cooking spray. Layer one-quarter of potatoes and onions on bottom of slow cooker.

4. Top with one-quarter of soup mixture. Repeat layers 3 times.

5. Cover. Cook on low 6-8 hours, or until potatoes are tender and most of liquid is absorbed.

6. Sprinkle with paprika before serving.

—— PER SERVING ——
• 210 calories
  (35 calories from fat)
• 4g total fat
  (1.5g saturated, 1g trans)
• 10mg cholesterol
• 620mg sodium
• 36g total carbohydrate (4g fiber, 4g sugar)
• 11g protein
• 10%DV vitamin A
• 20%DV vitamin C
• 10%DV calcium
• 8%DV iron

It's quite convenient to use a slow cooker to cook potatoes for salads or for fried potatoes or as baked potatoes. Just fill the slow cooker with cleaned potatoes and cook all day until done. Darla Sathre, Baxter, MN

Mustard Potatoes

Frances Musser
Newmanstown, PA

Makes 6 servings

Prep. Time: 15 minutes after potatoes are cooked
Cooking Time: 3-4 hours
Ideal slow-cooker size: 4-qt.

½ cup onions, chopped
1 Tbsp. butter
1½ tsp. prepared mustard
1 tsp. salt
¼ tsp. black pepper
½ cup fat-free, *or* 2%, milk
¼ lb. low-fat cheese
6 medium potatoes, cooked and grated

1. Sauté onion in butter in skillet. Add mustard, salt, pepper, milk, and cheese.
2. Place potatoes in slow cooker. Do not press down.
3. Pour mixture over potatoes.
4. Cover. Cook on low 3-4 hours.
5. Toss potatoes with a large spoon when ready to serve.

—— PER SERVING ——
• 230 calories
   (30 calories from fat)
• 3.5g total fat
   (2g saturated, 0g trans)
• 10mg cholesterol
• 430mg sodium
• 40g total carbohydrate
   (5g fiber, 4g sugar)
• 10g protein
• 4%DV vitamin A
• 30%DV vitamin C
• 20%DV calcium
• 10%DV iron

Variation:
   If you like an unmistakable mustardy taste, and your diet allows, you can double the amount of mustard.

Extra-Good Mashed Potatoes

Zona Mae Bontrager, Kokomo, IN
Mary Jane Musser, Manheim, PA
Elsie Schlabach, Millersburg, OH
Carol Sommers, Millersburg, OH
 Edwina Stoltzfus, Narvon, PA
Barbara Hershey, Lancaster, PA

Makes 12 servings

Prep. Time: 45 minutes
Cooking Time: 4-6 hours
Ideal slow-cooker size: 5- to 6-qt.

5 lbs. potatoes, peeled and cooked
2 cups fat-free milk, heated to scalding
2 Tbsp. butter, melted in hot milk
8-oz. pkg. fat-free cream cheese, softened
1½ cups fat-free sour cream
1 tsp. onion, *or* garlic, salt
1 tsp. salt
¼-½ tsp. pepper

1. Mash all ingredients together in a large mixing bowl until smooth.
2. Pour into slow cooker.
3. Cover. Cook on low 4-6 hours, or until heated through.

—— PER SERVING ——
• 220 calories
   (20 calories from fat)
• 2.5g total fat (1.5g
   saturated, 0g trans)
• 10mg cholesterol
• 470mg sodium
• 41g total carbohydrate
   (3g fiber, 5g sugar)
• 8g protein
• 4%DV vitamin A
• 35%DV vitamin C
• 15%DV calcium
• 4%DV iron

Tip:
   These potatoes may be prepared 3-4 days in advance of serving and kept in the refrigerator until ready to use.

Do-Ahead Mashed Potatoes

Shari and Dale Mast
Harrisonburg, VA

Makes 8 servings

Prep. Time: 50 minutes
Chilling Time: 8 hours or overnight
Cooking Time: 3-4 hours
Ideal slow-cooker size: 6-qt.

12 medium-sized potatoes, washed, peeled, and quartered
1 small, *or* medium-sized, onion, chopped
4 ozs. Neufchatel, *or* fat-free cream cheese
1 tsp. salt
¼ tsp. black pepper
1 cup skim milk

1. In a saucepan, cover potatoes and onion with water. Bring to a boil, and then simmer over medium-low heat for 30 minutes or so, until fully softened. Drain.
2. Mash potatoes and onion with potato masher to remove chunks.
3. In large mixing bowl, combine partially mashed potatoes, cream cheese, salt, pepper, and milk. Whip together on high for 3 minutes.
4. Transfer potatoes into slow cooker. Cover and refrigerate overnight.
5. Cook on low 3-4 hours.

—— PER SERVING ——
- 280 calories
  (5 calories from fat)
- 0.5g total fat
  (0g saturated, 0g trans)
- 0mg cholesterol
- 400mg sodium
- 59g total carbohydrate
  (7g fiber, 5g sugar)
- 10g protein
- 0%DV vitamin A
- 60%DV vitamin C
- 10%DV calcium
- 15%DV iron

Variation:

If your diet allows, you may want to increase the salt to 1¼ or 1½ tsp. in Step 3.

Potato Filling

Miriam Nolt
New Holland, PA

Makes 20 servings

Prep. Time: 25 minutes
Cooking Time: 3 hours
Ideal slow-cooker size: 2 5-qt. cookers

1 cup celery, chopped fine
1 medium-sized onion, minced
1 stick (½ cup) butter
2 15-oz. pkgs. low-fat bread cubes
6 eggs, beaten
1 qt. fat-free milk
1 qt. mashed potatoes
3 tsp. salt
2 pinches saffron
1 cup boiling water
1 tsp. black pepper

1. Sauté celery and onion in butter in skillet until transparent.
2. Combine sautéed mixture with bread cubes. Stir in remaining ingredients.

Add more milk if mixture isn't very moist.
3. Pour into large, or several medium-sized, slow cookers. Cook on high 3 hours, stirring up from bottom every hour or so to make sure the filling isn't sticking.

—— PER SERVING ——
- 260 calories
  (45 calories from fat)
- 5g total fat (2.5g
  saturated, 0g trans)
- 65mg cholesterol
- 510mg sodium
- 70g total carbohydrate
  (4g fiber, 4g sugar)
- 10g protein
- 0%DV vitamin A
- 10%DV vitamin C
- 10%DV calcium
- 20%DV iron

Tip:

This recipe can be cut in half successfully.

Slow-Cooker Stuffing with Poultry

Pat Unternahrer
Wayland, IA

Makes 18 servings

Prep. Time: 20 minutes
Cooking Time: 5-6 hours
Ideal slow-cooker size: 6- or 7-qt., or 2 4-qt. cookers

1 large loaf low-fat bread, cubed and allowed to dry
2 cups chopped, cooked turkey, *or* chicken, skin removed
1 large onion, chopped
3 ribs celery with leaves, chopped
½ stick (¼ cup) butter, melted
4 cups fat-free chicken broth
1 Tbsp. poultry seasoning
1 tsp. salt
4 eggs, beaten
½ tsp. black pepper

1. Mix together all ingredients. Pour into slow cooker.
2. Cover and cook on high 1 hour, then reduce to low 4-5 hours.

—— PER SERVING ——
- 110 calories
  (40 calories from fat)
- 4.5g total fat
  (1.5g saturated,
  0g trans)
- 60mg cholesterol
- 270mg sodium
- 12g total carbohydrate
  (4g fiber, 1g sugar)
- 10g protein
- 0%DV vitamin A
- 0%DV vitamin C
- 6%DV calcium
- 10%DV iron

Fresh Herb Stuffing

Barbara J. Fabel
Wausau, WI

Makes 8 servings

Prep. Time: 30-45 minutes
Cooking Time: 4-5 hours
Ideal slow-cooker size: 6-qt.

3 Tbsp. butter
3 onions, chopped
4 celery ribs, chopped
½ cup chopped fresh parsley
1 Tbsp. chopped fresh rosemary
1 Tbsp. chopped fresh thyme
1 Tbsp. chopped fresh marjoram
1 Tbsp. chopped fresh sage
1 tsp. salt
½ tsp. freshly-ground black pepper
1 loaf stale low-fat sourdough bread, cut in 1-inch cubes
2 cups fat-free chicken broth

1. Sauté onions and celery in butter in skillet until transparent. Remove from heat and stir in fresh herbs and seasonings.

2. Place bread cubes in large bowl. Add onion/herb mixture. Add enough broth to moisten. Mix well but gently. Turn into greased slow cooker.

3. Cover. Cook on high 1 hour. Reduce heat to low and continue cooking 3-4 hours.

—— PER SERVING ——
• 100 calories
  (45 calories from fat)
• 5g total fat
  (3g saturated, 0g trans)
• 10mg cholesterol
• 420mg sodium
• 11g total carbohydrate
  (2g fiber, 3g sugar)
• 3g protein
• 6%DV vitamin A
• 6%DV vitamin C
• 4%DV calcium
• 8%DV iron

Irish Mashed Potatoes

Esther J. Yoder
Hartville, OH

Makes 9 servings

Prep. Time: 30-45 minutes
Cooking Time: 2½-4 hours
Ideal slow-cooker size: 5-qt.

3 lbs. peeled Yukon gold, *or* red potatoes, cubed
2½ cups chopped cabbage
3-6 garlic cloves, peeled, according to your taste preference
2 cups fat-free, low-sodium chicken broth
½ cup (4 ozs.) low-fat cream cheese, at room temperature
⅓ cup fat-free, *or* low-fat, sour cream
¼ cup skim, *or* 2%, milk
½ tsp. kosher salt
¼ tsp. black pepper

1. Combine potatoes, cabbage, garlic cloves, and chicken broth in slow cooker.

2. Cook on high 2½-4 hours, or until vegetables are soft.

3. Drain. Add remaining ingredients and mash.

4. The potatoes are now ready to serve, or you may pour them back into the slow cooker and set the cooker on low until you're ready to serve.

—— PER SERVING ——
• 160 calories
  (5 calories from fat)
• 0.5g total fat
  (0g saturated, 0g trans)
• 0mg cholesterol
• 260mg sodium
• 31g total carbohydrate
  (4g fiber, 3g sugar)
• 7g protein
• 4%DV vitamin A
• 30%DV vitamin C
• 8%DV calcium
• 10%DV iron

Variation:

1. If you prefer more seasoning, and your diet allows, you may want to increase the kosher salt to 1 tsp.

2. If you put the mashed potatoes back into the cooker to keep them warm, stir them up from the bottom and away from the sides before serving.

Potato Stuffed Cabbage

Jeanette Oberholtzer
Manheim, PA

Makes 10 servings

Prep. Time: 25-30 minutes
Cooking Time: 4-6 hours
Ideal slow-cooker size: 6-qt.

half a large head cabbage, sliced thin
2½ lbs. potatoes (6 or 7 medium-sized), peeled and grated
1 onion, sliced
¼ cup long-grain rice, uncooked
1 apple, peeled and sliced
½-1 tsp. dried dill, according to your taste preference
¼-½ tsp. black pepper, according to your taste preference
¼ tsp. ground ginger
1 egg white
14¼-oz. can tomatoes

1. Spray inside of cooker with nonfat cooking spray. Then begin layering vegetables into cooker. Place one-third of cabbage, one-third of potatoes, one-third of onion, one-third of rice, one-third of apple, and one-third of spices and seasonings into cooker.
2. Repeat twice.
3. Beat egg white until frothy. Fold into tomatoes. Spoon over top of vegetables.
4. Cover. Cook on low 4-6 hours, or until vegetables jag tender.

— PER SERVING —
• 120 calories
(0 calories from fat)
• 0g total fat
(0g saturated, 0g trans)
• 0mg cholesterol
• 135mg sodium
• 28g total carbohydrate
(5g fiber, 5g sugar)
• 4g protein
• 4%DV vitamin A
• 40%DV vitamin C
• 8%DV calcium
• 8%DV iron

Baked Potatoes

Mary Jane Musser
Manheim, PA

Makes 6 servings

Prep. Time: 5-10 minutes
Cooking Time: 3-8 hours
Ideal slow-cooker size: 4- or 5-qt.

6 medium-sized baking potatoes
nonfat cooking spray

1. Prick potatoes with fork.
2. Coat each potato with cooking spray. Place potatoes in slow cooker.
3. Cover. Cook on low 6-8 hours or on high 3-4 hours, or until potatoes jag tender and are not browned.

— PER SERVING —
• 160 calories
(0 calories from fat)
• 0g total fat
(0g saturated, 0g trans)
• 0mg cholesterol
• 15mg sodium
• 37g total carbohydrate
(5g fiber, 2g sugar)
• 4g protein
• 0%DV vitamin A
• 30%DV vitamin C
• 2%DV calcium
• 10%DV iron

Pizza Potatoes

Dorothy VanDeest
Memphis, TN

Makes 6 servings

Prep. Time: 20-25 minutes
Cooking Time: 4-6 hours
Ideal slow-cooker size: 3½-qt.

6 medium-sized potatoes, peeled and thinly sliced
1 large onion, thinly sliced
1 Tbsp. olive oil
1 oz. sliced pepperoni
¼ lb. grated low-fat mozzarella cheese
8-oz. can fat-free pizza sauce

1. In large skillet, sauté potato and onion slices in oil until onion becomes transparent. Stir constantly to prevent browning or sticking. Drain well.
2. Combine potatoes and onions with pepperoni and cheese in slow cooker.
3. Pour pizza sauce over top.
4. Cover and cook on low 4-6 hours.

— PER SERVING —
• 280 calories
(70 calories from fat)
• 8g total fat
(3g saturated, 0g trans)
• 15mg cholesterol
• 300mg sodium
• 43g total carbohydrate
(6g fiber, 5g sugar)
• 11g protein
• 6%DV vitamin A
• 40%DV vitamin C
• 15%DV calcium
• 15%DV iron

Variations:
If your diet allows, you may want to add ½ tsp. salt and ¼ tsp. black pepper to Step 2.

Hot German Potato Salad

Char Hagner
Montague, MI
Penny Blosser
Beavercreek, OH

Makes 8 servings

Prep. Time: 25-30 minutes
Cooking Time: 3-8 hours
Ideal slow-cooker size: 3½- or 4-qt.

6-7 cups potatoes, sliced
1 cup onions, chopped
1 cup celery, chopped
1 cup water
⅓ cup vinegar
¼ cup sugar
2 Tbsp. quick-cooking
   tapioca
1 tsp. salt
1 tsp. celery seed
¼ tsp. black pepper
6 slices lean turkey bacon,
   cooked and chopped
¼ cup fresh parsley

1. Combine potatoes, onions, and celery in slow cooker.
2. In a bowl, combine water, vinegar, sugar, tapioca, salt, celery seed, and black pepper.
3. Pour over potatoes. Mix together gently.
4. Cover. Cook on low 6-8 hours or on high 3-4 hours.
5. Stir in bacon and parsley just before serving.

—— PER SERVING ——
• 170 calories
  (20 calories from fat)
• 2.5g total fat
  (0.5g saturated,
  0g trans)
• 10mg cholesterol
• 440mg sodium
• 32g total carbohydrate
  (3g fiber, 8g sugar)
• 4g protein
• 0%DV vitamin A
• 25%DV vitamin C
• 4%DV calcium
• 8%DV iron

Candied Sweet Potatoes

Julie Weaver
Reinholds, PA

Makes 8 servings

Prep. Time: 50 minutes
Cooking Time: 4 hours
Ideal slow-cooker size: 3½-qt.

8 medium-sized sweet
   potatoes
½ tsp. salt
20-oz. can unsweetened,
   crushed pineapples,
   undrained
2 Tbsp. brown sugar
1 tsp. ground nutmeg
1 tsp. ground cinnamon

1. Cook sweet potatoes until soft. Peel. Slice and place in slow cooker.
2. Combine remaining ingredients. Pour over sweet potatoes.
3. Cover. Cook on low 4 hours.

—— PER SERVING ——
• 130 calories
  (0 calories from fat)
• 0g total fat
  (0g saturated, 0g trans)
• 0mg cholesterol
• 160mg sodium
• 32g total carbohydrate
  (4g fiber, 25g sugar)
• 2g protein
• 200%DV vitamin A
• 20%DV vitamin C
• 4%DV calcium
• 10%DV iron

Rosy Sweet Potatoes

Evelyn L. Ward
Greeley, CO

Makes 8 servings

Prep. Time: 5 minutes
Cooking Time: 3-4 hours
Ideal slow-cooker size: 3½- or 4-qt.

40-oz. can unsweetened
   sweet potato chunks,
   drained
21-oz. can lite apple pie
   filling
⅓ cup brown sugar
⅓ cup red hots
1 tsp. ground cinnamon

1. Combine all ingredients in slow cooker sprayed with nonfat cooking spray.
2. Cover. Cook on low 3-4 hours.

—— PER SERVING ——
• 280 calories
  (25 calories from fat)
• 3g total fat
  (1g saturated, 0g trans)
• 5mg cholesterol
• 220mg sodium
• 62g total carbohydrate
  (3g fiber, 46g sugar)
• 4g protein
• 400%DV vitamin A
• 2%DV vitamin C
• 6%DV calcium
• 15%DV iron

Sweet Potato Fruit Compote

Ilene Bontrager
Arlington, KS

Makes 8 servings

Prep. Time: 45 minutes
Cooking Time: 5-6 hours
Ideal slow-cooker size: 3½-qt.

4 cups sweet potatoes,
   peeled and cubed
3 tart cooking apples,
   peeled and diced
20-oz. can unsweetened
   pineapple chunks,
   undrained
¼ cup brown sugar
1 cup miniature
   marshmallows, *divided*

1. Cook sweet potatoes
in small amount of water in
saucepan until almost soft.
Drain.
2. Combine sweet potatoes,
apples, and pineapples in
slow cooker.
3. Sprinkle with brown sugar
and ⅔ cup marshmallows.
4. Cover. Cook on low 5-6
hours.
5. Thirty minutes before
serving, top potatoes and
fruit with remaining ⅓ cup
marshmallows. Cover and
continue cooking.

—— PER SERVING ——
• 200 calories   • 49g total carbohydrate
   (0 calories from fat)   (4g fiber, 31g sugar)
• 0g total fat   • 2g protein
   (0g saturated, 0g trans) • 400%DV vitamin A
• 0mg cholesterol   • 20%DV vitamin C
• 15mg sodium   • 4%DV calcium
                        • 6%DV iron

Sweet Potato- Cranberry Casserole

Mary E. Wheatley
Mashpee, MA

Makes 12 servings

Prep. Time: 20-30 minutes
Cooking Time: 3-4 hours
Ideal slow cooker size: 4- to 6-qt.

¼ cup orange juice
¼ stick (2 Tbsp.) butter
3 Tbsp. brown sugar
1 tsp. ground cinnamon
1½ cups fresh, *or* frozen,
   cranberries
salt
4 lbs. sweet potatoes, *or*
   yams, peeled if you wish
   and cut into 1" pieces

1. Place all ingredients
except sweet potatoes in slow
cooker. Mix together.
2. Cover. Cook on high
while preparing potatoes.
3. Add potato pieces to
warm mixture.
4. Cover. Cook on high 3-4
hours.
5. When potatoes are soft,
stir until they're mashed and
then serve.

—— PER SERVING ——
• 120 calories   • 25g total carbohydrate
   (20 calories from fat)   (4g fiber, 10g sugar)
• 2g total fat   • 2g protein
   (1.5g saturated,   • 370%DV vitamin A
   0g trans)   • 30%DV vitamin C
• 5mg cholesterol   • 4%DV calcium
• 45mg sodium   • 6%DV iron

Green Beans with Dill

Rebecca Leichty
Harrisonburg, VA

Makes 8 servings

Prep. Time: 5 minutes
Cooking Time: 3-4 hours
Ideal slow-cooker size: 3½- or 4-qt.

2 qts. fresh cut green beans,
   or 4 14½-oz. cans cut
   green beans
2 tsp. beef bouillon granules
½ tsp dill seed
¼ cup water

1. Spray slow cooker with
fat-free cooking spray.
2. Add all ingredients and
mix well.
3. Cook on high 3-4 hours,
or until beans are done to
your liking.

—— PER SERVING ——
• 35 calories   • 8g total carbohydrate
   (0 calories from fat)   (4g fiber, 3g sugar)
• 0g total fat   • 2g protein
   (0g saturated, 0g trans) • 15%DV vitamin A
• 0mg cholesterol   • 20%DV vitamin C
• 310mg sodium   • 4%DV calcium
                        • 6%DV iron

Variations:
1. If you like, add 2 Tbsp.
minced onions to Step 2.
2. If your sodium counter
allows, you may want to add
1 tsp. garlic salt to Step 2.

Green Bean Supper

Beverly Flatt-Getz
Warriors Mark, PA

Makes 24-28 servings

Prep. Time: 15-20 minutes
Cooking Time: 6-8 hours
Ideal slow-cooker size: 6- or 7-qt.

2 lbs. new potatoes, *or* 5 white potatoes halved and scrubbed
6-lb. 5-oz. can green beans, drained
15-oz. can whole corn, drained
1 large onion, *or* 2 medium onions, diced
5-oz. can lean chunk ham in water
10¾-oz. can fat-free, low-sodium chicken broth
½ tsp. garlic powder
½ tsp. onion powder
1 chicken bouillon cube

1. Place potatoes in slow cooker.
2. Add remainder of ingredients.
3. Fill pot half-full of water.
4. Cook 6-8 hours on low, or until the vegetables are done to your liking.

—— PER SERVING ——
- 70 calories
  (0 calories from fat)
- 0g total fat
  (0g saturated, 0g trans)
- 0mg cholesterol
- 510mg sodium
- 14g total carbohydrate
  (3g fiber, 3g sugar)
- 3g protein
- 6%DV vitamin A
- 10%DV vitamin C
- 2%DV calcium
- 6%DV iron

Variations:
You can use fresh green beans in place of the canned ones. You may need to increase cooking time to 8-10 hours on low.

Slow-Cooker Ratatouille

Nanci Keatley
Salem, OR

Makes 6 servings

Prep. Time: 35-40 minutes
Cooking Time: 6-7 hours
Ideal slow-cooker size: 5- or 6-qt.

1 Tbsp. olive oil
1 large onion, chopped
6 large garlic cloves, minced
1 green bell pepper, cut into strips
1 red bell pepper, cut into strips
1 medium-sized eggplant, cubed, peeled *or* not
2 cups mushrooms, thickly sliced
4 tomatoes, cubed
1 cup low-sodium tomato purée
¼ cup dry red wine, *or* wine vinegar
1 Tbsp. lemon juice
2 tsp. dried thyme
1 tsp. dried oregano
1 tsp. ground cumin
½-1 tsp. salt
¼-½ tsp. black pepper
4 Tbsp. minced fresh basil
¼ cup fresh parsley, chopped

1. Turn slow cooker on high for 2 minutes.
2. Pour oil into slow cooker and add remaining ingredients, except parsley and fresh basil.
3. Cover. Cook on high 2 hours, then on low 4-5 hours.
4. Stir in fresh basil. Sprinkle with parsley. Serve.

—— PER SERVING ——
- 120 calories
  (30 calories from fat)
- 3g total fat
  (0g saturated, 0g trans)
- 0mg cholesterol
- 30mg sodium
- 20g total carbohydrate
  (6g fiber, 10g sugar)
- 4g protein
- 30%DV vitamin A
- 50%DV vitamin C
- 6%DV calcium
- 15%DV iron

Variations:
1. This is delicious over whole wheat pasta or brown rice! It also makes great pizza topping.
2. You may substitute 1 rounded Tbsp. dried basil for the fresh basil. If you do that, then add the basil to Step 2.

Mediterranean Eggplant

Willard E. Roth
Elkhart, IN

Makes 8 servings

Prep. Time: 25-30 minutes
Cooking Time: 5-6 hours
Ideal slow-cooker size: 5-qt.

1 medium-sized red onion, chopped
2 cloves garlic, crushed
1 cup fresh mushrooms, sliced
2 Tbsp. olive oil

1 eggplant, unpeeled, cubed

2 green bell peppers, coarsely chopped

28-oz. can crushed tomatoes

28-oz. can garbanzos, drained and rinsed

2 Tbsp. fresh rosemary

1 cup fresh parsley, chopped

½ cup kalamata olives, pitted and sliced

1. Sauté onion, garlic, and mushrooms in olive oil in skillet over medium heat. Transfer to slow cooker coated with nonfat cooking spray.

2. Add eggplant, peppers, tomatoes, garbanzos, rosemary, and parsley to cooker.

3. Cover. Cook on low 5-6 hours.

4. Stir in olives just before serving.

5. Serve with couscous or polenta.

— PER SERVING —

• 250 calories
  (70 calories from fat)
• 8g total fat
  (1g saturated, 0g trans)
• 0mg cholesterol
• 370mg sodium
• 38g total carbohydrate
  (9g fiber, 8g sugar)
• 11g protein
• 10%DV vitamin A
• 40%DV vitamin C
• 15%DV calcium
• 30%DV iron

Eggplant Italian

Melanie Thrower
McPherson, KS

Makes 6-8 servings

Prep. Time: 30 minutes
Cooking Time: 4 hours
Ideal slow-cooker size: 4- or 5-qt., (an oval cooker works best!)

2 eggplants

¼ cup Egg Beaters

24 ozs. fat-free cottage cheese

¼ tsp. salt

black pepper to taste

14-oz. can tomato sauce

2-4 Tbsp. Italian seasoning, according to your taste preference

1. Peel eggplants and cut in ½"-thick slices. Soak in salt-water for about 5 minutes to remove bitterness. Drain well.

2. Spray slow cooker with fat-free cooking spray.

3. Mix Egg Beaters, cottage cheese, salt, and pepper together in bowl.

4. Mix tomato sauce and Italian seasoning together in another bowl.

5. Spoon a thin layer of tomato sauce into bottom of slow cooker. Top with about one-third of eggplant slices, and then one-third of egg/cheese mixture, and finally one-third of remaining tomato sauce mixture.

6. Repeat those layers twice, ending with seasoned tomato sauce.

7. Cover. Cook on high 4 hours. Allow to rest 15 minutes before serving.

— PER SERVING —

• 120 calories
  (10 calories from fat)
• 1g total fat
  (0g saturated, 0g trans)
• 30mg cholesterol
• 940mg sodium
• 17g total carbohydrate
  (4g fiber, 11g sugar)
• 11g protein
• 15%DV vitamin A
• 4%DV vitamin C
• 8%DV calcium
• 4%DV iron

Variation:

For more spice, add red pepper seasoning to taste in Step 4.

Caponata

Katrine Rose
Woodbridge, VA

Makes 10 servings

Prep. Time: 25-30 minutes
Cooking Time: 5-6 hours
Ideal slow-cooker size: 4-qt.

1 medium-sized eggplant, peeled and cut into ½″ cubes
14-oz. can low-sodium diced tomatoes
1 medium-sized onion, chopped
1 red bell pepper, cut into ½″ pieces
¾ cup low-sodium salsa
¼ cup olive oil
2 Tbsp. capers, drained
3 Tbsp. balsamic vinegar
3 garlic cloves, minced
1¼ tsp. dried oregano
⅓ cup chopped fresh basil

1. Combine all ingredients except basil in slow cooker.
2. Cover. Cook on low 5-6 hours, or until vegetables are tender.
3. Stir in basil. Serve over slices of toasted French bread.

—— PER SERVING ——
• 340 calories
  (70 calories from fat)
• 8g total fat
  (1.5g saturated,
  0.5g trans)
• 0mg cholesterol
• 830mg sodium
• 58g total carbohydrate
  (5g fiber, 5g sugar)
• 10g protein
• 2%DV vitamin A
• 10%DV vitamin C
• 10%DV calcium
• 15%DV iron

Eggplant & Zucchini Casserole

Jennifer Dzialowski
Brighton, MI

Makes 6 servings

Prep. Time: 25-30 minutes
Cooking Time: 5-6 hours
Ideal slow-cooker size: 5-qt.

2 egg whites
1 medium-sized eggplant
1 medium-sized zucchini
1½ cups bread crumbs
1 tsp. garlic powder
1 tsp. low-sodium Italian seasoning
48-oz. jar fat-free, low-sodium spaghetti sauce
8-oz. bag low-fat shredded mozzarella cheese

1. Beat egg whites in small bowl.
2. Slice eggplant and zucchini. Place in separate bowl.
3. Combine in another bowl bread crumbs, garlic powder, and Italian seasoning.
4. Dip sliced veggies in egg white and then in bread crumbs. Layer in slow cooker, pouring sauce and sprinkling cheese over each layer. (Reserve ½ cup cheese). Top with sauce.
5. Cover. Cook on low 5-6 hours, or until vegetables are tender.
6. Top with remaining cheese during last 15 minutes of cooking.

—— PER SERVING ——
• 280 calories
  (100 calories from fat)
• 11g total fat (4.5g
  saturated, 0g trans)
• 20mg cholesterol
• 1380mg sodium
• 30g total carbohydrate
  (6g fiber, 15g sugar)
• 15g protein
• 20%DV vitamin A
• 20%DV vitamin C
• 30%DV calcium
• 15%DV iron

Variation:

For added flavoring, sprinkle chopped onions and minced garlic over each layer of vegetables.

Zucchini Special

Louise Stackhouse
Benten, PA

Makes 4 servings

Prep. Time: 20 minutes
Cooking Time: 5-6 hours
Ideal slow-cooker size: 3-qt.

1 medium-to-large zucchini, peeled and sliced
1 medium-sized onion, sliced
1 qt. low-sodium stewed tomatoes with juice, *or* 2 14½-oz. cans low-sodium stewed tomatoes with juice
¼ tsp. salt
1 tsp. dried basil
8 ozs. fat-free mozzarella cheese, shredded

1. Layer zucchini, onion, and tomatoes in slow cooker.
2. Sprinkle with salt and basil.
3. Cover. Cook on low 5-6 hours.
4. Sprinkle with cheese 15 minutes before end of cooking time.

—— PER SERVING ——
• 170 calories
  (0 calories from fat)
• 0g total fat
  (0g saturated, 0g trans)
• 5mg cholesterol
• 620mg sodium
• 20g total carbohydrate
  (5g fiber, 15g sugar)
• 19g protein
• 20%DV vitamin A
• 20%DV vitamin C
• 90%DV calcium
• 20%DV iron

Zucchini in Sour Cream

Lizzie Ann Yoder
Hartville, OH

Makes 6 servings

Prep. Time: 20 minutes
Cooking Time: 1-1½ hours
Ideal slow-cooker size: 3- or 4-qt.

4 cups zucchini, unpeeled, sliced
1 cup fat-free sour cream
¼ cup skim milk
1 cup onions, chopped
1 tsp. salt
1 cup grated low-fat sharp cheddar cheese

1. Cook zucchini in microwave on high 2-3 minutes. Turn into slow cooker sprayed with nonfat cooking spray.
2. Combine sour cream, milk, onions, and salt. Pour over zucchini and stir gently.
3. Cover. Cook on low 1-1½ hours.
4. Sprinkle cheese over vegetables 30 minutes before serving.

—— PER SERVING ——
• 100 calories
  (20 calories from fat)
• 2g total fat
  (1g saturated, 0g trans)
• 10mg cholesterol
• 430mg sodium
• 12g total carbohydrate
  (1g fiber, 7g sugar)
• 8g protein
• 10%DV vitamin A
• 0%DV vitamin C
• 20%DV calcium
• 4%DV iron

Vegetable Acorn Squash

Janet Roggie
Lowville, NY

Makes 6 servings

Prep. Time: 5 minutes
Cooking Time: 8 hours
Ideal slow-cooker size: 4-qt.

1 large acorn squash
½ tsp. salt
¼ tsp. ground cinnamon
1 Tbsp. butter

1. Wash squash.
2. Cook on low 8 hours.
3. Split in half and remove seeds.
4. Cut each half into 3 wedges.
5. Sprinkle wedges with salt and cinnamon. Dot with butter.

—— PER SERVING ——
• 45 calories
  (20 calories from fat)
• 2g total fat
  (1g saturated, 0g trans)
• 5mg cholesterol
• 0mg sodium
• 7g total carbohydrate
  (1g fiber, 2g sugar)
• 1g protein
• 6%DV vitamin A
• 8%DV vitamin C
• 2%DV calcium
• 2%DV iron

Squash and Apples

Sharon Miller
Holmesville, OH

Makes 6 servings

Prep. Time: 25 minutes
Cooking Time: 6-8 hours
Ideal slow-cooker size: 6-qt.

1 large butternut squash, peeled, seeded, and cut into ¼" slices
2 medium-sized cooking apples, cored and cut into ¼" slices
3 Tbsp. raisins, *optional*
3 Tbsp. reduced-calorie pancake syrup
dash of ground cinnamon *and/or* nutmeg
¼ cup apple cider, *or* apple juice

1. Layer half of these ingredients in slow cooker: squash, apples, and raisins.
2. Drizzle with half the syrup.
3. Repeat layers.
4. Pour cider over top.
5. Cook on low 6-8 hours or until squash is tender.

— PER SERVING —
• 130 calories
  (0 calories from fat)
• 0g total fat
  (0g saturated, 0g trans)
• 0mg cholesterol
• 10mg sodium
• 34g total carbohydrate
  (8g fiber, 15g sugar)
• 2g protein
• 200%DV vitamin A
• 20%DV vitamin C
• 10%DV calcium
• 8%DV iron

Creamy Broccoli Casserole

Jeanne Allen
Rye, CO

Makes 4 servings

Prep. Time: 15 minutes
Cooking Time: 2-4 hours
Ideal slow-cooker size: 4-qt.

2 10-oz. pkgs. frozen broccoli spears, thawed and cut in pieces
10¾-oz. can 98% fat-free cream of celery soup
1½ cups reduced-fat cheddar cheese, *divided*
¼ cup yellow onions, finely chopped
1 cup baked potato chips, crushed

1. Combine broccoli, soup, 1 cup cheese, and onions in slow cooker sprayed with nonfat cooking spray.
2. Cover. Cook on low 3-4 hours or on high 2 hours, or until broccoli is done to your liking.
3. Mix remaining ½ cup cheese and crushed potato chips together and sprinkle on top of casserole 30 minutes before end of cooking time. Leave cooker uncovered during this final half hour of cooking.

— PER SERVING —
• 390 calories
  (80 calories from fat)
• 8g total fat
  (3g saturated, 0.5g trans)
• 15mg cholesterol
• 1200mg sodium
• 61g total carbohydrate
  (9g fiber, 8g sugar)
• 22g protein
• 40%DV vitamin A
• 60%DV vitamin C
• 50%DV calcium
• 10%DV iron

Cheesy Broccoli Casserole

Dorothy Van Deest
Memphis, TN

Makes 6 servings

Prep. Time: 10 minutes
Cooking Time: 3-5 hours
Ideal slow-cooker size: 3-qt.

10-oz. pkg. frozen chopped broccoli
6 eggs, beaten
24-oz. carton fat-free small-curd cottage cheese
6 Tbsp. flour
8 ozs. fat-free mild cheese of your choice, diced
2 green onions, chopped
½ tsp. salt

1. Place frozen broccoli in colander. Run cold water over it until it thaws. Separate into pieces. Drain well.
2. Combine remaining ingredients in large bowl and mix until well blended. Stir in broccoli. Pour into slow cooker sprayed with fat-free cooking spray.
3. Cover. Cook on high 1 hour. Stir well, then resume cooking on low 2-4 hours.

— PER SERVING —
• 250 calories
  (40 calories from fat)
• 4.5g total fat (1.5g saturated, 0g trans)
• 200mg cholesterol
• 980mg sodium
• 20g total carbohydrate
  (4g fiber, 8g sugar)
• 32g protein
• 20%DV vitamin A
• 20%DV vitamin C
• 35%DV calcium
• 8%DV iron

Variation:
You can use fresh broccoli instead of frozen.

Broccoli and Bell Peppers

Frieda Weisz
Aberdeen, SD

Makes 8 servings

Prep. Time: 20 minutes
Cooking Time: 4-5 hours
Ideal slow-cooker size: 3½- or 4-qt.

2 lbs. fresh broccoli, trimmed and chopped into bite-size pieces
1 clove garlic, minced
1 green, *or* red, bell pepper, cut into thin slices
1 onion, cut into slices
4 Tbsp. light soy sauce
½ tsp. salt
dash of black pepper
1 Tbsp. sesame seeds, *optional*, as garnish

1. Combine all ingredients except sesame seeds in slow cooker.
2. Cook on low for 4-5 hours. Top with sesame seeds.
3. Serve on brown rice.

—— PER SERVING ——
• 50 calories
  (10 calories from fat)
• 1 total fat
  (0g saturated, 0g trans)
• 0mg cholesterol
• 300mg sodium
• 9g total carbohydrate
  (4g fiber, 3g sugar)
• 4g protein
• 50%DV vitamin A
• 150%DV vitamin C
• 6%DV calcium
• 15%DV iron

Broccoli Delight

Nancy Wagner Graves
Manhattan, KS

Makes 4-6 servings

Prep. Time: 25 minutes
Cooking Time: 2-6 hours
Ideal slow-cooker size: 3½- or 4-qt.

1-2 lbs. broccoli, chopped
2 cups cauliflower, chopped
10¾-oz. can 98% fat-free cream of celery soup
½ tsp. salt
¼ tsp. black pepper
1 medium-sized onion, diced
2-4 garlic cloves, crushed, according to your taste preference
½ cup vegetable broth

1. Combine all ingredients in slow cooker.
2. Cook on low 4-6 hours or on high 2-3 hours.

—— PER SERVING ——
• 110 calories
  (20 calories from fat)
• 2.5 total fat
  (0.5g saturated, 0.5g trans)
• 5mg cholesterol
• 740mg sodium
• 19g total carbohydrate
  (5g fiber, 5g sugar)
• 6g protein
• 300%DV vitamin A
• 100%DV vitamin C
• 10%DV calcium
• 10%DV iron

Sweet-Sour Red Cabbage

Kaye Taylor
Florissant, MO

Makes 8 servings

Prep. Time: 30-45 minutes
Cooking Time: 3-4 hours
Ideal slow-cooker size: 3½-qt.

4 slices turkey bacon, diced
¼ cup brown sugar
2 Tbsp. flour
1 tsp. salt
⅛ tsp. pepper
½ cup water
¼ cup vinegar
1 medium head red cabbage shredded (8 cups)
1 small onion, finely chopped

1. Sauté bacon in nonstick skillet until crispy. Set bacon aside.
2. In slow cooker combine sugar, flour, salt, and pepper. Stir in water and vinegar.
3. Add cabbage and onion. Mix together well.
4. Cover. Cook on low 3-4 hours, or until cabbage and onion are as tender as you like them.
5. Sprinkle cooked bacon on top just before serving.

—— PER SERVING ——
• 70 calories
  (15 calories from fat)
• 1.5g total fat
  (0g saturated, 0g trans)
• 5mg cholesterol
• 420mg sodium
• 12g total carbohydrate
  (2g fiber, 7g sugar)
• 3g protein
• 15%DV vitamin A
• 70%DV vitamin C
• 4%DV calcium
• 4%DV iron

To make your own cream of mushroom or celery soup, please turn to pages 264-265.

Never-Fail Rice

Mary E. Wheatley
Mashpee, MA

Makes 6 servings

Prep. Time: 5 minutes
Cooking Time: 2-6 hours
Ideal slow-cooker size: 1- or 2-qt.

1 cup uncooked long-grain
  rice
2 cups water
½ tsp. salt
½ Tbsp. butter

1. Combine all ingredients
in small slow cooker.
2. Cover. Cook on low 4-6
hours or on high 2-3 hours, or
until rice is just fully cooked.
3. Fluff with fork. Serve.

—— PER SERVING ——
• 120 calories
  (10 calories from fat)
• 1g total fat
  (0.5g saturated,
  0g trans)
• 5mg cholesterol
• 200mg sodium
• 25g total carbohydrate
  (0g fiber, 0g sugar)
• 2g protein
• 0%DV vitamin A
• 0%DV vitamin C
• 2%DV calcium
• 8%DV iron

Herb Rice

Frieda Weisz
Aberdeen, SD

Makes 6 servings

Prep. Time: 5-10 minutes
Cooking Time: 4-6 hours
Ideal slow-cooker size: 3½-qt.

3 chicken bouillon cubes
3 cups water
1½ cups uncooked long-
  grain rice
1 tsp. dried rosemary
½ tsp. dried marjoram
¼ cup dried parsley,
  chopped
1 Tbsp. butter
¼ cup onions, diced
½ cup slivered almonds,
  optional

1. Combine all ingredients
in slow cooker.
2. Cook on low 4-6 hours,
or until rice is fully cooked.

—— PER SERVING ——
• 70 calories
  (20 calories from fat)
• 2g total fat
  (1g saturated, 0g trans)
• 5mg cholesterol
• 610mg sodium
• 10g total carbohydrate
  (0.5g fiber, 1g sugar)
• 1g protein
• 4%DV vitamin A
• 2%DV vitamin C
• 2%DV calcium
• 6%DV iron

Variation:

If you prefer, you may use
24 ozs. (or 3 cups) fat-free
low-sodium chicken broth
instead of bouillon cubes and
water.

Wild Rice Pilaf

Susan Kasting
Jenks, OK

Makes 6 servings

Prep. Time: 10 minutes
Cooking Time: 2½-3 hours
Ideal slow-cooker size: 4-qt.

1½ cups wild rice,
  uncooked
3 cups low-sodium, nonfat
  chicken stock
3 Tbsp. orange zest
2 Tbsp. orange juice
½ cup raisins (I like golden
  raisins)
1½ tsp. curry powder
1 tsp. butter, softened
½ cup fresh parsley
2 Tbsp. chopped pecans
½ cup chopped green
  onion

1. Mix rice, chicken stock,
orange zest, orange juice,
raisins, curry powder, and
butter in slow cooker.
2. Cover and cook on high
2½-3 hours, or until rice is
tender and has absorbed most
of liquid, but is not dry.
3. Stir in parsley, pecans,
and green onion just before
serving.

—— PER SERVING ——
• 240 calories
  (25 calories from fat)
• 3g total fat
  (0.5g saturated,
  0g trans)
• 0mg cholesterol
• 60mg sodium
• 47g total carbohydrate
  (4g fiber, 9g sugar)
• 8g protein
• 10%DV vitamin A
• 25%DV vitamin C
• 4%DV calcium
• 10%DV iron

Wild Rice

Ruth S. Weaver
Reinholds, PA

Makes 5 servings

Prep. Time: 15 minutes
Cooking Time: 2½-3 hours
Ideal slow-cooker size: 3-qt.

1 cup wild rice, *or* wild rice mixture, uncooked
½ cup sliced fresh mushrooms
½ cup diced onions
½ cup diced green, *or* red, bell peppers
1 Tbsp. oil
½ tsp. salt
¼ tsp. black pepper
2½ cups fat-free, low-sodium chicken broth

1. Layer rice and vegetables in slow cooker. Pour oil, salt, and pepper over vegetables. Stir.

2. Heat chicken broth. Pour over ingredients in slow cooker.

3. Cover. Cook on high 2½-3 hours, or until rice is soft and liquid is absorbed.

—— **PER SERVING** ——
- 180 calories
  (30 calories from fat)
- 3.5g total fat
  (0g saturated, 0g trans)
- 0mg cholesterol
- 300mg sodium
- 31g total carbohydrate
  (3g fiber, 2g sugar)
- 9g protein
- 0%DV vitamin A
- 10%DV vitamin C
- 2%DV calcium
- 10%DV iron

Wild Rice and Veggies

Darla Sathre
Baxter, MN

Makes 10 servings

Prep. Time: 15 minutes
Cooking Time: 3 hours
Ideal slow-cooker size: 3-qt.

6 cups cooked wild rice
3.8-oz. can sliced black olives, drained
4-oz. can sliced button mushrooms, rinsed and drained
1 large onion chopped (about 2 cups)
1 pint (2 cups) grape, *or* cherry, tomatoes, halved
8-oz. pkg. fat-free cheddar cheese, cubed
1½ Tbsp. olive oil
black pepper to taste, *optional*

1. Mix all ingredients together gently in slow cooker.

2. Cover. Cook on low 3 hours.

—— **PER SERVING** ——
- 170 calories
  (25 calories from fat)
- 3g total fat
  (0g saturated, 0g trans)
- 5mg cholesterol
- 300mg sodium
- 25g total carbohydrate
  (3g fiber, 3g sugar)
- 12g protein
- 10%DV vitamin A
- 8%DV vitamin C
- 20%DV calcium
- 6%DV iron

Tips:

1. The proportions of this recipe can be adjusted to your personal preferences quite easily.

2. When we have just a small amount of leftovers of this recipe, we use it as a pizza topping, and it is delicious!

Elegant Carrots with Onions

Dorothy VanDeest
Memphis, TN

Marjorie Yoder Guengerich
Harrisonburg, VA

Makes 6 servings

Prep. Time: 15-20 minutes
Cooking Time: 3-7 hours
Ideal slow-cooker size: 3- or 4-qt.

1 cube chicken bouillon
1 cup boiling water
2 medium-sized onions, sliced
1 Tbsp. butter
1 Tbsp. flour
pinch of salt, *optional*
6 carrots, pared and cut into julienne strips
1 Tbsp. sugar, *optional*

1. Dissolve bouillon cube in boiling water. Set aside.
2. In a large skillet, sauté onions in butter until transparent, stirring to separate rings.
3. Add flour and salt to onions in skillet. Add slightly cooled bouillon. Cook until thickened.
4. Combine carrots and onion sauce in slow cooker, stirring to coat carrots
5. Cover and cook on high one hour, then turn to low for 2-6 hours, or until carrots are done to your liking.
6. If desired, add sugar just before serving.

— PER SERVING —
- 35 calories
  (15 calories from fat)
- 1.5 total fat
  (1g saturated, 0g trans)
- 5mg cholesterol
- 330mg sodium
- 5g total carbohydrate
  (1g fiber, 2g sugar)
- 1g protein
- 2%DV vitamin A
- 4%DV vitamin C
- 2%DV calcium
- 2%DV iron

Orange-Glazed Carrots

Cyndie Marrara
Port Matilda, PA

Makes 6-8 servings

Prep. Time: 5-10 minutes
Cooking Time: 4-6 hours
Ideal slow-cooker size: 3½-qt.

32-oz. pkg. baby carrots
¼ cup packed brown sugar
½ cup orange juice
1 Tbsp. butter
½-¾ tsp. ground cinnamon, according to your taste preference
¼ tsp. ground nutmeg
2 Tbsp. cornstarch
¼ cup water

1. Combine all ingredients except cornstarch and water in slow cooker.
2. Cover. Cook on low 4-6 hours, or until carrots are done to your liking.
3. Put carrots in serving dish and keep warm, reserving cooking juices. Put reserved juices in small saucepan. Bring to boil.
4. Mix cornstarch and water in small bowl until blended. Add to juices. Boil one minute or until thickened, stirring constantly.
5. Pour over carrots and serve.

— PER SERVING —
- 130 calories
  (25 calories from fat)
- 3g total fat
  (1.5g saturated, 0g trans)
- 5mg cholesterol
- 60mg sodium
- 26g total carbohydrate
  (3g fiber, 18g sugar)
- 1g protein
- 300%DV vitamin A
- 20%DV vitamin C
- 4%DV calcium
- 8%DV iron

Baked Tomatoes

Lizzie Ann Yoder
Hartville, OH

Makes 4 servings

Prep. Time: 10 minutes
Cooking Time: 45 minutes-1 hour
Ideal slow-cooker size: 2½- or 3-qt.

2 tomatoes, each cut in half
½ Tbsp. olive oil
½ tsp. parsley, chopped, *or*
¼ tsp. dry parsley flakes
¼ tsp. dried oregano
¼ tsp. dried basil

1. Place tomato halves in slow cooker sprayed with nonfat cooking spray.
2. Drizzle oil over tomatoes. Sprinkle with remaining ingredients.
3. Cover. Cook on high 45 minutes-1 hour.

— PER SERVING —
- 30 calories
  (20 calories from fat)
- 2g total fat
  (0g saturated, 0g trans)
- 0mg cholesterol
- 5mg sodium
- 4g total carbohydrate
  (0.5g fiber, 2g sugar)
- 1g protein
- 4%DV vitamin A
- 10%DV vitamin C
- 0%DV calcium
- 2%DV iron

Stewed Tomatoes

Michelle Showalter
Bridgewater, VA

Makes 12 servings

Prep. Time: 10 minutes
Cooking Time: 3-4 hours
Ideal slow-cooker size: 4-qt.

2 qts. low-sodium canned
  tomatoes
¼ cup sugar
1 tsp. salt
dash of black pepper
2 Tbsp. butter
2 cups bread cubes

1. Place tomatoes in slow cooker.
2. Sprinkle with sugar, salt, and pepper.
3. Lightly toast bread cubes in melted butter in skillet on top of stove. Spread over tomatoes.
4. Cover. Cook on high 3-4 hours

—— PER SERVING ——
- 90 calories
  (20 calories from fat)
- 2.5g total fat (1.5g saturated, 0g trans)
- 5mg cholesterol
- 650mg sodium
- 15g total carbohydrate
  (2g fiber, 9g sugar)
- 2g protein
- 10%DV vitamin A
- 10%DV vitamin C
- 10%DV calcium
- 4%DV iron

Tip:

If you prefer bread that is less moist and soft, add bread cubes 15 minutes before serving and continue cooking without the lid.

Cranberry-Orange Beets

Jean Butzer
Batavia, NY

Makes 6 servings

Prep. Time: 15-20 minutes
Cooking Time: 3½-7½ hours
Ideal slow-cooker size: 6-qt.

2 lbs. medium-sized beets,
  peeled and quartered
½ tsp. ground nutmeg
1 cup cranberry juice
1 tsp. orange peel, finely
  shredded, *optional*
2 Tbsp. butter
2 Tbsp. sugar
4 tsp. cornstarch

1. Place beets in slow cooker. Sprinkle with nutmeg.
2. Add cranberry juice and orange peel. Dot with butter.
3. Cover. Cook on low 6-7 hours or on high 3-3½ hours.
4. In small bowl, combine sugar and cornstarch.
5. Remove ½ cup of cooking liquid and stir into cornstarch.
6. Stir mixture into slow cooker.
7. Cover. Cook on high 15-30 minutes.

—— PER SERVING ——
- 150 calories
  (35 calories from fat)
- 4g total fat
  (2.5g saturated,
  0g trans)
- 10mg cholesterol
- 120mg sodium
- 26g total carbohydrate
  (4g fiber, 19g sugar)
- 2g protein
- 4%DV vitamin A
- 20%DV vitamin C
- 2%DV calcium
- 8%DV iron

Harvard Beets

Marjorie Yoder Guengerich
Harrisonburg, VA

Makes 6 servings

Prep. Time: 10 minutes
Cooking Time: 1 hour
Ideal slow-cooker size: 3-qt.

⅓ cup sugar
2 Tbsp. flour
¼ cup beet juice, *or* water
¼ cup vinegar
2 16-oz. cans sliced beets,
  drained

1. Mix sugar and flour in small bowl. Stir in beet juice and vinegar. Mix well.
2. Place beets in slow cooker. Pour sugar and vinegar mixture over beets. Stir to coat.
3. Cover. Cook on high 1 hour. Turn to low until ready to serve.

—— PER SERVING ——
- 100 calories
  (0 calories from fat)
- 0g total fat
  (0g saturated, 0g trans)
- 0mg cholesterol
- 75mg sodium
- 24g total carbohydrate
  (3g fiber, 17g sugar)
- 2g protein
- 0%DV vitamin A
- 0%DV vitamin C
- 0%DV calcium
- 8%DV iron

Brussels Sprouts with Pimentos

Donna Lantgon
Rapid City, SD

Makes 8 servings

Prep. Time: 10 minutes
Cooking Time: 6 hours
Ideal slow-cooker size: 3½- or 4-qt.

2 lbs. Brussels sprouts
¼ tsp. dried oregano
½ tsp. dried basil
2-oz. jar pimentos, drained
¼ cup, *or* 1 small can, sliced black olives, drained
1 Tbsp. olive oil
½ cup water

1. Combine all ingredients in slow cooker.
2. Cook on low 6 hours, or until sprouts are just tender.

—— PER SERVING ——
- 70 calories
  (20 calories from fat)
- 2.5g total fat
  (0g saturated, 0g trans)
- 0mg cholesterol
- 25mg sodium
- 11g total carbohydrate
  (3g fiber, 5g sugar)
- 3g protein
- 20%DV vitamin A
- 100%DV vitamin C
- 4%DV calcium
- 10%DV iron

Corn and Macaroni

Kristine Martin
Newmanstown, PA

Makes 6 servings

Prep. Time: 5 minutes
Cooking Time: 2½ hours
Ideal slow cooker size: 3-qt.

15½-oz. can whole-kernel corn, drained
15½-oz. can creamed corn
1 cup uncooked macaroni
1 cup fat-free longhorn cheese, shredded
1 Tbsp. butter, cut in pieces
1 Tbsp. onion powder
1 tsp. salt
¾ fat-free cup milk

1. Spray interior of slow cooker with cooking spray.
2. Mix all ingredients together in slow cooker.
3. Cover. Cook on high 2½ hours, or until macaroni is soft but not mushy.

—— PER SERVING ——
- 220 calories
  (30 calories from fat)
- 3g total fat (1.5g saturated, 0g trans)
- 10mg cholesterol
- 930mg sodium
- 40g total carbohydrate
  (3g fiber, 7g sugar)
- 12g protein
- 8%DV vitamin A
- 8%DV vitamin C
- 20%DV calcium
- 4%DV iron

Note:
This helps children to eat their vegetables!

Baked Corn

Velma Stauffer
Akron, PA

Makes 8 servings

Prep. Time: 5-10 minutes
Cooking Time: 3 hours
Ideal slow-cooker size: 3-qt.

1 qt. corn (be sure to thaw and drain if using frozen corn)
2 eggs, beaten
1 tsp. salt
1 cup fat-free milk
⅛ tsp. black pepper
2 tsp. oil
2 Tbsp. sugar
3 Tbsp. flour

1. Combine all ingredients well in slow cooker sprayed with fat-free cooking spray.
2. Cover. Cook on high 3 hours.

—— PER SERVING ——
- 140 calories
  (25 calories from fat)
- 3g total fat
  (0.5g saturated, 0g trans)
- 45mg cholesterol
- 320mg sodium
- 25g total carbohydrate
  (2g fiber, 6g sugar)
- 5g protein
- 0%DV vitamin A
- 0%DV vitamin C
- 4%DV calcium
- 4%DV iron

Spicy Corn Casserole

Beth Nafziger
Lowville, NY

Makes 10 servings

Prep. Time: 20-30 minutes
Cooking Time: 3 hours
Ideal slow cooker size: 4-qt.

¼ stick (2 Tbsp.) butter
1 large onion, chopped
2 medium green bell
   peppers, chopped
¼ cup flour
2 cups fresh, *or* frozen, corn
2 cups cooked long-grain
   brown rice
14½-oz. can low-sodium
   diced tomatoes with
   liquid
2 hard-cooked eggs, chopped
2½ cups low-fat shredded
   sharp cheese
2 Tbsp. Worcestershire
   sauce
2-3 tsp. hot pepper sauce
½ tsp. salt
½ tsp. pepper

1. In large skillet, melt butter. Sauté onion and peppers until tender.

2. Stir in flour and remove from heat.

3. Place sautéed vegetables in slow cooker. Add all remaining ingredients. Mix together gently.

4. Cover. Cook on low 2-3 hours. If the corn becomes drier than I like while cooking, I add some tomato juice.

—— PER SERVING ——
- 200 calories
  (60 calories from fat)
- 6g total fat
  (3g saturated, 0g trans)
- 55mg cholesterol
- 420mg sodium
- 25g total carbohydrate
  (3g fiber, 5g sugar)
- 12g protein
- 15%DV vitamin A
- 45%DV vitamin C
- 15%DV calcium
- 8%DV iron

Note:

I serve this casserole when I'm looking for a spicy, meatless meal. This recipe is a family favorite that we enjoy over and over and never tire of.

Cheesy Hominy

Michelle Showalter
Bridgewater, VA

Makes 14 servings

Prep. Time: 5-10 minutes
Cooking Time: 3½-9 hours
Ideal slow-cooker size: 5- or 6-qt.

2 cups cracked hominy
6 cups water
2 Tbsp. flour
1½ cups fat-free milk
4 cups fat-free sharp
   cheddar cheese, grated
1½ tsp. salt
¼ tsp. black pepper
2 Tbsp. butter

1. Combine hominy and water in slow cooker.

2. Cover. Cook on high 3-4 hours, or on low 6-8 hours.

3. Stir in remaining ingredients.

4. Cover. Cook on high 30 minutes, or on low 60 minutes.

—— PER SERVING ——
- 90 calories
  (15 calories from fat)
- 2g total fat
  (1g saturated, 0g trans)
- 10mg cholesterol
- 620mg sodium
- 7g total carbohydrate
  (0.5g fiber, 1g sugar)
- 12g protein
- 10%DV vitamin A
- 0%DV vitamin C
- 30%DV calcium
- 2%DV iron

Tips:

Cheesy Hominy is a nice change if you're tired of the same old thing. It's wonderful with ham, slices of bacon, or meatballs. Add a green vegetable and you have a lovely meal. Hominy is usually available at bulk-food stores.

Mushrooms in Red Wine

Donna Lantgen
Rapid City, SD

Makes 4 servings

Prep. Time: 20-30 minutes
Cooking Time: 6 hours
Ideal slow-cooker size: 2- or 3-qt.

1 lb. fresh mushrooms, stemmed, trimmed, and cleaned
4 cloves garlic, minced
¼ cup onion
1 Tbsp. olive oil
1 cup red wine

1. Combine all ingredients in slow cooker.
2. Cook on low 6 hours.

—— PER SERVING ——
- 110 calories
  (35 calories from fat)
- 4g total fat (0.5g saturated, 0g trans)
- 0mg cholesterol
- 10mg sodium
- 7g total carbohydrate
  (2g fiber, 2g sugar)
- 4g protein
- 0%DV vitamin A
- 6%DV vitamin C
- 2%DV calcium
- 8%DV iron

Tips:
1. You can serve this as a side dish or as a condiment.
2. You can also use it as the base for a sauce to which you can add steak tips or ground beef, as well as 2 cups chopped onions, 2 tsp. dried oregano, 1½ tsp. salt, ½ tsp. black pepper, and 4 cloves minced garlic. You can also add a quart of spaghetti sauce and serve the mixture over a pound of your favorite pasta.

Wild Mushrooms Italian

Connie Johnson
Loudon, NH

Makes 5-7 servings

Prep. Time: 30-45 minutes
Cooking Time: 6-8 hours
Ideal slow-cooker size: 5-qt.

2 large onions, chopped
3 large red bell peppers, chopped
3 large green bell peppers, chopped
2 Tbsp. oil
12-oz. pkg. oyster mushrooms, cleaned and chopped
4 garlic cloves, minced
3 fresh bay leaves
10 fresh basil leaves, chopped
1½ tsp. salt
1½ tsp. black pepper
28-oz. can low-sodium Italian plum tomatoes, crushed *or* chopped

1. Sauté onions and peppers in oil in skillet until soft. Stir in mushrooms and garlic. Sauté just until mushrooms begin to turn brown. Pour into slow cooker.
2. Add remaining ingredients. Stir well.
3. Cover. Cook on low 6-8 hours.

—— PER SERVING ——
- 180 calories
  (60 calories from fat)
- 7g total fat
  (1g saturated, 0g trans)
- 0mg cholesterol
- 1040mg sodium
- 29g total carbohydrate
  (8g fiber, 6g sugar)
- 7g protein
- 50%DV vitamin A
- 150%DV vitamin C
- 8%DV calcium
- 25%DV iron

Tip:
This dish is good as an appetizer or on pita bread, or served over rice or pasta for a main dish.

Frequently Asked Questions about Slow-Cooker Cooking

Q. Is it important to spray the inside of the cooking vessel, the part that lifts out of the electrical unit, before putting the food in?

A. Doing so will make clean-up easier. And if you do that, you aren't creating used plastic liners which need to be disposed of.
One caution—when you've emptied the cooking vessel of the cooked food, let the vessel cool to room temperature before running water into it or putting it—or its lid—into dish water. And never put the electrical unit in water.

Desserts

Baked Apples with Dates

Mary E. Wheatley
Mashpee, MA

Makes 8 servings

Prep. Time: 20-25 minutes
Cooking Time: 2-6 hours
Ideal slow-cooker size: 6-qt. oval, or large enough cooker that the apples can each sit on the floor of the cooker, rather than being stacked

8 medium-sized baking apples

Filling:
   ¾ cup coarsely chopped dates
   3 Tbsp. chopped pecans
   ¼ cup, *or less,* brown sugar

Topping:
   1 tsp. ground cinnamon
   ½ tsp. ground nutmeg
   1 Tbsp. butter
   ½ cup water

1. Wash, core, and peel top third of apples.
2. Mix dates and chopped nuts with small amount of brown sugar. Stuff into centers of apples where cores had been.
3. Set apples upright in slow cooker.
4. Sprinkle with cinnamon and nutmeg. Dot with butter.
5. Add water around inside edge of cooker.
6. Cover. Cook on low 4-6 hours or on high 2-3 hours, or until apples are as tender as you like them.

—— PER SERVING ——
- 120 calories
   (20 calories from fat)
- 2g total fat
   (0g saturated, 0g trans)
- 0mg cholesterol
- 0mg sodium
- 26g total carbohydrate
   (2g fiber, 23g sugar)
- 1g protein
- 0%DV vitamin A
- 0%DV vitamin C
- 0%DV calcium
- 0%DV iron

"Bake" cakes in a cake pan set directly on the bottom of your slow cooker. Cover the top with 4-5 layers of paper towels to help absorb the moisture from the top of the cake. Tilt the cooker lid open slightly to let extra moisture escape.
Eleanor J. Ferreira, North Chelmsford, MA

Baked Apples with Cranberries

Stacy Schmucker Stoltzfus
Enola, PA

Rebecca Meyerkorth
Wamego, KS

Makes 4 servings

Prep. Time: 20-30 minutes
Cooking Time: 2½-3 hours
Ideal slow-cooker size: 5- or
6-qt. oval

¼ cup toasted chopped
  pecans, *or* walnuts
3 Tbsp. dried cranberries,
  or currants
3 Tbsp. brown sugar
¾ tsp. ground cinnamon,
  divided
¾ tsp. ground nutmeg
4 medium-sized Granny
  Smith apples, cored
1 cup brown sugar, packed
¾ cup apple cider
2 Tbsp. maple syrup, *or*
  1 tsp. maple flavoring

1. Combine nuts, dried cranberries, and 3 Tbsp. brown sugar. Add ¼ tsp. cinnamon and all of nutmeg.

2. Peel top third of each apple. Remove each apple's core, but keep apples whole. Place upright in slow cooker.

3. Spoon nut and fruit mixture into center of each apple, where core had been.

4. Combine remaining cinnamon, 1 cup brown sugar, cider, and maple syrup in small bowl. Stir well. Pour over apples.

5. Cover. Cook on low 2½-3 hours.

6. Remove apples with a spoon into individual serving bowls. Pour remaining juice over each apple.

—— PER SERVING ——
- 430 calories
  (50 calories from fat)
- 5g total fat (0.5g
  saturated, 0g trans)
- 0mg cholesterol
- 35mg sodium
- 99g total carbohydrate
  (4g fiber, 93g sugar)
- 1g protein
- 0%DV vitamin A
- 0%DV vitamin C
- 8%DV calcium
- 10%DV iron

Tip:

If you wish, and diets allow, serve apples with low-fat frozen yogurt.

Apple Cranberry Compote

Charlotte Shaffer
East Earl, PA

Makes 8 servings

Prep. Time: 15-20 minutes
Cooking Time: 4-6 hours
Ideal slow cooker size: 3- to 4-qt.

6 apples, peeled and sliced
1 cup fresh cranberries
¾ cup sugar
½ tsp. grated orange peel
½ cup water
¼ cup port wine
low-fat sour cream, *optional*

1. Combine apples and cranberries in slow cooker. Sprinkle evenly with sugar. Stir in orange peel, water, and wine.

2. Cover. Cook on low 4-6 hours.

3. Serve with dollops of sour cream on individual servings if you wish.

—— PER SERVING ——
- 160 calories
  (0 calories from fat)
- 0g total fat
  (0g saturated, 0g trans)
- 0mg cholesterol
- 0mg sodium
- 40g total carbohydrate
  (4g fiber, 34g sugar)
- 0g protein
- 2%DV vitamin A
- 15%DV vitamin C
- 2%DV calcium
- 2%DV iron

Country Apples

Betty K. Drescher
Quakertown, PA

Makes 8 servings

Prep. Time: 25 minutes
Cooking Time: 4-6 hours
Ideal slow-cooker size: 2½-qt.

4-5 cups apples, peeled and
  sliced
2 Tbsp. flour
¼ cup sugar
⅓ cup raisins
¼ tsp. ground cinnamon
⅔ cup dry oatmeal, rolled
  or quick
1 cup water
2 Tbsp. butter, melted
⅓ cup brown sugar

1. Coat apples in flour and white sugar. Stir in raisins, cinnamon, and oatmeal.
2. Pour water into slow cooker. Add apple mix.
3. Pour melted butter over apples. Sprinkle with brown sugar.
4. Cover. Cook on low 4-6 hours.
5. Serve over vanilla ice cream as a dessert, over oatmeal for breakfast, or use as a filling for crepes.

—— PER SERVING ——
• 160 calories
  (30 calories from fat)
• 3g total fat
  (2g saturated, 0g trans)
• 10mg cholesterol
• 5mg sodium
• 35g total carbohydrate
  (2g fiber, 26g sugar)
• 1g protein
• 0%DV vitamin A
• 0%DV vitamin C
• 2%DV calcium
• 4%DV iron

Chunk-Style Applesauce

Miriam Nolt, New Holland, PA
Judi Manos, West Islip, NY
Jean Butzer, Batavia, NY
Janet Roggie, Lowville, NY
Michelle Steffen, Harrisonburg, VA

Makes 8 servings

Prep. Time: 25 minutes
Cooking Time: 3-8 hours
Ideal slow-cooker size: 3½-qt.

8 large cooking apples,
  peeled, cored, and sliced
  or cut into chunks
½ cup water
1 tsp. cinnamon
½ cup sugar

1. Combine all ingredients in slow cooker.
2. Cover. Cook on low 8 hours or on high 3-4 hours.
3. Serve warm. (This sauce is also delicious served chilled!)

—— PER SERVING ——
• 110 calories
  (0 calories from fat)
• 0g total fat
  (0g saturated, 0g trans)
• 0mg cholesterol
• 0mg sodium
• 30g total carbohydrate
  (3g fiber, 26g sugar)
• 0g protein
• 0%DV vitamin A
• 0%DV vitamin C
• 2%DV calcium
• 2%DV iron

Healthy Harvest Applesauce

Dawn Day
Westminster, CA

Makes 12 servings

Prep. Time: 30-35 minutes
Cooking Time: 8 hours
Ideal slow-cooker size: 5-qt.

10 medium-sized apples
  (Rome, McIntosh,
  Pippin, *or* a variety that
  holds its shape well)
3 fresh pears
1 cup fresh, *or* frozen,
  cranberries
½ cup apple cider
3 tsp. ground cinnamon
¼ tsp. ground nutmeg
¼ tsp. ground cloves
juice of 1 lemon
½ cup brown sugar, *optional*

1. Peel and chop apples and pears into ¼" cubes. Place in slow cooker.
2. Mix in cranberries and remaining ingredients.
3. Cover. Cook on low 8 hours.

—— PER SERVING ——
• 100 calories
  (0 calories from fat)
• 0g total fat
  (0g saturated, 0g trans)
• 0mg cholesterol
• 0mg sodium
• 28g total carbohydrate
  (6g fiber, 20g sugar)
• 0g protein
• 2%DV vitamin A
• 2%DV vitamin C
• 4%DV calcium
• 4%DV iron

Tips:
1. You may add a little more cider for a saucier consistency.
2. Serve hot or cold as a side dish with pork or chicken, or chilled as a dessert.

Spiced Apples

Shari and Dale Mast
Harrisonburg, VA

Makes 10-12 servings

Prep. Time: 30-40 minutes
Cooking Time: 4-5 hours
Ideal slow-cooker size: 6-qt.

16 cups sliced apples, peeled
 or **unpeeled,** *divided*
½ cup brown sugar, *divided*
3 Tbsp. minute tapioca,
 divided
1 tsp. ground cinnamon,
 divided

1. Layer half of sliced apples, sugar, tapioca, and cinnamon in slow cooker.
2. Repeat, making a second layer using remaining ingredients.
3. Cover. Cook on high 4 hours or on low 5 hours.
4. Stir before serving. Delicious hot or cold.

—— PER SERVING ——
- 130 calories
  (0 calories from fat)
- 0g total fat
  (0g saturated, 0g trans)
- 0mg cholesterol
- 0mg sodium
- 33g total carbohydrate
  (3g fiber, 27g sugar)
- 0g protein
- 0%DV vitamin A
- 0%DV vitamin C
- 2%DV calcium
- 2%DV iron

Caramel Pears 'n' Wine

Sharon Timpe
Jackson, WI

Makes 6 servings

Prep. Time: 20-30 minutes
Cooking Time: 4-6 hours
Ideal slow-cooker size: 6-qt.

6 medium-sized fresh
 pears with stems
1 cup white wine (sautérne
 works well) *
½ cup sugar
½ cup water
3 Tbsp. lemon juice
2 apple cinnamon sticks,
 each about 2½-3" long
3 whole dried cloves
¼ tsp. ground nutmeg
6 Tbsp. fat-free caramel
 apple dip

1. Peel pears, leaving whole with stems intact.
2. Place upright in slow cooker. Shave bottom if needed to level fruit.
3. Combine wine, sugar, water, lemon juice, cinnamon, cloves, and nutmeg. Pour over pears.
4. Cook on low 4-6 hours, or until pears are tender.
5. Cool pears in liquid.
6. Transfer pears to individual serving dishes. Place 2 tsp. cooking liquid in bottom of each dish.
7. Microwave caramel dip for 20 seconds and stir. Repeat until heated through.
8. Drizzle caramel over pears and serve.

—— PER SERVING ——
- 290 calories
  (25 calories from fat)
- 2.5 total fat
  (0g saturated, 0g trans)
- 0mg cholesterol
- 140mg sodium
- 62g total carbohydrate
  (4g fiber, 42g sugar)
- 2g protein
- 0%DV vitamin A
- 4%DV vitamin C
- 15%DV calcium
- 6%DV iron

* For a non-alcoholic option, use apple juice or white grape juice instead of white wine.

Leave the lid on while the slow cooker cooks. The steam that condenses on the lid helps cook the food from the top. Every time you take the lid off, the cooker loses steam. After you put the lid back on, it takes one to 20 minutes to regain the lost steam and temperature. That means it takes longer for the food to cook. Pam Hochstedler, Kalona, IA

Golden Fruit Compote

Cindy Krestynick
Glen Lyon, PA
Judi Manos
West Islip, NY

Makes 8 servings

Prep. Time: 5-10 minutes
Cooking Time: 6-8 hours
Ideal slow-cooker size: 3-qt.

1-lb. 13-oz. can light
   peach, *or pear, slices,*
   undrained
½ cup dried apricots
¼ cup golden raisins
⅛ tsp. ground cinnamon
⅛ tsp. ground nutmeg
¾ cup orange juice

1. Combine undrained
peach or pear slices, apricots,
raisins, cinnamon, and
nutmeg in slow cooker. Stir
in orange juice. Completely
immerse fruit in liquid.
2. Cover and cook on low
6-8 hours.
3. Serve cold with angel
food cake or fat-free ice
cream. Serve warm as a side
dish in the main meal.

—— PER SERVING ——
• 70 calories
   (0 calories from fat)
• 0g total fat
   (0g saturated, 0g trans)
• 0mg cholesterol
• 0mg sodium
• 17g total carbohydrate
   (2g fiber, 13g sugar)
• 1g protein
• 2%DV vitamin A
• 10%DV vitamin C
• 2%DV calcium
• 4%DV iron

Variation:
   If you prefer a thicker
compote, mix together 2
Tbsp. cornstarch and ¼ cup

cold water until smooth.
Stir into hot fruit 15 minutes
before end of cooking time.
Stir until absorbed in juice.

Hot Fruit Compote

Sue Williams
Gulfport, MS

Makes 4-6 servings

Prep. Time: 10 minutes
Cooking Time: 3-8 hours
Ideal slow-cooker size: 4-qt.

1 lb. dried plums
1⅓ cups dried apricots
13½-oz. can unsweetened
   pineapple chunks,
   undrained
1-lb. can unsweetened
   pitted dark sweet
   cherries, undrained
¼ cup dry white wine
2 cups water
⅓ cup sugar

1. Mix together all ingredients in slow cooker.
2. Cover and cook on low
7-8 hours or on high 3-4 hours.
3. Serve warm.

—— PER SERVING ——
• 600 calories
   (10 calories from fat)
• 1g total fat
   (0g saturated, 0g trans)
• 0mg cholesterol
• 15mg sodium
• 148g total carbohydrate
   (13g fiber, 112g sugar)
• 6g protein
• 50%DV vitamin A
• 10%DV vitamin C
• 10%DV calcium
• 40%DV iron

Hot Fruit Salad

Judi Manos
West Islip, NY

Makes 16 servings

Prep. Time: 30 minutes
Cooking Time: 3-4 hours
Ideal slow-cooker size: 4-qt.

25-oz. can unsweetened
   chunky applesauce
21-oz. can light cherry pie
   filling
20-oz. can light pineapple
   chunks, undrained
15¼-oz. can light sliced
   peaches, undrained
15½-oz. can light apricot
   halves, undrained
15-oz. can light mandarin
   oranges, undrained
½ cup brown sugar, packed
1 tsp. ground cinnamon

1. Combine applesauce
and all canned fruit in slow
cooker. Stir gently.
2. Combine brown sugar
and cinnamon. Sprinkle over
fruit mixture.
3. Cover. Cook on low 3-4
hours.

—— PER SERVING ——
• 150 calories
   (0 calories from fat)
• 0g total fat
   (0g saturated, 0g trans)
• 0mg cholesterol
• 25mg sodium
• 37g total carbohydrate
   (2g fiber, 34g sugar)
• 1g protein
• 10%DV vitamin A
• 10%DV vitamin C
• 2%DV calcium
• 4%DV iron

Note:
   This recipe is very easy. It
is especially great around the
holidays. The aroma it creates
in the house is wonderful.

Hot Fruit Dessert

Pat Unternahrer
Wayland, IA

Makes about 8-9 servings

Prep. Time: 15-20 minutes
Cooking Time: 4 hours
Ideal slow-cooker size: 5-qt.

3 grapefruit, peeled and sectioned
11-oz. can mandarin orange segments, drained
16-oz. can unsweetened sliced peaches, drained
16-oz. can unsweetened fruit cocktail, drained
20-oz. can unsweetened pineapple chunks, drained
3 bananas, sliced
1 Tbsp. lemon juice
21-oz. can low-fat cherry pie filling

1. Combine all ingredients in slow cooker.
2. Cover. Cook on low 4 hours.
3. Chill and serve.

—— PER SERVING ——
• 120 calories
  (0 calories from fat)
• 0g total fat
  (0g saturated, 0g trans)
• 0mg cholesterol
• 15mg sodium
• 31g total carbohydrate
  (3g fiber, 24g sugar)
• 1g protein
• 2%DV vitamin A
• 30%DV vitamin C
• 2%DV calcium
• 2%DV iron

Tip:
This is an excellent topping for angel-food cake, if diets allow.

Strawberry Rhubarb Sauce

Tina Snyder
Manheim, PA

Makes 8 servings

Prep. Time: 25 minutes
Cooking Time: 6-7 hours
Ideal slow-cooker size: 3½-qt.

6 cups sliced rhubarb
¾ cup sugar
1 cinnamon stick, *optional*
½ cup white grape juice
2 cups sliced strawberries, unsweetened

1. Place rhubarb in slow cooker. Pour sugar over. Add cinnamon stick if you wish, and grape juice. Stir well.
2. Cover and cook on low 5-6 hours, or until rhubarb is tender.
3. Stir in strawberries. Cook 1 hour longer.
4. Remove cinnamon stick if you've used it. Chill.

—— PER SERVING ——
• 120 calories
  (0 calories from fat)
• 0g total fat
  (0g saturated, 0g trans)
• 0mg cholesterol
• 10mg sodium
• 29g total carbohydrate
  (3g fiber, 26g sugar)
• 1g protein
• 0%DV vitamin A
• 30%DV vitamin C
• 10%DV calcium
• 4%DV iron

Tip:
Serve as is, or, if diets allow, over cake or ice cream.

Rhubarb Sauce

Esther Porter
Minneapolis, MN

Makes 6 servings

Prep. Time: 20 minutes
Cooking Time: 4-5 hours
Ideal slow-cooker size: 4½-qt.

1½ lbs. rhubarb
⅛ tsp. salt
½ cup water
½ cup sugar
pinch of baking soda

1. Cut rhubarb into ½"-thick slices.
2. Combine all ingredients except baking soda in slow cooker. Cook on low 4-5 hours. Stir in baking soda.
3. Serve chilled.

—— PER SERVING ——
• 90 calories
  (0 calories from fat)
• 0g total fat
  (0g saturated, 0g trans)
• 0mg cholesterol
• 55mg sodium
• 22g total carbohydrate
  (2g fiber, 19g sugar)
• 1g protein
• 0%DV vitamin A
• 0%DV vitamin C
• 10%DV calcium
• 2%DV iron

Variation:
You may want to add 1 pint sliced strawberries about 30 minutes before end of cooking time.

Pineapple Sauce

Elizabeth L. Richards
Rapid City, SD

Makes 8 servings

Prep. Time: 10 minutes
Cooking Time: 2 hours
Ideal slow-cooker size: 3-qt.

4 cups apple juice
15-oz. can light crushed
   pineapples, undrained
1½ cups golden raisins
½ tsp. ground cinnamon
½ tsp. ground allspice
½ cup sugar
¼ cup cornstarch

1. Combine all ingredients
in slow cooker. Mix well.
2. Cover. Cook on high 2
hours.
3. Serve as a topping for
dessert, as topping for baked
ham, or as a side dish during
holidays.

—— PER SERVING ——
• 250 calories   • 63g total carbohydrate
  (0 calories from fat)   (2g fiber, 53g sugar)
• 0g total fat   • 1g protein
  (0g saturated, 0g trans) • 0%DV vitamin A
• 0mg cholesterol   • 60%DV vitamin C
• 10mg sodium   • 2%DV calcium
           • 8%DV iron

Cranberry Sauce with Red Wine and Oranges

Donna Treloar
Muncie, IN

Makes 6 servings

Prep. Time: 5-10 minutes
Cooking Time: 2-2½ hours
Ideal slow cooker size: 2-qt.

12-oz. bag fresh
   cranberries, rinsed
1¼ cups sugar
1 cup dry red wine
1 cinnamon stick
grated zest of one orange,
   then cut orange in half
4 whole cloves

1. Combine cranberries,
sugar, wine, cinnamon, and
zest in slow cooker.
2. Place 2 cloves in each
orange half. Push down into
cranberry mixture.
3. Cover. Cook on high 2-2½
hours, or until cranberries pop.
Turn off cooker.
4. Discard cinnamon stick
and orange halves with cloves.
5. Remove lid and let Sauce
cool to room temperature.
Serve chilled or at room
temperature over low-fat
frozen yogurt or angel food
cake.

—— PER SERVING ——
• 220 calories   • 51g total carbohydrate
  (0 calories from fat)   (3g fiber, 44g sugar)
• 0g total fat   • 0g protein
  (0g saturated, 0g trans) • 0%DV vitamin A
• 0mg cholesterol   • 20%DV vitamin C
• 0mg sodium   • 0%DV calcium
           • 2%DV iron

Just Rice Pudding

Mrs. Audrey L. Kneer
Williamsfield, IL

Makes 10 servings

Prep. Time: 10-15 minutes
Cooking Time: 2½ hours
Ideal slow-cooker size: 5-qt.

1 cup long-grain white rice,
   uncooked
1 cup sugar
8 cups skim milk
¾ cup fat-free, cholesterol-
   free egg product
1 cup skim milk
2 tsp. vanilla
¼ tsp. salt
¼ tsp. ground nutmeg, *or*
   cinnamon

1. Combine rice, sugar,
and 8 cups skim milk in slow
cooker.
2. Cover. Cook on high
2 hours, or just until rice is
tender.
3. Beat together egg-
substitute, 1 cup skim milk,
vanilla, and salt. Add to slow
cooker. Stir.
4. Cover. Cook on high
25-30 minutes.
5. Sprinkle with nutmeg or
cinnamon and serve warm.

—— PER SERVING ——
• 200 calories   • 36g total carbohydrate
  (20 calories from fat)   (0g fiber, 30g sugar)
• 2g total fat   • 10g protein
  (0.5g saturated,   • 4%DV vitamin A
  0g trans)   • 0%DV vitamin C
• 70mg cholesterol   • 30%DV calcium
• 190mg sodium   • 4%DV iron.

Vanilla Bean Rice Pudding

Michele Ruvola
Selden, NY

Makes 12 servings

Prep. Time: 10 minutes
Cooking Time: 2½-4 hours
Ideal slow-cooker size: 4-qt.

6 cups fat-free milk
1½ cups uncooked
  converted rice
1 cup sugar
1 cup raisins
1 Tbsp. butter, melted
½ tsp. salt
1 vanilla bean, split
1 large egg
½ tsp. ground cinnamon
8-oz. carton fat-free sour
  cream

1. Combine milk, rice, sugar, raisins, butter, and salt in slow cooker. Stir well.
2. Scrape seeds from vanilla bean. Add seeds and bean to milk mixture.
3. Cover and cook on high 2½-4 hours, or just until rice is tender and most of liquid is absorbed.
4. Place egg in small bowl. Stirring well with a whisk, gradually add ½ cup hot rice mixture to egg.
5. Return egg mixture to slow cooker, stirring constantly with whisk. Cook 1 minute while stirring. Remove inner vessel from slow cooker.
6. Let stand 5 minutes. Mix in cinnamon and sour cream. Discard vanilla bean.
7. Serve warm, not hot, or refrigerate until fully chilled.

—— PER SERVING ——
- 270 calories
  (15 calories from fat)
- 2g total fat
  (1g saturated, 0g trans)
- 20mg cholesterol
- 180mg sodium
- 55g total carbohydrate
  (0.5g fiber, 33g sugar)
- 8g protein
- 8%DV vitamin A
- 2%DV vitamin C
- 20%DV calcium
- 8%DV iron

Tip:

If your diet permits, you may top individual servings with light, or fat-free, vanilla-flavored whipped topping.

Deluxe Tapioca Pudding

Michelle Showalter
Bridgewater, VA

Makes 16 servings

Prep. Time: 20-30 minutes
Cooking Time: 3½-4½ hours
Chilling Time: 5-6 hours
Ideal slow-cooker size: 4-qt.

2 qts. fat-free milk
¾ cup dry small pearl
  tapioca
1 cup sugar
¾ cup Egg Beaters
2 tsp. vanilla
3 cups fat-free frozen
  whipped topping, thawed

1. Combine milk, tapioca, and sugar in slow cooker.
2. Cook on high 3-4 hours, or until tapioca is tender.
3. Add a little hot tapioca-milk mixture to Egg Beaters. Stir. Whisk Egg Beaters into full tapioca-milk mixture. Add vanilla.
4. Cover. Cook on high 20-30 minutes.
5. Cool. Chill in refrigerator. When fully chilled, beat with hand mixer to fluff pudding.
6. Fold in whipped topping.

—— PER SERVING ——
- 150 calories
  (10 calories from fat)
- 1g total fat
  (0g saturated, 0g trans)
- 40mg cholesterol
- 80mg sodium
- 29g total carbohydrate
  (0g fiber, 20g sugar)
- 5g protein
- 0%DV vitamin A
- 0%DV vitamin C
- 15%DV calcium
- 2%DV iron

Cook your favorite "Plum Pudding" recipe in a can set inside a slow cooker on a metal rack or trivet. Pour about 2 cups warm water around it. The water helps steam the pudding. Cover the can tightly with foil to help keep the cake dry. Cover the cooker with its lid. Cook on High.

Eleanor J. Ferreira, North Chelmsford, MA

Cinnamon Raisin Bread Pudding

Penny Blosser
Beavercreek, OH

Makes 8 servings

Prep. Time: 15 minutes
Cooking Time: 2½-3 hours
Ideal slow-cooker size: 4-qt.

10 slices cinnamon bread,
   cut into cubes
1 cup raisins
1 cup fat-free, cholesterol-
   free egg product
1½ cups warm water
1 tsp. vanilla
½ tsp. ground cinnamon
16-oz. can fat-free
   sweetened condensed
   milk

1. Place bread cubes
and raisins in greased slow
cooker. Mix together gently.
2. Mix remaining ingredi-
ents together and pour over
top.
3. Cover. Cook on high 30
minutes, then on low 2-2½
hours.

—— PER SERVING ——
• 360 calories   • 69g total carbohydrate
   (50 calories from fat)   (3g fiber, 53g sugar)
• 6g total fat   • 12g protein
   (1.5g saturated,   • 0%DV vitamin A
   0g trans)   • 0%DV vitamin C
• 110mg cholesterol   • 20%DV calcium
• 240mg sodium   • 10%DV iron

White Chocolate Bread Pudding

Linda E. Wilcox
Blythewood, SC

Makes 9 servings

Prep. Time: 30 minutes
Cooking Time: 1¾ hours
Cooling Time: 30 minutes, and
then 1-2 hours
Ideal slow-cooker size: 3- or 4-qt.

½ cup dried cranberries, *or*
   dried cherries
3 Tbsp. apple cider, *or*
   brandy
2 ozs. white chocolate, in
   bar form
6 cups stale French bread,
   cubed, *divided*
1 cup Egg Beaters
½ cup sugar
1 cup fat-free half-and-half
1 tsp. vanilla

1. Combine dried fruit with
cider or brandy in microwave-
safe bowl.
2. Microwave on high 30
seconds. Set aside to cool
(about 30 minutes).
3. Coarsely chop chocolate.
Set aside.
4. Drain dried fruit. Set
aside.
5. Spray interior of slow
cooker with cooking spray.
6. Cover bottom of slow
cooker with half the bread
cubes.
7. Sprinkle half the chocolate and half the fruit over
bread cubes.
8. Layer in remaining
bread cubes. Top with a layer

of remaining fruit and a layer
of remaining chocolate.
9. In a bowl beat Egg Beaters with sugar, half-and-half,
and vanilla. Mix together
thoroughly.
10. Pour over bread
mixture and press to make
sure egg mixture covers all
bread.
11. Cover and cook on high
1¾ hours.
12. Cool until warm or at
room temperature.

—— PER SERVING ——
• 220 calories   • 41g total carbohydrate
   (25 calories from fat)   (1g fiber, 23g sugar)
• 3g total fat (1.5g   • 7g protein
   saturated, 0g trans) • 2%DV vitamin A
• 5mg cholesterol   • 0%DV vitamin C
• 300mg sodium   • 6%DV calcium
                        • 8%DV iron

Note:
   My grandchildren love this
dessert.

Home-Style Bread Pudding

Lizzie Weaver
Ephrata, PA

Makes 6 servings

Prep. Time: 10-15 minutes
Cooking Time: 2-3 hours
Ideal slow-cooker size: large enough to hold your baking insert

⅓ cup Egg Beaters
2¼ cups fat-free milk
½ tsp. ground cinnamon
¼ tsp. salt
⅓ cup brown sugar
1 tsp. vanilla
2 cups 1"-square bread cubes
½ cup raisins

1. Combine all ingredients in bowl. Pour into slow-cooker baking insert. Cover baking insert. Place on metal rack (or rubber jar rings) in bottom of slow cooker.

2. Pour ½ cup hot water into cooker around outside of insert.

3. Cover slow cooker. Cook on high 2-3 hours.

4. Serve pudding warm or cold.

—— **PER SERVING** ——
- 170 calories
  (15 calories from fat)
- 2g total fat
  (0.5g saturated,
  0g trans)
- 50mg cholesterol
- 70mg sodium
- 33g total carbohydrate
  (0g fiber, 26g sugar)
- 6g protein
- 0%DV vitamin A
- 0%DV vitamin C
- 15%DV calcium
- 6%DV iron

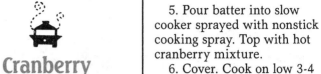

Cranberry Pudding Cake

Sue Hamilton
Minooka, IL

Makes 6 servings

Prep. Time: 15-20 minutes
Cooking Time: 3-4 hours
Ideal slow-cooker size: 2-qt.

1½ cups fresh, *or frozen,* cranberries
1¾ cups water
.3-oz. box sugar-free orange gelatin
½ cup Splenda
1 cup flour
1½ tsp. baking powder
½ cup Splenda
1 tsp. vanilla extract
¼ tsp. baking soda
½ cup skim milk
½ tsp. almond extract

1. In a microwaveable bowl, combine cranberries and water.

2. Cook in microwave 4-5 minutes on high until cranberries pop.

3. Stir in gelatin and ½ cup Splenda until dissolved. Set aside.

4. In another bowl, combine flour, baking powder, ½ cup Splenda, vanilla extract, baking soda, milk, and almond extract. Mix until dry ingredients are moistened.

5. Pour batter into slow cooker sprayed with nonstick cooking spray. Top with hot cranberry mixture.

6. Cover. Cook on low 3-4 hours.

7. This is best served warm or cold rather than hot.

—— **PER SERVING** ——
- 180 calories
  (5 calories from fat)
- 0.5g total fat
  (0g saturated,
  0g trans)
- 0mg cholesterol
- 500mg sodium
- 25g total carbohydrate
  (2g fiber, 3g sugar)
- 10g protein
- 2%DV vitamin A
- 2%DV vitamin C
- 8%DV calcium
- 6%DV iron

Pumpkin Pie Pudding

Sue Hamilton
Minooka, IL

Makes 8 servings

Prep. Time: 5-10 minutes
Cooking Time: 3 hours
Ideal slow-cooker size: 3-qt.

15-oz. can pumpkin
12-oz. can evaporated skim milk
¾ cup Splenda
½ cup low-fat buttermilk baking mix
2 eggs, beaten, *or* 6 egg whites
2 tsp. pumpkin pie spice
1 tsp. lemon zest

1. Combine all ingredients in slow cooker sprayed with cooking spray. Stir until lumps disappear.
2. Cover. Cook on low 3 hours.
3. Serve warm or cold.

—— PER SERVING ——
- 140 calories
  (30 calories from fat)
- 3.5g total fat
  (1g saturated, 0g trans)
- 50mg cholesterol
- 220mg sodium
- 21g total carbohydrate
  (2g fiber, 7g sugar)
- 7g protein
- 200%DV vitamin A
- 2%DV vitamin C
- 15%DV calcium
- 8%DV iron

Tip:
If you like, and your diet permits, add a spoonful of low-fat whipped topping to each serving.

Apple Crisp

Mary Jane Musser
Manheim, PA

Makes 6 servings

Prep. Time: 15-20 minutes
Cooking Time: 2-4 hours
Ideal slow-cooker size: 3-qt.

6 cups cooking apples, peeled, cored, and sliced
½ cup dry quick oatmeal
½ cup brown sugar
½ cup flour
1½ Tbsp. butter, softened
½ tsp. ground cinnamon

1. Place apples in slow cooker sprayed with nonfat cooking spray.
2. Combine remaining ingredients in mixing bowl until crumbly.
3. Sprinkle mixture over apples.
4. Cover. Cook on low 4 hours or on high 2 hours.

—— PER SERVING ——
- 260 calories
  (40 calories from fat)
- 4.5g total fat
  (0.5g saturated, 0g trans)
- 0mg cholesterol
- 55mg sodium
- 53g total carbohydrate
  (4g fiber, 32g sugar)
- 3g protein
- 0%DV vitamin A
- 0%DV vitamin C
- 2%DV calcium
- 8%DV iron

Tip from Tester:
The next time you do a major cleaning in your kitchen, clear your kitchen shelves of those high-fat items you haven't used in a while. When they are out of the house they won't be a temptation.

Low-Fat Apple Cake

Sue Hamilton
Minooka, IL

Makes 8 servings

Prep. Time: 20 minutes
Cooking Time: 2½-3 hours
Ideal slow-cooker size: 4-qt.

1 cup flour
¾ cup sugar
2 tsp. baking powder
1 tsp. ground cinnamon
¼ tsp. salt
4 medium-sized cooking apples, chopped
⅓ cup Egg Beaters
2 tsp. vanilla

1. Combine flour, sugar, baking powder, cinnamon, and salt.
2. Add apples, stirring lightly to coat.
3. Combine Egg Beaters and vanilla. Add to apple mixture. Stir until just moistened. Spoon into lightly greased slow cooker.
4. Cover. Bake on high 2½-3 hours.
5. Serve warm.

—— PER SERVING ——
- 180 calories
  (10 calories from fat)
- 1g total fat
  (0g saturated, 0g trans)
- 35mg cholesterol
- 85mg sodium
- 41g total carbohydrate
  (2g fiber, 26g sugar)
- 3g protein
- 0%DV vitamin A
- 0%DV vitamin C
- 6%DV calcium
- 6%DV iron

Cherry Cobbler

Penny Blosser
Beavercreek, OH

Makes 6 servings

Prep. Time: 5-10 minutes
Cooking Time: 1½-2 hours
Ideal slow-cooker size: 3½-qt.

21-oz. can low-fat, low-
    sodium cherry pie filling
1 cup flour
¼ cup sugar
half a stick (¼ cup) butter,
    melted
½ cup skim milk
1½ tsp. baking powder
½ tsp. almond extract
¼ tsp. salt

1. Pour pie filling into greased slow cooker.

2. Combine remaining ingredients in bowl. Beat until smooth. Spread over pie filling.

3. Cover. Cook on high 1½-2 hours on high.

—— PER SERVING ——
- 230 calories
  (5 calories from fat)
- 0.5g total fat
  (0g saturated, 0g trans)
- 0mg cholesterol
- 125mg sodium
- 54g total carbohydrate
  (1g fiber, 33g sugar)
- 3g protein
- 0%DV vitamin A
- 0%DV vitamin C
- 10%DV calcium
- 8%DV iron

Slow-Cooker Berry Cobbler

Wilma Haberkamp
Fairbank, IA
Virginia Graybill
Hershey, PA

Makes 8 servings

Prep. Time: 15-20 minutes
Cooking Time: 2-2½ hours
Ideal slow-cooker size: 5-qt.

1¼ cups all-purpose flour,
    divided
2 Tbsp. sugar, plus 1 cup
    sugar, *divided*
1 tsp. baking powder
¼ tsp. ground cinnamon
1 egg, lightly beaten
¼ cup skim milk
2 Tbsp. canola oil
⅛ tsp. salt
2 cups unsweetened rasp-
    berries, fresh, *or* thawed
    if frozen, and drained
2 cups unsweetened
    blueberries, fresh, *or*
    thawed if frozen, and
    drained

1. In mixing bowl, combine 1 cup flour, 2 Tbsp. sugar, baking powder, and cinnamon.

2. In a separate bowl, combine egg, milk, and oil. Stir into dry ingredients until moistened. Batter will be thick.

3. Spray slow cooker with cooking spray. Spread batter evenly on bottom of slow cooker.

4. In another bowl combine salt, remaining flour, remaining sugar, and berries. Toss to coat berries.

5. Spread berries over batter.

6. Cook on high 2-2½ hours, or until toothpick inserted into cobbler comes out clean.

—— PER SERVING ——
- 260 calories
  (40 calories from fat)
- 4.5g total fat
  (0g saturated, 0g trans)
- 25mg cholesterol
- 50mg sodium
- 52g total carbohydrate
  (4g fiber, 34g sugar)
- 3g protein
- 2%DV vitamin A
- 10%DV vitamin C
- 6%DV calcium
- 8%DV iron

Tip:
    If your diet permits, eat in soup bowl with cold milk poured over.

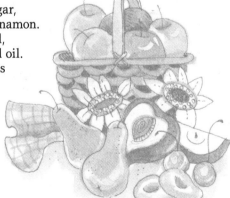

Quick Yummy Peaches

Willard E. Roth
Elkhart, IN

Makes 6 servings

Prep. Time: 5-20 minutes
Cooking Time: 5 hours
Ideal slow-cooker size: 3-qt.

⅓ cup low-fat buttermilk
   baking mix
⅔ cup dry quick oats
⅓ cup brown sugar
1 tsp. ground cinnamon
4 cups sliced peaches,
   canned, *or* fresh
½ cup water

1. Mix together baking mix, dry oats, brown sugar, and cinnamon in greased slow cooker.

2. Stir in peaches and water.

3. Cook on low for at least 5 hours. (If you like a drier cobbler, remove lid for last 15-30 minutes of cooking.)

—— PER SERVING ——
• 270 calories   • 57g total carbohydrate
  (25 calories from fat)   (1g fiber, 42g sugar)
• 2.5g total fat   • 3g protein
  (0.5g saturated,   • 10%DV vitamin A
  0g trans)   • 0%DV vitamin C
• 0mg cholesterol   • 4%DV calcium
• 230mg sodium   • 6%DV iron

Tip:
   If diets allow, serve with fat-free frozen yogurt or ice cream.

Gingerbread Pudding Cake

Katrina Eberly
Wernersville, PA

Makes 12 servings

Prep. Time: 20 minutes
Cooking Time: 2-2½ hours
Standing Time: 15 minutes
Ideal slow cooker size: 3-qt.

3 Tbsp. butter, softened
¼ cup sugar
1 egg white
1 tsp. vanilla extract
½ cup molasses
1 cup water
1¼ cups flour
¾ tsp. baking soda
½ tsp. ground cinnamon
½ tsp. ground ginger
¼ tsp. salt
¼ tsp. ground allspice
⅛ tsp. ground nutmeg

1. Spray interior of slow cooker with cooking spray.

2. In large mixing bowl, cream 3 Tbsp. butter and sugar until light and fluffy. Beat in egg white and vanilla.

3. In separate bowl, combine molasses and water until blended.

4. In another bowl, combine flour, baking soda, and spices. Add to creamed mixture alternately with molasses mixture, beating well after each addition.

5. Spoon into slow cooker.

6. Cover. Cook on high 2-2½ hours, or until toothpick inserted in center of cake comes out clean.

7. Turn off cooker. Let stand 15 minutes. Serve cake warm.

—— PER SERVING ——
• 150 calories   • 29g total carbohydrate
  (25 calories from fat)   0g fiber, 16g sugar)
• 3g total fat   • 2g protein
  (2g saturated, 0g trans)   • 2%DV vitamin A
• 10mg cholesterol   • 0%DV vitamin C
• 160mg sodium   • 4%DV calcium
                • 8%DV iron

Tip from Tester:
   I used blackstrap molasses, and the flavor didn't overpower the cake.

Chocolate Mud Cake

Marci Baum
Annville, PA

Makes 8 servings

Prep. Time: 20 minutes
Cooking Time: 1-2 hours
Cooling Time: 25 minutes
Ideal slow-cooker size: 4-qt.

1 cup flour
2 tsp. baking powder
2 Tbsp. butter
2 ozs. semisweet chocolate,
   or ⅓ cup chocolate chips
1 cup sugar, *divided*
3 Tbsp. plus ⅓ cup Dutch-
   processed cocoa
1 Tbsp. vanilla extract
¼ tsp. salt
⅓ cup skim milk
1 egg yolk
⅓ cup brown sugar
1½ cups hot water

1. Coat inside of slow cooker with nonfat cooking spray.

2. In mixing bowl, whisk together flour and baking powder. Set aside.

3. In large microwave-safe mixing bowl, melt butter and chocolate in microwave. Mix well.

4. Whisk in ⅔ cup sugar, 3 Tbsp. cocoa, vanilla, salt, milk, and egg yolk.

5. Add flour mixture. Stir until thoroughly mixed.

6. Pour batter into slow cooker. Spread evenly.

7. Whisk together remaining sugar, cocoa, and hot water until sugar is dissolved. Pour over batter in slow cooker. Do not stir.

8. Cover. Cook on high 1-2 hours. The cake will be very moist and floating on a layer of molten chocolate when it's done. And you'll know it is done cooking when nearly all the cake is set and its edges begin to pull away from the sides of the pot.

9. Turn off slow cooker and remove lid. Try not to let condensed steam from the lid drip onto the cake.

10. Let cool for 25 minutes before cutting and spooning onto individual plates.

—— PER SERVING ——
• 370 calories
  (60 calories from fat)
• 7g total fat (3.5g
  saturated, 0g trans)
• 35mg cholesterol
• 150mg sodium
• 72g total carbohydrate
  (2g fiber, 53g sugar)
• 9g protein
• 0%DV vitamin A
• 0%DV vitamin C
• 25%DV calcium
• 8%DV iron

Tip:
If diets permit, serve the cake with low-fat or fat-free frozen yogurt.

You can use a 2-lb. coffee can, 2 1-lb. coffee cans, 3 16-oz. vegetable cans, a 6-7 cup mold, or a 1½-2-quart baking dish for "baking" cakes in a slow cooker. Leave the cooker lid slightly open to let extra moisture escape.
Eleanor J. Ferreira, North Chelmsford, MA

Appetizers, Snacks, and Spreads

Prairie Fire Dip

Cheri Jantzen
Houston, TX

Makes 1¼ cups, or 10 servings

Prep. Time: 5-10 minutes
Cooking Time: 1-3 hours
Ideal slow-cooker size: 2-qt.

**1 cup refried fat-free beans
(half a 15-oz. can)**
**½ cup shredded fat-free
Monterey Jack cheese**
¼ cup water
1 Tbsp. minced onion
1 clove garlic, minced
2 tsp. chili powder
hot sauce as desired

1. Combine all ingredients in slow cooker.

2. Cover. Cook on high 1 hour, or on low 2-3 hours. Serve with baked tortilla chips.

—— PER SERVING ——
- 45 calories
  (0 calories from fat)
- 0g total fat
  (0g saturated, 0g trans)
- 0mg cholesterol
- 190mg sodium
- 6g total carbohydrate
  (2g fiber, 0g sugar)
- 5g protein
- 6%DV vitamin A
- 0%DV vitamin C
- 15%DV calcium
- 4%DV iron

Tip:
This recipe can easily be doubled.

Chili Cheese Dip

Vicki Dinkel
Sharon Springs, KS

Makes 8 servings

Prep. Time: 10-15 minutes
Cooking Time: 4 hours
Ideal slow-cooker size: 2 qt.

---

1 onion, diced
**8-oz. pkg. fat-free cream
cheese, cubed**
**2 15-oz. cans lowfat
vegetarian chili without
beans**
2 tsp. garlic salt
1½ cups salsa

1. Lightly brown onion in skillet sprayed with nonfat cooking spray. Transfer to slow cooker.

2. Stir in cream cheese, chili, garlic salt, and salsa.

3. Cover. Cook on low 4 hours, stirring occasionally.

4. Serve with baked tortilla chips.

—— PER SERVING ——
- 230 calories
  (15 calories from fat)
- 2g total fat
  (0g saturated, 0g trans)
- 0mg cholesterol
- 1420mg sodium
- 40g total carbohydrate
  (8g fiber, 2g sugar)
- 15g protein
- 10%DV vitamin A
- 4%DV vitamin C
- 10%DV calcium
- 10%DV iron

Kickin' Dip

Rose Hankins
Stevensville, MD

Makes 3-4 cups, or 12-16 servings

Prep. Time: 15 minutes
Cooking Time: 3-4 hours
Ideal slow cooker size: 4-qt.

4 cups (16 oz.) low-fat
  shredded cheddar cheese
14-oz. can diced tomatoes,
  drained, with juice
  reserved
7-oz. can chopped green
  chilies, drained
1 cup chopped onions
1 Tbsp. cumin
1 tsp. chili powder
1 tsp. hot pepper sauce
baked tortilla chips

1. Mix all ingredients
except chips in slow cooker.
2. Cover. Cook on low 3-4
hours.
3. Stir before serving. If
Dip is stiffer than you like,
stir in some of reserved
tomato juice
4. Serve with baked tortilla
chips for dipping

—— PER SERVING ——
• 60 calories
  (20 calories from fat)
• 2g total fat
  (1g saturated, 0g trans)
• 5mg cholesterol
• 260mg sodium
• 3g total carbohydrate
  (1g fiber, 1g sugar)
• 7g protein
• 6%DV vitamin A
• 15%DV vitamin C
• 15%DV calcium
• 4%DV iron

Nacho Dip

Susan Tjon
Austin, TX

Makes 8 servings

Prep. Time: 10 minutes
Cooking Time: 2 hours
Ideal slow-cooker size: 3-qt.

8 ozs. fat-free cream cheese
1 cup shredded reduced-fat
  cheddar cheese
½ cup mild, *or* medium,
  chunky salsa
¼ cup fat-free, *or* 2%, milk
8-oz. bag baked tortilla
  chips, *or* assorted fresh
  vegetables

1. Cut cream cheese into
chunks.
2. Combine cream cheese,
cheddar cheese, salsa, and
milk in slow cooker.
3. Cook on low 2 hours.
Stir to blend.
4. When smooth and
hot, serve with baked
tortilla chips or assorted fresh
vegetables.

—— PER SERVING ——
• 170 calories
  (25 calories from fat)
• 2.5 total fat
  (1g saturated, 0g trans)
• 5mg cholesterol
• 430mg sodium
• 27g total carbohydrate
  (2g fiber, 1g sugar)
• 10g protein
• 8%DV vitamin A
• 4%DV vitamin C
• 20%DV calcium
• 4%DV iron

Tip:
  You may double this recipe
successfully. Just be sure to
allow extra cooking time.

Meatless Pizza Fondue

Virginia Graybill
Hershey, PA

Makes 4 cups, or 16 servings

Prep. Time: 5-10 minutes
Cooking Time: 3 hours
Ideal slow cooker size: 3-qt.

29-oz. jar low-fat, low-sodium
  meatless spaghetti sauce
2 cups (8 oz.) fat-free
  shredded mozzarella
  cheese
¼ cup shredded reduced-fat
  Parmesan cheese
2 tsp. dried oregano
1 tsp. dried minced onion
¼ tsp. garlic powder
1 lb. unsliced loaf Italian
  bread, cut into cubes

1. Combine spaghetti
sauce, cheeses, oregano,
onion, and garlic powder in
slow cooker.
2. Cover. Cook on low
3 hours, or until cheese is
melted and sauce is hot.
3. Serve with bread cubes
for dunking.

—— PER SERVING ——
• 150 calories
  (25 calories from fat)
• 2.5g total fat
  (1g saturated, 0g trans)
• 5mg cholesterol
• 310mg sodium
• 22g total carbohydrate
  (2g fiber, 5g sugar)
• 8g protein
• 10%DV vitamin A
• 0%DV vitamin C
• 20%DV calcium
• 8%DV iron

Tip from Tester:
  I had some leftover sauce
that I served as a topping
for steamed cauliflower.
My family loved it!

Salsa

Wilma J. Haberkamp
Fairbank, IA

*Makes 6-7 pints, or 48 or
more 4-Tbsp.-size servings*

Prep. Time: 45-50 minutes
Cooking Time: 3 hours
Ideal slow-cooker size: 6- or 7-qt.

13 tomatoes, peeled and
  seeded
1 tsp. salt
4 tsp. white vinegar
2 6½-oz. cans tomato paste
⅔ cup Louisiana Pure Hot
  Sauce
1 large yellow onion,
  chopped
1 large red onion, chopped
1 green bell pepper, seeded
  and chopped
1 red bell pepper, seeded
  and chopped
1 yellow bell pepper,
  seeded and chopped
1, or 2, hot peppers, seeded
3 banana peppers, seeded
  and chopped

1. Combine all ingredients
in large bowl and mix well.
Ladle into 6-qt., or larger,
slow cooker.

2. Cook on high 1 hour,
and then reduce to low for 2
hours.

3. Pour into sterilized jars
and follow directions from
your canner for sealing and
preserving.

Tip from Tester:

When I served the salsa, I
stirred in some fresh chopped
cilantro to add taste and
lively green color. I served it
as an appetizer, and 8 people
almost finished a pint jar!

Fruit Salsa

Joyce Shackelford
Green Bay, WI

Makes 4 cups, or 16 servings

Prep. Time: 30-45 minutes
Cooking Time: 2 hours
Ideal slow-cooker size: 2- or 3-qt.

11-oz. can mandarin
  oranges
8½-oz. can unsweetened
  sliced peaches,
  undrained
8-oz. can unsweetened
  pineapple tidbits,
  undrained
1 medium-
  sized onion,
  chopped
half a medium-
  sized green
  bell pepper,
  chopped
half a medium-
  sized red bell
  pepper, chopped

half a medium-sized
  yellow bell pepper,
  chopped
3 garlic cloves, minced
3 Tbsp. cornstarch
4 tsp. vinegar

1. Combine all ingredients
in slow cooker.

2. Cover. Cook on high 2
hours, stirring occasionally.

3. Serve with baked tortilla
chips.

Peach Chutney

Jan Mast
Lancaster, PA

Makes 32 servings

Prep. Time: 20 minutes
Cooking Time: 5-8 hours
Ideal slow-cooker size: 4-qt.

2 29-oz. cans (about 6 cups)
  peaches in sugar-free
  syrup, diced
1 cup raisins
1 small onion, chopped
1 garlic clove, minced
1 Tbsp. ground mustard
  seeds
1 tsp. dried red chilies,
  chopped
2 oz. crystallized ginger,
  chopped
1 tsp. salt
¾ cup vinegar
½ cup brown sugar

1. Combine all ingredients
in slow cooker.
2. Cover. Cook on low 4-6
hours.
3. Remove lid. Stir chutney.
Cook on high, uncovered, an
additional 1-2 hours.

—— PER SERVING ——
• 45 calories
  (0 calories from fat)
• 0g total fat
  (0g saturated, 0g trans)
• 0mg cholesterol
• 75mg sodium
• 11g total carbohydrate
  (1g fiber, 9g sugar)
• 0g protein
• 6%DV vitamin A
• 2%DV vitamin C
• 0%DV calcium
• 2%DV iron

Tip:
This is a great accompani-
ment to curried chicken or
lamb.

Texas Dip

Donna Lantgen
Rapid City, SD

Makes 8 servings

Prep. Time: 15-20 minutes
Cooking Time: 6 hours
Ideal slow-cooker size: 1½-qt.

1 cup onions, chopped
4-oz. can diced green chilies
16-oz. can Rotel tomatoes,
  diced, *or* 2 cups fresh
  tomatoes, diced
1½ cups cubed Velveeta
  Light cheese

1. Combine all ingredients
in slow cooker.
2. Cook on low 6 hours.

—— PER SERVING ——
• 120 calories
  (40 calories from fat)
• 4.5 total fat
  (3g saturated, 0g trans)
• 20mg cholesterol
• 900mg sodium
• 11g total carbohydrate
  (2g fiber, 7g sugar)
• 9g protein
• 15%DV vitamin A
• 15%DV vitamin C
• 30%DV calcium
• 2%DV iron

Tip:
Serve with lowfat tortilla
chips, or cut-up fresh vegetables.

Italiano Spread

Nanci Keatley
Salem, OR

Makes 24 servings

Prep. Time: 20-30 minutes
Cooking Time: 2-3 hours
Ideal slow-cooker size: 2-qt.

2 8-oz. pkgs. fat-free cream
  cheese, softened
½ cup reduced-fat
  prepared pesto
3 medium fresh tomatoes,
  chopped
½ cup fresh basil, chopped
1 cup reduced fat
  mozzarella cheese,
  shredded
½ cup reduced fat
  Parmesan cheese,
  shredded

1. Spread cream cheese on
bottom of slow cooker.
2. Spread pesto over cream
cheese.
3. Add layer of chopped
tomatoes over cream cheese
and pesto.
4. Sprinkle with chopped
basil.
5. Sprinkle cheeses on top
of basil.
6. Cook on low 2-3 hours,
or until cheese is melted.
7. Spread on baked crackers
or thin slices of Italian bread.

—— PER SERVING ——
• 70 calories
  (25 calories from fat)
• 3g total fat
  (1g saturated, 0g trans)
• 10mg cholesterol
• 250mg sodium
• 4g total carbohydrate
  (0g fiber, 2g sugar)
• 6g protein
• 4%DV vitamin A
• 6%DV vitamin C
• 15%DV calcium
• 0%DV iron

Slim Dunk

Vera Smucker
Goshen, IN

Makes 3 cups, or 12 servings

Prep. Time: 20 minutes
Cooking Time: 1 hour
Ideal slow-cooker size: 1½-qt.

2 cups fat-free sour cream
¼ cup fat-free Miracle
Whip salad dressing
10-oz. pkg. frozen chopped
spinach, thawed and
squeezed dry
1.8-oz. envelope dry leek
soup mix
¼ cup red bell pepper,
minced

1. Combine all ingredients in slow cooker. Mix well.
2. Cover. Cook on high 1 hour.
3. Serve with fat-free baked tortilla chips.

—— PER SERVING ——
- 70 calories (10 calories from fat)
- 1 total fat (0.5g saturated, 0g trans)
- 5mg cholesterol
- 310mg sodium
- 11g total carbohydrate (0.5g fiber, 4g sugar)
- 3g protein
- 25%DV vitamin A
- 10%DV vitamin C
- 10%DV calcium
- 4%DV iron

Cheesy Spinach and Bacon Dip

Amy Bauer
New Ulm, MN

Makes 3½ cups, or 20 servings

Prep. Time: 20-30 minutes
Cooking Time: 1 hour
Ideal slow cooker size: 3-qt.

10-oz. pkg. frozen chopped
spinach, thawed and
squeezed dry
1 lb. Velveeta Light, *or* your
choice of soft low-fat
cheese, cut into ½" cubes
3-oz. pkg. fat-free cream
cheese, softened
14½-oz. can Rotel diced
tomatoes and green
chilies, undrained
4 slices turkey bacon,
cooked crisp
crudites

1. Combine all ingredients except bacon and crudites in slow cooker.
2. Cover. Heat on low 1 hour, or until cheeses have melted and Dip is heated through. Stir occasionally if you're around to do so.
3. Just before serving, stir in crumbled bacon.
4. Serve warm with crudites.

—— PER SERVING ——
- 70 calories (30 calories from fat)
- 3g total fat (2g saturated, 0g trans)
- 10mg cholesterol
- 530mg sodium
- 4g total carbohydrate (1g fiber, 2g sugar)
- 6g protein
- 40%DV vitamin A
- 4%DV vitamin C
- 15%DV calcium
- 2%DV iron

Variation:

This is also tasty with half a 10-oz. package of frozen chopped spinach, thawed and squeezed dry.

Prepare an appetizer in another little slow cooker and keep your guests busy with dipping into it while you finish the final prep of the main meal.

Creamy Artichoke Dip

Jessica Stoner
West Liberty, OH

Makes 7-8 cups, or 28-32 servings

Prep. Time: 15-20 minutes
Cooking Time: 1 hour
Ideal slow cooker size: 3-qt.

2 14-oz. cans water-packed artichoke hearts, coarsely chopped (drain one can; stir juice from other can into Dip)
2 cups (8 oz.) shredded, low-fat part-skim mozzarella cheese
8-oz. pkg. fat-free cream cheese, softened
1 cup grated reduced-fat Parmesan cheese
½ cup shredded low-fat Swiss cheese
½ cup fat-free mayonnaise
2 Tbsp. lemon juice
2 Tbsp. fat-free plain yogurt
1 Tbsp. seasoned salt
1 Tbsp. chopped seeded jalapeño pepper
1 tsp. garlic powder
Dippers: baked tortilla chips

1. In slow cooker, combine artichoke hearts, cheeses, mayonnaise, lemon juice, yogurt, salt, jalapeño pepper, and garlic powder.

2. Cover. Cook on low 1 hour, or until cheeses are melted and Dip is heated through.
3. Serve with baked tortilla chips.

—— PER SERVING ——
• 60 calories   • 6g total carbohydrate
  (25 calories from fat)   (2g fiber, 1g sugar)
• 2.5g total fat   • 5g protein
  (1g saturated, 0g trans) • 2%DV vitamin A
• 10mg cholesterol   • 4%DV vitamin C
• 320mg sodium   • 10%DV calcium
   • 0%DV iron

Variation:

Add 2 10-oz. pkgs. frozen chopped spinach, thawed and squeezed dry, to Step 1.
Steven Lantz
Denver, CO

To make your own cream of mushroom or celery soup, please turn to pages 264-265.

Broccoli Cheese Dip

Carla Koslowsky
Hillsboro, KS

Makes 6 cups, or about 23 2-oz. servings

Prep. Time: 25-30 minutes
Cooking Time: 2 hours
Ideal slow-cooker size: 3- or 4-qt.

1 cup chopped celery
½ cup chopped onions
10-oz. pkg. frozen chopped broccoli, cooked
1 cup cooked rice
10¾-oz. can fat-free, sodium-free cream of mushroom soup
16-oz. jar fat-free cheese spread

1. Combine all ingredients in slow cooker.
2. Cover. Heat on low 2 hours.
3. Serve with snack breads or crackers.

—— PER SERVING ——
• 60 calories   • 7g total carbohydrate
  (15 calories from fat)   (0g fiber, 1g sugar)
• 1.5g total fat   • 6g protein
  (1g saturated, 0g trans) • 0%DV vitamin A
• 5mg cholesterol   • 0%DV vitamin C
• 110mg sodium   • 15%DV calcium
   • 2%DV iron

Tips:

1. If you're an onion-lover, you may want to increase the chopped onions to ¾ cup.
2. If you prefer your vegetables soft rather than crunchy, you may want to cook the onions and celery before adding them to the cooker.

Hot Artichoke Dip

Mary E. Wheatley
Mashpee, MA

---

*Makes 7-8 cups, or
28 2-oz. servings*

Prep. Time: 15 minutes
Cooking Time: 1-4 hours
Ideal slow-cooker size: 3-qt.

---

2 14¾-oz. jars marinated
artichoke hearts,
drained
1½ cups fat-free
mayonnaise
1½ cups fat-free sour
cream
1 cup water chestnuts,
chopped
¼ cup grated Parmesan
cheese
¼ cup finely chopped
scallions

1. Cut artichoke hearts
into small pieces. Add
mayonnaise, sour cream,
water chestnuts, cheese, and
scallions. Pour into slow
cooker.
2. Cover. Cook on high 1-2
hours or on low 3-4 hours.
3. Serve with crackers or
crusty French bread.

—— PER SERVING ——
• 60 calories
(20 calories from fat)
• 2.5g total fat
(0g saturated, 0g trans)
• 5mg cholesterol
• 240mg sodium
• 8g total carbohydrate
(2g fiber, 2g sugar)
• 2g protein
• 0%DV vitamin A
• 10%DV vitamin C
• 4%DV calcium
• 0%DV iron

Tomato-Zucchini Ratatouille

Barb Yoder
Angola, IN

Makes about 3½ cups, or 13 servings

Prep. Time: 20-30 minutes
Cooking Time: 7-8 hours
Ideal slow cooker size: 4-qt.

1½ cups chopped onion
6-oz. can tomato paste
1 Tbsp. olive oil
2 minced cloves garlic (1 tsp.)
1½ tsp. crushed dried basil
½ tsp. dried thyme
15-oz. can chopped low-
sodium tomatoes, with
juice drained but reserved
1 large zucchini, halved
lengthwise and sliced
thin
salt and pepper to taste,
optional
26 slices French bread, *or*
baguette

1. Mix all ingredients in
slow cooker, except bread.
2. Cover. Cook on low 7-8
hours.
3. If mixture is stiffer than
you wish, stir in some reserved
tomato juice.
4. Serve hot or cold on top
of French bread or baguette
slices.

—— PER SERVING ——
• 230 calories
(20 calories from fat)
• 2.5g total fat
(0.5g saturated,
0g trans)
• 0mg cholesterol
• 570mg sodium
• 44g total carbohydrate
(3g fiber, 5g sugar)
• 9g protein
• 10%DV vitamin A
• 20%DV vitamin C
• 6%DV calcium
• 20%DV iron

Mexican Dip

Marla Folkerts
Holland, OH

Makes 15 servings

Prep. Time: 15-20 minutes
Ideal slow-cooker size: 3-qt.

---

1 lb. low-fat ground beef,
or turkey
8-oz. pkg. no-fat Mexican
cheese, grated
16-oz. jar mild, thick and
chunky picante salsa, *or*
thick and chunky salsa
16-oz. can vegetarian
refried beans

1. Brown meat in nonstick
skillet. Do not drain.
2. Add remaining ingredi-
ents to meat in skillet. Stir until
mixed and hot.
3. Keep warm in slow
cooker. Serve with lowfat
tortilla chips.

—— PER SERVING ——
• 110 calories
(25 calories from fat)
• 3g total fat
(1g saturated, 0g trans)
• 15mg cholesterol
• 400mg sodium
• 7g total carbohydrate
(2g fiber, 1g sugar)
• 12g protein
• 6%DV vitamin A
• 8%DV vitamin C
• 25%DV calcium
• 8%DV iron

Turkey Meatballs in Cranberry Barbecue Sauce

Mary Ann Bowman
East Earl, PA

Makes 12 servings

Prep. Time: 30-45 minutes
Cooking Time: 3½ hours
Ideal slow cooker size: 3-qt.

16-oz. can jellied cranberry sauce
½ cup barbecue sauce
1 egg white
1 lb. 95% fat-free ground turkey
1 green onion with top, sliced
2 tsp. grated orange peel
1 tsp. reduced-sodium soy sauce
¼ tsp. black pepper
⅛ tsp. ground red pepper, *optional*

1. Combine cranberry sauce and barbecue sauce in slow cooker.
2. Cover. Cook on high 20-30 minutes until cranberry sauce is melted and mixture is hot, stirring every 10 minutes.
3. Meanwhile, place egg white in medium bowl and beat lightly. Add remainder of ingredients, mixing well with hands until well blended. Shape into 24 balls.
4. Spray large nonstick skillet with nonstick cooking spray. Add meatballs to skillet and cook over medium heat 8-10 minutes, or until meatballs are no longer pink in center, carefully turning to brown evenly.
5. Add to heated sauce in slow cooker. Stir gently to coat evenly with sauce.
6. Reduce heat to low. Cover. Cook 3 hours.
7. When ready to serve, transfer meatballs to serving plate. Garnish if desired. Serve with decorative picks.

— PER SERVING —
- 130 calories
  (15 calories from fat)
- 2g total fat
  (0.5g saturated,
  0g trans)
- 25mg cholesterol
- 190mg sodium
- 19g total carbohydrate
  (1g fiber, 12g sugar)
- 8g protein
- 0%DV vitamin A
- 2%DV vitamin C
- 0%DV calcium
- 4%DV iron

Hot Hamburger Dip

Kristi See
Weskan, KS

Makes 12 servings

Prep. Time: 20 minutes
Cooking time: 2 hours
Ideal slow-cooker size: 4- or 5-qt.

½ lb. lean ground beef
2 small onions, chopped
½ lb. Velveeta Light cheese, cubed
10-oz. can green chilies and tomatoes
2 tsp. Worcestershire sauce
½ tsp. chili powder
1 tsp. garlic powder
½ tsp. black pepper
10¾-oz. can low-sodium tomato soup
10¾-oz. can 98% fat-free mushroom soup

1. Brown beef and onions in nonstick skillet. Place in slow cooker. Drain off drippings.
2. Add remaining ingredients to cooker and stir well.
3. Cover. Cook on low until cheese is melted, about 2 hours.

— PER SERVING —
- 110 calories
  (40 calories from fat)
- 4.5g total fat
  (2.5g saturated,
  1g trans)
- 15mg cholesterol
- 620mg sodium
- 9g total carbohydrate
  (0g fiber, 3g sugar)
- 8g protein
- 6%DV vitamin A
- 6%DV vitamin C
- 15%DV calcium
- 4%DV iron

A slow cooker is great for taking food to a potluck supper, even if you didn't prepare it in the cooker.
Irma H. Schoen, Windsor, CT

Mexican Cheesecake

Janie Steele
Moore, OK

Makes 20 servings

Prep. Time: 10-15 minutes
Cooking Time: 1 hour
Ideal slow-cooker size: 2-qt.

3 8-oz. pkgs. fat-free cream cheese, softened
½ cup Egg Beaters
2 tsp. low-sodium chicken bouillon
½ cup hot water
4-oz. can green chilies, chopped
½-1½ tsp. chili powder, depending upon how much heat you enjoy
½ tsp., *or* less, hot sauce, *optional*
1 cup cooked skinless chicken breast, chopped

1. Combine all ingredients in slow cooker until smooth.
2. Cook on high 1 hour.
3. Turn to low to keep warm while serving.
4. Serve with baked tortilla chips or crackers, or crudités.

—— PER SERVING ——
• 50 calories
  (5 calories from fat)
• 0.5g total fat
  (0g saturated, 0g trans)
• 10mg cholesterol
• 280mg sodium
• 3g total carbohydrate
  (0g fiber, 2g sugar)
• 8g protein
• 2%DV vitamin A
• 2%DV vitamin C
• 10%DV calcium
• 2%DV iron

Chicken Cheese Dip

Sheridy Steele
Ardmore, OK

Makes 10 servings

Prep. Time: 15 minutes
Cooking Time: 1-2 hours
Ideal slow-cooker size: 1- or 1½ qt.

½ lb. Velveeta cheese
12-oz. can tomatoes with chilies
1 cup cooked skinless chicken breast, diced and shredded
½ cup bell peppers, chopped

1. Cube cheese.
2. Combine cheese, tomatoes, chicken, and peppers in slow cooker.
3. Cook on low 1-2 hours.
4. Serve with baked chips.

—— PER SERVING ——
• 270 calories
  (45 calories from fat)
• 5g total fat
  (2g saturated, 0g trans)
• 30mg cholesterol
• 830mg sodium
• 43g total carbohydrate
  (4g fiber, 2g sugar)
• 15g protein
• 8%DV vitamin A
• 10%DV vitamin C
• 20%DV calcium
• 6%DV iron

Tips:
1. To add color, use a mixture of chopped red, yellow, and green bell peppers.
2. For a thicker dip, drain tomatoes with chilies before mixing them in.

Buffalo Chicken Dip

Gail Skiff
Clifton Park, NY

Makes 3-4 cups, 12-16 servings

Prep. Time: 30-40 minutes
Cooking Time: 1 hour
Ideal slow-cooker size: 2- to 3-qt.

8-oz. pkg. fat-free cream cheese, softened
½ cup fat-free bleu cheese dressing
½ cup bleu cheese crumbles
½ cup buffalo wing sauce (I use Anchor Bar Buffalo Wing Sauce)
1 lb. boneless skinless chicken breasts, cooked and shredded
celery sticks *and/or* your favorite baked chips

1. Mix cream cheese, dressing, blue cheese crumbles, and sauce in slow cooker.
2. Stir in chicken.
3. Cover. Heat on low 1 hour, or until cheeses melt and Dip is heated through. Stir several times during the hour if you're home and able to do so.
4. Serve warm with celery sticks and/or your favorite baked chips.

—— PER SERVING ——
• 70 calories
  (20 calories from fat)
• 2g total fat
  (1g saturated, 0g trans)
• 20mg cholesterol
• 450mg sodium
• 4g total carbohydrate
  (0g fiber, 2g sugar)
• 9g protein
• 4%DV vitamin A
• 0%DV vitamin C
• 8%DV calcium
• 2%DV iron

Tangy Cocktail Franks

Linda Sluiter
Schererville, IN

Makes 12 servings

Prep. Time 5 minutes
Cooking Time: 1-2 hours
Ideal slow-cooker size: 3-qt.

14-oz. jar currant jelly
¼ cup prepared mustard
3 Tbsp. dry sherry
¼ tsp. ground allspice
30-oz. can unsweetened
  pineapple chunks
6-oz. pkg. low-sodium
  cocktail franks

1. Melt jelly in slow cooker turned on high. Stir in seasonings until blended.
2. Drain pineapple chunks and any liquid in cocktail franks package. Discard juice. Gently stir pineapple and franks into slow cooker.
3. Cover. Cook on low 1-2 hours.

—— PER SERVING ——
• 160 calories   • 28g total carbohydrate
  (40 calories from fat)   (0.5g fiber, 25g sugar)
• 4g total fat   • 2g protein
  (2g saturated, 0g trans) • 0%DV vitamin A
• 10mg cholesterol   • 0%DV vitamin C
• 170mg sodium   • 2%DV calcium
                           • 4%DV iron

Hot Crab Dip

Karen Waggoner
Joplin, MO

Makes 5 cups

Prep. Time: 15 minutes
Cooking Time: 3-4 hours
Ideal slow-cooker size: 2-qt.

⅓ cup salsa
½ cup fat-free milk
2 8-oz. pkgs. imitation
  crabmeat, flaked finely
¾ cup green onions, thinly
  sliced
4-oz. can chopped green
  chilies
3 8-oz. pkgs. fat-free cream
  cheese, cubed
10 ozs. stone wheat
  crackers

1. Spray slow cooker with fat-free cooking spray.
2. Mix salsa and milk in cooker.
3. Stir in all remaining ingredients except crackers.
4. Cover. Cook on low 3-4 hours.
5. Stir approximately every half hour.
6. Serve with crackers or raw vegetables.

—— PER SERVING ——
• 520 calories   • 65g total carbohydrate
  (110 calories from fat)   (8g fiber, 4g sugar)
• 12g total fat   • 38g protein
  (3g saturated, 0g trans) • 20%DV vitamin A
• 55mg cholesterol   • 10%DV vitamin C
• 1410mg sodium   • 35%DV calcium
                           • 15%DV iron

Seafood Dip

Joan Rosenberger
Stephens City, VA

Makes 24 servings of 2 Tbsp. each

Prep. Time: 5-10 minutes
Cooking Time: 3 hours
Ideal slow-cooker size: 3½-qt.

10-oz. pkg. fat-free cream
  cheese
8-oz. pkg. imitation crab
  strands
2 Tbsp. onion, finely
  chopped
4-5 drops hot sauce
¼ cup walnuts, finely
  chopped
1 tsp. paprika

1. Blend all ingredients except nuts and paprika until well mixed.
2. Spread in slow cooker. Sprinkle with nuts and paprika.
3. Cook on low 3 hours.

—— PER SERVING ——
• 70 calories   • 7g total carbohydrate
  (10 calories from fat)   (0g fiber, 3g sugar)
• 1.5g total fat   • 7g protein
  (0g saturated, 0g trans) • 6%DV vitamin A
• 5mg cholesterol   • 0%DV vitamin C
• 370mg sodium   • 4%DV calcium
                           • 0%DV iron

Tip:
Serve with crackers.

Cheesy New Orleans Shrimp Dip

Kelly Amos
Pittsboro, NC

Makes 3-4 cups dip or 24 servings

Prep. Time: 20-30 minutes
Cooking Time: 1 hour
Ideal slow-cooker size: 2-qt.

1 slice lean turkey bacon
3 medium-sized onions,
    chopped
1 garlic clove, minced
4 jumbo shrimp, peeled
    and deveined
1 medium-sized tomato,
    peeled and chopped
3 cups low-fat Monterey
    Jack cheese, shredded
4 drops Tabasco sauce
⅛ tsp. cayenne pepper
dash of black pepper

1. Cook bacon until crisp.
Drain on paper towel. Cut
fine.
2. Sauté onion and garlic
in bacon drippings. Drain on
paper towel.
3. Coarsely chop shrimp.
4. Combine all ingredients
in slow cooker.
5. Cover. Cook on low 1
hour, or until cheese is melted.
Thin with milk if too thick.
6. Serve with chips.

—— PER SERVING ——
• 130 calories   • 12g total carbohydrate
  (5 calories from fat)   (1g fiber, 4g sugar)
• 0.5g total fat   • 18g protein
  (0g saturated, 0g trans) • 10%DV vitamin A
• 10mg cholesterol   • 0%DV vitamin C
• 520mg sodium   • 60%DV calcium
      • 2%DV iron

Spiced Pear Butter

Betty Moore
Plano, Il

Makes 2 pints

Prep. Time: 25-30 minutes
Cooking Time: 1 hour
Cooling Time: 13 hours
Ideal slow-cooker size: 5-qt.

10 large, well-ripened pears
    (4 lbs.)
2 Tbsp. frozen orange juice
    concentrate
2 cups sugar
1 tsp. ground cinnamon
1 tsp. ground cloves
½ tsp. ground allspice

1. Peel and quarter pears.
Place in slow cooker.
2. Cover. Cook on low 12
hours. Drain thoroughly and
then discard liquid.
3. Mash or purée pears.
Add remaining ingredients.
Mix well and return to slow
cooker.
4. Cover. Cook on high 1
hour.
5. Place in hot sterile jars and
process according to canner
manufacturer's instructions.

—— PER SERVING ——
• 100 calories   • 26g total carbohydrate
  (0 calories from fat)   (2g fiber, 23g sugar)
• 0g total fat   • 0g protein
  (0g saturated, 0g trans) • 0%DV vitamin A
• 0mg cholesterol   • 0%DV vitamin C
• 0mg sodium   • 0%DV calcium
      • 0%DV iron

Tip:
If the butter is too soupy
after cooking on low 12
hours, you may want to cook
it uncovered during Step 4
in order to create a stiffer
consistency.

Saucy Pear Butter

Dorothy Miller
Gulfport, MI

Makes 6 pints

Prep. Time: 5 minutes
Cooking Time: 10-12 hours
Ideal slow-cooker size: 5-qt.

8 cups pear sauce
3 cups brown sugar
1 Tbsp. lemon juice
1 Tbsp. cinnamon

1. Combine all ingredients
in slow cooker.
2. Cover. Cook on high
10-12 hours.

—— PER SERVING ——
• 40 calories   • 10g total carbohydrate
  (0 calories from fat)   (0g fiber, 10g sugar)
• 0g total fat   • 0g protein
  (0g saturated, 0g trans) • 0%DV vitamin A
• 0mg cholesterol   • 0%DV vitamin C
• 0mg sodium   • 0%DV calcium
      • 0%DV iron

Tip:
To make pear sauce, peel,
core, and slice 12 large,
well-ripened pears. Place
in slow cooker with ¾ cup
water. Cover and cook on low
8-10 hours, or until very soft.
Stir to blend.

251

Chunky Sweet Spiced Apple Butter

Jennifer Freed
Harrisonburg, VA

Makes 4 cups, or 64 1 Tbsp. servings

Prep. Time: 20 minutes
Cooking Time: 8 hours
Ideal slow-cooker size: 2- or 3-qt.

4 cups (about 1¼ lbs.) peeled, chopped Granny Smith apples
¾ cup packed dark brown sugar
2 Tbsp. balsamic vinegar
¼ stick (2 Tbsp.) butter, *divided*
1 Tbsp. ground cinnamon
½ tsp. salt
¼ tsp. ground cloves
1½ tsp. vanilla

1. Combine apples, sugar, vinegar, 1 Tbsp. butter, cinnamon, salt, and cloves in slow cooker.
2. Cover. Cook on low 8 hours.
3. Stir in remaining 1 Tbsp. butter and vanilla.
4. Cool completely before serving, storing, or giving away.

—— **PER SERVING** ——
• 15 calories
  (0 calories from fat)
• 0g total fat
  (0g saturated, 0g trans)
• 0mg cholesterol
• 20mg sodium
• 4g total carbohydrate
  (0g fiber, 3g sugar)
• 0g protein
• 0%DV vitamin A
• 0%DV vitamin C
• 0%DV calcium
• 0%DV iron

Apple Butter – for Your Toast

Alix Nancy Botsford
Seminole, OK

Makes 8 pints

Prep. Time: 30-45 minutes
Cooking Time: 4-5 hours
Ideal slow-cooker size: 5- or 6-qt.

108-oz. can (#8 size) unsweetened applesauce
2 cups cider
1 Tbsp. ground cinnamon
1 tsp. ground ginger
½ tsp. ground cloves, *or* 1 tsp. ground nutmeg, *optional*

1. Combine applesauce and cider in slow cooker.
2. Cover. Cook on high 3-4 hours.
3. Add spices.
4. Cover. Cook 1 hour more.
5. Sterilize cup- or pint-size jars. Heat lids.
6. Fill jars with apple butter. Clean rims with damp paper towel. Put on lids.
7. Place in canner and cook according to manufacturer's instructions.

—— **PER SERVING** ——
• 180 calories
  (0 calories from fat)
• 0g total fat
  (0g saturated, 0g trans)
• 0mg cholesterol
• 15mg sodium
• 46g total carbohydrate
  (5g fiber, 38g sugar)
• 1g protein
• 0%DV vitamin A
• 60%DV vitamin C
• 2%DV calcium
• 4%DV iron

Notes:
1. This is better than any air freshener. When anyone comes home I receive a hug and then a question: "Where's the toast?"
2. It also tastes wonderful on plain yogurt!

Beverages

Hot Mulled Cider

Betty K. Drescher
Quakertown, PA

Makes 8 servings

Prep. Time: 10 minutes
Cooking Time: 3-6 hours
Ideal slow-cooker size: 3½-qt.

1 tsp. whole cloves
¼ cup brown sugar
2 qts. cider
1 3"-long cinnamon stick
1 orange, sliced

1. Tie cloves in cheesecloth or put in tea strainer.
2. Combine all ingredients in slow cooker.
3. Cover. Cook on low 3-6 hours.

—— PER SERVING ——
- 160 calories
  (0 calories from fat)
- 0g total fat
  (0g saturated, 0g trans)
- 0mg cholesterol
- 30mg sodium
- 39g total carbohydrate
  (0.5g fiber, 34g sugar)
- 0g protein
- 0%DV vitamin A
- 8%DV vitamin C
- 2%DV calcium
- 2%DV iron

Hot Apple Cinnamon Drink

Marla Folkerts
Holland, OH

Makes 24 servings

Prep. Time: 5 minutes
Cooking Time: 3-5 hours
Ideal slow-cooker size: 6-qt.

1 gallon cider
2 liters diet ginger ale
4 ozs. hard candies—your choice of flavors
cinnamon sticks, *optional*

1. Combine all ingredients in slow cooker.
2. Cover. Simmer on low 3-5 hours.

—— PER SERVING ——
- 100 calories
  (0 calories from fat)
- 0g total fat
  (0g saturated, 0g trans)
- 0mg cholesterol
- 30mg sodium
- 25g total carbohydrate
  (0g fiber, 20g sugar)
- 0g protein
- 0%DV vitamin A
- 0%DV vitamin C
- 0%DV calcium
- 0%DV iron

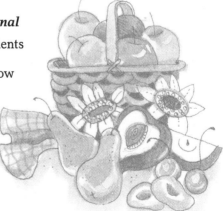

253

Christmas Wassail

Linda Sluiter
Schererville, IN

Makes 8 servings

Prep. Time: 5-10 minutes
Cooking Time: 1-2 hours
Ideal slow-cooker size: 3-qt.

1 qt. apple cider
½ cup orange, *or*
    pineapple, juice
2 cups water
3 orange pekoe tea bags
¼ cup brown sugar
¼ tsp. ground cinnamon
¼ tsp. ground cloves
oranges

1. Combine all ingredients except oranges in slow cooker.
2. Cover. Cook on high 1-2 hours.
3. Slice oranges to float on top. Serve in mugs.

— PER SERVING —
- 160 calories
  (0 calories from fat)
- 0g total fat (0g saturated, 0g trans)
- 0mg cholesterol
- 20mg sodium
- 45g total carbohydrate
  (7g fiber, 35g sugar)
- 1g protein
- 2%DV vitamin A
- 100%DV vitamin C
- 8%DV calcium
- 4%DV iron

Note:
  Your kitchen will smell great!

Peachy Spiced Cider

Joyce Shackelford
Green Bay, WI

Makes 8 small servings

Prep. Time: 10 minutes
Cooking Time: 4-6 hours
Ideal slow-cooker size: 2-qt.

4 5½-oz. cans peach nectar
2 cups unsweetened apple juice
½ tsp. ground ginger
¼ tsp. ground cinnamon
¼ tsp. ground nutmeg
4 fresh orange slices, cut ¼" thick and then halved

1. Combine peach nectar, apple juice, ginger, cinnamon, and nutmeg in slow cooker.
2. Top with orange slices.
3. Cover. Cook on low 4-6 hours.
4. Remove orange slices and stir before serving.

— PER SERVING —
- 180 calories
  (0 calories from fat)
- 0g total fat
  (0g saturated, 0g trans)
- 0mg cholesterol
- 15mg sodium
- 44g total carbohydrate
  (3g fiber, 41g sugar)
- 1g protein
- 6%DV vitamin A
- 100%DV vitamin C
- 4%DV calcium
- 6%DV iron

Cran-Apple Juice

Anita Troyer
Fairview, MI

Makes 9 servings

Prep. Time: 15 minutes
Cooking Time: 1-1½ hours
Ideal slow cooker size: 3-qt.

6 cups Cran-Apple juice
3 cups water
3 Tbsp. sugar
3 Tbsp. red hots
9 whole cloves
9 tendrils mace
¾ tsp. nutmeg

1. Mix all ingredients in slow cooker.
2. Cover. Heat on medium 1-1½ hours.
3. Before serving, remove cloves and mace.

— PER SERVING —
- 140 calories
  (0 calories from fat)
- 0g total fat
  (0g saturated, 0g trans)
- 0mg cholesterol
- 5mg sodium
- 35g total carbohydrate
  (0g fiber, 31g sugar)
- 0g protein
- 0%DV vitamin A
- 110%DV vitamin C
- 0%DV calcium
- 0%DV iron

Autumn Tea

Shelia Heil
Lancaster, PA

Makes 12 servings

Prep. Time: 15 minutes
Cooking Time: 2-3 hours
Ideal slow-cooker size: 4- or 5-qt.

5 individual tea bags
5 cups boiling water
5 cups unsweetened apple juice
2 cups low-sugar cranberry juice
⅓ cup lemon juice
⅓ cup sugar
½ tsp. pumpkin pie spice

1. Place tea bags in slow cooker. Pour in boiling water. Cover and steep for 10 minutes.
2. Remove and discard tea bags.
3. Add juices, sugar, and pumpkin pie spice.
4. Stir until sugar is dissolved.
5. Heat in slow cooker 2-3 hours on high or low, or until flavors have blended and tea is heated through. Serve warm.

—— PER SERVING ——
• 80 calories
  (0 calories from fat)
• 0g total fat
  (0g saturated, 0g trans)
• 0mg cholesterol
• 10mg sodium
• 20g total carbohydrate
  (0g fiber, 17g sugar)
• 0g protein
• 0%DV vitamin A
• 30%DV vitamin C
• 0%DV calcium
• 0%DV iron

Cranberry Punch

Betty B. Dennison
Grove City, PA

Makes 8 servings

Prep. Time: 15-25 minutes
Cooking Time: 4 hours
Ideal slow-cooker size: 4-qt.

8 whole cardamom pods
2 sticks cinnamon
12 whole cloves
4 cups dry red wine
2 6-oz. cans frozen cranberry concentrate
2⅔ cups water
½ cup honey, *or to taste*
1 orange sliced into 8 thin crescents

1. Make a spice packet of these items: Pinch open cardamom pods to release seeds. Place seeds on a piece of cheesecloth or paper coffee filter. Add cinnamon sticks and cloves. Tie with a string to make a bag.
2. Pour wine, cranberry concentrate, water, and honey into slow cooker. Heat on low.
3. Submerge spice packet in liquid. Heat but do not boil.
4. Let punch steep on low for up to 4 hours.
5. To serve, remove and discard spice bag. Divide punch among cups. Float an orange slice in each cup. Serve warm.

—— PER SERVING ——
• 240 calories
  (0 calories from fat)
• 0g total fat
  (0g saturated, 0g trans)
• 0mg cholesterol
• 30mg sodium
• 40g total carbohydrate
  (3g fiber, 33g sugar)
• 2g protein
• 4%DV vitamin A
• 20%DV vitamin C
• 8%DV calcium
• 10%DV iron

Pomegranate Punch

Lindsey Spencer
Marrow, OH

Makes 6 servings

Prep. Time: 5-7 minutes
Cooking Time: 1-2 hours
Ideal slow cooker size: 3-qt.

3 cups pomegranate juice
1½ cups reduced-sugar cranberry juice cocktail
½ cup orange juice
3"-long cinnamon stick
1 tsp. grated ginger

1. Put all ingredients in slow cooker.
2. Cover. Cook on low 1-2 hours, or until heated through.
3. Serve hot or chilled, depending on the time of year.

—— PER SERVING ——
• 90 calories
  (0 calories from fat)
• 0g total fat
  (0g saturated, 0g trans)
• 0mg cholesterol
• 15mg sodium
• 23g total carbohydrate
  (0g fiber, 21g sugar)
• 1g protein
• 0%DV vitamin A
• 45%DV vitamin C
• 2%DV calcium
• 0%DV iron

Spiced Apricot Cider

Joyce Shackelford
Green Bay, WI
Mary Longenecker
Bethel, PA

Makes 6 servings

Prep. Time: 10 minutes
Cooking Time: 2 hours
Ideal slow-cooker size: 2½-qt.

2 12-oz. cans apricot nectar
2 cups water
¼ cup lemon juice
¼ cup sugar
2 whole cloves
2 3"-long cinnamon sticks

1. Combine all ingredients in slow cooker.
2. Cover. Cook on high 2 hours.
3. Remove cloves and cinnamon sticks before serving.

—— PER SERVING ——
• 140 calories
  (0 calories from fat)
• 0g total fat
  (0g saturated, 0g trans)
• 0mg cholesterol
• 40mg sodium
• 35g total carbohydrate
  (1g fiber, 27g sugar)
• 1g protein
• 20%DV vitamin A
• 80%DV vitamin C
• 2%DV calcium
• 4%DV iron

Orange Ginger Tea

Jeanne Heyerly
Chenoa, IL

Makes 8-10 servings

Prep. Time: 5-10 minutes
Cooking Time: 4-6 hours
Ideal slow-cooker size: 2½-qt.

2 qts. water
3 1"-squares fresh gingerroot, sliced
3 Tbsp. brown sugar, *or* honey
1 orange, sliced

1. Place water and gingerroot in slow cooker.
2. Cover. Cook on high 2 hours; then on low 2-4 hours.
3. Add sugar or honey and sliced orange 1 hour before serving.

—— PER SERVING ——
• 20 calories
  (0 calories from fat)
• 0g total fat
  (0g saturated, 0g trans)
• 0mg cholesterol
• 10mg sodium
• 6g total carbohydrate
  (0g fiber, 5g sugar)
• 0g protein
• 0%DV vitamin A
• 8%DV vitamin C
• 2%DV calcium
• 0%DV iron

Note:
This tea makes cold-sufferers feel better!

Green Grape Ginger Tea

Evelyn Page
Gillette, WY

Makes 8 cups

Prep. Time: 5-15 minutes
Cooking Time: 2 hours
Ideal slow cooker size: 3-qt.

4 cups boiling water
15 single green tea bags
4 cups white grape juice
1 Tbsp. honey
1 Tbsp. minced fresh gingerroot

1. Place boiling water and tea bags in slow cooker. Cover and let stand 10 minutes. Discard tea bags.
2. Stir in juice, honey, and gingerroot.
3. Cover. Cook on low 2 hours, or until heated through.
4. Strain if you wish before pouring into individual cups.

—— PER SERVING ——
• 90 calories
  (0 calories from fat)
• 0g total fat
  (0g saturated, 0g trans)
• 0mg cholesterol
• 15mg sodium
• 22g total carbohydrate
  (0g fiber, 21g sugar)
• 0g protein
• 0%DV vitamin A
• 60%DV vitamin C
• 0%DV calcium
• 0%DV iron

Slow-Cooker Chai

Kathy Hertzler
Lancaster, PA

Makes 18 servings

Prep. Time: 10 minutes
Cooking Time: 1-1½ hours
Ideal slow-cooker size: 6-qt.

16 regular black tea bags
1 gallon water
8 opened cardamom pods
9 whole cloves
3 Tbsp. gingerroot, freshly grated, *or* chopped fine
3 cinnamon sticks
8-oz. can fat-free sweetened condensed milk
12-oz. can fat-free evaporated milk

1. Pour one gallon water into slow cooker. Turn cooker to high and bring water to a boil.
2. Tie tea bag strings together. Remove paper tags. Place in slow cooker, submerging in boiling water.
3. Place cardamom seeds and pods, cloves, and ginger in a tea ball.
4. Place tea ball and cinnamon sticks in boiling water in slow cooker. Reduce heat to warm and steep, along with tea bags, for 10 minutes.
5. After 10 minutes, remove tea bags. Allow spices to remain in cooker. Increase heat to medium.
6. Add condensed milk and evaporated milk. Bring mixture to a boil.
7. Immediately turn back to warm. Remove spices 30 minutes later.

8. Serve tea from slow cooker, but do not allow it to boil.

—— PER SERVING ——
- 50 calories (0 calories from fat)
- 0g total fat (0g saturated, 0g trans)
- 0mg cholesterol
- 40mg sodium
- 11g total carbohydrate (0g fiber, 10g sugar)
- 2g protein
- 2%DV vitamin A
- 0%DV vitamin C
- 8%DV calcium
- 0%DV iron

Note:
We love this after leaf-raking or for a fall party, especially when we serve it with muffins and fruit.

Vanilla Steamer

Anita Troyer
Fairview, MI

Makes 8 servings

Prep. Time: 5-10 minutes
Cooking Time: 2-3 hours
Ideal slow cooker size: 3-qt.

8 cups fat-free milk
⅛ tsp. cinnamon, *or* 2 3"-long cinnamon sticks
2 Tbsp. Splenda
2 Tbsp. vanilla
pinch of salt
pinch of nutmeg
1 Tbsp. per serving fat-free whipped topping, *optional*
sprinkling of ground cinnamon, *optional*

1. Put all ingredients except whipped topping and sprinkling of ground cinnamon in slow cooker.

2. Cover. Cook on low 2-3 hours, taking care to make sure it doesn't boil.
3. Garnish individual servings with whipped topping and a sprinkling of cinnamon if you wish.

—— PER SERVING ——
- 90 calories (0 calories from fat)
- 0g total fat (0g saturated, 0g trans)
- 5mg cholesterol
- 120mg sodium
- 13g total carbohydrate (0g fiber, 13g sugar)
- 8g protein
- 10%DV vitamin A
- 0%DV vitamin C
- 30%DV calcium
- 0%DV iron

Tip:
I usually make a larger recipe than I will need, and then refrigerate the leftovers. We like it either reheated, or as creamer in our coffee. This drink is very soothing and helps everyone relax!

Almond Tea

Frances Schrag
Newton, KS

Makes 10-11 servings

Prep. Time: 10 minutes
Cooking Time: 1 hour
Ideal slow-cooker size: 4½-qt.

10 cups boiling water
1 Tbsp. instant tea
⅔ cup lemon juice
6 Tbsp. sugar
1 tsp. vanilla
1 tsp. almond extract

1. Mix together all ingredients in slow cooker.
2. Turn to high and heat thoroughly (about 1 hour). Turn to low while serving.

—— PER SERVING ——
• 30 calories
  (0 calories from fat)
• 0g total fat
  (0g saturated, 0g trans)
• 0mg cholesterol
• 5mg sodium
• 8g total carbohydrate
  (0g fiber, 7g sugar)
• 0g protein
• 0%DV vitamin A
• 0%DV vitamin C
• 0%DV calcium
• 0%DV iron

Spiced Coffee

Joyce Shackelford
Green Bay, WI

Makes 8 servings

Prep. Time: 15 minutes
Cooking Time: 2-3 hours
Ideal slow-cooker size: 3-qt.

8 cups brewed coffee
⅓ cup sugar
¼ cup low-fat chocolate syrup
½ tsp. anise extract
4 cinnamon sticks, halved
1½ tsp. whole cloves

1. Combine coffee, sugar, chocolate syrup, and anise extract in slow cooker.
2. Place cinnamon sticks and cloves in cheesecloth bag. Place in slow cooker.
3. Cover. Cook on low 2-3 hours.
4. Discard spice bag.
5. Ladle coffee into mugs. Garnish each with half a cinnamon stick.

—— PER SERVING ——
• 70 calories
  (10 calories from fat)
• 1g total fat
  (0g saturated, 0g trans)
• 0mg cholesterol
• 20mg sodium
• 17g total carbohydrate
  (0.5g fiber, 14g sugar)
• 0g protein
• 6%DV vitamin A
• 2%DV vitamin C
• 2%DV calcium
• 10%DV iron

Viennese Coffee

Evelyn Page
Gillette, WY

Makes 4 servings

Prep. Time: 15 minutes
Cooking Time: 3 hours
Ideal slow cooker size: 1½- or 2-qt.

3 cups strong brewed coffee
3 Tbsp. low-fat chocolate syrup
1 tsp. sugar
⅓ cup fat-free half-and-half
¼ cup crème de cacao, *or* Irish cream liqueur
fat-free whipped topping, thawed, *optional*
chocolate curls, *optional*

1. In a slow cooker, combine coffee, chocolate syrup, and sugar.
2. Cover. Cook on low 2½ hours.
3. Stir in half-and-half and crème de cacao.
4. Cover. Cook 30 minutes more, or until heated through.
5. Ladle into mugs. Garnish if you wish with whipped topping and chocolate curls.

—— PER SERVING ——
• 110 calories
  (25 calories from fat)
• 3g total fat
  (1.5g saturated, 0g trans)
• 10mg cholesterol
• 55mg sodium
• 16g total carbohydrate
  (0g fiber, 12g sugar)
• 1g protein
• 2%DV vitamin A
• 0%DV vitamin C
• 2%DV calcium
• 0%DV iron

Breads and Breakfast Dishes

Overnight Apple Oatmeal

Frances Musser
Newmanstown, PA

John D. Allen
Rye, CO

Makes 4 servings

Prep. Time: 10 minutes
Cooking Time: 6-8 hours
Ideal slow-cooker size: 2-qt.

2 cups skim, *or* 2%, milk
2 Tbsp. honey, *or* ¼ cup brown sugar
¾ Tbsp. butter
¼ tsp. salt
½ tsp. ground cinnamon
1 cup dry rolled oats
1 cup apples, chopped
½ cup raisins, *optional*
¼ cup walnuts, chopped
½ cup fat-free half-and-half

1. Spray inside of slow cooker with nonfat cooking spray.

2. Combine all ingredients except half-and-half in cooker.

3. Cover and cook on low overnight, ideally 6-8 hours. The oatmeal is ready to eat in the morning.

4. Stir in half-and-half just before serving.

—— PER SERVING ——
• 240 calories
  (60 calories from fat)
• 6g total fat
  (1g saturated, 0g trans)
• 0mg cholesterol
• 240mg sodium
• 37g total carbohydrate
  (4g fiber, 21g sugar)
• 10g protein
• 8%DV vitamin A
• 6%DV vitamin C
• 20%DV calcium
• 8%DV iron

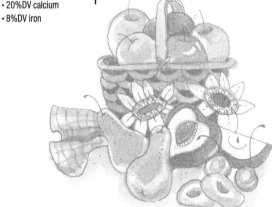

Almond-Date Oatmeal

Darla Sathre
Baxter, MN

Makes 8 servings

Prep. Time: 5-10 minutes
Cooking Time: 4-6 hours
Ideal slow-cooker size: 3-qt.

2 cups dry rolled oats
½ cup dry Grape-Nuts cereal
½ cup almonds, slivered
¼ cup dates, chopped
4 cups water

1. Combine all ingredients in slow cooker.
2. Cook on low 4-6 hours.
3. Serve with fat-free milk.

—— PER SERVING ——
- 160 calories
  (45 calories from fat)
- 5g total fat
  (0g saturated, 0g trans)
- 0mg cholesterol
- 50mg sodium
- 26g total carbohydrate
  (4g fiber, 5g sugar)
- 5g protein
- 2%DV vitamin A
- 0%DV vitamin C
- 2%DV calcium
- 15%DV iron

Oatmeal Morning

Barbara Forrester Landis
Lititz, PA

Makes 6 servings

Prep. Time: 5 minutes
Cooking Time: 2½-6 hours
Ideal slow cooker size: 3-qt.

1 cup uncooked rolled oats
1 cup dried cranberries
2½ Tbsp. broken walnuts
½ tsp. salt
1 Tbsp. cinnamon
4 cups liquid—fat-free milk, water, *or* combination of the two

1. Combine all dry ingredients in slow cooker. Stir well.
2. Pour in liquid ingredient(s). Mix together well.
3. Cover. Cook on high 2½ hours, or on low 5-6 hours.

—— PER SERVING ——
- 190 calories
  (30 calories from fat)
- 3g total fat
  (0g saturated, 0g trans)
- 5mg cholesterol
- 260mg sodium
- 35g total carbohydrate
  (3g fiber, 22g sugar)
- 8g protein
- 6%DV vitamin A
- 0%DV vitamin C
- 20%DV calcium
- 4%DV iron

Variation:

If you wish, substitute fresh or dried blueberries, or raisins, for the dried cranberries.

Eggs 'n' Spinach

Shirley Unternahrer
Wayland, IA

Makes 8 servings

Prep. Time: 20 minutes
Cooking Time: 1½-8 hours
Ideal slow cooker size: 6-qt.

½ lb. turkey sausage
1½ 10-oz. pkgs. frozen chopped spinach, thawed and squeezed dry
⅓ cup, plus 2 Tbsp., fat-free grated Parmesan cheese, *divided*
2 cups Egg Beaters
⅛ tsp. black pepper, ground *or* cracked

1. Sauté turkey sausage in nonstick skillet until browned.
2. Coat interior of slow cooker with cooking spray. Drain sausage and place in slow cooker.
3. Stir spinach into slow cooker.
4. Stir in ⅓ cup low-fat Parmesan cheese.
5. Spoon Egg Beaters over mixture in slow cooker. Do not stir.
6. Cover. Cook on high 1½ hours, or on low up to 8 hours (you can turn it on right before you go to bed).
7. Sprinkle with pepper and 2 Tbsp. Parmesan cheese before serving.

Breakfast Bake

Audrey L. Kneer
Williamsfield, IL

Makes 10 servings

Prep. Time: 15 minutes
Cooking Time: 3-4 hours
Ideal slow-cooker size: 4- or 5-qt.

3 cups Egg Beaters
1½ cups fat-free cheese, shredded
1 cup cooked low-fat ham, diced
1 cup fat-free milk
1 tsp. salt
½ tsp. pepper

1. Spray slow cooker with nonstick spray.
2. Pour Egg Beaters into slow cooker.
3. In a bowl mix together cheese, ham, milk, salt, and pepper.
4. Pour into Egg Beaters. Stir gently.
5. Cover and cook on low 3 to 4 hours.

Breakfast Apple Cobbler

Virginia Graybill
Hershey, PA

Makes 8-10 servings

Prep. Time: 20-25 minutes
Cooking Time: 2-6 hours
Ideal slow-cooker size: 5- or 6-qt.

8 medium-sized tart apples
½ cup sugar
2 Tbsp. fresh lemon juice
1-2 tsp. grated lemon rind
dash of ground cinnamon
half a stick (¼ cup) butter, melted
1½ cups natural fat-free cereal mixed with fruit and nuts

1. Spray interior of cooker lightly with nonfat cooking spray.
2. Core, peel, and slice apples into slow cooker.
3. Add sugar, lemon juice, rind, and cinnamon.
4. Mix cereal and melted butter together.
5. Add to ingredients in slow cooker. Mix thoroughly.
6. Cover. Cook on low 6 hours, or on high 2-3 hours.

Tips:
   You can serve this with fat-free milk for breakfast. If diets permit, you can also serve it as a dessert with fat-free frozen yogurt instead.

Slow cookers come in a variety of sizes, from 2- to 8- quarts. The best size for a family of four or five is a 5-6 quart-size. — Dorothy M. Van Deest, Memphis, TN

Breakfast Fruit Compote

Betty K. Drescher
Quakertown, PA

Makes 8-9 servings

Prep. Time: 5 minutes
Cooking Time: 2-7 hours
Ideal slow-cooker size: 3- or 4-qt.

12-oz. pkg. dried apricots
12-oz. pkg. pitted dried
  plums
11-oz. can mandarin
  oranges in light syrup,
  undrained
29-oz. can sliced peaches
  in light syrup, undrained
¼ cup white raisins
10 maraschino cherries

1. Combine all ingredients
in slow cooker. Mix well.
2. Cover. Cook on low 6-7
hours, or on high 2-3 hours.

—— PER SERVING ——
• 300 calories
  (0 calories from fat)
• 0g total fat
  (0g saturated, 0g trans)
• 0mg cholesterol
• 40mg sodium
• 74g total carbohydrate
  (5g fiber, 42g sugar)
• 3g protein
• 30%DV vitamin A
• 10%DV vitamin C
• 4%DV calcium
• 15%DV iron

Tip:
  If the fruit seems to be
drying out as it cooks, you
may want to add up to 1 cup
water.

Blueberry-Apple Waffle Topping

Willard E. Roth
Elkhart, IN

Makes 10-12 servings

Prep. Time: 10 minutes
Cooking Time: 3 hours
Ideal slow-cooker size: 3½- or 4-qt.

1 qt. natural applesauce,
  unsweetened
2 Granny Smith apples,
  unpeeled, cored, and
  sliced
1 pt. fresh, *or* frozen,
  blueberries
½ Tbsp. ground cinnamon
½ cup pure maple syrup
1 tsp. almond flavoring
½ cup walnuts, chopped

1. Stir together applesauce,
apples, and blueberries in
slow cooker sprayed with
nonfat cooking spray.
2. Add cinnamon
and maple syrup.

3. Cover. Cook on low 3
hours.
4. Add almond flavoring and
walnuts just before serving.

—— PER SERVING ——
• 130 calories
  (35 calories from fat)
• 3.5g total fat
  (0g saturated, 0g trans)
• 0mg cholesterol
• 0mg sodium
• 25g total carbohydrate
  (3g fiber, 20g sugar)
• 2g protein
• 0%DV vitamin A
• 20%DV vitamin C
• 2%DV calcium
• 4%DV iron

Tip:
  If your diet allows, this
is also delicious served over
cake or fat-free frozen yogurt.

Boston Brown Bread

Virginia Graybill
Hershey, PA

Makes 1 loaf

Prep. Time: 15-20 minutes
Cooking Time: 4-5 hours
Cooling Time: 1 hour
*Ideal slow-cooker size: tall 4- or
  5-qt.*

½ cup flour
½ tsp. baking powder
½ tsp. baking soda
½ tsp. salt
  ½ cup yellow cornmeal
  ½ cup whole wheat
    flour
  ¼ cup walnuts,
    chopped
  6 Tbsp. unsulfured
    molasses
  1 cup low-fat
    buttermilk, *or*
    sour milk
½ cup raisins

1. Sift flour with baking powder, baking soda, and salt.

2. Stir in cornmeal and whole wheat flour.

3. Add remaining ingredients. Beat well.

4. Pour batter into greased and floured 2-lb. coffee can.

5. Pour 2 cups water into slow cooker. Set can inside cooker on top of metal rack or several rubber jar rings.

6. Place aluminum foil over top of can, folding it down around edge of can. Cover cooker.

7. Cook on high 4-5 hours, until a skewer inserted in center of bread comes out clean.

8. Remove can from cooker. Lay it on its side to cool. Keep can covered 1 hour before unmolding.

9. Slice and serve.

—— **PER SERVING** ——
- 80 calories
  (10 calories from fat)
- 1g total fat
  (0g saturated, 0g trans)
- 0mg cholesterol
- 105mg sodium
- 16g total carbohydrate
  (0.5g fiber, 7g sugar)
- 2g protein
- 0%DV vitamin A
- 0%DV vitamin C
- 4%DV calcium
- 4%DV iron

Parmesan Garlic Quick Bread

Leona Miller
Millersburg, OH

Makes 8 servings

Prep. Time: 10-15 minutes
Cooking Time: 1 hour
Ideal slow-cooker size: 2- or 3-qt.

1½ cups reduced-fat
  buttermilk baking mix
2 egg whites
½ cup skim milk
1 Tbsp. minced onions
1 Tbsp. sugar
1½ tsp. garlic powder
¼ cup reduced-fat
  Parmesan cheese

1. Combine baking mix, egg whites, milk, onions, sugar, and garlic powder in mixing bowl.

2. Spray slow cooker with cooking spray. Spoon dough into cooker.

3. Sprinkle dough with Parmesan cheese.

4. Cook on high 1 hour.

—— **PER SERVING** ——
- 120 calories
  (20 calories from fat)
- 2g total fat
  (1g saturated, 0g trans)
- 0mg cholesterol
- 330mg sodium
- 19g total carbohydrate
  (0g fiber, 4g sugar)
- 4g protein
- 0%DV vitamin A
- 0%DV vitamin C
- 4%DV calcium
- 4%DV iron

Tip:
This bread is great with hot soup, Italian dishes, or salads.

Cottage Cheese Bread

Leona Miller
Millersburg, OH

Makes 8 servings

Prep. Time: 10 minutes
Cooking Time: 2 hours
Ideal slow-cooker size: 3-qt.

1 cup fat-free cottage
  cheese
4 egg whites
1 cup sugar
¾ cup fat-free, *or* 2%, milk
1 tsp. vanilla
2¾ cups reduced-fat
  buttermilk baking mix
½ cup raisins, *or* dried
  cranberries
½ tsp. orange zest

1. Combine all ingredients in mixing bowl.

2. Pour into greased slow cooker.

3. Cook on high 2 hours.

—— **PER SERVING** ——
- 320 calories
  (25 calories from fat)
- 3g total fat
  (0.5g saturated, 0g trans)
- 0mg cholesterol
- 510mg sodium
- 63g total carbohydrate
  (0.5g fiber, 34g sugar)
- 10g protein
- 0%DV vitamin A
- 0%DV vitamin C
- 6%DV calcium
- 10%DV iron

Making Cream of Mushroom/ Celery Soup from Scratch

When I first began making cookbooks, I was a purist. No canned cream-of-xxx soups for me, whether I was working on cookbooks or making dinner. I resolutely turned any reference to canned creamed soups into a multi-step process, which wasn't too bad if I took a magazine along to the stove or the microwave. I would do Steps 1-4 (on next page); then I'd whip out the magazine while I stirred. It made the time fly.

But when I became a mom, I began to compromise on a few things. It was a little harder to hold a wiggly child than it was to read a magazine while I stirred up a creamy soup.

Then I heard from other people who were juggling things that didn't always allow them to stand and read while stirring. So I switched and began to permit canned soups in recipes.

If you like to know exactly what you are eating, and if you have the time, I applaud your making cream soups and bases from scratch. Here is a recipe for doing this on the stove-top or in the microwave.

If you're tight time-wise, or aren't sure you want to make the extra effort to create a creamy soup or base, you'll find canned cream soups in the ingredient lists of many recipes in this cookbook. Because my first intent is to make sure you can make a meal at home and serve it to your friends and family, no matter how full or chaotic your life is.

Homemade Cream of Mushroom Soup –on the stove

Makes about 1¼ cups (10 oz.)

3 Tbsp. butter
¼ cup mushrooms, chopped
1 Tbsp. onion, chopped
3 Tbsp. flour
1 cup milk (skim, 1%, 2%, *or* whole)

1. In a small saucepan, melt butter.

2. Sauté mushrooms and onion in butter until tender. Stir frequently.

3. Add flour and stir until smooth. Cook over low heat for a minute or so to cook off the raw flour taste.

4. Continuing over low heat, gradually add milk, stirring the whole time.

5. Stir frequently to keep soup from sticking. When soup begins to bubble, stir continuously until it thickens to a creamy consistency.

Homemade Cream of Mushroom Soup –in the microwave

Makes about 1¼ cups (10 oz.)

3 Tbsp. butter
¼ cup mushrooms, chopped
1 Tbsp. onion, chopped
3 Tbsp. flour
1 cup milk (skim, 1%, 2%, *or* whole)

1. In a 1- or 2-qt. microwave-safe container, melt 3 Tbsp. butter on high for 30 seconds.

2. Stir chopped mushrooms and onions into melted butter.

3. Microwave on high for 1 minute, or just enough to make the vegetables tender.

4. Stir in flour until well blended.

5. Microwave on high for 1 minute, just enough to overcome the raw flour taste.

6. Gradually stir in milk until as well blended as possible.

7. Microwave on Power 5 for 45 seconds.

8. Stir until well blended.

9. Microwave on Power 5 for another 45 seconds. The mixture should be starting to bubble and thicken.

10. Stir again until well blended.

11. If the mixture isn't fully bubbling and thickened, microwave on high for 20 seconds.

12. Stir. If the mixture still isn't fully bubbling and thickened, microwave on high for 20 more seconds.

13. Repeat Step 12 if needed.

Note:

If your microwave is fairly new and powerful, you will probably have a creamy soup by the end of Step 8 or 10 below. If you're working with an older, less powerful, microwave, you will likely need to go through Step 12, and maybe Step 13.

To make cream of celery soup, substitute ¼ cup finely chopped celery for the ¼ cup chopped mushrooms.

Equivalent Measurements

dash = little less than ⅛ tsp.

3 teaspoons = 1 Tablespoon

2 Tablespoons = 1 oz.

4 Tablespoons = ¼ cup

5 Tablespoons plus 1 tsp. = ⅓ cup

8 Tablespoons = ½ cup

12 Tablespoons = ¾ cup

16 Tablespoons = 1 cup

1 cup = 8 ozs. liquid

2 cups = 1 pint

4 cups = 1 quart

4 quarts = 1 gallon

1 stick butter = ¼ lb.

1 stick butter = ½ cup

1 stick butter = 8 Tbsp.

Beans, 1 lb. dried = 2-2½ cups (depending upon the size of the beans)

Bell peppers, 1 large = 1 cup chopped

Cheese, hard (for example, cheddar, Swiss, Monterey Jack, mozzarella), 1 lb. grated = 4 cups

Cheese, cottage, 1 lb. = 2 cups

Chocolate chips, 6-oz. pkg. = 1 scant cup

Crackers (butter, saltines, snack), 20 single crackers = 1 cup crumbs

Herbs, 1 Tbsp. fresh = 1 tsp. dried

Lemon, 1 medium-sized = 2-3 Tbsp. juice

Lemon, 1 medium-sized = 2-3 tsp. grated rind

Mustard, 1 Tbsp. prepared = 1 tsp. dry or ground mustard

Oatmeal, 1 lb. dry = about 5 cups dry

Onion, 1 medium-sized = ½ cup chopped

Pasta

Macaronis, penne, and other small or tubular shapes, 1 lb. dry = 4 cups uncooked

Noodles, 1 lb. dry = 6 cups uncooked

Spaghetti, linguine, fettucine, 1 lb. dry = 4 cups uncooked

Potatoes, white, 1 lb. = 3 medium-sized potatoes = 2 cups mashed

Potatoes, sweet, 1 lb. = 3 medium-sized potatoes = 2 cups mashed

Rice, 1 lb. dry = 2 cups uncooked

Sugar, confectioners, 1 lb. = 3½ cups sifted

Whipping cream, 1 cup unwhipped = 2 cups whipped

Whipped topping, 8-oz. container = 3 cups

Yeast, dry, 1 envelope (¼ oz.) = 1 Tbsp.

Substitute Ingredients
for when you're in a pinch

For one cup **buttermilk**—use 1 cup plain yogurt; or pour 1⅓ Tbsp. lemon juice or vinegar into a 1-cup measure. Fill the cup with milk. Stir and let stand for 5 minutes. Stir again before using.

For 1 oz. **unsweetened baking chocolate**—stir together 3 Tbsp. unsweetened cocoa powder and 1 Tbsp. butter, softened.

For 1 Tbsp. **cornstarch**—use 2 Tbsp. all-purpose flour; or 4 tsp. minute tapioca.

For 1 **garlic clove**—use ¼ tsp. garlic salt (reduce salt in recipe by ⅛ tsp.); or ⅛ tsp. garlic powder.

For 1 Tbsp. **fresh herbs**—use 1 tsp. dried herbs.

For ½ lb. **fresh mushrooms**—use 1 6-oz. can mushrooms, drained.

For 1 Tbsp. **prepared mustard**—use 1 tsp. dry or ground mustard.

For 1 **medium-sized fresh onion**—use 2 Tbsp. minced dried onion; or 2 tsp. onion salt (reduce salt in recipe by 1 tsp.); or 1 tsp. onion powder. Note: These substitutions will work for meat balls and meat loaf, but not for sautéing.

For 1 cup **sour milk**—use 1 cup plain yogurt; or pour 1 Tbsp. lemon juice or vinegar into a 1-cup measure. Fill with milk. Stir and then let stand for 5 minutes. Stir again before using.

For 2 Tbsp. **tapioca**—use 3 Tbsp. all-purpose flour.

For 1 cup canned **tomatoes**—use 1⅓ cups diced fresh tomatoes, cooked gently for 10 minutes.

For 1 Tbsp. **tomato paste**—use 1 Tbsp. ketchup.

For 1 Tbsp. **vinegar**—use 1 Tbsp. lemon juice.

For 1 cup **heavy cream**—add ⅓ cup melted butter to ¾ cup milk. *Note: This will work for baking and cooking, but not for whipping.*

For 1 cup **whipping cream**—chill thoroughly ⅔ cup evaporated milk, plus the bowl and beaters, then whip; or use 2 cups bought whipped topping.

For ½ cup **wine**—pour 2 Tbsp. wine vinegar into a ½-cup measure. Fill with broth (chicken, beef, or vegetable). Stir and then let stand for 5 minutes. Stir again before using.

Assumptions about Ingredients

flour = unbleached *or* white, and all-purpose

oatmeal or oats = dry, quick *or* rolled (old-fashioned), unless specified

pepper = black, finely ground

rice = regular, long-grain (not minute or instant unless specified)

salt = table salt

shortening = solid, not liquid

sugar = granulated sugar (not brown and not confectioners)

Three Hints

1 If you'd like to cook more at home — without being in a frenzy — go off by yourself with your cookbook some evening and make a week of menus. Then make a grocery list from that. Shop from your grocery list.

2 Thaw frozen food in a bowl in the fridge (not on the counter-top). If you forget to stick the food in the fridge, put it in a microwave-safe bowl and defrost it in the microwave just before you're ready to use it.

3 Let roasted meat, as well as pasta dishes with cheese, rest for 10-20 minutes before slicing or dishing. That will allow the juices to redistribute themselves throughout the cooked food. You'll have juicier meat, and a better presentation of your pasta dish.

Index

Index

Index

Index

Index

Index

Index

Index

About the Author

Phyllis Good is a *New York Times* bestselling author whose books have sold nearly 11 million copies.

Good is the author of the nationally acclaimed *Fix-It and Forget-It* slow-cooker cookbooks, several of which have appeared on *The New York Times* bestseller list, as well as the bestseller lists of *USA Today*, *Publishers Weekly*, and *Book Sense*. In addition to this book, the series includes:

- *Fix-It and Forget-It Cookbook (Revised and Updated)*
  700 Great Slow-Cooker Recipes

- *Fix-It and Forget-It Christmas Cookbook*
  600 Slow-Cooker Holiday Recipes

- *Fix-It and Forget-It 5-Ingredient Favorites*
  Comforting Slow-Cooker Recipes

- *Fix-It and Forget-It Slow Cooker Diabetic Cookbook (Revised and Updated)* 550 Slow Cooker Favorites—to include everyone (with the American Diabetes Association)

- *Fix-It and Forget-It Vegetarian Cookbook*
  565 Delicious Slow-Cooker, Stove-Top, Oven, and Salad Recipes, plus 50 Suggested Menus

- *Fix-It and Forget-It PINK Cookbook*
  More than 700 Great Slow-Cooker Recipes!

- *Fix-It and Forget-It Kids' Cookbook*
  50 Favorite Recipes to Make in a Slow Cooker

- *Fix-It and Forget-It New Cookbook*
  250 New Delicious Slow Cooker Recipes!

- *Fix-It and Forget-It Slow Cooker Magic*
  550 Amazing Everyday Recipes

Good is also the author of the *Fix-It and Enjoy-It* series, a "cousin" series to the phenomenally successful *Fix-It and Forget-It* cookbooks. There are currently four books in that series:

- *Fix-It and Enjoy-It Cookbook*
  All-Purpose, Welcome-Home Recipes

- *Fix-It and Enjoy-It 5-Ingredient Recipes*
  Quick and Easy—for Stove-Top and Oven!

- *Fix-It and Enjoy-It Diabetic Cookbook*
  Stove-Top and Oven Recipes—for Everyone!
  (with the American Diabetes Association)

- *Fix-It and Enjoy-It Church Suppers Diabetic Cookbook*
  500 Great Stove-Top and Oven Recipes—for Everyone!
  (with the American Diabetes Association)

- *Fix-It and Enjoy-It Healthy Cookbook*
  400 Great Stove-Top and Oven Recipes
  (with nutritional expertise from Mayo Clinic)

- *Fix-It and Enjoy-It Potluck Heaven*
  543 Recipes That Everyone Loves

Phyllis Pellman Good is Executive Editor at Good Books. (Good Books has published hundreds of titles by more than 135 authors.) She received her B.A. and M.A. in English from New York University. She and her husband, Merle, live in Lancaster, Pennsylvania. They are the parents of two adult daughters.

For a complete listing of books by Phyllis Good, as well as excerpts and reviews, visit www.Fix-ItandForget-It.com or www.GoodBooks.com.

Rhubarb Sauce, page 232

Sausage-Sweet Potato Bake,
page 101